Mogollon
Culture
in the
Forestdale Valley
East-central
Arizona

Mogollon
Culture
in the
Forestdale Valley
East-central
Arizona

EMIL W. HAURY

The University of Arizona Press
Tucson, Arizona
1985

About the Author . . .

EMIL W. HAURY, one of the early originators of the
Mogollon concept in the classification of southwestern
prehistoric groups, has been actively contributing to
archaeological advancements for sixty years. Haury became Head of the Anthropology Department at the
University of Arizona in 1937 and was appointed Director of the Arizona State Museum in 1938. He continued
in these two positions until 1964, and during that time
established highly successful archaeological field schools
that trained many future professional archaeologists.
The excavations of Mogollon sites reported on in this
volume were conducted at the early (1939–1941) field
schools in Forestdale, Arizona. From 1970 to 1980, Haury
held the Fred A. Riecker Distinguished Professorship in
Anthropology at the University of Arizona, and he became Professor Emeritus in 1980. Preeminent among his
numerous honors and awards was his election to the
National Academy of Sciences and the American Philosophical Society. Major publications by Haury include *The
Stratigraphy and Archaeology of Ventana Cave, Arizona;
Excavations at Snaketown, Material Culture* (with
others); and *The Hohokam: Desert Farmers and Craftsmen;* and he has authored a multitude of professional
monographs and articles.

THE UNIVERSITY OF ARIZONA PRESS

Copyright © 1985
The Arizona Board of Regents
All Rights Reserved

Manufactured in the U.S.A.

Library of Congress Cataloging in Publication Data

Haury, Emil W. (Emil Walter), 1904-
    Mogollon culture in the Forestdale Valley, east-central
Arizona.

    Bibliography: p.
    Includes index.
    1. Mogollon culture. 2. Indians of North America—
Arizona—Forestdale Valley—Antiquities. 3. Forestdale Valley
(Ariz.)—Antiquities. 4. Arizona—Antiquities.
I. Title.
E99.M76H3   1985   979.1   84-28058

ISBN 0-8165-0894-1

Dedicated with respect to

ALCHESAY

Defender of his branch of the Apache tribe and of its territorial rights while relating amicably with an alien White people, and the last native American leader who shared dramatically in the 1800-year history of the Forestdale Valley.

CONTENTS

Prologue: The Mogollon Concept xv

Part I. Tla Kii Ruin,
         Forestdale's Oldest Pueblo 1
         Preface 3
         Archaeology in the
            Forestdale Valley 7
         The Forestdale Valley and
            Tla Kii Ruin 12
         Tla Kii Ruin 20
         The Significance of Tla Kii Ruin 132

Part II. Excavations in the Forestdale Valley,
          East-central Arizona 135
          Introduction 139
          The Bear Ruin 142
          General Discussion and
             Conclusions 254
          Appendix: The Skeletal Remains
             of the Bear Ruin 264
                Norman E. Gabel
          Bibliography 271

Part III. An Early Pit House Village of the
           Mogollon Culture, Forestdale Valley,
           Arizona 281
                Emil W. Haury and E. B. Sayles
           Acknowledgments 283
           Introduction 285
           The Bluff Site 285
           Summary and Conclusions 360
           Appendix: Analysis of
              Soil Samples 368
                 T. F. Buehrer
           Bibliography 370

Part IV. The Forestdale Valley
Cultural Sequence 373
Dating the Forestdale Phases 376
Hilltop Phase 377
Cottonwood Phase 380
Forestdale Phase 382
Corduroy Phase 383
Dry Valley Phase 385
Carrizo Phase 386
Linden Phase 388
Pinedale Phase 391
Canyon Creek Phase 392
Skidi Phase 396
Alchesay Phase 397
Regional Note 401

Epilogue: The Mogollon and Anasazi 403

References: Prologue, Parts I and IV,
and Epilogue 409

Appendix A. A Sequence of Great Kivas in the
Forestdale Valley, Arizona 415
Emil W. Haury

Appendix B. New Tree-Ring Dates from the
Forestdale Valley,
East-central Arizona 423
Emil W. Haury

Appendix C. Checking the Date of Bluff Ruin,
Forestdale; A Study in Technique ... 427
A. E. Douglass

Appendix D. Tabulation of Dates for Bluff Ruin,
Forestdale, Arizona 433
A. E. Douglass

Appendix E. Some Implications of the Bluff
            Ruin Dates 441
                    Emil W. Haury

     Index   443

ILLUSTRATIONS

Part I Figures
1. Map of Forestdale Valley and environs 14
2. Map of Tla Kii Ruin in relation to terrace
    system 18
3. Views of Tla Kii Ruin 21
4. Map of Tla Kii Ruin and related structures 22
5. Pit House 1, Corduroy Phase 24
6. Plan and sections of Pit House 1 25
7. Pit House 2, Corduroy Phase 26
8. Plan and sections of Pit House 2 27
9. Pit House 3 and Unit Structure 1 28
10. Plan and section of Pit House 3 29
11. Plan and section of Storage Structure (?) 1 30
12. Unit Structure 2 32
13. Plan and sections of Unit Structure 2 33
14. Ground plan and section of Tla Kii Ruin 35
15. Tla Kii Ruin building episodes 36
16. Shaped building blocks and masonry detail 38
17. Masonry details 40
18. Masonry details 41
19. Hearth and corner detail 44
20. Plan and section of Great Kiva (Kiva 1) 48
21. Great Kiva and Great Kiva bench wall 49
22. Great Kiva entrance and rock-lined posthole 50
23. Plan and section of Kiva 2 53
24. Plan and section of Storage Pit 1 55
25. Plan and section of Storage Pits 2 and 3 56
26. Storage Pit 2; Pit 14 57
27. Tla Kii Ruin 61

28. Burial 3; Burial 10 66
29. Alma Neck Banded 74
30. Corduroy Black-on-white 76
31. Corduroy Black-on-white vessels 77
32. Corduroy Black-on-white vessel forms 77
33. Corduroy Black-on-white rim forms 78
34. Miscellaneous gray and brown wares 80
35. Alma Incised 83
36. Neck Corrugated pottery 84
37. Black-on-white, Black Mesa style 86
38. Black-on-white, Dry Valley Phase 87
39. Black-on-white jars 88
40. Trade Pottery, Dry Valley Phase 90
41. Corrugated Pottery, Carrizo Phase 94
42. Corrugated Pottery, vessel forms 95
43. McDonald Corrugated bowl forms 96
44. McDonald Corrugated 96
45. Black-on-white, Carrizo Phase 98
46. Black-on-white, Snowflake Style 99
47. Black-on-white, Puerco Style 100
48. Black-on-white, vessel shapes 101
49. Bowl design panels, Room 13-15 102
50. Trade Pottery, Carrizo Phase 105
51. Pottery associated with Burial 13 108
52. Pottery associated with Burial 3 109
53. Diagram of brown ware-gray ware merger 110
54. Miscellaneous clay objects 112
55. Metates 114
56. Manos 115
57. Miscellaneous stone tools 117
58. Stone ornaments 118
59. Technology of steatite bead manufacture 120
60. Composite bird effigy 122
61. Painted stone slab 123
62. Percussion flaked tools 124
63. Pressure flaked tools 125
64. Knives 126
65. Projectile points 128
66. Bone objects 130
67. Shell jewelry 133

Part II Plates

I. Forestdale Valley and the Bear Ruin 136
II. House 1 and House 5 156
III. Houses 13 and 14 and Houses 2 and 3 161
IV. House 4 and House 6 165
V. House 8 and House 12 169
VI. A seventh century kiva in the Bear Ruin,
and floor trench in kiva 178
VII. Hearth stones on old surface,
and burnt rock mound 187
VIII. Deep hearth with undercut sides 189
IX. Mortuary offerings, and adult burial
showing normal burial position 195
X. Flexed burials, and infant burial
with offerings 199
XI. Intrusive pottery in Bear Ruin 213
XII. Skulls of Burials 5 and 12 265

Part II Figures

1. Map of east-central Arizona and
west-central New Mexico 143
2. Map of Forestdale Valley at Bear Ruin 145
3. Plan of Bear Ruin 150
4. Profile of subsurface conditions
at Bear Ruin 151
5. Plan and section of House 1 153
6. Plan and section of House 5 155
7. Plan and section of Houses 13 and 14 158
8. Plan and section of Houses 2 and 3 159
9. Plan and section of House 4 162
10. Plan and section of House 6 164
11. Plan and section of House 7 166
12. Plan and section of House 8 168
13. Plan and section of House 9 170
14. Plan and section of House 10 171
15. Plan and section of House 11 172
16. Plan and section of House 12 173
17. Plan and section of Storage Room 1 175
18. Plan and section of Storage Room 2 176
19. Plan and section of Bear Ruin Kiva 177

20. Roof reconstructions of houses 185
21. Hearth types 191
22. Table on Bear Ruin burials 197
23. Alma Plain vessel forms 203
24. Alma Plain handle and lug types 204
25. Forestdale Smudged bowl forms 206
26. Forestdale Plain vessel forms 208
27. Forestdale Red vessel forms 210
28. Neck Banding in Anasazi and
    Mogollon cultures 215
29. Maps showing spread of smudging technique ... 222
30. Diagram showing percent changes in
    pottery types in four sites 224
31. Chart showing priority of Mogollon ceramic
    traits 226
32. Correlation chart of intrusive pottery 228
33. Metate types 231
34. Mano types 232
35. Grinding slabs, pestles, and mortars 234
36. Miscellaneous stone implements 235
37. Ornaments and chipped blades 237
38. Projectile points 239
39. Flake implements 240
40. Bone tools 246
41. Bone objects 248
42. Clay objects 250
43. Worked potsherds 251
44. Diagram of Bear Ruin trait alignments 257

Part III Plates
  I. Northern face of the bluff from the valley floor,
     and eastern slope,
     showing shallow depressions 282
 II. Starting excavations, and general
     view toward the southwest 288
III. Bedrock wall of House 7,
     and House 1 partially cleared 292
 IV. House 2, and House 3 during excavation 295
  V. Houses 4 and 4A, and House 5, western half 297
 VI. House 6, and House 7 301
VII. House 9, and House 11,
     a Basketmaker type slab-house 309

VIII.   Early type metate built into wall of
        House 11, and House 14 311
  IX.   Burial 1, and telephoto view across the
        Forestdale Valley to the Red Hill Site 325

Part III Figures
  1. Map of Forestdale Valley 286
  2. Topographic map of the Bluff Site 291
  3. Plan and section of House 1 294
  4. Plans and sections of Houses 4 and 4A 298
  5. Plan and section of House 5 300
  6. Plan and sections of House 6 303
  7. Plan and section of House 7 304
  8. Plan and sections of House 8 305
  9. Plan and section of House 9 307
 10. Plan and section of House 10 308
 11. Plan and sections of House 11 310
 12. Plan and profile of trash fill in House 12 312
 13. Plan and sections of House 13 313
 14. Plan and sections of House 14 315
 15. Plan and sections of House 15 316
 16. Plan and sections of Houses 19 and 19A 318
 17. Table summarizing essential features of
        Bluff Ruin house types 321
 18. Plan and section of Hearth 1 323
 19. Vessel forms of Alma Plain, Bluff Variety 327
 20. Vessel forms of Alma Plain,
        Forestdale Variety 329
 21. Jar rim sherd, and potsherd tray 329
 22. The phase scheme of Bluff and Bear ruins,
        showing ceramic components 339
 23. Chart suggesting the relative time of
        appearance of pottery in the Anasazi,
        Mogollon, and Hohokam cultures 340
 24. Pueblo I pottery scraper from Hearth 2 341
 25. Clay figurine fragments 342
 26. Metate types 343
 27. Mano types 345
 28. Stone implements 347
 29. Stone objects 349
 30. Percussion flaked tools 350
 31. Pressure flaked and ground-edge tools 351

32. Projectile points and knives 353
33. Drills 354
34. Phase chart correlating three early
    branches of the Mogollon complex 363

Part IV Figures
 1. Linden phase black-on-white pottery 390
 2. Mormon log structure built in 1881 399

Appendix A Figure
 1. Chart summarizing essential data on
    Forestdale Valley Great Kivas
    and Kinishba Plaza 419

Appendix C Figure
 1. Tree-ring specimens dating the Bluff Ruin 431

Appendix D Figure
 1. Early ring record at Bluff Site 438

TABLES

Part I
 1. Phases in the Forestdale Valley 15
 2. Grave data for Tla Kii Ruin burials 64
 3. Faunal occurrences in Forestdale Valley sites ... 68
 4. Corduroy phase intrusive pottery 81
 5. Dry Valley phase intrusive pottery 91
 6. Carrizo phase intrusive pottery 103
 7. Shell from Tla Kii Ruin 132

Part IV
 1. Phase chronology in the Forestdale Valley 377

Appendix B
 1. Tree-ring dates from the Bear Ruin 424

Appendix D
 1. Tree-ring dates from the Bluff Site 434
 2. Distribution of tree-ring specimens
    from the Bluff Site 439

PROLOGUE: THE MOGOLLON CONCEPT

The late 1920s and the 1930s were times of expanding horizons in southwestern archaeology. Neither before nor since have so many events taken place to guide and stimulate the direction of prehistoric studies. The first milestone was reached in 1927, when most of the archaeologists active in the region, brought together by A. V. Kidder at Pecos, New Mexico, codified in outline form what was then known about the order and nature of development of the past people who formerly lived on the Colorado Plateau. At that time, it was well understood that all of the archaeological manifestations in the other parts of the Southwest were not accommodated by what came to be known as the Pecos Classification.

Increasing attention to those other areas, the arid desert to the southwest and the verdant mountains to the south and east, was being given by the staff members of newly-founded private institutions devoted to archaeology. The Laboratory of Anthropology in Santa Fe, the Museum of Northern Arizona in Flagstaff, the Amerind Foundation in Dragoon, and Gila Pueblo in Globe, all established in close order, brought new vigor to archaeological studies. Their findings quickly reinforced the beliefs that the records of the past in the mountainous and desertic regions did not fit the Plateau mold as outlined at Pecos.

The outcome of these beliefs was the conclusion among many investigators that if the Pecos agreement was to apply to the Southwest as a whole, either its guidelines would need modification to accommodate the later findings or new categories in the system of classification were necessary. The steady accumulation of information soon demonstrated that the latter alternative was the route to pursue. The result was the addition of two new entities believed by their proponents to have the same classificatory value as Basketmaker-Pueblo or Anasazi.

The first of these entities was Hohokam, a word taken from the Pima language to identify the Desert people of prehistory, and the second was Mogollon, the Spanish surname borrowed from a mountain range in New Mexico, an appropriate label for the people who made a mountain habitat their home in the past.

Up to this time in southwestern studies, in the 1930s, archaeologists had not given much heed to what might be termed

larger "tribal" groups, or at least had not examined the ele-
mental criteria that could be indicative of the existence of more
than one "basic" cultural unit. Therefore, the proposal to add
two new groups to the taxonomy in quick succession brought
speedy and highly vocal protests. The risks of expanding the
structure of the Southwest's past had not been apparent before,
but it was now clear that this touched sensitive nerves. The
proposals, however, did have the salutary effect of stimulating
the thinking of investigators along new lines. To those who preferred the simple arrangement, the unitary cultural complex
that encompassed the Southwest, the notion of several entities
seemed cumbersome and unwarranted. Yet the solution to the
conflicting data demanded an equally searching answer, if the
archaeological evidence was being read correctly and the per-
ceived differences in cultural vestiges were to be accommodated.

It always seemed paradoxical to me that there should have
been so much resistance to recognizing multiple cultural
groups in antiquity, when historically we can tally a dozen or
more Indian tribes in the Southwest with almost as many life
styles and half as many distinct language groupings. The
ethnologists' advantage, of course, is that they have available
information such as language and can directly observe social,
political, and religious behavior of the living as the basis for
identifying different peoples, an advantage that is denied
archaeologists. The contrasting life ways of today's groups can
and must guide archaeologists in reaching conclusions of likes
and dislikes among past people based on the far leaner records
with which they must work.

Kidder, in his landmark publication of 1924, *An Introduction
to Southwestern Archaeology* (pp. 105–106), said the following of
the Gila Basin in southern Arizona: "The archaeological remains
are . . . unlike those of any of our other districts and are in some
ways so aberrant that, were it not for the pottery, we should be
forced to consider that we had overstepped the limits of the
Southwestern culture area." That statement was surely partly
responsible for the early, though reluctant, acceptance of the
label Hohokam. The remains of these people in the climax days
of their culture, around A.D. 800 to 1000, marked by an absence
of pueblo architecture, no kivas, open-grain villages, no black-
on-white pottery, and a host of other distinctive attributes, could
not possibly be incorporated in the model of a cultural style as
seen in the contemporaneous pueblos of Chaco Canyon.

The Mogollon concept, however, was another matter. What justification was there for seeing the Mountain people as different from those of the pre-A.D. 800 Plateau people when they both lived in pit houses, practiced agriculture and grew the same crops, and in later times lived in stone pueblos, with some making black-and-white pottery mindful of that of the north? Their developmental histories were thought to run parallel courses. The observed differences were more attributable to environmental than to cultural forces.

Yet, the advocates for the Mogollon idea held that there were a number of adequate, if in some cases subtle, contrasting elements to warrant separation of the remains in a taxonomic sense. Most notable were the highly disparate characteristics that marked the two ceramic fabrics. Mogollon pottery ran to grays, reds, and browns in color, the product of residual clays, fixed in oxidizing firings, and initially decorated, if at all, with red paint. In contrast, the primary kaolinitic clays of the Plateau, under often reducing firing conditions, lead to a dominantly gray-to-white bodied pottery carrying black painted patterns, as the rule, and in certain locales in late prehistory evolving into flamboyant polychromes.

I am well aware that pottery cannot always be used as a certain identifier of a people, but one need look only at the pottery produced today by southwestern Indians to realize that there is a one-to-one correlation between type and tribe for most of the vessels produced. I believe that this situation obtained in antiquity as well, and that the inference that Anasazi-Mogollon ceramic differences denote "tribal" differences is sound.

The Forestdale Valley investigations came at a most propitious time, from 1939 to 1941, when the debate over the Mogollon concept was at its peak. Urgently needed were new data to bring the problem into sharper focus. This the excavations in the Bear and Bluff ruins did. They not only yielded data to expand the substance of the culture, but also to establish several developmental stages revealing changes through time. Above all, the contrasting nature between Mogollon and Anasazi archaeology was heightened by the fact that the Forestdale Valley lay at the front doorstep of the vast Anasazi domain. The environment alone could not be blamed for the differences one saw. It was clear that some other force was at work, and that had to be an inheritance of cultural values that coursed along a different track than that of the Anasazi.

At this time too, Paul S. Martin's promptly reported findings in the Pine Lawn area of west-central New Mexico provided significant support for the maturing Mogollon concept by demonstrating that the remains of the group in question had territorial breadth and that once again a local chronology could be established.

At this juncture in the unfolding of the fascinating, if vexing, drama of the Mogollon, tree-ring dating entered the picture to play a crucial role. Because the well-preserved architectural beams from many Anasazi ruins figured prominently in developing Douglass' prehistoric tree-ring calendar, it followed logically that those Anasazi ruins, and many others soon after, were the first to be dated in terms of the Christian Calendar. Among the many intriguing and basic bits of information that emerged from this monumental achievement was the fact that Anasazi pottery was not made before about A.D. 400. Yet the tree-ring dated woods from the Forestdale sites indicated pottery was already at hand a few centuries before, and the primacy of Mogollon pottery was further supported by Martin's findings. So in this respect, reliable dating of one cultural attribute strongly supported once again the notion that two sets of people had separate histories.

Today, in 1983, almost fifty years after the term "Mogollon Culture" was formally launched, the validity of the concept is no longer debated. The people working in the Mogollon area and the amount of work done matches or even outstrips that being done in either the Hohokam or Anasazi regions. An annual Mogollon conference attracts several hundred people and numerous papers enumerate in excruciating detail a host of aspects of the complex. At last, respectability has come to the Mogollon as a rightful subject for study. But a frightening aspect of the burgeoning interest to me is that far more is now included in the framework of the Mogollon than I ever envisioned. This, no doubt, is a natural consequence of a new idea when it is espoused by many people. The time has come, it would seem, to once again look at what we mean by Mogollon, to redefine the concept, and to reassess the role of those people in the greater Southwest.

Perhaps we can see in the long delay between the innovation of an idea and its acceptance a healthy built-in conservatism in the minds of investigators, a well-placed skepticism that demands "show-me" before the cause is joined. As long as that condition prevails, the discipline is in sound health.

The reissuance of out-of-print reports on the Bluff and Bear ruins in the Forestdale Valley, together with the long overdue and never published report on our work in the Tla Kii Ruin (long referred to as the Forestdale Ruin) in 1940 and 1941, is a matter of great personal satisfaction. The significant role the Forestdale ruins played in bringing credence to the Mogollon concept is thereby heightened. Further, the Tla Kii Ruin calls attention to a continuing and vexing problem of the hybridization of Anasazi and Mogollon in the eleventh century, a problem explored in the Epilogue. The products of this cultural blending are viewed differently by almost every investigator, resulting in a currently confused state of affairs in Mogollon studies. Perhaps in another half century that, too, will have reached a state of broad acceptability and equilibrium.

Parts II and III of this book are photoreproductions of the original reports published in 1940 and 1947, with new page numbers added. The various appendixes are reprinted with the kind permission of the Southwest Parks and Monuments Association and the Tree-Ring Society. References for the Prologue, Parts I and IV, and the Epilogue are listed after the Epilogue.

My gratitude is expressed to the University of Arizona Press, directed by Stephen Cox, for its interest and support in publishing this material as a single volume, and my special thanks to Carol Gifford for her skillful editorial merging of old and new texts.

Emil W. Haury
6 September 1983

PART I
Tla Kii Ruin
Forestdale's Oldest Pueblo

PREFACE

For a variety of reasons, the final report on the archaeological studies conducted by the Arizona State Museum and the Department of Anthropology, University of Arizona, in the Forestdale Valley of east-central Arizona, has long been delayed. The first two treatises (Haury 1940a, Part II herein; and Haury and Sayles 1947, Part III herein), dealt with the initial village dwellers whose remains were preserved in the Bear Ruin and the Bluff Site, spanning roughly the time from A.D. 200 to 700. The noteworthiness of those findings centered on the fact that the people were members of the Mogollon culture closely bordering the southern threshold of the cultural domain of the Anasazi. This report reviews the findings in site Arizona P:16:2, which, with data from other sites, builds the succession of cultural stages upward in time from A.D. 700 to the historic present (see Part IV). Further, this study draws attention to that moment in Southwestern prehistory when two readily identifiable cultural streams, Mogollon and Anasazi, coalesced to produce a blend that has both vexed and, in some measure, clarified the thinking of archaeologists concerned with cultural processes.

Arizona P:16:2, named Tla Kii Ruin, was investigated from July 1 to August 7, 1940, and from June 17 to August 9, 1941. During the latter season, excavations were carried on concurrently in the Bluff Site about 1 km to the southwest, where the archaeological record as we know it begins. Several groups of students, listed below, and a small crew of Apache Indians made up the labor force. The latter were paid with funds made available to us by William Donner, then Superintendent of the Fort Apache Indian Reservation, drawn from the Indian Division of the Civilian Conservation Corps. Two grants from the Penrose Fund of the American Philosophical Society, Philadelphia (Haury 1940b, 1941), are also acknowledged with thanks. Permits to excavate came from the U.S. Department of the Interior, carrying also the approval of the Apache Tribal Council.

The Forestdale activities were conducted as a field school, and I am happy to acknowledge the contributions of the students in all phases of the work except the final writing. Their labors in the ruins, notes, drawings, and observations have been most helpful. P. E. Vickrey's detailed architectural analysis of Tla

Kii Ruin was especially useful. Bird bone identifications were made by the late Lyndon L. Hargrave. I am obligated also to Linda Carey for effective drafting and art services and to Helga Teiwes, Arizona State Museum photographer, for the studio pictures of artifacts. Ida Edwards prepared the readable typescript and organized the bibliography.

As I look back on those early efforts in the Forestdale Valley and compare what we did then with what is expected of archaeologists in the 1980s, I am conscious of serious omissions in field methodology. One cannot be held liable, however, for not having taken certain steps, made observations, or collected samples, the values of which had not then been suspected or demonstrated. The marvel is that, with the tools at hand, we extracted from the ground as much information as we did. An important contributor to that success was the ideal nature of the archaeological remains. The sites are geographically closely related, little disturbed, and they yield contrasting cultural attributes, including convincing information about their ages that permits arranging them chronologically. That our venture went so well must be credited to the students who shared in the work, who demonstrated so much enthusiasm and such keen eagerness to learn what the valley offered about the past. I have had few seasons in the field with young people that gave me so much pleasure with so few logistical headaches. And even if we be accused of having missed a few "tricks," I doubt if those investigators today, pressing to stretch the archaeological data to and beyond their capacity to deliver, can possibly be having more splanchnic and cerebral satisfaction in the pursuit of archaeology than we did.

Roster of Participants in the Forestdale Field School

1939
Bear Ruin

Students:
Wilfrid C. Bailey   Frederick H. Scantling
Gordon C. Baldwin   James Schaeffer
Florence M. Connolly   Margaret Schaeffer
Edward B. Danson   Frederick W. Sleight
Grace M. Eaton   Arnold M. Withers

Cook:
Sergeant "Sarge" Brown

1940
Bear Ruin and
Tla Kii Ruin

Students:
Brigham A. Arnold
Wilfrid C. Bailey
Jane Chesky
Allison Clement
Edward B. Danson
Clifford Evans
Richard B. Langenwalter
R. Kepler Lewis
May Belle Olea
Penelope P. Pattee
David W. Rice
Albert H. Schroeder
Margaret Shreve

Assistants:
Florence M. Connolly
Arnold M. Withers

Cook:
"Sarge" Brown

1941
Tla Kii Ruin
and Bluff Site

Students:
Brigham A. Arnold
David M. Bigelow
Marion A. Brown
Jane Chesky
M. Phyllis Cubberley
Doris Dayton
Philippa Dunham
John Gallovich
Charles H. Hewitt
Margaret C. Houghton
Richard K. Merrill
Jacqueline R. Newman
Ruth DeEtte Simpson
Irene S. Vickrey
Ruth E. Warner

Assistants:
Florence M. Connolly
Ralph T. Patton
Parke E. Vickrey

Cook:
"Sarge" Brown

May those named above derive pleasure from knowing that their labors contributed significantly to unraveling the human story of a little mountain valley that had a big impact on our understanding of the prehistory of the Southwest.

TLA KII RUIN
FORESTDALE'S OLDEST PUEBLO

ARCHAEOLOGY IN THE FORESTDALE VALLEY

One of the early goals of the Gila Pueblo Archaeological Foundation, established in Globe, Arizona, in 1928, was to inventory the ruins in the Southwest and to develop a sample of materials from them, notably pottery, as a basis for devising problem-oriented research. In the summer of 1931, Russell Hastings and I were sent by Harold S. Gladwin, Gila Pueblo's Director, to search for ruins in the threshold regions of the White Mountains in east-central Arizona. One aspect of this endeavor was to define the eastern limits of the Hohokam culture, to which much thought was being given at the time. We started near Heber along the Mogollon Rim and worked in a southeasterly direction as far as the White River country, the seat of the White Mountain Apache Reservation. We next moved to the San Francisco River drainage in west-central New Mexico, establishing a base near Reserve. The final step in the effort was to do a minimum sampling of the archaeological resources in the Mimbres Valley, ending an extended summer's activity.

Early in the survey it became clear to us that we were well beyond the eastern bounds of the Hohokam and into a rich archaeological zone of another kind. Although numerous stone ruins of pueblos were visited with the usual complements of black-on-white and sometimes polychrome pottery, we were struck by the fact that almost everywhere we looked, there were also extensive surface scatterings of broken pottery, predominantly brown and red in color, much of it smudged. For the most part, painted pottery was absent. These areas, we noted, were devoid of piles of stone rubble marking the site of collapsed buildings. In some places we saw depressions that were assumed to be pit houses. Troubles arose when we tried to apply the rules of the day in assigning these plain ware-producing sites to a place in the then-accepted classification of southwestern cultures. The sites particularly in question were Arizona P:16:1 (Bear Ruin) in the Forestdale Valley, a number in the Pine Lawn Valley of New Mexico, Mogollon 1:15 (Mogollon Village) along the San Francisco River north of

Alma, and New Mexico Q:1:14 (Harris Site) in the Mimbres Valley. All of them shared certain environmental and ceramic similarities, and it was assumed that they must have preceded in time the omnipresent and often large, demolished stone pueblos. They could not be accommodated under the rubric of Basketmaker.

After reviewing the summer's findings in the laboratory during the winter of 1931-1932, the Gila Pueblo staff decided that the question of what the cultural manifestation meant, and how it might be related to what was then known in the Southwest, warranted further investigation. Excavation of the Mogollon Village in 1933 and the Harris Site in 1934 launched this new interest at Gila Pueblo and provided the information that was written into *Medallion Paper* 20 (Haury 1936a; references follow the Epilogue), proposing the time had come to recognize a new complex, the Mogollon culture.

These efforts left the Forestdale Valley site untouched but not forgotten. In the mid-1930s the suggestion was made to Earl Morris, a key contributor to the Basketmaker story, that he should consider shifting his interest farther south to the Forestdale Valley to evaluate through his eyes what the differences between the early Plateau and more southerly cultural evidences meant. Although he expressed interest in doing this, the opportunity to carry out his intent never came. In the meantime, having returned to the faculty of the University of Arizona, I selected the Forestdale Valley in 1939 as an ideal spot for a summer school to acquaint students first-hand with field work in archaeology. The Bear Ruin (AZ P:16:1) was the first village to be studied. That work (Haury 1940a, reprinted herein as Part II), together with subsequent investigations in the Bluff Site (AZ P:16:20; Haury and Sayles 1947, reprinted herein as Part III), demonstrated that a cultural bond did seem to exist in these mountain-based villages from New Mexico into Arizona. Furthermore, the proximity of the Forestdale sites to those of Basketmaker vintage not far to the north on the Colorado Plateau emphasized the contrasts between them.

The good fortune of being in an area favorable to applying the tree-ring technique and, better still, the recovery during excavations of adequate tree-ring samples for dating, provided us early in the investigations with the information needed to establish a chronological base for the complex. Dates reaching back to the third and fourth centuries A.D. came as a surprise to many people. But those dates, along with later ones extending into the eighth and ninth centuries, added a significant and much needed dimension to the problem. The geographic extent of the complex was now known also to have a respectable time depth.

When the Forestdale studies were launched, our concern was with the emerging Mogollon problem. The thought that the later villages, the large stone pueblos such as Tundastusa and nearby AZ P:16:9, were then better known persuaded us not to spend much time on them. While in retrospect that now seems an unwise choice, as a partial compensation the study of the small pueblo, Tla Kii (AZ P:16:2), was a positive move. That decision was reached because it was believed to be the earliest stone structure seen during the survey. Furthermore, a heavy concentration of plain brown pottery near the pueblo suggested that information on the relationship between the Mogollon and the Anasazi might be forthcoming by excavating it. The transition from one complex to the other, whether continuous and smooth or whether of short duration and abrupt, were questions of interest. This report, then, is a belated accounting of the work in the Tla Kii pueblo and its environs.

HISTORICAL NOTE

One aspect of the work in the Forestdale Valley, which was mentioned in the Prologue, is the role it played in the unfolding of ideas about the Mogollon culture. Historically, the Forestdale studies built on the findings in the Mogollon and Harris villages. The solid chronological information, as well as data on the nature of the remains collected during those efforts, stimulated interest in the Mogollon and curiosity, if not skepticism, about it among colleagues. A review of my log of the four seasons of work in the valley reveals a few crumbs of history worth incorporating in this record.

In 1938, Paul S. Martin of the Field Museum of Natural History, Chicago, having completed his investigations in the Lowry Ruin of southwestern Colorado, visited Gila Pueblo ". . . for the purpose of keeping abreast of the work being done by its staff and of obtaining counsel on the choice of new sites for study" (Martin and others 1940: 8). His interest in the plain ware sites of the Pine Lawn region near Reserve, New Mexico, was kindled at that time. The prospects of having another investigator in the Mogollon region was warmly welcomed by Gila Pueblo. Martin proceeded to develop a base camp in the Pine Lawn Valley from which he launched many years of highly productive work in sites of the Mogollon culture, becoming one of its ardent proponents.

Martin was visiting Gila Pueblo in June of 1939 while his camp in the Pine Lawn Valley was being assembled by Joe Weckler and John Rinaldo, his chief assistants. Having learned that we were to start our work in the Forestdale Valley, he expressed a desire to visit the region to see the sites and to keep informed of our plans. On June 11, I picked him up in Globe as we headed for Forestdale to establish our camp. Visits back and forth and season-end contacts provided opportunities for sharing information and exchanging ideas.

A serious concern of mine was that as many colleagues as possible should see first-hand the nature of Forestdale archaeology. The Mogollon and Harris village studies had attracted few professional peers. Early in July, 1939, Ernst Antevs arrived at Forestdale, at our invitation, to examine the physiography and geology of the valley, and to interpret the terrace system and its bearing on the archaeological record. In mid-July, J. O. Brew and Harriet Cosgrove appeared for a visit, coming from Awatovi where those important studies were in full swing. A review of the structures then open and other evidence persuaded Brew to admit freely that what he saw could not be classified as Basketmaker. This did not mean, however, that he endorsed the Mogollon concept, as his later writings made clear.

Although by July 22 and 23 we did not yet have tree-ring data for the Bear Ruin, perhaps it was prophetic that our camp should play host to the Fifth Annual Tree-Ring Conference (Lassetter 1939). Present were: A. E. Douglass, Gordon C. Baldwin, Paul Ezell, I. F. Flora, H. T. Getty, Thomas Hale, Edward T. Hall, L. L. Hargrave, Roy Lassetter, Albert Schroeder, Edmund Schulman, Donovan Senter, Florence Hawley Senter, and W. S. Stallings, Jr. Apart from settling Tree-Ring Society business, the conferees were fully acquainted with our findings.

Earl Morris paid us a brief call on July 24, 1939. His disappointment at not being able to work in the Forestdale Valley was heightened after seeing the site. He expressed his view by saying, "There's something different going on here."

By early August, not long before the summer's work was to end, the time was right to compare notes with co-workers. Invitations brought the following people to the Forestdale camp: Paul Martin and his assistants, Joe Weckler and John Rinaldo; Paul Nesbitt, then digging on the Three Circle Ranch; John McGregor; Erik Reed; and E. B. Sayles. The pros and cons of what we were dealing with in relation to other manifestations in the Southwest were discussed in depth. Efforts to categorize the essence of the Mogollon were attempted, trait lists were developed, and we had near-unanimous agreement that the people of the Mogollon culture, although "colorless, living on a relatively low cultural plane, built houses, had pottery and a few other elements which left their imprint on later Southwestern developments." Nesbitt remained unconvinced, though he offered no alternative solution and found it difficult to answer certain questions put to him. The group agreed (before tree-ring dates became available) that the Forestdale site should date in the late A.D. 700s and that smudged pottery found there was not only indigenous, but the oldest yet seen and undoubtedly one of the main hallmarks of the Mogollon. While agreements in views do not necessarily establish the correctness of a situation, the plausibility of the interpretation nevertheless is enhanced thereby.

During the 1940 season, work on the Bear Ruin was completed, including clearing the proto Great Kiva, which added a new feature to the complex, and the Tla Kii studies went into full swing. While the findings in the pueblo lacked the excitement of the 1939 work, we were satisfied that the post-A.D. 900 additions to the chronology were essential in binding together the several chapters in the valley's prehistory.

In the summer of 1941, our investigation of Tla Kii Ruin was finished, and preliminary testing was started on the Bluff Site (AZ P:16:20), then believed to be Apache. We were under the impression that the earliest evidence of occupation in the valley had been tapped in the Bear Ruin, and that efforts to bridge the late prehistoric Pueblo and early historic Apache histories would add significantly to the story. Hough's (1903, Pl. 2) designation of the bluff top as an Apache fort and our own investigations showed that some use of the bluff had indeed been made by the Apache as a refuge and burial place. However, excavations immediately revealed a depth of refuse and extent of surface topographic alterations that did not fit our concepts of Apache activities (Haury and Sayles 1947: 11). We were soon to learn that the remains on the bluff carried the Mogollon complex deeper into antiquity, and that stages antecedent to and forerunners of the oldest Bear Ruin materials were being viewed. This was a most welcome turn of events, because at that moment in Southwestern archaeological investigations the question of time depth was uppermost in many minds, and new data were needed if the credibility of the Mogollon was to be established. Important in reaching that decision were pit houses hewn into native rock, indicative of village stability; food processing tools reflecting an agricultural base; a ceramic technology, simple with respect to range of types and extremely low in frequency of production; and lesser attributes that were not only non-Apache but reflective of items we had seen somewhat better developed in the younger horizon of the Bear Ruin. Most importantly, analysis of tree-ring specimens supported our belief by providing dates in the third and fourth centuries A.D. These tantalizing findings made us eager to expand the investigations, digging in the remaining parts of the site. But the season's end had come and we returned to Tucson.

Then came the war, putting a halt to the work until 1944. A welcome grant from the Viking Fund, one of its first, persuaded Sayles and me to return to Forestdale, using an Apache labor crew. The discovery of several houses, later than the rank and file of those that had been opened earlier, revealed certain Basketmaker characteristics that focused attention on the question we had already asked as to the nature and the beginning of an amalgamation between the Anasazi and Mogollon complexes. Hypothetically, this had to take place if the people of the later pueblos were descended in an unbroken line from such cultural stages as those manifested in the Bear and Bluff villages.

The Forestdale years and my connection with them represented a deep personal involvement in the shaping of a concept then new to the Southwest. Whether right or wrong was less important than trying to understand the remains being studied and how they related to the larger picture of Southwestern prehistory. Heated debates, overt expressions of disbelief, and questionings of one's own thoughts characterized the times. Eventually, the ever-increasing amount of excavation in the brown ware-producing sites, refinement of our knowledge of the substance and age of the culture, and an expanded view of the pan-Southwest, brought respectability to the concept, which, after experiencing exceptional birth pangs, seems to be here to stay.

THE FORESTDALE VALLEY AND TLA KII RUIN

The Mogollon Rim looms as an impressive feature on the landscape in central Arizona. Earth-shaping processes left behind a south-facing escarpment from 500 m to 800 m high that appears south of Flagstaff and slashes its way southeasterly for about 150 km, where it loses itself in the massif of the White Mountains. The Rim forms the southern limit of the Colorado Plateau, a vast area stretching north and east into the adjoining states of Utah, Colorado, and New Mexico. As a topographic feature, the Rim holds fascination for the traveler because from its top one gains a magnificent view of central Arizona. While not a significant geographic barrier, the Rim may be recognized as a symbol of a cultural boundary, for in the early centuries of the Christian era the people on the Plateau and those in the mountains south of it appear to have been different, as reflected by the hardware of culture they left behind. As time progressed, a spilling over of people, largely from north to south, resulted in an amalgamation of the two groups, thereby posing a set of exceptionally interesting problems for the archaeologist.

The Mogollon Rim, rising to an elevation of 2200 m and more in a few places (7000+ feet), constitutes a watershed between drainages that feed north to the Little Colorado River and those trending south to discharge collected waters into the Salt River, ultimately reaching the Gila River near Phoenix, thence to the Colorado River and the Gulf of California. The head branches of Forestdale Canyon begin under the Rim, 5 km (3 miles) due south of Show Low. Dropping sharply, they soon coalesce to form Forestdale Creek at about 660 m (6100 feet) above sea level, where the gradient of the stream flattens and the valley floor opens in a series of subtle terraces. At this point the topography becomes suitable for agriculture (Fig. 1).

Compared with most other southwestern valleys, such as those of the Chaco Wash, Puerco River, Little Colorado and Mimbres rivers, the Forestdale Valley is narrow and short, and the ruins in it are limited in number. The rich bottom lands, barely 6.5 km (4 miles) in extent, were nevertheless a plum worth picking by agriculturists. The lower end of the valley is choked by a lava flow, and at about that point Forestdale Creek joins Corduroy Creek. The shortness of the valley and the hills crowding in from the sides forced the population to live in comparatively close quarters.

The physical discreteness of the valley was one of the qualities that attracted us to it, for the archaeological problems could thereby be more easily contained, and we foresaw the possibility of developing a notion of valley prehistory in the time and with the resources available to us.

Gila Pueblo's survey of the Forestdale Valley in 1931 was expanded during our four seasons of digging, and a few more sites have been added to the inventory in recent years as the result of highway construction. In aggregate, the site list enumerates 73 places where man left traces of his presence. These include villages large and small, identified by tumbled-down houses of stone, scatterings of pottery and other debris without

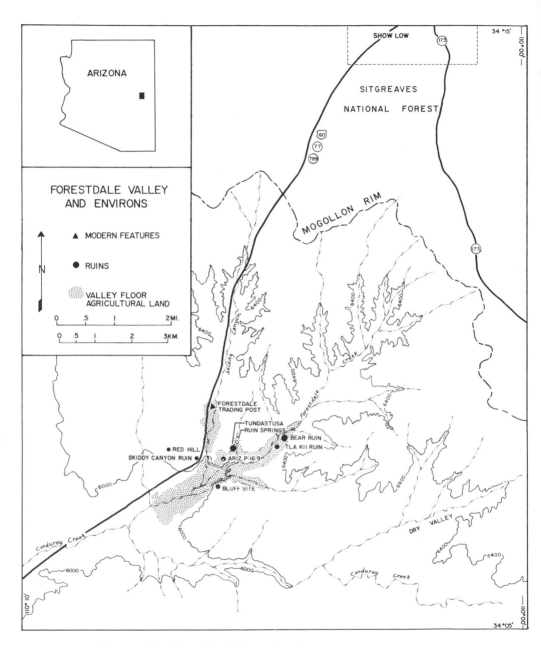

Figure 1. The Forestdale Valley and environs.
Only the principal sites are shown.

Table 1
PHASES IN THE FORESTDALE VALLEY

Date	Phase	Site
1900	Alchesay	Mormon "temple"
1800		
1700	Skidi	
1600		
1500	—hiatus—	
1400	Canyon Creek	Show Low Ruin (AZ P:12:3), also Red Rock House, Grasshopper Pueblo, Canyon Creek Ruin
1300	Pinedale	Pinedale Ruin (AZ P:12:2)
1200	Linden	
1100	Carrizo	Tla Kii Ruin (AZ P:16:2)
1000	Dry Valley	Tla Kii Ruin (AZ P:16:2)
900	Corduroy	Tla Kii Ruin (AZ P:16:2)
800		
700	Forestdale	Bear Ruin (AZ P:16:1)
600		
500	Cottonwood	Bluff Site (AZ P:16:20)
400		
300	Hilltop	Bluff Site (AZ P:16:20)
200		
100		
A.D. 1		

architectural evidence, and the remains of Apache wickiups. We can be certain that the major areas of prolonged pre-Apache residence in the valley have been found. Although there was little overbuilding through time, we need not go far to find remains centuries apart in time. Succeeding generations seem to have avoided establishing their buildings on the ruins of those already there.

The range of time represented by the sites is estimated to be from the second or third century of the Christian era to the twentieth century, with a major discontinuity from about A.D. 1450 to 1850 (Table 1). Sound judgments about population increases and decreases, and variations in the subsistence base, are not easily made. Certainly, agriculture was always a part of the economic pattern, supplemented at all times by gathering and hunting practices. The large architectural complexes, notably Tundastusa, hint that in late times, between 1200 and 1400, farming reached its peak in the per capita yield of plant food.

Site distribution points out a simple fact: well-drained places were selected for residence. There is evidence, however, that during the oldest horizon, the Hilltop phase, high prominences were chosen, most likely because they offered better opportunities for self-protection, whether against human foes or adverse natural conditions (Haury and Sayles 1947; see Part III, *Additional Sites*). The Bluff Site and the Red Knoll Site (AZ P:16:58) are examples. The ready availability of water in the valley from the stream and springs made that resource only a nominal factor in site location. Tundastusa, it should be noted, was situated adjacent to a reliable and free-flowing spring. In short, practical reasons of safety from foes or floods, nearness to water and arable land, determined residence location.

The presence of Hohokam pottery in the Hilltop phase and early Anasazi types in phase contexts thereafter clearly reveals that contacts with other Southwestern groups were enjoyed throughout prehistory. Intensification of contacts, for whatever reasons, may be assumed to have taken place during the Pinedale and Canyon Creek phases, the time of greatest population in the White Mountains generally, but I see nothing in site placement that could be taken as evidence of a conscious choice of location to improve intervillage relationships.

A simple correlation between architectural form and ceramic typology can be made that reflects the trend of cultural advances. Brown and smudged plain ware, an absence of indigenous painted pottery, and pit houses (no surface stone houses) constitute a small group of sites (three) in which the Hilltop, Cottonwood, and Forestdale phases have been recognized. Next in the sequence are probably six sites containing the same pottery complex as before but with the addition of Corduroy Black-on-white, the first locally produced painted pottery, and neck-banded vessels still associated with pit houses. That was the time of the Corduroy phase. In the ensuing horizon, the Dry Valley phase, stone architecture in the form of small houses and an increased amount of and more developed black-on-white pottery appear. About 16 sites fit this group. Then follows a roughly equal number of sites containing a complement of black-on-white, black-on-red, plain brown, and smudged wares, with an abundance of corrugated pottery (including the beginning of McDonald Corrugated), related to pueblos ranging from 10 to 20 rooms—the Carrizo phase. In the succeeding Linden phase, although the number of ruins drops to 10, village size increases to at least 100 rooms, and the ceramic complex is enriched by the first three-color pottery, St. Johns Polychrome. Finally, in the Pinedale and Canyon Creek phases, the population coalesced into a single large pueblo of several hundred rooms, except for a few scattered outlying structures, and the pottery inventory was further elaborated by the addition of a variety of late polychromes: Pinedale, Gila, and Fourmile. The five Apache wickiups, noted in the survey, are not fully reflective of the extent of Apache use of the valley, but they do demonstrate the radical change in cultural type after the withdrawal of the pueblo-building Indians.

Perhaps as many as 600 domestic rooms are represented in the sites listed in the survey. A subjective prorating of rooms by phase would show a curve indicating a population increase early to late, but my confidence in exact quantification is so low that I do not have the courage to put the figures down on paper. What one sees transpiring.in the Forestdale Valley, with respect to subsistence and population, appears to be a microcosm of what happened in the Southwest generally.

In a description of the Forestdale Valley, Hough (1903: 291) includes mention of a small stone pueblo on the south bank of Forestdale Creek about 1 km east of the principal ruin, Tundastusa. Our survey designated that pueblo as AZ P:16:2. To be consistent with earlier practices of naming sites in which extensive work was done and to avoid the cumbersomeness of a code designation, a search was made for an appropriate Apache term for the site. Although English-speakers find difficulty in pronouncing many Apache words, two single-syllable words suggested by Keith Basso, łąą 'many' and kįįh 'rooms' should present no insurmountable obstacles to oral and written communication. The International Phonetic Alphabet used may be simplified for our needs as Tla Kii, pronounced to rhyme with "baa key." The name suitably recognizes the first appearance of tightly clustered houses in the long evolution of Forestdale architecture.

The 6080–foot contour (1853 m) runs directly through the site (Fig. 1). The Bear Ruin (AZ P:16:1) lies about 250 m to the north north-east on the same plain (Part II), which is the surface of the first or oldest terrace in the valley's terrace system. The obvious architectural mound and differences in the pottery scattered about the Tla Kii Ruin suggested to us that excavations here might lead to evidences that would contribute to the valley's cultural sequence.

The dating of the set of terraces formed by Forestdale Creek has been greatly helped by the archaeological remains resting upon or affected by them (see Part II, *Terraces*). Because nature's way of building and destroying terraces has played an important role in the status of Tla Kii Ruin as we see it today, a review of the evidence is worthwhile. Figure 2 represents

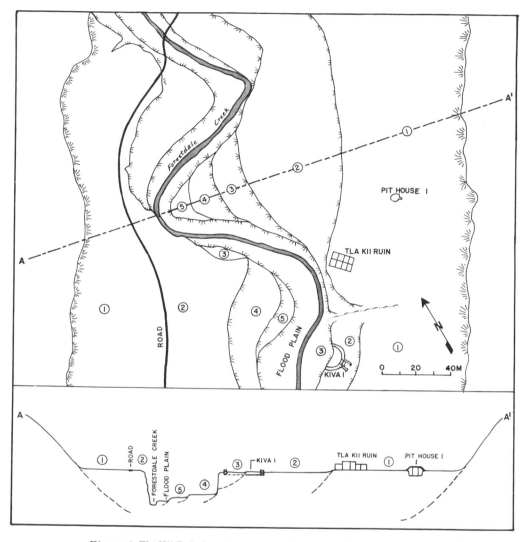

Figure 2. Tla Kii Ruin in relation to the Forestdale Valley terrace system. The profile is a composite; archaeological features have been moved to the cross-section line to show the relationship of Man's activities to terrace-building and destruction. Vertical scale exaggerated. Terraces indicated by circled number.

schematically a cross-section of the terrace system at the site. The upper terrace (1) is the oldest, dating far into the past. Terrace 1 was well established when the Bear village settlers moved in around A.D. 600. Most of the Tla Kii Ruin, as nearly as can be determined, also rests on that terrace. However, the

Great Kiva (Kiva 1), detached from the room cluster, was built
into Terrace 2, which formed sometime after A.D. 600, but that
was well established when the kiva was built soon after A.D.
1115. As is noted later, during the excavation of the structure we
were puzzled when the outer rock wall, the bench, and well-
packed and easily followed floor suddenly played out. We were
hard pressed to understand what happened until deeper excavations, at the point where the architectural features disappeared,
revealed the bank of an old arroyo. During a previous erosion
cycle, natural forces bit into the kiva, carrying a little more than
half of it down stream (see Fig. 4, plan), thereby destroying a
part of the archaeological record. Later on, when down-cutting
was replaced by a period of aggradation, nature played an
uncommon trick by restoring the landscape to its exact former
level. The surfaces of Terrace 2 and the newly developed Terrace
3 coincided, leaving no evidence superficially to suggest any
difference in the morphology of the deposits. Evidence was clear
that the kiva was destroyed by fire, presumably during the
period of its use. The further destruction by erosion probably
took place after the abandonment of the pueblo. Antevs, who
studied the terrace system for us, suggested that the cutting of
the arroyo was associated with the dry cycle recorded in the
tree-rings from A.D. 1276 to 1299. The pottery types in Tla Kii
Ruin indicate that the abandonment took place in the latter half
of the 1100s.

After the restoration of Terrace 3, Forestdale Creek ran in a
shallow channel, willow-lined, as it was seen by the early White
settlers. Long-time residents of the area told us that the creek
could be crossed anywhere by wagon and that trout fishing was
one of the local pastimes. By about 1910 a new period of down-
cutting began, which, by 1939, had reached a depth of 3 m in the
vicinity of Tla Kii Ruin. Meandering of the stream brought its
destructive forces to the ruin once again, washing away portions
of Rooms 5 and 19 (see Fig. 3b) and exposing Burial 2. How much
more of the occupational evidence was removed, we do not know.

Further shifts in the stream channel have resulted in Terraces 4 and 5, both weak structures, dating since 1910. These
have no bearing on the archaeology.

Paleoenvironmental and land form changes since the Southwestern valleys were first inhabited by humans are becoming of
increasing interest not only for archaeologists, but for investigators in other disciplines. Knowledge of them is essential if we
are to understand how people responded to changes in the land
and whether or not they were a causal factor in producing those

changes. The recent studies on Black Mesa (Euler and others 1979), the Cochise studies of Sayles and Antevs (1941), and Hack's (1942) work in the Hopi area are examples. With respect to the Forestdale terrace system, the time represented in their formation was relatively short. Alterations in the topography of considerable magnitude can be demonstrated as having taken place in only a few centuries. I do not sense, recognizing the incompleteness of the data, that the land-form changes we see in the valley are grounds for claiming any major impacts on the life-ways of the local populace. People, undoubtedly, were forced to make adjustments, perhaps less with respect to residence than to where they planted and where the trails up and down the valleys were deployed. The continuity of the archaeological record to about A.D. 1450 does not support a claim for intermittency of occupation or modifications of the subsistence base caused by environmental factors. The fifteenth century abandonment of the area is another matter.

TLA KII RUIN

ARCHITECTURAL REMAINS

The mound of rocks formed by Tla Kii Ruin rose approximately 1 m above the surrounding plain, and its longest axis, about 25 m, trended northwest-southeast (Fig. 3a). Before excavation, wall outlines were not sufficiently clear to provide an accurate basis for judging the number of rooms in the structure. The channel of Forestdale Creek, in 1941, was cutting into the northwest end of the building (Fig. 3b), although when occupied the pueblo must have been located at what was regarded as a safe distance from the flowing stream from which the occupants drew their domestic water.

A short distance northeast of the pueblo, a slight rise in the ground surface, well sprinkled with potsherds, suggested the presence of a rubbish heap. Here a mixture of early and late sherds occurred that gave rise to the hope that somewhere in the area overlapping of late on early remains would be found. Testing eventually proved this to be the case, revealing old pit houses and associated trash. The significance of this situation became apparent when we determined that the residue of occupation on which the pueblo was superimposed was more recent than that of the Bear Ruin proper (Forestdale phase), and that in all, three cultural stages were discernible on the basis of architecture and ceramics. These were named the Corduroy, Dry Valley, and

Figure 3. The Forestdale Valley: *a*, view to the west with Tla Kii Ruin in *lower right*; *b*, Tla Kii Ruin in relation to the east bank of Forestdale Creek in 1941.

Carrizo phases. Figure 4 shows the general relationships of the architectural features. In order to keep the horizons well separated, there follows first the description and discussion of the older pit house remains in the environs of the pueblo, followed by a review of the pueblo itself.

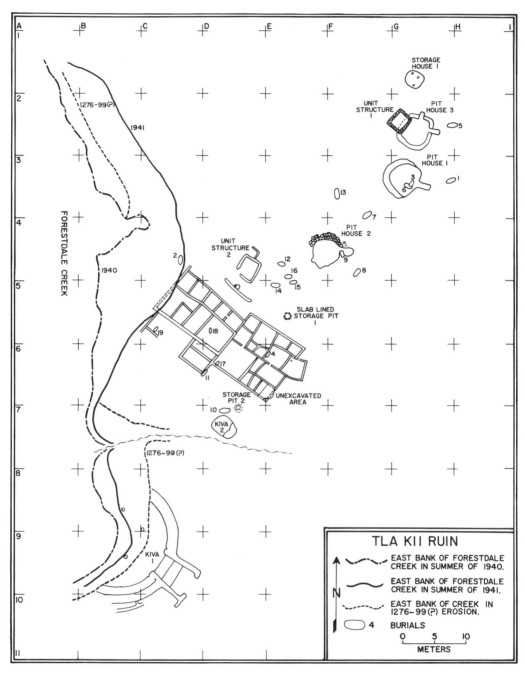

Figure 4. Tla Kii Ruin and nearby kivas, unit structures,
and pit houses. Burial locations are also shown.

PIT HOUSES

House 1 (Figs. 5, 6)
  Shape. Roughly circular; maximum diameter, 5.5 m.
  Walls. Unplastered black native clay; eroded, apparently
    from standing open after abandonment.
  Bench. Three-quarter type, away from entrance; 0.65 m above
    floor.
  Floor. Black clay, rough; depth below present surface, 1.2 m,
    below ground level at time of construction, probably 1 m.
  Firepit. Large, centrally located basin, scooped out of clay.
  Entrance. Lateral, east-southeast, sloping toward surface,
    departs room with low step; length 1.75 m.
  Pits. Four, all containing some rocks; large pit along south
    margin partially filled with heat-fractured stones, though
    pit itself showed no burning. This is regarded as a "warm-
    ing area" for which stones were heated outside. Pit along
    west side slightly undercut wall and penetrated sand,
    probably for storage.
  Postholes. Four primary, arranged on quadrate plan, set in
    from wall; average depth 0.25 m. None located at entrance
    or on bench.
  Roof. No direct evidence; probably flat central part with
    leaning parts.
  Tree-ring material. None.
  Pottery. Unmixed assemblage of Corduroy Black-on-white,
    Forestdale Smudged, Forestdale Red, and a strong
    dominance of Alma Plain and some Alma Neck-banded.
    If sample was quantified, the data have been lost.
  Phase. Corduroy.
  Comments. Circumstances force the use of associational data
    only in determining the age of this room. Two Corduroy
    phase burials (Numbers 3 and 6), both with mortuary
    offerings, at a depth of 0.55 m or halfway down in the fill,
    point to a Corduroy phase assignment or earlier. In the
    former case, the structure might be regarded as dating
    from the early part of the phase, or the burials date late in
    this horizon. The field analysis of the pottery from this
    house reflects only the Corduroy phase complex. Since
    the ceramic components of the Forestdale and Corduroy
    phases differ chiefly in the addition of black-on-white
    pottery to the brown, red, and smudged wares of the
    earlier horizon, the structure could be somewhat earlier
    than here supposed. (See Fig. 52 for Burial 3 grave
    furniture.)

Figure 5. Pit House 1, Corduroy phase.

House 2 (Figs. 7, 8)

Shape. Circular, maximum diameter, 4.0 m.

Walls. Native clay, no plaster evident.

Bench. North margin of house has rock paving on what might have been bench level, but further extension of this level about perimeter of house not traceable. Stones could be resting on ground surface at time house was inhabited.

Floor. Irregular and pitted.

Firepit. Centrally located, oblong, floor depression.

Entrance. Lateral, east orientation, pear-shaped; floor slopes upward slightly, ending in step of about 0.5 m to old surface; length 2.6 m.

Pits. Four. Two along north and west walls, respectively undercut and excavated to sandy silt; former has smaller pit within the larger one. Rock-filled pit between firepit and entry contained no ash, but stones were fire-stained. Possibly a warming oven.

Postholes. Two primary only; depth 0.2 m.

Roof. No data.

Tree-ring material. None.

Pottery. See comments for House 1.

Phase. Corduroy.

Comments. House 2 is the only structure in either the For-

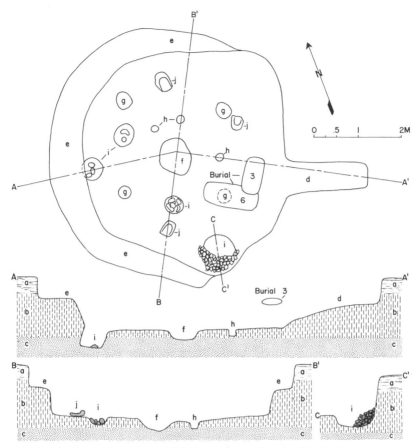

Figure 6. Plan and sections of Pit House 1: *a*, silt and refuse; *b*, black clay; *c*, yellow sandy silt; *d*, entrance; *e*, bench; *f*, firepit; *g*, primary postholes; *h*, secondary postholes; *i*, floor pits; *j*, metates on floor.

estdale or Corduroy phases in which any appreciable stone work was seen. The rimming of the pit with rocks of various sizes, although only partially, would appear to forecast a more-developed form of this principle seen in Unit Structure 2 of the Dry Valley phase. Equivalent use of peripheral stones is reported by Breternitz (1959: 5-6) in the Nantack Village in a time period approximately the age of House 2. Burial 9, judged to be late Corduroy phase by the associated pottery, was intruded into the entry after the house was vacated and became filled. The house did not burn.

Figure 7. Pit House 2, Corduroy phase. Rocks represent
early architectural use of stone.

House 3 (Figs. 9, 10)

Shape. Roughly quadrate; maximum diameter, 4.5 m,
exclusive of bench.

Walls. Black native clay, no evidence of plaster.

Bench. Completely encircles pit, sides eroded; 0.4 m above
floor, excavated through black clay into sandy-silt layer.

Floor. Rough and unplastered; depth below present surface
1.25 m, below old ground level about 1 m.

Firepit. Central, circular depression in sand.

Deflector. Fallen flat rock at northeast margin of firepit
probably represents deflector.

Ventilator. To north, short, interrupts bench; four small posts
probably supported protective cover; width 0.5 m.

Entrance. Lateral, east-southeast, sloping toward surface
and slightly expanded distally; leaves pit near primary
roof support post; length 2.0 m.

Pits. One, shallow, south of hearth.

Postholes. Four primary, arranged on quadrate plan, set
away from wall; average depth 0.25 m.

Roof. No data.

Tree-ring material. None.

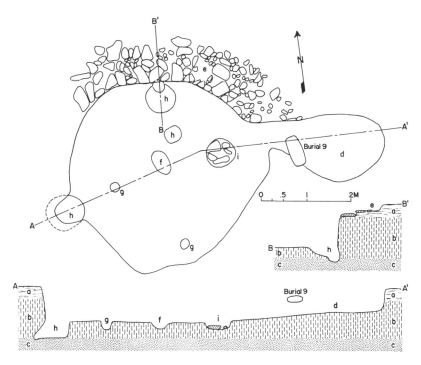

Figure 8. Plan and sections of Pit House 2: *a*, silt and refuse; *b*, black clay; *c*, yellow sandy silt; *d*, entrance; *e*, rock paving; *f*, firepit; *g*, primary postholes; *h*, floor pits; *i*, probable warming oven.

Pottery. Pottery yield of fill about 1300 fragments, represents the Corduroy phase complex in the following gross percentages: Alma Plain (75%); Forestdale Smudged (10%); Forestdale Red (3%); Corduroy Black-on-white (5%); other, including Alma Neck-banded, Forestdale Plain, Woodruff Smudged, White Mound Black-on-white, Lino Gray, and intrusive Hohokam (5%); pottery of later phases (2%).

Phase. Corduroy.

Comments. A peculiarity of this house is that it was equipped with an entryway and a ventilator. House 4 of the Bear Ruin, Forestdale phase (see Part II, *Domestic Structures*), was similarly arranged, establishing the tradition at an earlier time level than indicated here. Unit Structure 1, of masonry, stratigraphically overlaps

Figure 9. Pit House 3, Corduroy phase. Unit structure 1
was built later, probably during the Carrizo phase.

House 3, indicating that by the time it was built,
probably during the Carrizo phase, the older house pit
was already filled.

STORAGE STRUCTURE 1

About 5 m north of House 3, a circular structure (Fig. 11)
came to light lacking entryway, hearth, and other features
normally associated with domestic structures. Several holes in
the floor may have engaged posts. The small diameter, 3.5 m,
and absence of hearth and floor artifacts suggest a usage other
than for living, hence the idea that it served storage needs.
Sherds removed from the fill include Alma Plain, Forestdale
Plain, red and smudged wares, Alma Neck-banded and Corduroy Black-on-white, on which the structure is assigned to the
Corduroy phase.

UNIT STRUCTURES

Structure 1 (Figs. 9, 10)

Shape. Rectangular; width 1.65 m, length 2.25 m.

Walls. Unshaped sandstone blocks, poorly laid; west wall
base 0.15 m above floor; foundation only remaining.

Floor. Excavated to black clay level in that part of structure
lying outside of Pit House 3, not well-packed or readily
definable.

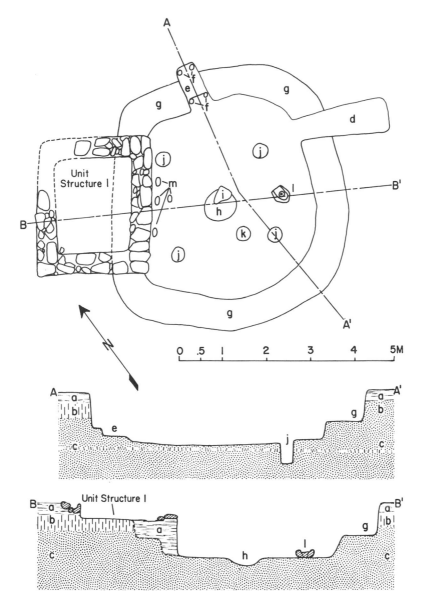

Figure 10. Plan and sections of Pit House 3: *a*, silt and refuse; *b*, black clay; *c*, yellow sandy silt; *d*, entrance; *e*, ventilator; *f*, support posts for ventilator cover; *g*, bench; *h*, firepit; *i*, deflector stone; *j*, primary postholes; *k*, shallow pit; *l*, metate-mortar; *m*, manos.

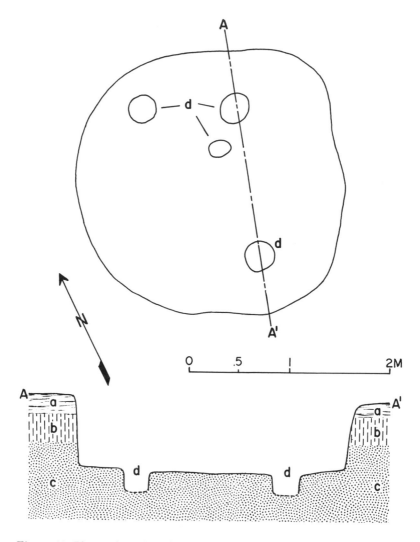

Figure 11. Plan and section of Storage Structure (?) 1: *a*, silt and refuse; *b*, black clay; *c*, yellow sandy silt; *d*, probable postholes.

Firepit, Entrance. No evidence.

Pottery. Only 57 sherds recovered, predominantly Corduroy phase.

Phase. Carrizo (?)

Comments. On the basis of form, masonry construction, and stratigraphic lateness, Unit Structure 1 is assigned to the Carrizo phase. The small sample of pottery, although including a few late (Carrizo phase) black-on-white and corrugated fragments, consisted mainly of Corduroy phase types. This is a good illustration of the fact that pottery associated with an architectural feature may be deceptive and unreliable as a means of dating.

The isolation of this unit from the main structure and lack of a hearth and artifacts hint at a special function, perhaps that of a menstrual hut.

Structure 2 (Figs. 12, 13)

Shape. Square; 2.90 m by 3.0 m.

Walls. Lower 0.35 m, yellow sandy silt, unplastered and without masonry face; upper part masonry, mostly of unshaped angular sandstone blocks, roughly laid up along the edge of excavation with black clay mortar and small chinking stones. Stones set vertically, as in annex, were shaped by percussion flaking. Incompleteness of such walls indicates stone salvaging by later residents. Pueblo walls show random distribution of identically shaped stones.

Bench. Along northeast wall only, width and height, 0.35 m. Bench is native yellow sandy silt, left during course of house excavation; partially destroyed during clearing.

Floor. Unplastered and irregular.

Firepit. Original pit circular with clay coping, later remodeled into a square slab-lined fire box; located near southwest wall.

Entrance. No clear evidence for side entrance, though several interruptions in masonry wall occurred. Roof entrance probable.

Pits. Two; shallow small hole next to hearth and a basin-shaped pit, diameter 0.4 m, near south corner, filled with clean sand.

Postholes. None.

Roof. No data; walls probably supported beams.

Tree-ring material. None.

Pottery. See comments below.

Phase. Dry Valley.

Comments. Several aspects of this structure should be noted.

1. The architectural form, combining both the old idea of a pit and the newer tradition of stone walls, places it, typologically at least, between the pit houses of the Corduroy

Figure 12. Unit Structure 2. A roughly laid stone wall
tops the edge of the excavations into subsoil.

phase and the pueblo of the Carrizo phase. For its probable chronological position, we must rely wholly on
ceramics from the room. The principal types present—
black-on-white in the Reserve and Snowflake style of
painting, corrugated vessels, and small amounts of red,
smudged, and plain types—are the components of the Dry
Valley phase. They also constitute the complex taken
from the storage pits below and therefore antedating the
pueblo, giving support to the time placement stated
above. This is not to imply that the evolution of subsurface to surface living took place here, only that the trend,
widely seen in the Southwest, is also reflected here.

2. Consideration has been given to the idea that Unit
   Structure 2 may have been a kiva, due to the presence of
   a bench, a floor pit filled with sand, a pit near the hearth
   that might be construed as a *sipapu*, and the subsurface
   nature of the room. If so, it lacked the ventilator and the
   formality usually associated with kivas. The idea is
   rejected because of the following observations.

3. The small annex near the north corner may have been a
   storage structure, often associated with domestic rooms
   and not kivas. The wing-wall 1.5 m to the southwest,
   with its related firepit, appears by its location to have

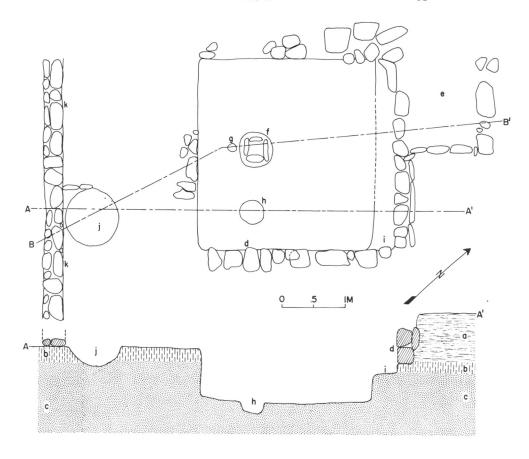

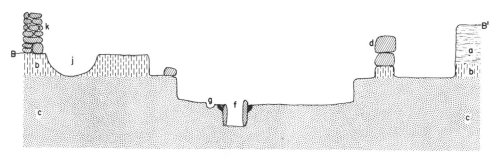

Figure 13. Plan and sections of Unit Structure 2: *a*, silt and refuse; *b*, black clay; *c*, yellow sandy silt; *d*, roughly laid masonry; *e*, annex structure; *f*, slab-lined hearth in clay hearth; *g*, floor pit; *h*, sand-filled pit; *i*, bench; *j*, large firepit; *k*, wing wall.

had some connection with the house unit. This wall is in the direction of the prevailing wind, and it would have given some protection for cooking and other outside activities.

The discovery of only one house does not provide us, of course, with the data needed to assess the architecture of the Dry Valley phase, but the type is not incongruous in the trend determined by both earlier and later local house forms.

THE PUEBLO

Figure 14 gives the ground plan of Tla Kii Ruin. The structure consists of a minimum of 21 compactly arranged rooms, all but one of which (Room 15) were completely excavated. An additional room or rooms may have existed at the west corner, indicated by a few wall footings. The axis of the pueblo trends northwest to southeast, and the grouping of the rooms indicates that a plaza as such did not exist as a part of the plan. Extensive trenching failed to reveal any outlying walls except the one apparently related to Unit Structure 2. During the winter of 1940, Forestdale Creek, deeply entrenched in its arroyo, cut into the northwestern end of the structure, partially destroying Rooms 5 and 19, and exposing Burial 2 and a trash-filled pit (Pit 12) below the floor of Room 19. The threatened destruction of the village by erosion was partly responsible for the redoubling of our efforts to complete work on it in 1941.

Order of Construction

Examination of wall junctures (Fig. 14) reveals that the construction of the 21 rooms in totality followed no preconceived plan. Enlargement of the nuclear core of rooms was done by the simple expedient of tacking on sets of rooms as they were needed. The nature of the wall junctures establishes the order of construction, at least for blocks of rooms. Because there is no reason to believe that more than a decade or two elapsed during which construction was done, the building sequence loses any possible period or phase significances, but the order does tell us something about the building habits of the people. In spite of the apparently short construction time, the masonry is surprisingly varied.

Ignoring for the present time such features as were left by earlier occupants, referring particularly to a wall footing

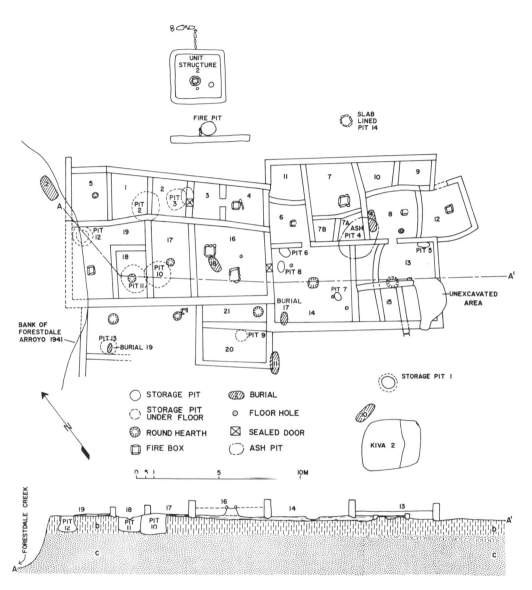

Figure 14. Ground plan and section of Tla Kii Ruin, showing some construction details and relationships to subfloor features: *a*, silt and refuse; *b*, black clay; *c*, yellow sandy silt. For location of Kiva 1 and pit houses, see Figure 4.

under the floors of Rooms 13 and 15, and a wall stub separating Rooms 20 and 21 that was later concealed or modified by pueblo remodeling, the construction order was as follows.

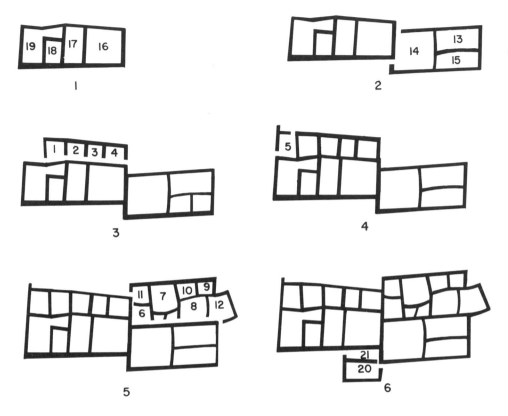

Figure 15. Construction of Tla Kii Ruin; six building episodes are evident.

1. Rooms 16, 17, 18, and 19, housing at least three families (Fig. 15a). Room 18, evidently an afterthought, was put inside of Room 19 and is suggestive of the storage cubicles sometimes seen in pueblo rooms. It did have its own hearth, however. Following this initial cluster of rooms, additions were made in the approximate order mentioned below.

2. Rooms 14 and 13, both large, the latter divided by a partition wall to create Room 15. This wall was built on 0.4 m of fill in Room 13, hence late in the life of the pueblo. A two-family addition.

3. Rooms 1, 2, 3, and 4; two families.

4. Probably Room 5, although this could have been erected at any time after Room 1; one family.

5. Rooms 6, 11, 7, 7A, 8, 9, 10, and 12; four families.

6. Rooms 20 and 21; one family.

Two hearths in a partially walled area (unnumbered) south of Rooms 17, 18, and 19 may represent two additional lots of rooms, though the absence of definable floors and little rock fall from walls suggest that these were outside hearths.

Growth was southeasterly, unimpeded by any topographic features. A small drainage to the south of the pueblo and Forestdale Creek toward the northwest discouraged expansion in those directions. We do not know whether growth by accretion was due to new families moving into the community or to normal population increase, but accretion by blocks of rooms more than by single room growth suggests immigration. Similar ceramics from all parts of the structure probably means that the families swelling Tla Kii's population did not come from far away, and the close clustering of tree-ring dates shows that the elapsed time between building episodes was short. The wall footings, mentioned earlier as antedating the pueblo, were related inferentially to the Dry Valley occupation.

Walls

Material. An outcrop of Coconino sandstone 75 m south and west of the pueblo was the chief source of building stone. Angular blocks of varying dimensions litter the surface on the slope of the outcrop today, produced by the weathering of the bedrock above. The builders of the pueblo would have had the choice of a wide range in stone sizes without resorting to quarrying. A few water-worn boulders from the creek and basalt blocks from a nearby side canyon were also present, especially in the wall footings. In their present weathered condition and after excavation, walls stood a maximum of 1 m in height. Wall thicknesses varied from 0.3 m to 0.5 m, with the thicker walls of the double-face type described below. No evidence of a second story was seen.

Shaping. Most of the building blocks, whether large or small, were not shaped, resulting in irregularly faced walls, the use of excessive amounts of mortar, and generally weak construction. Two kinds of stone shaping were observed: (1) percussion of large blocks that occurred at random and sparsely through the pueblo (Fig. 16a); (2) pecking and rubbing, seen best on some of the large blocks in the southwest wall of Rooms 14 and 15 (Fig. 16b). The stones in the pueblo that were broken by percussion may have been salvaged from Unit Structure 2, where the blocks set vertically in constructing the bin were similarly treated.

Figure 16. Wall stones and masonry detail, Tla Kii Ruin: *a*, building blocks shaped by percussion; *b*, outside wall of Room 14. In *b*, irregular footing stones were topped with roughly coursed blocks neatly spalled. Some blocks were modified by pecking and rubbing.

Masonry

An overall review of Tla Kii masonry leads quickly to the observation that an unexpected variety of quality and kinds of wall surface finishes characterize the site. Masonry types run the gamut from methodically laid stones (the exception), to walls of such inferior craftsmanship that one wonders how they stood up at all. Construction differences are sometimes helpful in arranging the history of a pueblo sequentially, but in Tla Kii Ruin the variations have been of no help in this respect. One would suppose that the clear growth stages of the structure, already described, and the incremental expansion by several family units would have resulted in a uniformity of wall type within a building stage. A further hope would be that such a situation might reflect the origins of the newly arrived groups. For example, a Chaco masonry type (Fig. 16*b*) might hint at affiliations with the people to the northeast. However, no such correlations are possible because several wall-face types may occur in the same room block. The problem is further complicated by the fact that oftentimes the same wall has two dissimilar faces, a kind of double-wall construction. Initially, it was thought the masonry surface finishes could be shown on a map, but this was given up as an ambiguous excercise. Tla Kii Ruin masonry differences are best credited to the individual preferences of the masons and possibly to the extent the builders were willing to go in expending energy to make a good wall.

Wall construction began either by positioning the basal layer of rocks directly on the ground or by placing them in a specially prepared foundation trench. When the latter procedure was followed, large angular blocks of stone were used without special care for selection or placement. This situation may be seen in Figure 16*b*, where our excavation extended 0.3 m below floor level.

A simplified masonry typology recognizes two kinds of walls.

1. Large block type: large individual stones generally make up the total width of the wall and both faces present the same appearance; varied mainly by the arrangement of the chinking stones (Fig. 17*a*).

2. Double-faced type: walls in this category have faces that may or may not resemble each other. Outer faces of room walls at the time of construction usually show large rocks, poorly fitted and roughly chinked (Fig. 17*b*), while the inner faces are

Figure 17. Masonry types, Tla Kii Ruin: *a*, large block wall in Room 7 with mortar and few chinking stones, both faces the same; *b*, inner face of southeast wall, Room 16, with mixed-stone veneering.

Figure 18. Masonry details, Tla Kii Ruin: *a*, open doorway between Rooms 14 and 16, with small stone veneering at right; *b*, normal mode wall juncture.

veneered with small rocks or a mixture of large and small rocks. The double-faced wall shown in Figure 16*b* has the best craftsmanship, with unmistakable Chacoan masonry affiliations. The style was little used, apparently degenerating into treatment as seen in Figure 18*a*.

Structurally, the double-faced wall was weak. Bonding between the layers was not enough to prevent frequent sloughing of one face, usually the thinner veneer of the two. If the surface texture of walls was originally covered with plaster (for which there is some evidence, especially on room interiors), then the different effect of wall faces was not inspired by aesthetics but possibly more by the availability of materials and the mood of the masons. The marvel is that the structurally weak, double-faced walls did not collapse during occupancy. Day-to-day maintenance must have been a considerable chore.

In the usual fashion of the pueblo mason, wall junctures and corners were seldom bonded; Rooms 9, 11, and 20 are exceptions. Butt joining of two walls was normal (Fig. 18b). Tying-in of walls was noted in one place only, in the southwest corner of Room 17, where rocks in the existing wall were broken out to allow for the insertion of stones of a cross wall.

Mortar

Binding material for walls varied from the black clay that underlies the area and dries hard and compact, to a clay-sand mixture, and, finally, in one of the last additions (Rooms 6 to 12), to a poor quality mortar containing potsherds, charcoal, and fragments of burned clay, evidently surface debris. The irregularities of the building blocks required liberal applications of mortar, and on the average the bearing was rock-on-mortar, rather than rock-on-rock.

Plaster

The only plaster remaining occurred on walls in room interiors. Clay, with sand added to reduce cracking while drying, was thickly (to 5 cm) applied to even wall surfaces. In Rooms 13 and 16, traces remained of thin (0.1 cm) coats, numbering up to five and varying in color from brownish-red to yellow. These were applied on the base layer and represented periodic refinishings of the walls.

Floors

The poor condition of the floors would justify believing that no special treatment was accorded them. Because most of the pueblo was built on a surface already littered with cultural refuse, the exact floor line was seldom clearly distinguishable. Wall bases and hearths were the chief clues of the floor level, or fire-staining where the rooms burned.

Multiple floor levels were recognized in Rooms 7, 13, and 16, with a maximum vertical difference of 0.5 m in Room 16. The indicated reoccupation of these rooms was within the single ceramic horizon noted in the pueblo as a whole.

Subfloor burial by room occupants was not practiced.

Firepits

Firepits were normally placed somewhat to the side of the geographic center of rooms, although there was no rule as to which side. Two styles were recognized:

1. Circular floor pit, clay lined, no coping; average diameter, 25 cm. Only one (Room 14), larger than normal, has a deflector slab along the northeast margin.
2. Rectangular or square stone-lined boxes (Fig. 19*a*); stones protrude above the floor 5 to 10 cm; diameter from 0.3 m to 0.5 m.

The choice as to which type was used seems to have been up to the room occupants. There is no apparent correlation between hearth type and room block additions.

Doors

Doors were used only for interroom access, but there were as many rooms without doors as there were with this feature. No doorways opened from rooms to the outside, unless a break in the north wall of Room 12 can be so interpreted. Only one door was found unsealed, between Rooms 14 and 16 (Fig. 18*a*), and four sealed doors were noted in the entire structure. Widths averaged 0.55 m, and the sill height above apparent floors averaged 0.6 m. Door heights were not preserved.

Hatchways

The absence of doors in the outer pueblo walls and the limited number of interconnecting doors mean that the normal mode of room access was by roof hatchways. That further implies the use of ladders to reach roof-tops. No evidence for either hatchways or ladders was seen.

Roofing

The nature of the roof was usually best preserved, paradoxically, when the rooms burned, but only a few of the rooms were so destroyed. The imprints of roofing elements in burnt clay tell us that primary timbers up to 0.3 m in diameter spanned the rooms, though the number in any one room could not be determined. These timbers were crossed by secondary beams of

Figure 19. Construction features: *a*, hearth in Room 16; *b*, Room 20, behind the pick, was annexed to Room 14 after the outside ground level had risen because of refuse accumulation.

about 0.1 m in diameter at unknown intervals, and split wood shakes or reeds were laid at right angles across the top of these as the base for a final topping of clay about 0.25 m thick.

Only Room 14 had holes in the floor, probably where posts were placed under sagging timbers in this large room.

Storage Pits

Although large pits occurred below the floors, these clearly antedate the pueblo and must be linked with an earlier occupation. Small pits in Rooms 13 and 14 may have been made at the time these dwellings were lived in, but in general subfloor pits are not one of the characteristics of this period. Large outside pits may have taken their place, though none assignable to the Carrizo phase were found.

Bins

Specially constructed bins, either for storage or for metates, were not seen. Small enclosures in rooms, made by erecting partition walls as in 7A and 7B, and small rooms like 9 and 10, may have taken the place of bins. Access to these units was over the tops of the low walls forming them, because a hatchway entrance for each of them does not appear logical.

Room Contents

How the Southwestern ruins became mounded, the rooms often filled with comparatively "clean" material, in my opinion, has never been adequately explained. Demolition of the structure itself provided some of the bulk, coming from building stones, mortar, and roofing clay. The dumping of refuse in abandoned rooms, wash from higher ground, and wind-blown material may be other contributing factors. But there are numerous cases in which these conditions do not fit and attention should be given to this problem. For Tla Kii Ruin, the explanation is simple, though there are one or two puzzling aspects. Here the bulk of room fill was building rock. This is well illustrated in Figure 18a, where the deposit in Room 16 is seen through the door of Room 14. We assume that the 1 m standing height of most walls at the time of excavation represents about half of the former full wall height. The volume of the roof clay, plus collapsed wall volume, would amount roughly to 75 percent or 80 percent of the bulk in the undemolished lower part of the room. The balance of the space must be taken up by wind-blown and washed material and by the loose fitting of the rocks in the matrix.

Lensed rubbish, with ash, was not detected in any of the rooms, but potsherds in numbers varying from 50 to over 1200 occurred. Few sherds are in the mortar of standing walls, hence this could not have been their source. The pottery may

have come from the heavy mat of roofing dirt and from roofs
themselves, which probably were not kept overly tidy and on
which traffic was heavy.

The 0.5 m accumulation between floors in Room 16 may have
been intentionally brought in to elevate the old floor. The soil
contained only a few sherds (235).

Floor artifacts were few in number, consisting mostly of
small articles easily misplaced. Whole vessels, and even the
bulkier stone tools such as manos and metates, were removed.
Abandonment of all rooms, however, was not simultaneous. A
skeleton of a young adult male (Burial 4) in Room 8, in the fill
0.2 m above the occupational floor, suggests the room was
uninhabited and used as a dump area while other rooms were
still occupied. Pottery associated with the burial was no
different from that found elsewhere in the pueblo. The absence
of signs of a hasty departure leads to the conclusion that
abandonment was orderly. Salvage of household goods, whether
kept on roofs or on house floors, was complete.

PRE-PUEBLO OCCUPATION

Inevitably, where extensive previous living has taken place,
old features will be hidden, even incorporated into later
construction. Old wall footings and a floor were found under
Rooms 13 and 15 (see Fig. 14), probably roughly equivalent in
age to Unit Structure 2. The stones of these walls, of the large
block type, were laid on culture-free subsoil. The pueblo walls,
on the other hand, exept where footing trenches were dug,
were laid on soil containing pottery and charcoal.

Other evidences of prior living were deep pits (Nos. 2, 3, 10,
11, and 13, discussed later), a large hearth area (Pit 4), and
four burials (Nos. 11, 17, 18, and 19) that apparently predated
the construction of the pueblo.

TRASH

Heavy concentrations of refuse left by the residents of the
pueblo, mounded or otherwise, were not found. Trash of the
period was thinly scattered about the premises, even before the
structure had reached its maximum extent (Fig. 19*b*), as
revealed by the high floor levels in Rooms 20 and 21. Even so,
there was not enough debris to account for all that must have
collected during the village's life. Most of the garbage may
have been dumped into the then-existing shallow arroyo of
Forestdale Creek or northwest of the pueblo on ground that has
since been washed away. Much trash may have been cast into
old storage pits that we did not find.

RELIGIOUS STRUCTURES

Kiva 1, Great Kiva (Figs. 20-22)

Location. 25 m south of pueblo.

Shape. Round, with wide lateral entrance to southeast, and one or more annexed rooms along south margin; maximum inside diameter including bench, 18.20 m; diameter excluding bench, 15.8 m; depth of floor below present surface, 1.25 m.

Walls. Rock facing of angular sandstone blocks laid against excavated vertical surface of bench; slight effort at coursing and spalling. Outer wall, south margin 1 m wide, elsewhere narrow and irregular. Foundation rocks remaining only, except in inner wall. Walls either were never high or stones were carried away after kiva fell into disuse.

Plaster. Traces on inside wall and walls of entrance passage.

Floor. Hard-packed clay, even.

Firepit. Destroyed by erosion.

Postholes. Three primary found, the fourth washed away; each stone-lined with large flat stones in bottom, diameters 0.5 m, depths 1.05 to 1.30 m (Fig. 22*b*). Two secondary posts (diameter 0.25 m) incorporated in bench wall on each side of entrance.

Bench. Probably completely encircled kiva except where broken by entrance; vertical stone facing, clay top; highest standing bench wall, 0.45 m; height above kiva floor, 0.9 m, average width 1.5 m.

Entrance. Oriented to southeast (Fig. 22*a*); width 3.5 m, extending to 4.6 m; length 6 m; masonry sides slightly expanded, ending in short, inwardly directed walls, reducing opening to 3.5 m width. Floor of entry has three low risers or steps, made by laying log treads on rock base; floor between risers slopes upward.

Roof. Four-post roof plan, forming a flat central plate, probably a sloping roof toward outer wall; secondary posts in wall at entrance evidently carried protective hood over opening.

Annex. One or more small rooms were added to exterior wall on the south. Details lacking.

Tree-ring material. Burning of the kiva produced some charcoal, but a disappointingly small amount in relation to the total number of beams that must have been incorporated in the massive roof. Eight fragmentary specimens were dated. Outer ring but not bark dates are A.D.

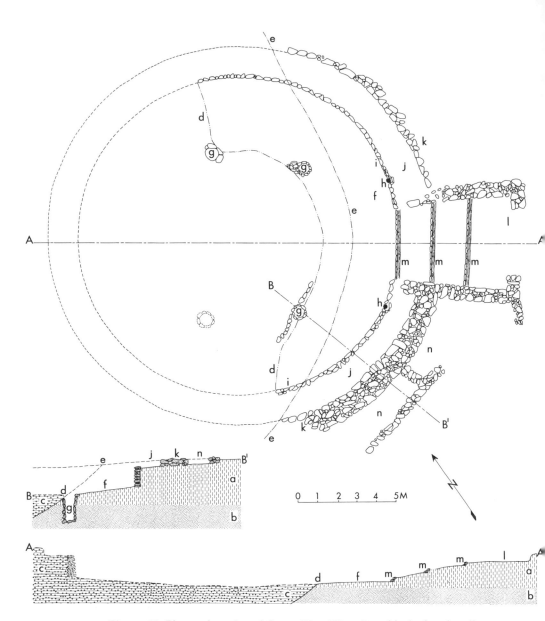

Figure 20. Plan and section of Great Kiva (Kiva 1): *a*, black clay; *b*, yellow sandy silt; *c*, sandy silt of third terrace; *d*, approximate edge of old arroyo at floor level; *e*, approximate edge of old arroyo at present surface level; *f*, floor; *g*, primary postholes; *h*, secondary posts in wall; *i*, bench face; *j*, bench surface; *k*, outer wall; *l*, entrance; *m*, stone and log risers; *n*, annexed rooms.

1008, 1069, 1070, 1088, 1102, 1105, 1114, and 1115 (Bannister, Gell, and Hannah 1966: 32). To repeat, these dates do not represent cutting dates, as there has been loss of the outer rings through shattering in every case.

a

b

Figure 21. The Great Kiva at Tla Kii Ruin: *a*, general view; *b*, disappearing bench wall (under figure) is near edge of old arroyo and vertical face of excavation; at left is the third terrace deposit dating from the twelfth century or later.

Figure 22. Architectural features of the Great Kiva: *a*, entrance, showing steps with stone and log risers; the presence of logs was revealed through impressions and charred remnants. *b*, rock-lined postholes; bottom of hole also rocked to keep weight of roof from pushing support posts into soft sand below. Inside diameter is 0.5 m.

The most recent date of A.D. 1115, therefore, probably comes nearest the time of construction. The general agreement of the dates from the kiva and those from the pueblo leaves no doubt as to the contemporaneity of the two, and there is no justification for stating that the kiva was built and used in the second or third decade of the twelfth century.

Comments. This kiva was found by the merest accident through the observation of a fire-stained floor in the bank of a small gully. A workman assigned to tracing it soon found a stone wall describing a large arc. As the structure unfolded, we saw that our effort was a good many centuries too late, for much of it was missing. In a previous erosion cycle, during which Forestdale Creek actively cut away its banks, about two-thirds of the kiva literally was swept away. To complicate matters for us, nature's cyclic swing from cutting to filling caused the creek capriciously to aggrade and to restore the volume of material removed earlier, even to matching the surface level of the old terrace.

Great Kivas, or at least analogous, if not homologous, structures were found in both the Bear and Bluff villages (Parts II, III), thereby establishing from the beginning of the Mogollon occupation that a building of large proportions and dedicated presumably to nonsecular functions was a part of the cultural complex. The construction of the Tla Kii Great Kiva at some distance from the domestic rooms may be seen as evidence of a belief that detachment was essential to functional fulfillment. That picture was to change, however, for by about A.D. 1200 the incorporation of large kivas within the domestic unit became the accepted procedure, leading progressively away from a formal structure to one approaching plaza characteristics, signs of a possible secularization of the feature (Haury 1950: 29-39).

Another matter of interest deals with the association of a Great Kiva with a small pueblo that housed no more than a dozen to fifteen families. The construction of the kiva, from the initial excavation to the engineering of the roof, was no small task and would appear to have required a larger labor force than the pueblo could muster. Could, therefore, this "super" kiva have been the gathering place for other communities in the valley as well? A recent survey in the Corduroy Valley adjacent to Forestdale has produced a site (AZ Q:13:1 ASU) similar to Tla Kii with a large kiva, though possibly attached to the pueblo, of about the same size and age (Stafford and Rice 1979), lending support to the notion that this arrangement between secular and other kinds of buildings was the normal pattern for the Carrizo phase. That they were built for, and served primarily as, redistribution centers for surplus commodities, as has been suggested (Plog 1974; Wilcox 1977), seems an unreasonable interpretation, considering the long history of the feature in both the Anasazi and Mogollon complexes, the regional and temporal specializations that seem far removed from economic factors, and the ethnological analogy of kiva use.

The flat rocks in the bottoms of the three remaining main postholes appear to have been functional, in that they helped prevent the weight of the roof from pushing the support posts into the relatively soft subsoil. Those stones, however, were smaller than the probable diameter of the posts. Their presence calls to mind the carefully shaped and heavy stone discs found in the bottoms of some Chaco Canyon Great Kiva postholes (Judd 1964: 208). An even stronger hint of an esoteric meaning is seen in the presence of carefully fashioned discs in the bottoms of postholes in the Great Kiva in the Turkey Creek Ruin, Point of Pines. These could be no more than symbolic of some belief held by the builders.

The formalized lateral entrance, consistently oriented to the southeast, whether in early or late kivas, round or rectangular, and whether detached from or incorporated in the domestic buildings, distinguishes White Mountain Great Kivas from most others, especially those from Zuni north and east. The presence of Great Kivas in communities so widely separated in space and time cannot be taken to mean that identical beliefs inspired them. Rather, the investigator must see in them a common denominator of a more generic kind, comparable to the forces that have driven mankind to erect in myriad variety the cathedrals, churches, temples, and shrines to his gods. The story of the Great Kiva, as seen in the earliest of the Mogollon and Anasazi villages, and later diverse forms of it, is yet to be written.

Kiva 2

Near the southeast corner of the pueblo and detached from it, our excavations opened a large pit containing

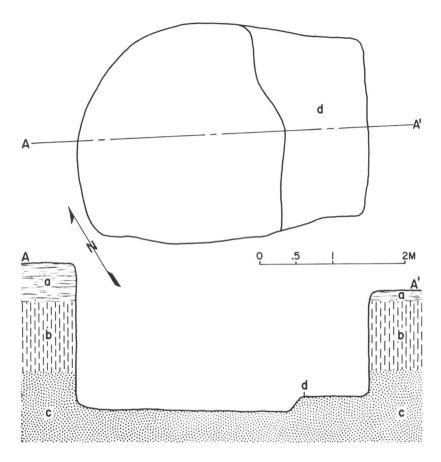

Figure 23. Plan and section of Kiva 2: *a*, silt and refuse;
b, black clay; *c*, yellow sandy silt; *d*, possible bench.

pueblo-age refuse (Carrizo phase), which we judged to be
an unfinished kiva (Fig. 23). The general form, the deep
excavation, and a bench with southeasterly orientation
are the only features that bring a kiva to mind. Absence
of masonry, hearth, and any other interior features, leads
to the conclusion that the structure was never completed.
Work on it may have been halted in favor of the building
of the Great Kiva.

The pit contained some burnt roof clay that undoubtedly
came from the pueblo as the result of a fire and rebuild-
ing there. The pit itself nowhere revealed fire stains.

A single fragment of charcoal from the fill yielded a date of A.D. 1035, but an indeterminate number of outer rings had been lost. Neither this clue nor the ceramic sample taken from the pit (235 sherds) is definitive as to the age. A Carrizo phase assignment is favored.

STORAGE PITS

A plausible explanation for a number of circular pits beneath the pueblo is that they were for storage to take care of surplus foods, a widespread and ancient custom. For the archaeologist, however, such pits often take on an additional meaning, because once the usefulness of a pit had passed it became an ideal depository for trash. The concentration of garbage in a limited pocket in sterile soil, collected over a comparatively short period of time, usually yields chronologically unmixed samples of cultural articles, most of which are broken pottery. The definition of ceramic horizons may be the more easily accomplished because of this phenomenon. Furthermore, the stratigraphic relationship of such pits to later structures where overbuilding took place is readily discerned. The contents of several such pits under Tla Kii Ruin provided our clearest understanding of the pottery of the Dry Valley phase, as little unmixed trash of that stage was found elsewhere.

Pit 1 (Fig. 24)

Located between Kiva 2 and the southeast corner of the pueblo, Pit 1 measurements were: mouth diameter, 0.75 m; maximum diameter near floor, 1.20 m; depth of original excavation, 1.35 m; floor depth below present surface, 2.05 m.

Bell-shaped, the pit sides bore no traces of plaster or burning, thereby eliminating the possibility that it was a roasting pit. The contents of the pit and the overlying stratigraphy permit a reasonably complete reconstruction of its story.

The pit was dug from a surface about on the same level as its definable mouth. After use and becoming filled with trash, the area was blanketed with a sheet of refuse of the same age, which itself was then capped with a 0.15 m thick layer of sterile yellow-sandy clay, the same material into which the pit was excavated. The origin of this deposit is undoubtedly related to digging the deep hole identified as Kiva 2 nearby. Finally, the stratigraphic column shows a 0.35 m thick layer of debris, silt, and building stones dating from the pueblo's occupation (Carrizo phase) and its subsequent destruction. The relationship of the pit to later deposits indicates a Dry Valley phase age

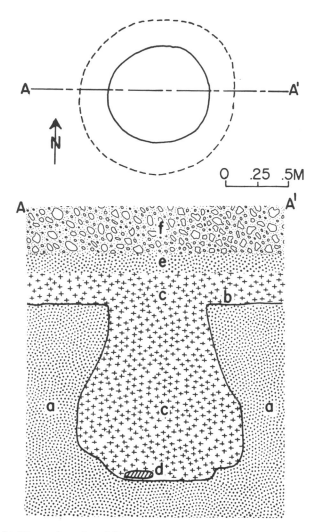

Figure 24. Plan and section of Storage Pit 1: *a*, yellow sandy silt; *b*, approximate surface at time pit was dug; *c*, Dry Valley phase trash; *d*, mano; *e*, sterile yellow-sandy silt, probably from Kiva 2 excavation; *f*, Carrizo phase debris and rubble from destruction of pueblo.

for it, a deduction borne out when the midden materials of the pit are examined. The pit contained flecks of charcoal, wood ash in irregular pockets and lenses, charred corn in small amounts, burnt architectural clay, animal bones, stone chips, a few large chunks of sandstone, a mano on the floor, and 254 potsherds. Of

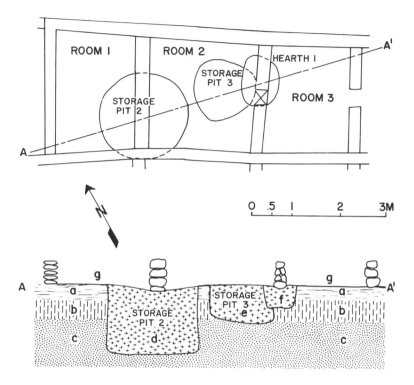

Figure 25. Plan and section of Storage Pits 2 and 3, and Hearth 1 under Rooms 1, 2, and 3: *a*, silt and refuse; *b*, black clay; *c*, yellow sandy silt; *d*, banded trash and soil fill; *e*, trash; *f*, ash; *g*, room floors.

the ceramic assemblage, 41 percent was black-on-white overwhelmingly of the Snowflake style, 12 percent was plain corrugated but no McDonald Corrugated, and the rest was smudged red and plain wares. The range of types, and roughly the quantities, matched the pottery associated with Unit Structure 2 of the Dry Valley phase.

Pit 2 (Figs. 25, 26*a*)

The presence of this pit, under the wall junctures of Rooms 1, 2, 17, and 19, was disclosed by a pronounced sag in the masonry, lowered by the settling of the pit contents. This pit, 1.8 m in greatest diameter, 1.35 m deep, flat bottomed, nearly vertically sided and unplastered, was dug into the subsoil from a level containing occupational debris predating the pueblo. The pit contents were well stratified, consisting of alternating bands from top to bottom of refuse, yellow sandy clay, refuse, yellow clay, and finally a densely packed layer of refuse. The only significance that may be attached to this is that as the pit was

Figure 26. Storage Pit 2 and Pit 14: *a*, Storage Pit 2 with dividing wall of Rooms 1 and 2 removed, revealing wall slumpage and soil disturbance (black layer at top of measuring stick); *b*, Pit 14, rock-lined feature.

filling, the dirt taken from nearby excavations, as would have come from Unit Structure 2, was thrown into it between the dumping of trash. The problems posed by tree-ring dates from the pit will be reviewed later.

Pits 3, 9, 10, 11, 13

There is no necessity to describe these pits individually. They ranged from 1 m to 2 m in diameter and in each case the depth was about one-third less than the diameter. The pottery from the trash contents justifies a late Dry Valley phase assignment, although the evidence in all cases is not without some contradiction, as will be reviewed below. Pit 4, under Rooms 7A, 8, 13, and 14, was shallow and contained much wood ash. Pits 5 (Room 13), 6, 7, and 8 (Room 14), all small and shallow, were related to the occupation of those rooms and therefore are Carrizo phase in age. Burial 19 in Pit 13 was the only instance of a burial in a storage pit.

Pit 12

Pit 12 was the deepest of all (1.9 m), located under the floor of Room 19. A meter in diameter at the mouth, the pit flared to form a bell shape with a curious undercut flare at the bottom. The maximum bottom diameter reached 1.5 m. No plastering of walls was seen. It was spotted initially when the arroyo bank was being studied to assess the damage done to the pueblo by Forestdale Creek. We estimated that a little less than half of the pit and its contents were lost. The stratigraphic relationship to Room 19 was clear, in that Pit 12 was present before the room was built. It equated stratigraphically, therefore, with the other pits predating the pueblo.

Removal of the trash content of the pit in several levels revealed no typological changes in the pottery top to bottom, suggesting the pit was quickly filled. The pottery yield amounted to 394 fragments and the upper part of a black-on-white jar that depicts a pair of birds whose long beaks connect with stylized flowers (see Fig. 39a).

Pit 14 (Fig. 26b)

Several meters north of Room 10, outside of the pueblo, a pit with sloping rock slab sides came to light. Its surface diameter was 1 m and its depth was 0.35 m. The chronological position of this feature was not certainly determined, though it was probably of pueblo (Carrizo phase) age. Similar constructions have been found repeatedly in later villages of the Salado people near Globe and in the Roosevelt Lake area. How pits of this type were put to use is not clear. No evidence of fire was seen.

Dating the Pits

The ambiguities referred to before must be reviewed in

assessing the age of the trash-filled pits. Some pits were clearly functioning while the rooms were in use and were integral parts of them. Others, except Pits 1 and 14, were underneath the pueblo and, therefore, stratigraphically older. The question is: how much older? For a possible answer, we must rely on tree-ring dates and pottery typology.

Charcoal fragments in Pit 2 yielded 6 dates: A.D. 1096, 1106, 1107 (2), and 1110 (2). From Pit 3, two dates were obtained, A.D. 1087 and 1093 (Bannister, Gell, and Hannah 1966: 32-33). Only the 1106 date from Pit 2 qualifies as a possible bark date; the rest are close to the final outside ring. The dates clearly lie within the 35-year period that characterizes the major building activity in the area, yet the pits by stratigraphy were present before the pueblo was built. More specifically, dates from Room 1 were A.D. 1103, and from Room 2, 1089 and 1093 (2), closely overlapping the dates from Pit 2. In fact, the 1110 dates from Pit 2 were later than any of the Room 1 and 2 dates. What can be the explanation for this phenomenon?

Pit 2 could not have been open when the rooms were in use because the walls of Rooms 1, 2, 17, and 19 intersected over it and were on top of the trash filling the pit. Figure 26*a* dramatically shows how the wall intersection slumped into the trash as it settled, presumably due to the reduction of trash volume as the organic materials decomposed. Our field records do not show the exact provenience of the charcoal specimens, but I suspect they were near the top of the fill in the pit. If that is so, the dates do not accurately reflect the age of the pit's contents. The cause of the suspected disturbance, if indeed it took place, cannot be determined now. Pit 3, with dates of A.D. 1087 and 1093, and Room 2 dates of 1089 and 1093 (2), demonstrate a similar overlap and an apparent conflict. Examining the stratigraphic situation in somewhat greater detail, we see in Figure 25 that Pit 3 was already present when a large ash-filled hearth, lying directly underneath the wall dividing Rooms 2 and 3, was used. These events need not have been separated by much time, but the tree-ring dates allow for no time between storage pit content accumulation, hearth use, and wall construction. Once again, to resolve an inconsistency, I must place more dependence on the stratigraphic record than on tree-ring data and conclude that some disturbance took place to confuse the issue. A review of field data sheets reveals no possible answers and one cannot know, at this late date, whether or not errors were made by the excavators or recorders by assigning the recovered materials to the wrong proveniences.

Unfortunately, ceramic typology, as a way of segregating Dry Valley from Carrizo phase materials, does not help much, because the black-on-white ceramics of the two stages were similar, though exhibiting subtle differences difficult to detect in sherds. Changing ratios of types, as between a reduction of Alma Plain offset by increasing production of corrugated pottery, are diagnostics, as are certain type absences. Neck corrugation is present, as is all-over corrugation of jars, but patterned and painted indentations in the coils, notably McDonald Corrugated, had not yet been developed. The pottery from Pits 2 and 3 reflects those differences and, on ceramic grounds, I am inclined to regard the tree-ring data as suspect. In all probability, however, the time difference between the pits and the pueblo construction was short, leading to a late Dry Valley phase assignment for the pits.

HEARTHS

The hearths occurring below the pueblo, and hence of earlier date, under the walls between Rooms 2 and 3 and Rooms 13 and 15, were basins scooped into the subsoil, up to 1 m in diameter. They were not connected with architectural units. Hearth 2, next to the wing wall near Unit Structure 2, has already been mentioned. Large roasting pits, as described for the Bear Ruin (see Part II, *Hearths*), were not found.

POPULATION SIZE

Judging the population size of a ruin like Tla Kii is, at best, an informed guess. Assuming that the presence of hearths indicates residence and that the occupants of any one room were a biological family, then it would appear that 13 families made up the community. Taking the modern pueblo Indian family size at about 4.5 persons, Tla Kii housed 55 to 60 people. There are problems with this calculation, however, because some of the rooms appear to be too small or ill-shaped (Room 21, for example) to have served as living quarters. Floor artifacts were too sparse to provide hints that small rooms such as 4 and 6 functioned differently than did large ones, as Rooms 14 (Fig. 27) and 16. It is generally believed that the smallest rooms in pueblos served as storage spaces and, indeed, those in Tla Kii are without hearths. The room number thus reduced suggests that 40 to 50 people lived in the pueblo.

BURIALS

Disposal of the dead was by earth burial during Tla Kii's three occupational phases. If cremation was ever practiced, no

Figure 27. Tla Kii Ruin: *a*, the northern section, looking northwest; *b*, overview from the southwest. The large room is No. 14.

traces were seen. The 19 burials recovered were widely scattered, and occurred under varying circumstances. Burials 1, 5, 7, 8, 12, 13, 14, 15, and 16 were in graves dug into the black clay near pit houses. Burials 3, 6, and 9 were in the fills of pit houses; Burials 2, 10, 11, 17, and 18 were near or under the pueblo; Burial 4 was interred in the fill of Room 8, and Burial 19 was put away in Storage Pit 13. The location of the graves, with respect to these surroundings and the associated mortuary offerings, has made possible reasonably convincing phase assignment. The number of graves for each phase so allocated are: Corduroy, 10; Dry Valley, 4; Carrizo, 4; and indeterminate, 1. The acid nature of the soil and the crushing of the bones by the overlying dirt damaged most of the skeletons so extensively that little remains for morphological study.

Grave data are given in Table 2. The small sample of burials, further reduced when each one is placed chronologically in one of three phases, does not provide the basis for extensive conclusions about burial customs. There is notable lack of consistency in body orientation and position. Regardless of the age, pottery offerings were present in every instance, usually placed about the head and shoulders. In the case of numerous pieces, as in Burial 3 (Fig. 28a; see also Fig. 52), pottery was located also at the sides. In one instance (Burial 10, Fig. 28b), the sherds of a single pot were strewn from head to pelvis. Grave goods, other than pottery, consisted mostly of personal ornaments of steatite, red stone, turquoise, and shell.

FAUNA

Table 3 provides a summary of the distribution of faunal occurrences in all excavations in the Forestdale Valley. The differences in the frequencies of species by phase are most likely attributed to sampling than to either environmental changes or cultural preferences.

Most of the animal bones from Tla Kii were recovered from the refuse in storage pits. The pit houses (Corduroy phase) themselves and the thinly scattered trash adjoining them yielded almost no bones. One may suppose, however, that there were no essential differences in food habits of the pit house and pueblo dwellers inasmuch as the animals taken, with the exception of birds, are all represented in the list of those recovered in the Bear Ruin of the Forestdale phase (see Part II, *Flora and Fauna*). The volume of bone from the entire operation aggregates less than 4.5 kg (10 pounds), a small amount in comparison with the returns from many other pueblo sites of comparable age on the Plateau. The following fauna were identified in Tla Kii Ruin:

Mammals
    Mule Deer (*Odocoileus hemionus*)
    Jack Rabbit (*Lepus* sp.)
    Cottontail (*Sylvilagus* sp.)
    Pocket Gopher (*Thomomys* sp.)
    Fox (*Urocyon* sp.)
    Bear (*Ursus* sp.)
Birds
    Sharp-shinned Hawk (*Accipiter striatus*)
    Harlequin Quail (*Cyrtonyx montezumae*)
    Turkey (*Meleagris gallopavo*)
    Band-tailed Pigeon (*Columba fasciata*)
    Mourning Dove (*Zenaidura macroura*)
    Black-billed Magpie (*Pica pica*)

The trash-filled storage pits (Dry Valley phase) contained elements from all or most of these animals. Comparable lots from the Corduroy and Carrizo phases do not exist and hence efforts to test temporal differences as to species cannot be made. Numbers of animals taken, as determined by the bone inventory, indicate that rabbits and deer were the chief suppliers of meat. Bones of turkey, a bird commonly found in the area even today, were rare, and no dog remains were encountered in the Tla Kii ruin.

The only surprise in the faunal list is the Black-billed Magpie, not now known from Arizona except in the extreme northeast corner of the State. It was doubtless prized for its feathers, as was also the Sharp-shinned Hawk. All other species, according to our standards, were edible.

FOOD

There is no reason to believe, from the information gathered in the Forestdale Valley, that there were any radical changes in ways of gaining a livelihood during the time of human occupancy covered by this work. The earliest pit house dwellers (Hilltop phase) were certainly growing corn, although no direct evidence of it was found. The metates were of forms usually associated with corn. There was no indication of bean and squash consumption. The increase in size of the settlements from early to late, culminating with Tundastusa (Canyon Creek phase), points to the probability that all of the valley's acreage was brought under cultivation with the passage of time, a logical consequence of the rising population. As is brought out later, however, agriculture may have fallen short of requirements, resulting in a greater dependence on hunting.

Table 2
GRAVE DATA FOR TLA KII RUIN BURIALS

Burial No.	Age			Sex		Head Direction							Body Position				Arms		
Skeleton (spanning)	Infant	Youth	Adult	Male	Female	North	Northeast	East	Southeast	West	Southwest	Indeterminate	Semi-flex	On back	On stomach	Indeterminate	At side	Mixed	Indeterminate
1			X	X							X		X	X			X		
2			X		X							X			X			X	
3			X	X	X								X	X			X	X	
4			X	X		X										X		X	
5			X		X		X						X	X			X		
6		X														X			X
7	X							X					X	X			X		
8	X															X			X
9	X															X	X		
10		X	X				X									X	X		
11			X	X	X								X	X				X	
12		X														X			X
13		X							X							X			X
14	X						X						X	X					X
15	X															X			X
16	X															X			X
17	X					X							X	X					X
18		X														X			X
19			X		X						X		X	X			X		

Considerable topographic relief in the region accounted for a diversity of plant life, which, in turn, made available certain plant food. Evidence exists for the collection of black walnuts, manzanita berries, and acorns; dependence on other seeds, vegetable greens, and roots can only be surmised. While no accurate means are available to assess the extent to which wild food products were exploited, there is no doubt that these were

Offerings													
Kind								Where					
Pottery	Clay figurine	Turquoise	Steatite or black stone beads	Flake scraper	Quartz crystal	Shell ornaments	Red stone beads	At head	At shoulder	At side	Feet	Indeterminate	Phase
X					X							X	Corduroy
X									X				Carrizo
X		X						X	X	X	X		Corduroy
X										X			Carrizo
X	X								X	X			Corduroy
X												X	Corduroy
X								X					Corduroy
X												X	Corduroy
X												X	Corduroy
X								X	X	X			Carrizo
X	X								X	X			Dry Valley?
X									X				?
X	X					X			X				Corduroy
X		X							X				Corduroy
X												X	Corduroy
X	X	X					X					X	Carrizo
X	X	X				X			X	X			Dry Valley?
X					X		X					X	Dry Valley?
X												X	Dry Valley

important in the economy, though superseded by agriculture based on maize. Regrettably, the kitchen refuse, much of it soft and destructible, is not preserved in open sites consistently enough to permit inferences of trends in vegetal food dependency. Animal foods, on the other hand, leave the hard residue of bone. Such information as we have for the taking of animal species through time is given in Table 3. The data represent presences

Figure 28. Grave offerings: *a*, Burial 3, Corduroy phase;
b, Burial 10, Carrizo phase.

only, not frequencies or numbers of animals taken, and for that
reason they fall short of revealing significant facts relating to
hunting. Nevertheless, a few noteworthy items appear.

First, the Forestdale Valley ruins show a curious anomaly in the amount of bone recoverable in early as opposed to late phases. In Hilltop and Cottonwood phase rubbish, bones are sparse and species few, while subsequent deposits produce an abundance of bones that are representative of the animals known to have been in the area historically. Because laboratory analysis demonstrated that soil conditions were not responsible for the disintegration of bone in the Bluff Site (T. F. Buehrer, see Part III, *Appendix*), we must assume that the early Mogollon people were much less hunters than farmers, or that the sparseness of bones in early times reflects a possible meat avoidance. This fact has been difficult to reconcile with a presumed primitive status in which food normally was obtained chiefly by hunting and gathering.

The finding of maize, or corn, in Bat Cave, New Mexico (Mangelsdorf and Smith 1949), associated with the Cochise culture and dated by radiocarbon means to several millennia B.C., indicates the introduction of this plant to the Southwest considerably earlier than heretofore has been supposed. While the early appearance of corn allowed ample time for the native people to develop a dependency on it, little or no progress was made toward a true agricultural state until new races of corn were introduced from the south shortly before the time of Christ. Still another point to be considered is the origin of the Mogollon. The notion is prevalent that the Mogollon people were derived from the old Cochise culture stock, in which a gathering economy was deeply rooted and which had for millennia the stone grinding tools needed to prepare natural plant foods. The adoption of corn was therefore an easy matter, for the same tools, with little modification, could be used to prepare dried corn for consumption. At the moment, this view appears to be an acceptable explanation. It is supported by the trend discerned in the ruins of the Pine Lawn Valley, New Mexico (Martin and Rinaldo 1950*b*: 566), when hunting became more important in the Georgetown to Three Circle phases, at a time roughly comparable with the observed change in the Forestdale Valley.

The swing to more hunting, beginning about A.D. 700, would have been the logical solution to the food problem where an increasing population, heavily dependent on agriculture, was faced with a shortage of arable land. It may be conjectured that all of Forestdale Valley's limited acreage was in use by the above date.

68   *PART I*

Table 3
FAUNAL OCCURRENCES IN FORESTDALE VALLEY SITES

Phase	Mule Deer	Antelope	Bison	Bear	Gray Fox	Racoon	Jack Rabbit	Cottontail	Prairie Dog	Wood Rat	Wild Cat	Pocket Gopher
Canyon Creek (1)	x	x			x						x	
Pinedale (2)												
Linden (3)	x	x										
Carrizo (4)	x			x	x		x	x				x
Dry Valley (5)												
Corduroy (6)												
Forestdale (7)	x		x	x	x	x	x	x	x	x		x
Cottonwood (8)	x	x										x
Hilltop (9)	x	x										x

1. Compiled from Hough 1903: 296, 301; Haury and Hargrave 1931: 21 (Tundastusa and Show Low Ruin).
2. No data.
3. Hough 1903: 299 (Pottery Hill Ruin).
4. Tla Kii Ruin (herein).
5. Tla Kii Ruin (herein). Entries for Carrizo phase may be specific for Dry Valley phase as well; clear phase allocation not possible.
6. No data.
7. Haury 1940*a*: 15 (Bear Ruin).
8, 9. Haury and Sayles 1947: 13 (Bluff Site).

Main dependence appears to have been on mule deer, antelope, and rabbits. Bones of elk do not occur until the late phases and we have only one record of bison from the Forestdale phase. This animal, probably never abundant in this timbered country, evidently was no longer available after about the seventh century.

At no time were bones sufficiently abundant to indicate much dependence on turkey, either for food or feathers, in spite of the fact that the turkey population then, as today, was doubtless high. No evidence in support of domestication can be noted. Our data are in agreement with Reed's observation that "The turkey certainly was not domesticated or kept by the Mogollon

										Fauna				
Elk	Mountain Lion	Beaver	Badger	Coyote	Dog	Mud Turtle	Turkey	Horned Owl	Eagle	Sharp-shinned Hawk	Harlequin Quail	Band-tailed Pigeon	Mourning Dove	Black-billed Magpie
X	X	X	X		X		X		X					
X							X							
							X			X	X	X	X	X
						X		X	X	X				
				X										

pueblo groups of the forested upland . . . and probably was not eaten by any of these Indians" (Reed 1951: 202). There is some likelihood, however, in the light of excavations in the Point of Pines area, that this statement will require modification for the period after about A.D. 1200, when turkey hunting, keeping, and possibly eating, appears to have taken hold in the later pueblos. This does not necessarily weaken Reed's general recognition of a difference between the habits of the San Juan Anasazi and the earlier Mogollon pueblo groups in their use of this bird.

Our records show only one late instance of the dog (Canyon Creek phase) for the area, an anomalous situation in view of the age-old and widespread possession of this animal.

Fish bones were not recovered, although the streams of the area, even Forestdale Creek, were well stocked with trout as recently as 1911.

There is no direct evidence from the Forestdale Valley concerning the seasoning of food. During the fourteenth century (Canyon Creek phase), salt was collected, probably from the salt banks on the Salt River (Haury 1934: 59-60), the nearest known source.

POTTERY

The task of presenting lucidly the pottery from a three-phase site is not an easy one. In thinking about the approach to the problem, it seems to me there are several distinct steps that must be followed: first, establishing the approximate chronological, or sequential, position of a pottery sample either through stratigraphic or tree-ring data and, as a supplementary aid, typology; second, detecting individual characters of form, design, color, paste, and presences or absences of types that are peculiar to the sample; third, grouping these attributes into clusters that establish a broad base for comparison of earlier or later clusters; fourth, determining trends by comparison with material both older and younger; fifth, applying available taxonomic controls; and, lastly, assessing the meaning of the *whole* in cultural terms.

To return to the first step, the precise chronological placement of numerous pottery samples from the Tla Kii Ruin was not always possible. Ceramic materials from the fill and floors of the pueblo and kivas, stratigraphically late and with a number of associated tree-ring dates, are located temporally about as convincingly as may be expected in the southwestern ruins. For the trash-filled storage pits under the pueblo and the unit structures, we rely on stratigraphy and ceramic association as the chief means of temporal placement. For pit houses, ceramic typology, distribution of the structures in relation to valley terraces and, to a limited extent, stratigraphy, assume time values.

Ever present is the question of mixture—of old materials intruded upward, of young materials intruded downward—to cloud the cluster of traits one is trying to establish for any one moment in the cultural stream. What does or does not legitimately occur together is best determined (Step 2) by the analysis of numerous samples of materials of equivalent age. In the case of Tla Kii, I believe we can demonstrate the horizon value of ceramic elements by the repetitiveness of the evidence. Step 3 logically follows, and again the repeated occurrences of clusters of elements lead to their acceptance as time markers.

The black-on-white Carrizo and Dry Valley phase pottery from the pueblo is particularly resistant to clear-cut taxonomic treatment. Variations from what may be considered "norms" in the eyes of a "splitter" would be enough to call for the establishment of new types. That temptation is being resisted and, instead, the black-on-whites are referenced with respect to styles of decoration, as, for example, Snowflake style. At the

moment that approach to understanding a mixed lot of ceramics appears to be the most useful. For a considerable residue of
the Corduroy phase material, however, although affinities are
clear, the technological aspects of the products are sufficiently
varied to warrant a new type of designation, a decision supported by the fact that the temporal position of this type makes
it a useful diagnostic.

Burials in Tla Kii Ruin contained most of the whole, or nearly
whole, pottery vessels in the collection. Houses at all times were
picked clean at the time of abandonment, eliminating the opportunity to relate directly specific kinds of pottery to domestic
quarters. Potsherds from all sources amount to about 18,000
pieces, and whole or restorable vessels aggregate 69 specimens.

How much of the pottery was produced locally and how much
was made elsewhere, and therefore should be labeled as intrusive, cannot be answered with certainty. In the discussion that
follows, pieces recognized as intrusive are clearly that. Given
the difficulty mentioned, specimens not so identified are considered as local products, although lithological studies of pastes in
the different kinds of pottery present have not been made. The
following review of Tla Kii ceramics departs from the manner
used in presenting other material culture, because an inventory
of pottery types or styles by phase more quickly and convincingly establishes the cluster of ceramic attributes that become
the phase hallmarks or, stated in another way, the most useful
vehicle for determining phases. Study materials for the Corduroy phase, the oldest in the site and the first to be considered,
amount to about 4000 sherds and 27 vessels.

CORDUROY PHASE, LOCAL TYPES

Alma Plain, Forestdale variety
(Parts II, III: *Pottery, Alma Plain*)

On the basis of the pottery content of Pit House 3 and from
the lowest level in Stratigraphic Test 1, this pottery type constitutes approximately 70 percent of the total sherd sample for the
Corduroy phase. After the three prior phases, Alma Plain was
still the predominant pottery of the area and expressive of the
Mogollon culture affiliation.

In form, finish, color, and vessel size, there are no observable
differences between the Alma Plain of this phase and that of
the Forestdale phase. Somewhat less in proportion to the total
pottery production appears to have been made, setting into
motion a trend that soon hereafter leads to the near extinction
of the type.

Forestdale Plain
(Part II: *Pottery, Forestdale Plain*)

This type, believed to be the result of a fusion of Lino Gray and Alma Plain, is present in minor amounts, about 5 percent of the total.

Forestdale Smudged
(Part II: *Pottery, Forestdale Smudged*)

This pottery is identical in all respects with the Forestdale Smudged of the Forestdale phase, though it occurred somewhat less commonly in the trash, 12 percent as opposed to 15 percent. The margin of error in these figures is great enough to cast doubt on any real difference in frequency.

Faint black lines in simple open scrolls and scrawls were seen on two of the Forestdale Smudged bowls, one associated with Burial 14, Corduroy phase, the other with Burial 16 dated to the Carrizo phase. They were put aside as curiosities and as probably having no typological significance. Wendorf (1953) described two similar pieces from the Twin Butte Site in the Petrified Forest National Monument and called them Forestdale Black-on-red, believing they had come from the Forestdale area. More recently, Ferg (1980) has located other examples in the Arizona State Museum collections, giving this unusual kind of pottery a somewhat broader base and prompting a detailed description.

The casual nature of the patterns, always in thin carbon paint applied with unconcerned and disorganized brushwork, suggests the bowls were the product of someone's doodling, but their appearance in four known sites hints there is more to it than that. In the Mogollon pottery of the Forestdale sequence, Forestdale Black-on-red is the first to exhibit attempts at painting. If it truly represents the initial Mogollon efforts at decorating by painting and has no functional specific value, then it is an impressive testimonial to Mogollon clumsiness with paint, the paint brush, and design layout. They had much catching-up to do and the trauma of the learning process is seen in much of the Corduroy Black-on-white pottery.

Forestdale Red
(Part II: *Pottery, Forestdale Red*)

The remarks made under Forestdale Smudged apply equally here; frequency is about 15 percent of the sample. The collection has one sherd decorated in the Forestdale Black-on-red style of painting.

Alma Neck-banded, Forestdale variety (Fig. 29)
(Haury 1936b: 35).

This type, first noted in the Forestdale Valley from the Bear Ruin (Forestdale phase), was regarded as foreign to the area because of its infrequent occurrence (Part II: *Intrusive Pottery, Mogollon Culture*). I am inclined now, however to believe that it was locally made, that as a clay treatment it was just being adopted in the Forestdale Valley during the period represented by the Bear Ruin, becoming somewhat more prevalent in the Tla Kii Ruin. It occupies the same typological and temporal position in the neck banded-neck corrugated to all-over corrugated sequence noted widely through the Southwest from the Mimbres region deep into Anasazi territory. The prevalence of neck-banding is difficult to express by percent because the body sherds would be included in Alma Plain, being no different in composition, color, and finish. The collection includes about 50 neck sherds and one whole vessel from Burial 14.

It should be noted that Kana-a Gray (Colton and Hargrave 1937: 195-196), with a similar neck treatment, does occur intrusively in Tla Kii in the Corduroy phase in the form of sherds from Pit House 2 and a whole vessel from Burial 9 (see Fig. 34b).

Because in paste and surface finish this type is difficult to differentiate from Alma Plain, Forestdale variety, it remains only to describe the neck banding and the form.

Neck-banding. Varies from a single rim coil (Fig. 29a) to about 10 coils (Fig. 29b-f), never extending below the maximum diameter of the vessel. Average width of coils is 1 cm; the range is 0.7-1.7 cm. Coils usually show considerable relief; the lower margin is sometimes flattened as though cut. Each coil was added as a unit, not spirally; coils are never scraped or polished. Occasionally the coils exhibit slight waviness from finger denting (Fig. 29j), and rarely "imbrication" (Fig. 29g), or fingernail tooling (Fig. 29h, i).

Forms. Bodies are spherical; vessels have wide mouths with pronounced necks or sometimes without necks (Fig. 29j).

Comparisons. Coils in Alma Neck-banded are scraped and polished, hence show less relief. For Kana-a Gray (Colton and Hargrave 1937: 195-196), these differences also apply and paste is gray.

Range. Forestdale Valley.

Figure 29. Alma Neck-banded, Forestdale variety, Corduroy phase.
Greatest dimension of d is 9.2 cm; diameter of j is 13.5 cm.

Remarks. The similarity of Alma Neck-banded and Kana-a Gray as a transitional technical treatment between an all-over untextured surface to an all-over corrugated surface suggests that pottery developments in the Mogollon and Anasazi regions were moving along the same paths. Yet, in all probability, the invention of Alma Neck-banded preceded Kana-a Gray (Part II: *Intrusive Pottery, Mogollon Culture*). The field evidence suggests that conclusion is borne out also by the greater age of Mogollon ceramics and the high level of production, variety, and excellence of execution seen in southern corrugated vessels.

Corduroy Black-on-white (new type)
(Figs. 30–33; see also Figs. 52 and 53)

Synonym. None.

Named for. Corduroy Valley, joining Forestdale Creek about three miles below Tla Kii Ruin.

Type specimens. Whole vessels A–2057 and A–2064, Arizona State Museum collection.

Type site. The pit houses of Tla Kii Ruin described herein.

Stage. Pueblo I.

Time. About A.D. 800 to 900, estimated.

Description.

Construction: coiled and scraped. *Firing:* probably chiefly reducing atmosphere but oxidizing atmosphere evident; extreme warping, especially in larger bowls (Fig. 31c). *Paste: Color*, predominantly light gray to gray (7.5 YR 7/0 through 7.5 YR 5/0), ranging to light reddish brown (5 YR 6/4) and reddish yellow (5 YR 6/8). *Temper*, particles are fine to medium, mostly rounded quartz sand, some angular white particles and other minerals abundant; some protrusion of temper particles through slip. *Carbon streak*, usually absent. *Paste texture*, rough. *Hardness*, 4.0–5.0 (Mohs' scale used throughout). *Fracture*, ragged, not crumbly. *Surface finish:* bowl exteriors scraped, bumpy and sandy to touch; interiors somewhat more carefully scraped, but not polished before application of slip; jar interiors show pronounced scraping marks, exteriors scraped but bumpy. Both bowl surfaces covered with chalky, soft white slip, show swabbing marks, poorly bonded and often almost entirely lost; jar exteriors slipped, extending below rim interiors for a few centimeters; slip mostly hand finished, rarely lightly

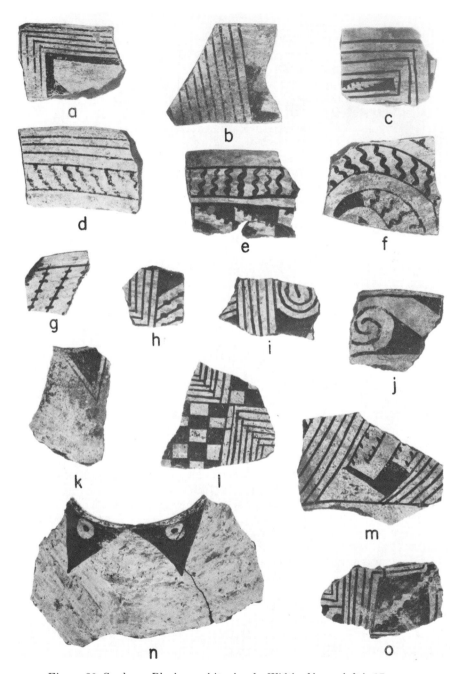

Figure 30. Corduroy Black-on-white sherds. Width of lower left is 17 cm.

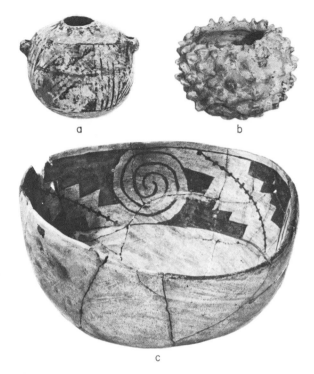

a　　　　　　b

c

Figure 31. Corduroy phase pottery: *a*, Corduroy Black-on-white canteen; *b*, knobbed vessel; *c*, Corduroy Black-on-white bowl, showing warping; diameter is 33.5 cm.

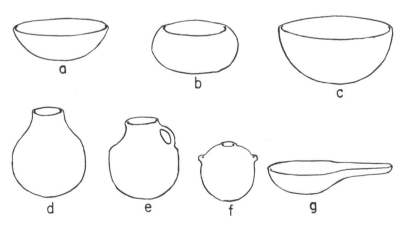

a　　　　　b　　　　　c

d　　　e　　　f　　　g

Figure 32. Corduroy Black-on-white vessel forms.

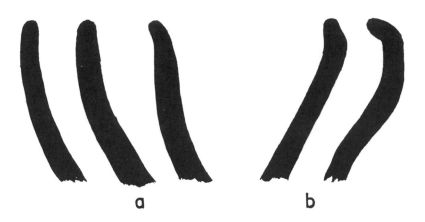

Figure 33. Corduroy Black-on-white rim forms: *a*, bowls; *b*, jars.

pebble polished, crazing common. *Surface color:* white (10 YR 8/1) to light gray (7.5 YR 7/0), latter predominating. *Fire clouds:* present on bowl exteriors, no uniformity as to placement; gray to very dark gray (2.5 YR 6/0 through 3/0). *Form* (Fig. 32): bowls, diameters 16.0-33.5 cm, averaging large; small-mouthed jars, bodies vertically elongated; pitchers, canteens, ladles, effigy (a single foot in the collection). *Vessel wall thickness: Bowls,* 4.5-7.0 mm (30 sherds), average 6.0 mm; *Jars,* 5.0-8.0 mm (15 sherds), average 6.0 mm. *Rims* (Fig. 33): Bowls, normally direct and rounded, occasionally show thinning or slight eversion; Jars, rounded or everted. *Decoration: Paint,* black inorganic, ranges to weak red (10 R 4/2), mat, although there are a few examples of glossy paint suggesting glaze; often lost due to weakly bonded slip, otherwise permanent. *Pigment,* not determined. *Design,* bowl interiors and jar exteriors; rim always black; "lifeline" observed in two instances; line work fine (1-3 mm), generally multiple lines in parallel series from 2 to 10, sometimes dotted; some wavy hachure; extensive use of solid triangles with one edge often sawtoothed or dotted; checker-board rare; negative parallelograms; interlocking scrolls. Brush mark lacks precision, lines variable in width; where lines join at an angle, may overlap or may not come together.

Comparisons. Kiatuthlanna Black-on-white from Kiatuthlanna and the Red Mesa sites (Roberts 1931: 114 *ff.*; Gladwin 1945: 41-42), paste and surface white, polished, vessels smaller and walls thinner, less use of large black areas; technically better in paste content and painting.

Range. At present known only as a dominant type in the Forestdale Valley. One sherd closely resembling Corduroy Black-on-white is in the surface collection from Kiatuthlanna (Arizona State Museum survey, AZ Q:3:1).

Remarks. Corduroy Black-on-white is the oldest painted pottery (about 3 percent of sherd samples) in the Forestdale Valley. The supposition that it was locally produced is based on the technical imperfections that hint that the potters were not familiar with a new paste and the art of applying paint. By design the derivation is clearly from Kiatuthlanna and Red Mesa Black-on-white. The presence of three Kiatuthlanna Black-on-white intrusive sherds in Pit Houses 2 and 3, and also Kana-a Gray, a companion type foreign to Tla Kii Ruin, is an indication of a rough temporal equivalency between Kiatuthlanna and Corduroy Black-on-white.

Knobbed Vessel. The curious vessel illustrated in Figure 31*b* was found among the grave offerings of Burial 3. The paste and thick white slip share the characteristics of Corduroy Black-on-white and there is a slight hint of black paint, the reason for including it here. The knobs were pinched outward from the vessel wall, a treatment occurring as early as the Gila Butte phase in the Hohokam (Haury 1976: 213) that preceded the Corduroy phase by at least one hundred years. The infrequent but widespread occurrence of vessels with this surface texturing suggests it was more than a casual potter's whim. Litzinger (1979) has argued convincingly that these "spiked" pottery vessels are copies of the *Datura* fruit, and he presents evidence of its use medicinally and ceremonially deep into prehistory.

CORDUROY PHASE, INTRUSIVE POTTERY

The examination of trade wares reveals the neighboring areas with which the Forestdale residents established contact and roughly at what time. A benefit of this inquiry is that the interchange of contemporaneous materials provides a basis for equating the Forestdale chronology with others. Although generally this can be done only in broad terms, if tree-ring or other precise ways of dating are applicable, a reasonably close correlation with the Christian calendar may be achieved. The cross-dating mechanism is of positive assistance in equating the Corduroy phase with other cultural manifestations, particularly those to the north.

Figure 34. Gray and brown wares: *a*, Lino Gray; *b*, Kana-a Gray; *c*, *d*, Alma Plain, Forestdale variety, Dry Valley phase; *e*, Alma Incised, Forestdale variety. Diameter of *c* is 25.6 cm.

Whole vessels recovered were: Lino Gray jar associated with Forestdale Smudged bowl in Burial 5; Lino Gray variety pitcher (Fig. 34*a*) and a Kana-a Gray pitcher (Fig. 34*b*) associated with Corduroy Black-on-white bowl in Burial 9.

With few exceptions, intrusive potsherds listed in Table 4 came from pit houses or nearby trash of Corduroy phase age, in contrast to the later trade materials that were found in and

Table 4
CORDUROY PHASE
INTRUSIVE POTTERY

	Number of Sherds					
Provenience	Lino Gray	Kana-a Gray	Kiatuthlanna Black-on-white	White Mound Black-on-white	Gila Plain	Gila Butte Red-on-buff
Pit House 1	5				10 +2 pots	
Pit House 2	5	1	1		1	
Pit House 3	6		2	1	1	
Test 4, Block G5		1			1	
Test, G5					1	
Test, F5						1
In pit house area			1		1	

near the pueblo. This geographical separation adds to the confidence placed in the trade pottery as time indicators.

The best estimated ages of the types in Table 4 are:

Lino Gray, A.D. 600–875 (Breternitz 1966: 83)
Kana-a Gray, A.D. 775–965 (Breternitz, 1966: 79)
Kiatuthlanna Black-on-white, A.D. 825–910 (Breternitz 1966: 80); A.D. 800–870 (Gladwin 1945: 45)
White Mound Black-on-white, A.D. 750–800 (Breternitz 1966: 102)
Gila Plain, duration too long to be helpful
Gila Butte Red-on-buff, A.D. 550–700 (Haury 1976: 338)

The comparatively long life of Lino Gray and Kana-a Gray somewhat reduces the dating value of these types. Their presence, nevertheless, suggests an A.D. 800 to 900 age for the local black-on-whites. Since White Mound Black-on-white occurred much more commonly in the Forestdale phase of the Bear Ruin (Part II: *Intrusive Pottery, Anasazi Culture*) than here, its earlier position seems clear, although its presence is not inconsistent with the temporal limits put on the White

Mound and Corduroy phases. Furthermore, the sherd in question was made into a pottery scraper that could well have been an heirloom. Gila Butte Red-on-buff also occurred with greater frequency in the Forestdale phase, agreeing better with the early age put on it. The village limits of the Bear Ruin and Tla Kii Ruin may well have overlapped. Kiatuthlanna Black-on-white, the inspiration in part for Corduroy Black-on-white, undoubtedly comes much nearer than the other intrusive forms as the marker for the age of the Corduroy phase, somewhat arbitrarily set at A.D. 800 to 900.

DRY VALLEY PHASE, LOCAL POTTERY

The definition of the Dry Valley phase ceramic complex is based entirely on the trash-filled storage pits that antedated the pueblo, on the sheet trash on which the pueblo was built, on the architectural units that typologically are between the pit houses and the pueblo, and on burial furnishings. Quantitatively, the sample includes approximately 2500 sherds and 14 whole or nearly whole vessels.

Alma Plain, Forestdale variety
(Fig. 34c, d)

By paste, color, and finish, not readily distinguished from earlier samples. Most sherds are from the plain parts of neck corrugated vessels, but some wholly plain vessels were still made. Forms include plates (Fig. 34c), small bowls, and jars (Fig. 34d). Alma Plain was waning by Dry Valley phase times, being replaced by corrugated pottery.

Alma Incised, Forestdale variety
(Figs. 34e, 35)

One whole vessel from Burial 19 in Storage Pit 13 and seven sherds, five from Storage Pit 2, represent this type. The paste is heavily tempered with quartz sand, and other characteristics are similar to Alma Plain, Forestdale variety. Surface incisions are in the nature of vertical lines in trios on the jar neck (Fig. 34e) and hastily done wavy lines on vessel bodies (Fig. 35). Postincision smoothing, probably by hand, has somewhat blurred the patterns.

Forestdale Smudged

Dry Valley phase sherd samples contain, on the average, about 6 percent smudged pottery, a sharp quantitative decrease from earlier phases. Qualitatively, the differences between late

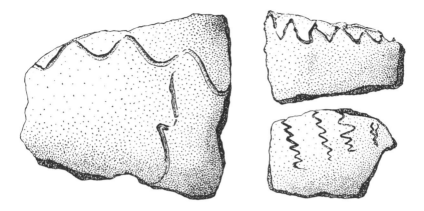

Figure 35. Alma Incised, Dry Valley phase. Width of *a* is 7.8 cm.

smudged pots, limited to bowls, and earlier forms are so minor as to make identification difficult.

Red Ware

All-over red pottery, as in the case of Forestdale Smudged, was diminishing in amount, a drop from about 3 percent to 1 percent of the pottery sample from Corduroy to Dry Valley phases. I do not regard the amount we have as adequate to firmly establish the differences that are apparent, or to propose a new type. Compared with Forestdale Red, this pottery is slipped, which gives it a richer red (7.5 R 4/4) than the earlier type. Vessel walls are also about 2 mm thicker on the average, 6 mm as compared to 4 mm, related possibly to a somewhat larger average vessel size. Fire clouds are not prominent. One sherd shows a black scrawl of the kind on Forestdale Black-on-red.

Neck Corrugated
(Fig. 36*a–c*)

This pottery is the logical outgrowth of Alma Neck-banded and is closely related to Three Circle Neck Corrugated (Haury 1936*b*: 36–37) and to Incised Corrugated of the Reserve area (Martin and Rinaldo 1950*b*: 500). In Tla Kii Ruin, the coils range from no indentation (Fig. 36*a*), to alternately plain and indented (Fig. 36*b*), to complete indentation (Fig. 36*c*). Incising and punching, common to the south and east, are absent. The amount of this pottery in Dry Valley phase contexts is small, but it nevertheless is a diagnostic of the phase. The plain body

Figure 36. Dry Valley phase corrugated pottery: *a–c*, neck corrugated; *d–k*, other kinds of corrugation. Width of *e* is 10.8 cm.

sherds from the bodies of jars are indistinguishable from Alma Plain, Forestdale variety, and are included in that category, artificially boosting the percent value.

Corrugated

Much of the culinary pottery (about 20 percent) of the Dry Valley phase was of the all-over corrugated variety. Acceptance of the idea of corrugating led to the production of much of it. Its differentiation from the brown-paste equivalent forms to the south and east is difficult, and could be done only by a carefully comparative lithological analysis. In general, the period of A.D. 1000 to 1100 was the time of considerable striving for effect in the way corrugations were produced, and seldom was the precision of indentation excelled in later times. This excellence is especially noticeable in the San Francisco River region (Martin and Rinaldo 1950*b*: 526–530) and in the Point of Pines area.

The range of corrugating techniques from Tla Kii Ruin is illustrated in Figure 36*d-k*. Vessel forms were chiefly large-mouthed, round-bodied jars, and hemispherical bowls, normally smudged interiorly. Paint on the exterior, producing McDonald Corrugated (Colton and Hargrave 1937: 61–62), does not occur. There are a few sherds of bowls slipped red inside and out over partially obliterated corrugations.

Black-on-white

Black-on-white pottery of the Dry Valley phase makes up about 40 percent of the sherd sample as compared with only 3 percent during the preceding Corduroy phase. This sharp numerical increase appears to reflect an all-out adoption of the gray ware painted tradition by the local potters. It was also accompanied by a bewildering multiplication of those decorative elements normally used to trace relationships. The product was a blend that is difficult to formalize. Rather than to complicate the ceramic taxonomy with a new type or types, I prefer to take notice only of the important features of the lot as a whole, attempting later to give a possible explanation.

Description.

> *Construction:* coil-scrape. *Firing:* reducing atmosphere; warping common (Fig. 38*a*). *Paste: Color,* dominantly white (7.5 YR 8/0). *Temper,* rounded quartz sand and mixed minerals, some black. *Carbon streak,* absent. *Hardness,* 5.0–6.0. *Surface finish:* all surfaces except jar interiors slipped white (7.5 YR 9/0 average); bowl interiors and jar exteriors pebble-polished, bowl exteriors

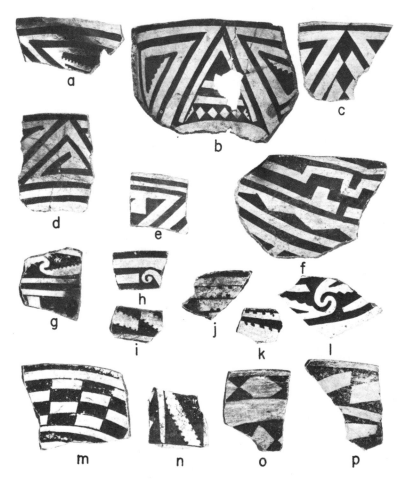

Figure 37. Black-on-white pottery of the Black Mesa style, with mat or glaze black mineral paint; Dry Valley phase. Width of *b* is 16.5 cm.

mostly hand-smoothed; surfaces occasionally bumpy from protruding temper particles; crazing and fire clouds present. *Form:* bowls (Fig. 38), jars (Fig. 39); pitchers with vertical necks and spherical bodies, stick or composite handles (no effigy handles noted); ladles of split-gourd type. *Decoration: Paint,* dense black, often with a glaze quality. Preliminary tests show copper and lead are absent, suggesting the glaze may be salt-derived;

Figure 38. Black-on-white pottery, Dry Valley phase: *a*, example of extreme warping; *b–d*, Reserve style (*b*, *c*, Cebolleta Black-on-white?); *e*, Snowflake style; *f*, Puerco style; *g*, unidentified style. Diameter of *g* is 29 cm.

reddish brown tint rare. Figures 37 and 38 illustrate the dominant decorative styles, the former related to Black Mesa Black-on-white, the latter also including the Puerco and Reserve styles of painting. The two fragmentary jars in Figure 39 have interesting, but not readily classifiable, patterns.

Comparisons. The design style illustrated in Figure 38*e* is generally called Snowflake (Gladwin and Gladwin 1934, Fig. 5; Martin and Willis, 1940, Pls. 121–122), with dull black paint. It is usually better polished than Puerco Black-on-white.

Range. Adequate comparative study not made.

Figure 39. Fragmentary black-on-white jars from Storage Pit 12, Dry Valley phase; *b* has glaze paint, diameter is 38 cm.

Remarks. The early, pre-A.D. 1000, black-on-white development in the Southwest lends itself to comparatively
simple taxonomic analysis. This condition was, in fact,
one of the bases for the original recognition by the Pecos
Conference of 1927 of such stages as Basketmaker III,
Pueblo I, and Pueblo II. Later, with the adoption of
phases as a classificatory device, we see such refinements
as Gladwin's (1945) proposed White Mound, Kiatuthlanna, Red Mesa sequence that encompasses a relatively
small area and evaluates cultural change in shorter time
intervals. After about A.D. 1000, however, pottery became
greatly complicated by the coming together of regional
styles and by the stimulus provided by a thriving art, if
not an industry. The archaeologist is often confronted
with a welter of decorative styles that do not lend
themselves to the kind of classification we have come to
expect or have believed to be desirable.

This situation certainly prevails for Tla Kii Ruin after
the Corduroy phase. By the eleventh century, the For-
estdale Valley potters were drifting along in a ceramic
current that was being generated by other people occupying a large arc from the northwest to the southeast.
From about A.D. 900 on, the pottery to the northwest,
dominated decoratively by the Black Mesa style of
Pueblo II (originally called Deadmans style, Colton and
Hargrave 1937: 16) and exemplified by Black Mesa
Black-on-white and variants such as Holbrook and Sosi
Black-on-white, was the inspiration for the Snowflake
Black-on-white style (Fig. 38*e*), which becomes the dominant decorative mode in the Carrizo phase. Corollary
evidence exists in the intrusion into the Forestdale Valley
of some of the aforementioned types.

The Puerco "style" (Fig. 38*f*), as yet, has not been so
clearly segregated, but it, too, must be recognized.
Finally, the closely related Reserve style (Fig. 38*b–d*;
Martin and Rinaldo 1950*b*: 499), culminating in the
Tularosa style to the east and southeast, also is in
evidence. Examples *b* and *c* in Figure 38 have been
identified by A. E. Dittert as Cebolleta Black-on-white,
most likely coming from the western part of the Acoma
province and dating near A.D. 1050. The resultant blending of these styles, in some cases, produced pottery that
is not quite like any of them, yet that in sherd form is
next to impossible to segregate.

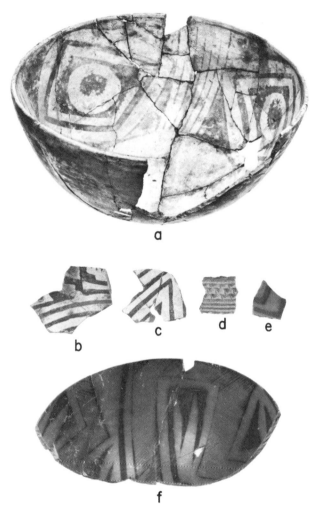

Figure 40. Trade pottery, Dry Valley phase: *a*, Black Mesa Black-on-white
(Puerco style); *b, c*, Holbrook Black-on-white; *d*, Tusayan Corrugated; *e*, Puerco
Black-on-red; *f*, Wingate Black-on-red. Diameter of *a* is 27.5 cm.

DRY VALLEY PHASE, INTRUSIVE POTTERY

The collection contains a single complete vessel certainly
foreign to the area, a bowl of Black Mesa Black-on-white (Fig.
40*a*), originally named Deadmans Black-on-white (Colton and
Hargrave 1937: 208–209; Colton 1955). It was associated with
Burial 11, partly under the wall of Room 20.

Table 5
DRY VALLEY PHASE INTRUSIVE POTTERY

	Number of Sherds						
Provenience	Holbrook Black-on-white	Black Mesa Black-on-white	Puerco Black-on-red	Wingate Black-on-red	Tusayan Corrugated	Deadmans Black-on-red	Cebolleta Black-on-white
Storage Pit 1	1	3		1			
Storage Pit 2		1					
Storage Pit 3					1		
Storage Pit 4	2	3					
Storage Pit 11					2		
Storage Pit 12		1	1	1			1
Unit Structure 2		1					1
Below floor, Room 7	1				1	1	
Below floor, Room 21	2	1		1			

Table 5 lists the proveniences of fragments of foreign pottery. Tree-ring dates assignable to them are:

Holbrook Black-on-white (Fig. 40*b*, *c*), A.D. 1070–1100 (Colton 1955); 1075–1130 (Breternitz 1966: 77–78)

Black Mesa Black-on-white (Fig. 40*a*), A.D. 875–1130, best 1000-1130 (Breternitz 1966: 70)

Puerco Black-on-red (Fig. 40*e*), A.D. 1030-1175, most abundant 1050–1125 (Breternitz 1966: 89)

Wingate Black-on-red (Fig. 40*f*), A.D. 1047–1200 (Breternitz 1966: 102); about 930–1000 (Gladwin 1945: 71–73, 76)

Tusayan Corrugated (Fig. 40*d*), A.D. 1075–1285 (Breternitz 1966: 100)

Deadmans Black-on-red (not shown), A.D. 775–1066 (Breternitz 1966: 73)

Cebolleta Black-on-white (Fig. 38*b*, *c*), about A.D. 1050 (Dittert 1959: 400)

In allotting arbitrary blocks of time to the phases in the Forestdale sequence, A.D. 900 to 1000 was assigned to the Dry Valley phase. Although the Corduroy–to–Dry Valley transition must have happened close to A.D. 900, most of the clues we have for Dry Valley indicate the last half of the 1000s to be more realistic. All of the associated trade pottery types, according to the best estimated tree-ring dates, indicate they were in vogue in the eleventh century and the tightest clustering of dates is after 1050.

CARRIZO PHASE, LOCAL POTTERY

Stratigraphically and by tree-ring dating, the latest constructions in the Tla Kii Ruin complex were the 21–room pueblo, the Great Kiva, and the unfinished small kiva. Pottery from the fills and floors of these structures and from four burials (2, 4, 10, and 16) is the material on which the following ceramic traits are based. About 60 percent (over 10,000 sherds) of the fragmentary pottery from the site is of this phase. Additionally, there are 28 whole or restorable vessels available for study.

Alma Plain, Forestdale variety

Approximately 15 percent of the fill and floor sherds from the pueblo are classifiable as Alma Plain. Some of these actually may be much older than the Carrizo phase but the amount, consistent in all rooms, strongly hints that some plain ware was still made. Because the neck corrugated vessel was now almost completely out-of-style, the presence of so many plain sherds cannot be explained as body fragments of such vessels. Jars, bowls, and plates are represented by rim sherds. Martin and Rinaldo (1950b: 500, 531) also note Alma Plain for the Reserve phase in the Reserve area, but they regard it as coming from neck corrugated vessels.

Forestdale Smudged and Reserve Smudged

Our field counts do not accurately distinguish between these two forms of smudged pottery. In the Forestdale Valley, Forestdale Smudged precedes and gives rise to Reserve Smudged, but it is not possible to establish a clear-cut separation. A Forestdale Smudged bowl was found with Burial 16, preserving the typically thin walls, reddish exterior, and sandy paste of the older pieces, and sherds also occurred in the trash. From these occurrences we reasoned that smudged pottery with early characteristics survived into the Carrizo phase. But most of the sherds are from bowls with thicker walls (average 6.0 mm), black to brown exteriors, less well formed and polished, with a harder paste containing sand and angular white temper particles, identified as Reserve Smudged (Martin and Rinaldo

1950*b*: 500). Rim fillets are lacking. The average frequency of smudged sherds of these two kinds from the pueblo rooms was 4.5 percent of a pottery sample of about 4500 pieces.

Red Ware

As during the Dry Valley phase, red ware is of infrequent occurrence (1 percent of the pueblo sherd sample) in this later phase. Shapes were predominantly bowls, and we have one fragment each of a solid-handle dipper and a "seed jar." A half-dozen bowl fragments show corrugated exteriors. The Forestdale Valley was near the northern limits of the undecorated red ware area, stretching in a wide region to the east, south and west, and little of it was ever produced here.

Corrugated

By the twelfth century, the Carrizo phase, about 40 percent of the pottery produced by Forestdale potters was corrugated in one of several ways. In general, both the width of the coils and the spacing of the indentation are narrower and finer than in the corrugated pottery of the preceding phase. A cross section of the principal techniques of pressing the coils together is given in Figure 41; for jars, examples *a* and *b* are the most prevalent, and *c-e* are variations. The flat, broad coils of *f* are exceptional, and *g-i* illustrate the zoning effect of indented and nonindented coils. Patterning by indentation (Fig. 41*j*) was not common, and paint was not used at this time to emphasize the design. Bowl interiors were smudged and highly polished, and the exterior shows a smoothing or light scraping (Fig. 41*k*, *l*) of the coils, a trait undoubtedly coupled with the frequent use of paint, as discussed under McDonald Corrugated. A few sherds of corrugated bowls, slipped red on both surfaces, occurred. The dominant vessel forms are illustrated in Figure 42: jars, *a-c*, with diameters from 12 cm to 37 cm; bowls, *d-e*, and plates, *f*, with diameters of 20 cm to 25 cm. The last are characterized by a high inner-surface finish and sloppiness of finish externally (Fig. 41*m-n*).

Much of the pottery is certainly Linden Corrugated (Colton and Hargrave 1937: 60–61), but the description does not cover the range of corrugation techniques present in the collection.

McDonald Corrugated
(Colton and Hargrave 1937: 61–62).

In every instance where painted corrugated pottery, or McDonald Corrugated, was found in a clearly defined stratigraphic context, it was assignable to the Carrizo phase. Dry

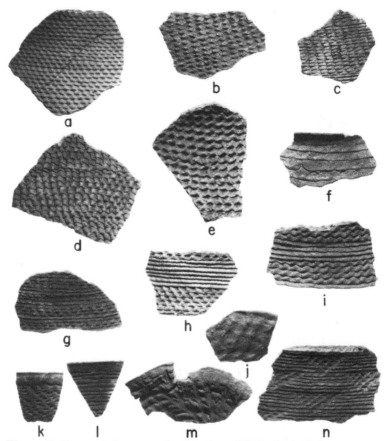

Figure 41. Corrugated pottery, Carrizo phase. Width of *a* is 12.5 cm.

Valley phase corrugated pottery never showed this characteristic, and we may take the introduction of the trait, about A.D.
1100, to be an important horizon marker. Just where, geographically, the custom of painting over the corrugation origi-
nated has not yet been determined. It should be noted that
examples occur as early, if not earlier, in the Point of Pines
region, where painting over textured surfaces ultimately
reached heights of variety and amounts not yet seen anywhere
else. The southern edge of the Colorado Plateau is the northern
distributional limit and it extends south as far as the Gila River
at Safford. The point of origin must lie somewhere between
these two extremes.

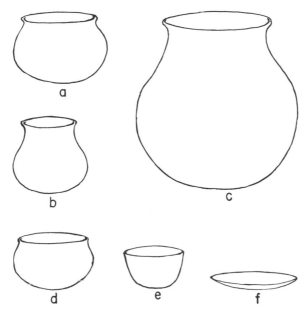

Figure 42. Corrugated pottery vessel forms, Carrizo phase.

In round numbers, McDonald Corrugated totaled 15 percent to 30 percent of all corrugated pottery in the samples from pueblo room fills and floors. The actual number of vessels produced in proportion to unpainted corrugated pots is not readily calculated, but it was sufficiently prevalent to regard it as an important element in the ceramic complex. The McDonald Corrugated from Tla Kii Ruin is limited to bowls (Fig. 43) and has a variety of decorative treatments, as shown in Figure 44. Interiors are always smudged and well polished, and exteriors are predominantly indented corrugated. Only occasionally are the coils unindented. Combinations of these two techniques, producing zones of texturing parallel to the rim, are common, but the indented paint-filled pattern is almost nonextant. A thick, white paint was applied, evidently with the finger, in broad stripes, rarely dots, to cover bowl exteriors with bold patterns. In many instances, after the application of the paint, the polishing tool was lightly applied, which not only compacted the creamy pigment, but faintly depressed the coils. It may be that this technique inspired the indented patterns and paint-filled grooves that became common in later times. A number of vessel exteriors were solidly coated with white pigment, in

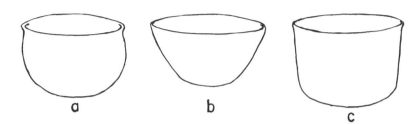

Figure 43. McDonald Corrugated bowl forms.

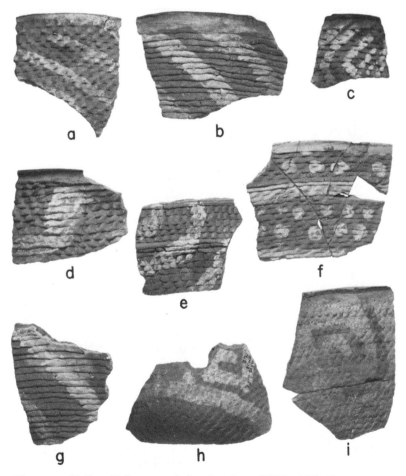

Figure 44. McDonald Corrugated, Carrizo phase. Width of *b* is 12 cm.

which case polishing was extensive, and in one instance a black design was added (Fig. 44*i*), producing a variant form of McDonald Corrugated.

Black-on-white

So far, the inventory of pottery from the Tla Kii Ruin has provided no clear proof, other than quantity, or in some cases conformity to the ceramic tradition, that the pottery was locally produced. Any doubts that may exist about the local production of black-on-white pottery during the Carrizo phase are dispelled by the recovery of several lots of untempered potters' clay, the kind that was used in producing gray ware, and two instances of unfired pots from pueblo room floors.

There is no difference in the frequency of black-on-white pottery between the Dry Valley and Carrizo phases, as in both it amounts to about 40 percent of the sherd sample. In most characteristics, it is indistinguishable from one phase to the other. There are some refinements in design execution, but the styles remain essentially the same. There is, however, a noticeable increase in the variety of vessel forms and a marked increase in the number of jars in proportion to bowls. Potters were still having trouble with warping during firing, resulting in misshapen vessels and blistered surfaces. Salt(?) glaze painting is common, though much of the black paint is mat. Evidently most, if not all, of the paint had the potential to produce a glaze effect, as in the same vessel the paint may range from mat to glaze.

The congeries of black-on-white pottery from the Carrizo phase further exemplify the assimilation of the artistic products developed by potters elsewhere. For example, the heaviness of the Black Mesa style was retained and built upon by making yet bolder patterns, loosely organized, and running to a gray background, as illustrated in Figure 45. There is some justification for believing that the Black Mesa style inspired the Snowflake style in its purest sense, which is also strongly represented in the collection (Fig. 46). Other strong design components are the Puerco style (Fig. 47*a–f*) and Reserve style (Fig. 47*g–s*). In the Reserve, well-executed wavy hatching, a derivation from earlier times, is common. Figure 45*b* is an oft-repeated decorative treatment in the region north of the White Mountains, not specifically assigned to any style.

The prevalence of glaze, the directional change in hatching of hatch-filled areas, the balancing of hatched and solid elements in the designs, and the precision of some of the brush

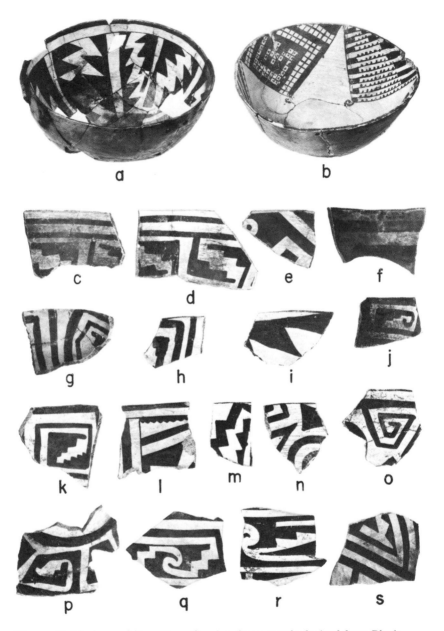

Figure 45. Black-on-white pottery, Carrizo phase; mostly derived from Black
Mesa Black-on-white (except *b*). Note: *a* and *b* are a different scale from *c–s*.
Diameter of *a* is 27.5 cm. Width of *c* is 13.0 cm.

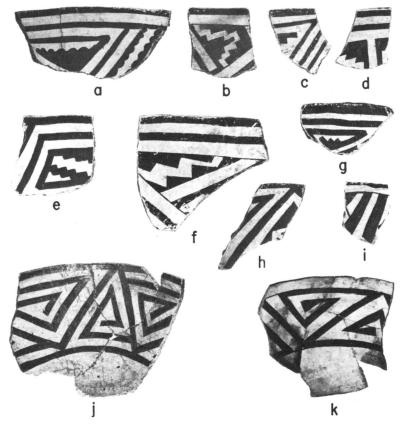

Figure 46. Black-on-white pottery, Snowflake style,
Carrizo phase. Width of *j* is 16 cm.

work forecast Pinedale Black-on-white of the thirteenth century
(Haury and Hargrave 1931: 62–63).

Shapes include bowls as illustrated in Figure 48*a–c*; jars of
the small-mouthed, spherical-bodied variety (Fig. 48*d–e*); pitchers with various handle treatments (Fig. 48*f*), including one of
the effigy type handle; a curious jar-in-bowl form (Fig. 48*g*)
occasionally seen in the White Mountain region; effigy vessels
represented by two fragments (Fig. 48*h*); and trough- and solid-
handled ladles (Fig. 48*i–j*). Corrugated black-on-white bowls
occur (Fig. 47*f, g*).

Rooms 13 and 15 were created when a large room was
divided by a partition wall. At the same time the floor level was

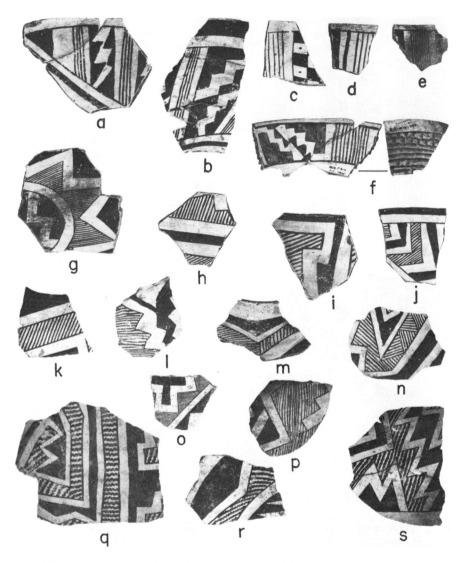

Figure 47. Black-on-white pottery: *a–f*, Puerco style; *g–s*,
Reserve style. Width of *s* is 16 cm.

raised, evidently intentionally, burying artifacts resting on the
deeper floor. Included among those were eight pottery bowls
that are of interest because of their similarity. The color of the
painted decoration, all in the Puerco style, grades from black to

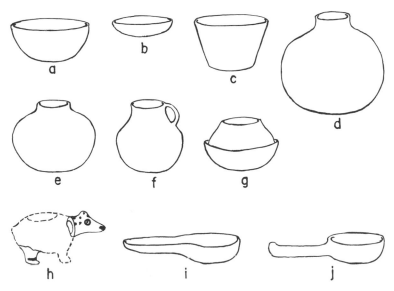

Figure 48. Black-on-white vessel shapes, Carrizo phase. Not to scale.

a weak red (2.5 YR 4/2) on a gray background (2.5 YR 6/0). Exterior surfaces are rough, but interior surfaces have a satinlike finish over a thin slip. The paste is exceptionally soft (2.0-2.5), containing sand and angular white fragments as tempering materials. Representative decorative panels are shown in Figure 49. The similarity of design layout, the nature of the brush work, the sameness of the clay, and the fact that the bowls were found together, indicate the vessels were the product of one potter. The absence of sherds of similar vessels in the general excavations suggests these vessels may have been produced in a single firing batch in which something went wrong, either in the firing process itself or in the mixing of the clay. While the uniqueness of these vessels might tempt designating them as a new type, that step is clearly not warranted. Rather, the significant points to be drawn from them are that pottery was locally made, which helps to explain the nature of the stylistic mixtures and derivatives therefrom evident in the Tla Kii Ruin, and also that the lot represents the preferred repertoire of a single potter. The technical similarities would appear to establish the basis of a rationale for efforts to identify individual pieces of pottery from different sources as the products of the same artist. The phase allocation of these specimens is Carrizo.

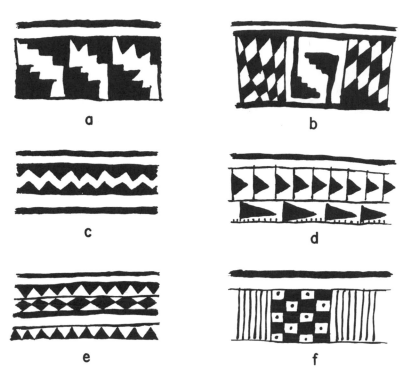

Figure 49. Design panels from six of eight vessels from Room 13–15, probably the product of a single potter.

    The dates for nearly all of these types have been given previously, and in most cases the terminal dates are about A.D. 1100 or later. White Mound Black-on-white, with an ascribed time of 750 to 800 (Breternitz 1966: 102), is out of context in the fill of a pueblo room, just as was an occasional sherd of Corduroy Black-on-white. Chaco Black-on-white of about 1050 to 1125 (Breternitz 1966: 71) and Showlow Black-on-red (Colton and Hargrave 1937: 78–79) with a date of 1030 to 1175 (Breternitz 1966: 95), come within the general range of the other trade pieces; Tularosa White-on-red and Tularosa Fillet Rim also are of about this same age. What this points to is merely the fact that the majority of the trade pottery is of an age that is in agreement with the tree-ring dates for the Tla Kii Ruin, and that it provides supportive evidence of the temporal equivalence of the design styles mentioned. Also, if trade pieces are regarded as evidence of actual contacts, the lines that connected the

Forestdale Valley people with others were mainly out to the north and east, as already noted for the ceramics of earlier phases.

Gila Plain

The single occurrence of Gila Plain means little chronologically because of its long life, but it does hint of contacts with the Hohokam far to the southwest. Actually, Hohokam pottery is more abundant in the earlier phases of the Forestdale sequence.

CARRIZO PHASE, INTRUSIVE POTTERY

Sherds from Pueblo room fills or floors, attributed to a Carrizo phase context, are listed in Table 6 (see also Fig. 50).

Table 6
CARRIZO PHASE INTRUSIVE POTTERY

Provenience	Holbrook Black-on-white	Black Mesa Black-on-white	Chaco Black-on-white	White Mound Black-on-white	Puerco Black-on-red	Wingate Black-on-red	Showlow Black-on-red	Deadmans Black-on-red	Tularosa White-on-red	Tularosa Fillet Rim	Gila Plain
Room 1					1						
3	1										
5	1				1						
8	2					1					
9						1					
10					1						
11					1	1		1			
12							1				
13	2	1	1	1	2	2	1				
14	1	1									
15		2									1
16	2	1								1	
17	3										
18					1						
20		1									
21	2	3									
General testing*	13	19	1		15	3	4			1	

*Sherds from tests may have come from either Dry Valley or Carrizo phase contexts, but most probably the latter.

GRAY WARE VERSUS BROWN WARE

A review of the ceramic assemblage, meaning the totality of the pottery known to the occupants of the Forestdale Valley, calls attention to an indisputable fact: the pottery made locally to the time of the Corduroy phase, or about A.D. 900, was brown, formed of alluvial clays containing considerable iron, and fired in an oxidizing atmosphere. Vessel surfaces carried no painted decoration. After the Corduroy phase, the monotony of that picture changed, for there was introduced a class of ceramics composed of kaolinitic clay, essentially iron-free and of sedimentary origin. The vessels made with it were baked in a controlled fire approaching a reducing atmosphere. The end product was a ware of white to gray color that provided an ideal contrast for black-painted patterns. Brown ware, although weakly present in the southern reaches of the Colorado Plateau, is the dominant pottery in the vast sub–Mogollon Rim country southward, the homeland of the Mogollon people. Gray paste pottery, on the other hand, whether painted or corrugated, is the hallmark of the Anasazi people of the Colorado Plateau.

The first question that must be answered is: are the differences we see environmentally determined, are they cultural, or a combination of both? The mountain zone where brown wares predominate is characterized by extensive vulcanism and complex orographic processes effecting largely metamorphic rocks of varying geologic ages. The clays in this region are mostly residual and alluvial in nature. The Colorado Plateau, on the other hand, except for only occasional volcanic intrusions, records a long sedimentary history of earth-forming processes through flat-lying strata of limestones, sandstones, shales, and clays. Sedimentary clays in the area tend to be kaolinitic. Immediately, therefore, it is clear that environment has been the basic determinant in clay type availability and hence the kinds of pottery produced. Cultural values, therefore, would seem to have been minimized. However, the two contrasting environmental zones, whether by choice or by accident, were occupied initially by people we recognize as having been somewhat different from each other on the basis of their material remains. The Mogollon appeared to have preferred a mountain setting, while the Anasazi seem to have felt more at home in the open reaches of the Plateau. Ceramics, then, by environmental constraints, came to be the hallmarks of people as well as of topographic zones.

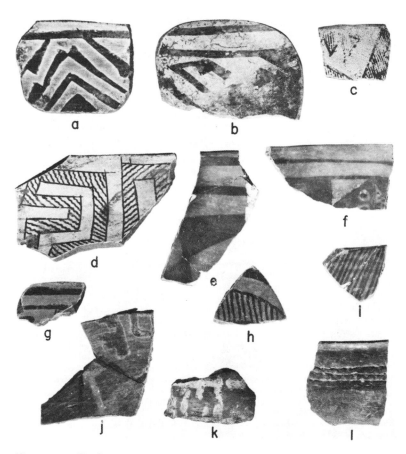

Figure 50. Trade pottery, Carrizo phase: *a*, *b*, Holbrook Black-on-white (scraping spoons); *c*, *d*, Chaco Black-on-white; *e*, *f*, Puerco Black-on-red; *g*, *h*, Wingate Black-on-red; *i*, *j*, Showlow Black-on-red; *k*, Tularosa White-on-red; *l*, Tularosa Fillet Rim. Width of *a* is 7.1 cm.

One must add to that factor the dimension of time. The pottery of the mountaineers was older than that of their Plateau neighbors by as much as about 800 years. That preeminence adds significantly to the cultural factor and somewhat reduces the importance of the environmental controls. Pottery, as a marker of cultural authorship and "tribal" presence, therefore, may be accepted with more confidence. The time and cultural factors combined add to the interest of the problem wherever the gray wares and brown wares come together.

In the Forestdale Valley, as elsewhere, the gray-white paste, smooth-surfaced pottery was painted with black pigment of mineral origin, producing black-on-white patterns that remained the dominant decorative form until the introduction of polychromes at about Pinedale phase times in the Forestdale sequence. Firing problems, resulting in the warping of vessels, and a certain clumsiness on the part of potters attempting to make a brand of painted pottery new to them, are evidences of the adaptive process. In time, the black-on-whites took on the ceramic quality of the surrounding areas, which means that the Forestdale potters either became equally as proficient as their neighbors, or there was a mixing of people bringing skilled potters to the valley, or, as a third possibility, the local craftsmen gave up and imported all painted vessels from a distance. We do not yet have certain answers to these several choices.

The brown pottery such as Alma Plain and a variety of corrugated types, as well as the miscalled red wares (actually brown wares), are generally classified as utility types, used for cooking and storage, while the painted vessels are believed to have served somewhat more sophisticated functions as "dinner" ware, perhaps ritual uses, or to dress up an otherwise dull collection of clay household containers. The intrusion, by whatever mechanism, of a painted pottery fabric into a much older tradition without painting, is a challenging problem of cultural transfer, and it deserves to be studied in depth of time, in geographical extent, and in typological variations. To do that lies beyond the scope of this report, though a few observations may be made.

First, the transfer meant the acceptance of a new kind of clay as well as a different firing technique. The manufacturing method remained essentially the same, for the coil-scrape system was used by the makers of both categories of wares. There are reasons to believe that the producers of brown wares, earlier by centuries than the gray wares, were also the inventors of corrugated pottery, that is, where the spiral coils were preserved exteriorly as a mode of surface texturing for practical or ornamental reasons. The priority of neck banding and neck corrugating, as a prelude to all-over corrugating in Mogollon sites, over similar treatments in the Anasazi area, has been noted (Part II: *Intrusive Pottery, Mogollon Culture*) but little heeded. The fact that technically the finest corrugated pottery ever produced in the Southwest and the greatest known range in treatment of the coils was centered in the White

Mountains and environs, the heartland of brown ware corrugation, bespeaks of a great time depth and an unusual preoccupation with the fictile nature of clay. Furthermore, the emphasis on clay texturing was offset by a weak concern, or even disregard, with the painting of pottery. This subject should be further elucidated when the full reports of the Point of Pines investigations become available.

The most significant attribute in the transfer process for our present needs was that design styles also were adopted along with the concept of painting the surface of a vessel. Those design styles were the ones used by the potters of the Colorado Plateau, where painting in black on a white or gray background had been well established and regional styles had also taken form. The most eligible and logical donor areas were those closest to the Forestdale Valley. It is not surprising, therefore, that the oldest black-on-white pottery in the Valley manifests patterns and treatments of decoration that reflect kinship to the pottery of the Kiatuthlanna, Black Mesa, Red Mesa, and Reserve areas.

To support this conclusion, the pottery associated with several burials is especially illuminating. Burial 13, the poorly preserved remains of an adult of indeterminate sex, was encountered near Pit Houses 1 and 2, in the area occupied during the Corduroy phase. The grave shallowly penetrated the undisturbed subsoil and the remains were covered with a soil-refuse mixture. The grave goods included turquoise beads (at lower arm, A-2874), a concretion (A-2861), shell ornaments, and six pottery vessels near the skull. Five of those, all bowls, were black-on-white in the Kiatuthlanna style of decoration (Fig. 51), and the sixth was a small pitcher of Forestdale Plain (A-2860). In contrast, Burial 3, a semiflexed adult, possibly female, was interred in the fill of Pit House 1, suggesting that the time of burial was late in the Corduroy phase, certainly before the Dry Valley phase came into full being. In addition to steatite beads (A-2065), grave accompaniments numbered ten clay vessels, six near the head, the others at the torso and legs (Fig. 52). Other than a small Forestdale Smudged bowl (A-2061) and a curious knobbed pot (Fig. 31*b*, A-2054), the vessels were black-on-white bowls, the designs in most cases seriously damaged by the acid soil and poor bonding of the slip. Enough painting remains, however, to illustrate a most interesting range in design styles (Fig. 52): Kiatuthlanna (*a–c*), Reserve (*d*), Black Mesa (*e*), Red Mesa (*f*), and two large misshapen vessels (*g, h*), the first with a disorganized quartered design, possibly

Figure 51. Black-on-white bowls, Kiatuthlanna style, associated with Burial 13. Diameter of *a* is 22.3 cm.

based on a contemporary Hohokam treatment even to the outside trailing line, and the second clearly inspired by the Red Mesa style. Quartering of the decorative field occurs in the Kiatuthlanna style, but the treatment of the quarters impresses one as being the work of a novice. These two pieces are believed to have been locally produced while the status of the others is not clear.

The lateness of Burial 3 compared with Burial 13, as indicated by the provenience data, is supported typologically by the pottery as well. Although we do not know what motivated the placing of these clay vessels with the dead and what their cultural affiliations were, the inference may be drawn that the painted pottery of the Kiatuthlanna area of the Kiatuthlanna

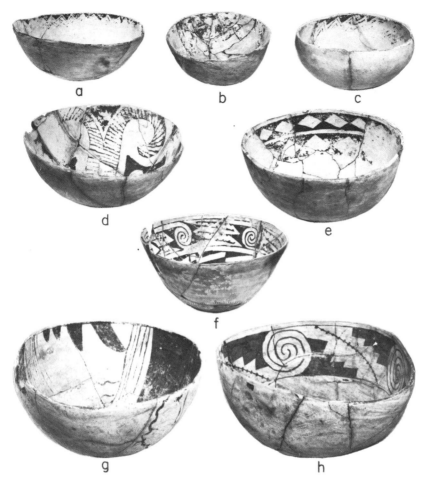

Figure 52. Black-on-white bowls associated with Burial 3, illustrating an exceptional range in design styles: *a–c*, Kiatuthlanna; *d*, Reserve; *e*, Black Mesa; *f*, Red Mesa; *g*, *h*, inept locally made Corduroy Black-on-white, *g* is possibly Hohokam inspired, *h* is of modified Red Mesa style. Diameter of *h* is 33 cm.

phase (Gladwin 1945: 41–48), roughly from A.D. 800 to 900, was the first to affect significantly the potters' products of the Forestdale Valley. Subsequently, the other influences converged on the valley to produce the combination of styles we see in Burial 3.

The process, diagrammed, is given in Figure 53. The Kiatuthlanna style, it should be noted, is derived from White Mound Black-on-white of late Basketmaker III times, roughly A.D. 700 to 800. Intrusives of that type occurred in the Bear Ruin during the Forestdale phase, a foretaste of the infusion of the gray ware ceramics into the Mogollon pottery tradition that was to follow.

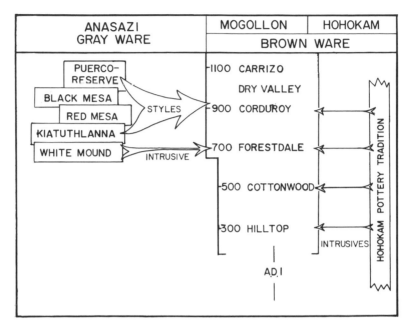

Figure 53. Diagram of initial merging of gray wares and brown wares in the Forestdale Valley, leading to the production of Corduroy Black-on-white pottery. Mogollon contact with the Hohokam is indicated by Gila Plain.

Not much has been said about the possible impact of the Hohokam ceramic tradition on the potters of the Forestdale Valley. We know that contacts of some kind were established from the beginning with the Desert tribe because Hohokam pottery has been found as foreign material in all early local phases. Although most of it was Gila Plain, some badly eroded, and therefore unclassifiable, painted fragments have been found as well. Given the sparseness of the data available, it is fruitless at this time to examine the question in detail. There is growing evidence, however, that the long-standing custom of painting pottery among the Hohokam, leading to the use of styles and motifs earlier in the desert than in the mountains and Plateau, did measurably influence what happened among the potters of the Mogollon and Anasazi.

Given these initial stimuli, the Forestdale potters and their neighbors produced decorative combinations unique to the Mogollon Rim and sub-Rim areas, but retaining qualities that reflect the melange of origins. In that respect, Forestdale was no different from all other parts of the Southwest, where borrowing and copying were always taking place to modify the potters' products. The change came at about the midpoint in the life span of brown ware. The valley was close to the southwestern limits where black-on-white pottery was made and, therefore, drew mainly on the ceramics of the north. A possible exception was the Tonto Basin, where Roosevelt Black-on-white appears to have been made well south of the Rim.

Immediately east of the White Mountain massif, the gray-paste pottery fabric occurs as Tularosa Black-on-white; and still farther south, in a modified form, as Mimbres Black-on-white and its antecedent form, Mimbres Boldface Black-on-white. Here the transition from the red-on-brown of Mogollon derivation to a black-on-white of Anasazi inspiration can be followed technologically through Three Circle Red-on-white. Paste changes, firing atmosphere modifications, and paint formula alterations were all in the direction of the northern potters' practices. Furthermore, decorative styles and elements reflected northern established features as well. Those, blended with relatively simple rectilinear layouts and elements long held by the Mogollon potters, coupled with the willingness of the Classic Mimbres potters to borrow from others, as from the Hohokam, and their incomparable inventiveness, led to the emergence of the renowned Mimbres school of potters. Alternative views, such as believing that Mimbres pottery evolved internally, require far more difficult-to-support interpretations of the data and the stretching of one's notion of cultural processes.

CLAY OBJECTS AND WORKED POTSHERDS

Miniature vessels (2; Fig. 54*a*, *b*)
> Brown, unpolished. Shallow bowl, diameter 2.2 cm; Unit Structure 2, Dry Valley phase. Fragmentary ladle, length 6.7 cm, Room 16, Carrizo phase.

Figurines (3)
> Animal (1; Fig 54*c*)
>> Light brown, fired, quadruped. Length 2.5 cm. Storage Pit 3, Dry Valley phase.

> Human (2; Fig. 54*d*, *e*)
>> Brown, fired; stylized and crudely fashioned. Figure 54*d* is 4.9 cm long, from the pit house area, probably Corduroy phase. Figure 54*e*, basal part only, is from Burial 5, Corduroy phase.

Figure 54. Miscellaneous clay objects. Length of *d* is 4.9 cm.

Worked Potsherds (46)
  Discs (16)
    Unperforated (13; Fig. 54*f*)
      Edges rough, occasionally ground down; diameters, 2.5-
      7.3cm. Pottery types by phase association are: Corduroy
      phase—Alma Plain (3), Forestdale Smudged (1), White
      Mound Black-on-white (1, Fig. 54*f*); Dry Valley phase—
      smudged brown ware (1), Reserve Black-on-white (1);
      Carrizo phase—Alma Plain (1), McDonald Corrugated
      (1), indeterminate black-on-white (1); phase uncertain—
      Alma Plain (1), indeterminate black-on-white (2).
        The White Mound Black-on-white sherd in Pit House
      3, Corduroy phase context, is of special interest as it is
      one of several clues to the approximate age of this
      horizon.

Perforated (3)

As above, but centrally drilled; diameters, 4.2–6.5 cm. Corduroy phase—Alma Plain (2); phase uncertain—Corduroy Black-on-white (1).

Ovals (3; Fig. 54*g*)

Lengths, 3.3–4.3 cm. Corduroy Phase—Alma Plain (1), Forestdale Smudged (1); phase uncertain—Alma Plain (1).

Square (1; Fig. 54*h*)

Dimensions, 1.9 by 1.9 cm. Phase association uncertain but probably Carrizo; pottery is red ware, derived from Forestdale Red.

Scraping spoons (26; Fig. 54*i, j*)

Maximum widths, 6.5–19.0 cm; greatest wear consistently on edge of convex surface. Corduroy phase—Corduroy Black-on-white (4), Alma Plain (1); Dry Valley phase—Reserve style black-on-white (3); Carrizo phase—black-on-white (8), Holbrook Black-on-white (4), Showlow Black-on-red (1), indeterminate red (1), McDonald Corrugated (1); phase uncertain—red ware (1), smudged (2).

It is worth noting that the types of pottery from which the scraping spoons were made are consistent with the phase contexts in which they occurred. In other words, Corduroy Black-on-white examples were not found in the pueblo, though they might occur there, and late types were not recovered in the pit houses. This is a minor confirmation of the dependability of the sherds from the fill in pit houses, rooms, and storage pits as stemming from different time periods. Of special interest are the four specimens of Holbrook Black-on-white, all from pueblo rooms.

MATERIAL CULTURE OTHER THAN CLAY PRODUCTS

The tools and various artifacts examined in the following section came mostly from random digging and from burials. Both pit houses and pueblo rooms were picked disappointingly clean before the structures were vacated, resulting in a sizeable number of objects for which we have no clear chronological association. Phase assignments are made where warranted; otherwise the placement is left open or, at the most, a guess is made as to the probable temporal position. Numerically, the number of specimens is small but they are helpful, nevertheless, in establishing continuities, trait beginnings and endings, or merely sporadic presences.

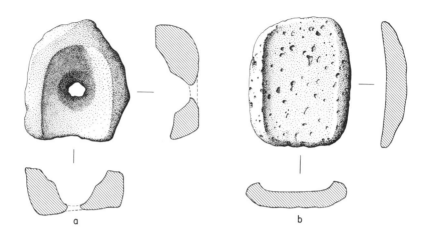

Figure 55. Metates: *a*, Pit House 3, Corduroy phase, converted to a mortar; *b*, Room 13, Carrizo phase. Length of *a* is 35.5 cm.

GROUND STONE ARTIFACTS

Metates (4; fragments not counted)
    Slab (1)

        Unshaped sandstone block with one smooth surface; length, 35 cm. Pit House 3, Corduroy phase.

    Trough, open one end (2; Fig. 55*a*)

        Basalt and lava; unshaped blocks, deeply concave grinding surface, with parallel sides. Example illustrated ultimately used as mortar; length 35.5 cm, width 34.5 cm, thickness 17.5 cm, from Pit House 3, Corduroy phase. Another example, lacking the mortar feature, came from Room 14, Carrizo phase.

    Trough, open both ends (1; Fig. 55*b*)

        Vesicular basalt; some shaping on sides and bottom; trough wide and shallow, nearly flat in both axes. Width, 35.0 cm; thickness, 11.0 cm. Room 13, Carrizo phase.

Manos (51)
    Oval, unifacial (16; Fig. 56*a*)

        Quartzite, sandstone, basalt; little or no edge trimming; grinding face convex, occasionally flat, but extends over ends, indicating manos were operated in trough. Lengths, 15.7-18.8 cm. Pit House 3 (13 specimens), Corduroy phase; Room 3 (3 specimens), Carrizo phase.

    Oval, bifacial (3; Fig. 56*b*)

        Quartzite, edges trimmed; grinding faces convex on

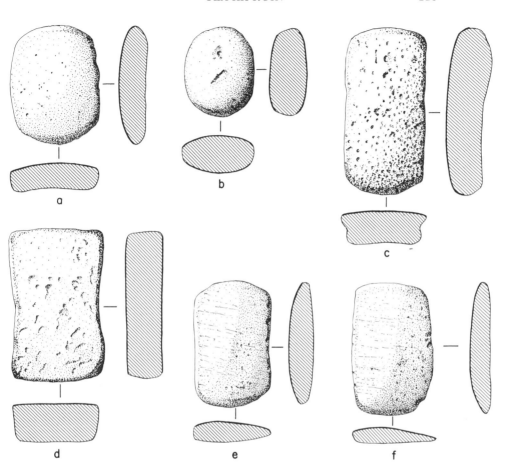

Figure 56. Manos. Length of *e* is 20 cm.

both axes. Length range, 11.9–14.2 cm. Storage Pit 11, Dry Valley phase; pueblo Rooms 2 and 7, Carrizo phase.

Rectangular, unifacial (21; Fig. 56c, *e*, *f*)

Quartzite, basalt, sandstone; former two rock types predominate. All edges trimmed; grinding surface nearly flat crosswise, slightly convex lengthwise, extends over ends; finger grooving noted in about half of sample; several have double-faceted surfaces and sharp trailing edge from long use (Fig. 56*f*). Lengths, 16–22 cm; widths, 8.8–12.5 cm; thicknesses, 2.5–5.4 cm. Pit House 3 (2), Corduroy phase; Storage Pit 11 (1), Dry Valley Phase; pueblo rooms (18), Corduroy phase.

Rectangular, bifacial (11; Fig. 56*d*)

Basalt, sandstone; generally possess some characteristics of preceding type except for double grinding surfaces. Example illustrated in Figure 56*d* has flat, parallel faces, not turned over on edges, indicating use on a flat slab metate. Edge indentations facilitate gripping. A few are worn to thin slabs. Size range is similar to that for unifacial rectangular manos. Three from pit house, Corduroy phase; one from Storage Pit 12, Dry Valley phase; seven from pueblo rooms, Carrizo phase.

Rubbing Stones (6)

Basalt; circular to oval in outline, usually bifacial. Diameters, 7–10 cm; thicknesses, 3–5 cm; designed for single hand operation. Four from Pit House 3, Corduroy Phase; two from pueblo rooms, Carrizo phase.

Polishing Stones (5)

Waterworn pebbles of varying materials, with one or more smooth facets, probably from polishing pottery. Diameters, 3.3–6.7 cm. All examples from pueblo rooms, Carrizo phase.

Hammerstones (29)

Angular (14)

Blocks of chert, quartzite, or basalt; show extensive fractured faces, sharp edges worn down by use; form is roughly spherical. Diameters, 5.5–7.5 cm. Four from Pit House 3, Corduroy phase; one from Storage Pit, Dry Valley phase; eight from pueblo rooms, Carrizo phase; one indeterminate.

Smooth (15)

Small elongate or oval stream pebbles, mostly quartzite; abrasion restricted to ends. Diameters, 4.3–6.7 cm. Five from pit houses, Corduroy phase; three from Storage Pits, Dry Valley phase; seven from pueblo rooms, Carrizo phase.

Small Metatelike Stone (1; Fig. 57*a*)

Block of unshaped sandstone with troughed groove, probably for sharpening axes. Length, 22.0 cm. Room 5, Carrizo phase.

Axe (Fig. 57*b*)

Fine-grained greenish crystalline stone; three-quarter groove, short-bitted and thick with ridge adjoining groove. Length, 13.5 cm. Room 14, Carrizo phase.

Mauls (4; Fig. 57*c–e*)

Basalt and quartzite, range from grooved angular block

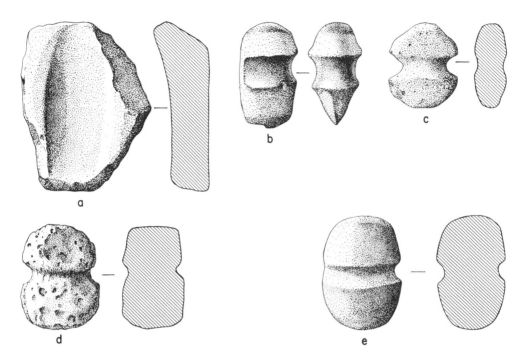

Figure 57. Stone tools: *a*, axe-sharpening stone; *b*, axe; *c–e*, mauls. Length of *a* is 22.0 cm.

to shaped thick-bodied form (Fig. 57*c*, *e*) and thin-bodied type (Fig. 57*d*); fully grooved except specimen *e*, which approaches three-quarter groove type. Lengths, 10.7–13.7 cm. Pit House 3 (1), Corduroy phase; pueblo room (1), Carrizo phase; indeterminate (2).

Vessels (2)

Basalt; circular, shaped externally, deep receptacles; both retain red paint inside. Diameters, 10.0–11.5 cm. Stratigraphic test 1, Level 1, Corduroy phase; Storage Pit 2, Dry Valley phase.

Ornaments

Pendants (3; Fig. 58*a*)

Turquoise; lengths, 1.5–2.0 cm. Roughly rectangular, tapered toward drilled end; all margins convex. All specimens with Burial 11, two at left wrist, one at left ear; Dry Valley phase.

Disc beads (13 lots)

Turquoise (6 lots)

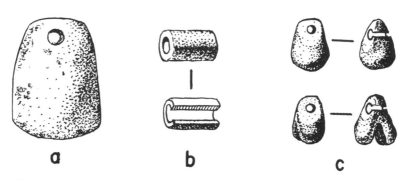

Figure 58. Stone ornaments. Length of *a* is 2.0 cm.

Diameters, 2.0–5.5 mm. String of 47 pale turquoise beads with Burial 13 at right wrist, Corduroy phase; four with Burial 16, Carrizo phase; others were surface or isolated finds.

Red Stone (4 lots)

Color ranges from pink to red; material is a highly metamorphosed rock type with fine quartz grains in close textured matrix. One lot of several hundred, diameter average 2.0 mm, with Burial 16, Carrizo phase; another lot of about 30 beads, diameter average 6.0 mm, with Burial 18, Dry Valley phase; isolated individual examples from Pit House 2, Corduroy phase, and Room 15, Carrizo phase.

Black Stone (3 lots)

One lot steatite (talc), 1.3 m when strung, average bead diameter 4.0 mm, with Burial 3, Corduroy phase. Two lots of black to gray stone, fine grain but apparently not steatite: string 0.5 m long, average bead diameter 2.5 mm, on lower left arm of Burial 17, Dry Valley phase; string 5.4 m long, average bead diameter 2.0 mm, with Burial 16, Carrizo phase.

Cylindrical beads (1 lot; Fig. 58*b*)

Red Stone (16)

Average diameter 5.5 mm, lengths from 3–11 mm; perforations are unusually large, of uniform diameter. With Burial 18, Dry Valley phase.

Tear drop beads (1 lot; Fig. 58*c*)

Wedge-shaped, rounded and polished lumps of steatite, resembling corn kernels, drilled at small end. Lengths, 8.5–12.0 mm. Three elements are birfurcate. Found as wristlet on left arm of Burial 14, Corduroy phase.

Note on Bead Manufacture

The abundance of black steatite (talc) beads in the ruins of the Mogollon Rim region from Heber and easterly has long suggested a local source for this early worked material. Recent surveys through the Wilson and Sloan Creek drainages and in the vicinity of Rock House, southeast of Young, have identified both outcroppings and surface scatters of the stone in question (information from Richard Lange). Ant hills about the Tla Kii Ruin produced many fragments of steatite, mostly the wastage of bead manufacture, as well as finished beads. The prevalence of the material suggests that the surrounding ground must be well saturated with it and that bead-manufacture was a local activity, dependent on a readily available supply of the stone. Tla Kii steatite products were associated with Corduroy phase features but none were seen in the Bear Ruin. Many ruins in the region comparable in age to Tla Kii contain much steatite, but the late large sites have so far produced little of it.

The debitage available from Tla Kii, and especially from ruins near Heber, is instructive in that the technique of bead production can be reconstructed with reasonable certainty. Figure 59 illustrates the main steps in the process (see also Cosgrove and Cosgrove 1932: 62-63). The equipment needed was an abrasive stone slab, a fine stone drill, and lumps of raw steatite. The tip of a remarkably tiny chipped-stone drill (11.5 mm long) was found with debitage on an ant hill near Heber, shown enlarged in Figure 59. Its tip fits the perforation in many beads.

Production steps were:

1. Reducing raw material into thin (2 mm to 3 mm) sheets by abrasion and incising one face to form squares 5 mm to 7 mm across.
2. Breaking out squares along cuts, making blanks. Broken squares and excess edges became wastage.
3. In some cases, blanks were rounded before drilling.
4. More commonly, squared blanks were drilled, and may have been hand-rounded after drilling.
5. Final rounding of beads was probably accomplished by stringing blanks and drawing them through a groove in an abrasive stone.

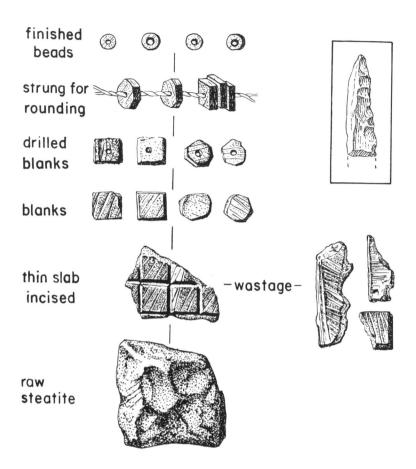

finished
beads

strung for
rounding

drilled
blanks

blanks

thin slab
incised

—wastage—

raw
steatite

Figure 59. Technology of steatite bead manufacture, based on material from Tla Kii and ruins near Heber, Arizona. Insert is enlarged tip of chipped drill, probably chalcedony. Maximum dimension of unworked lump is 3 cm.

Composite Bird Effigy

An ingeniously contrived pendant, made of at least three different materials, came from the refuse of Storage Pit 11 in Dry Valley phase context. The component parts, regrettably, were not removed from the ground with proper care and the proposed restoration, therefore, is based on the best "fits" possible with the fragments at hand. Some parts of this gem were either not in the ground to start with or were not recovered. Two old breaks on the core, or body part, suggest that the object had suffered extensive damage before it was lost or cast away.

Components
1. Body (Fig. 60a, a', a''), carved of dense siliceous hematite; cylindrical, broken end presumably carried head; thin wedge-shaped extensions rise from central core, flared at an angle of about 100^0, deeply grooved at base and joined with lateral groove behind presumed head position; these extensions form the supports for wings. Posteriorly, cylinder is drilled with a tapered pit, 3.5 mm deep and 3 mm in diameter, making mortise for tail. Underside drilled for suspension as shown in a'. Length, 22 mm; diameter of cylinder, 7 mm.
2. Tail (Fig. 60b, b'), same material as body; distal end broken; other end fitted with tapered tenon, off center, so when set into mortise on body, upper surface of tail unit is flush with upper surface of body cylinder. Length, 10 mm.
3. Wing plate (Fig. 60c), fine-grained, pink, ferruginous stone; diamond shaped, 14.0 mm on each side; thickness 1.5 mm; length of side and thickness coincide with length and width of cut at base of wings on body; edges beveled.
4. Turquoise ring (Fig. 60d), fragmentary, one edge lightly ground, other finely chipped; diameter, 6.5 mm; width, 3.3 mm. Perforation has same diameter as broken area at neck and probably was a half-collar around neck of bird.
5. Turquoise mosaic fragments, about 60; majority are rectangular to square, minimum and maximum dimensions 2.0 mm to 8.5 mm respectively (Fig. 60e); average thickness, 1.0 mm. Six fragments are trapezoidal (Fig. 60f) for angle fitting. All edges beveled away from polished face to provide more area for adhesive substance.
6. Red stone plate (Fig. 60g), rectangular, 6.5 mm by 8.5 mm. Position in assembly not known.

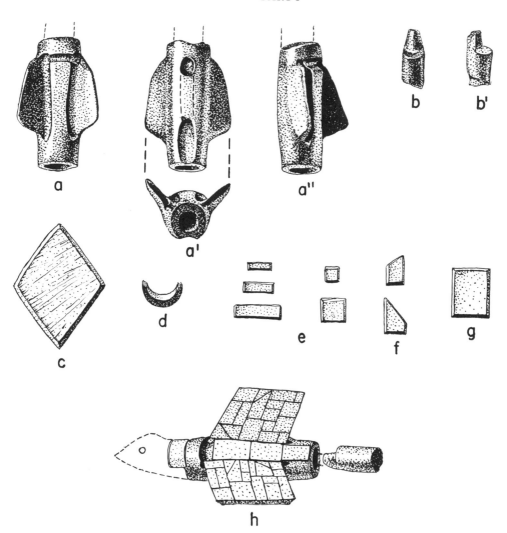

Figure 60. Composite bird effigy of siliceous hematite, red stone, and turquoise. Length of *a* is 22 mm. The restoration (*h*) is conjectural.

As stated before, we do not know exactly how the parts were assembled in this complicated piece of mosaic jewelry, but a likely restoration, not including the treatment of the tail, is shown in Figure 60*h*.

Painted Slab (1; Fig. 61)

Sandstone; rectangular slab shaped by percussion; one

Figure 61. Painted stone slab, red pigment. Length is 40 cm.

face shows red lateral bands of irregular width. Length, 40 cm; width, 32 cm; thickness, 3.4 cm. Room 13, between Floors 1 and 2, Carrizo phase. The provenience of this specimen provides no hints of its use and the simplicity of the decoration is equally mute.

CHIPPED STONE ARTIFACTS

Percussion Core Implements
  Chopper (1; Fig. 62a)
    Bulky block of quartzite made from a stream pebble;

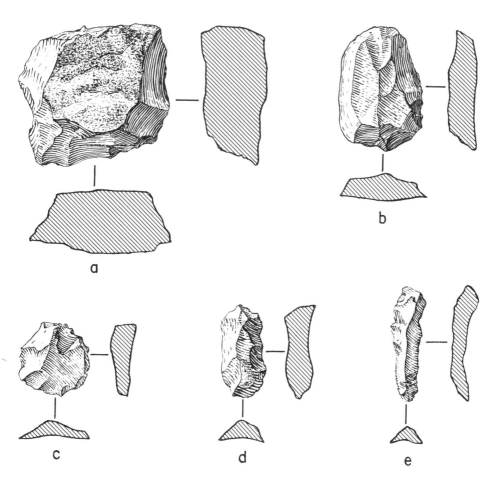

Figure 62. Percussion core (*a*) and flaked tools. Length of *b* is 8.6 cm.

edge partially and steeply trimmed from one face.
Diameter, 9.1 cm; thickness, 5.2 cm. Room 13, Pit 5,
Carrizo phase.

Percussion Flake Implements

Flake scrapers (6; Fig. 62*b*, *c*)

Quartzite or chert flakes with some directed edge trimming, but shape and size uniformity are lacking. Lengths,
3.9–8.6 cm. Pit House 3, Storage Pits 1 and 11, and
general testing; Corduroy and Dry Valley phases.

Flake scrapers, keeled (2; Fig. 62*d*, *e*)

Chert and petrified wood, elongate, end and edge trim-

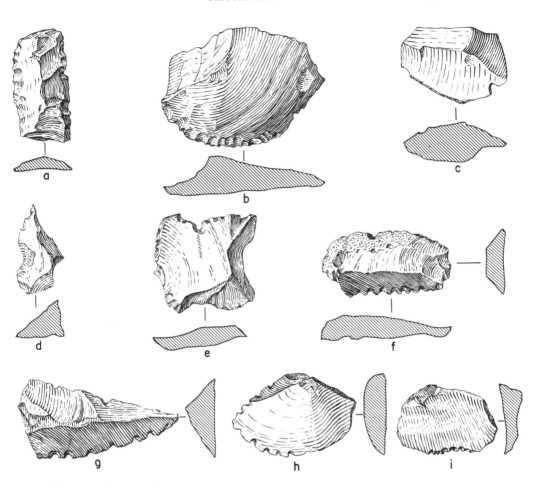

Figure 63. Pressure flaked and ground edge tools. Length of *g* is 9.0 cm.

ming. Lengths, 5.8, 7.9 cm. Room 16, and general testing; probably Carrizo phase.

Pressure Flake Implements (103)

Knives (9; Fig. 63*a*, *b*)

Chert and petrified wood; thin flakes; edge retouch appears to be intentional. Lengths, 3.2-7.4 cm. Unit Structure 2, Storage Pit 1, Room 16, general testing; undoubtedly from Corduroy, Dry Valley, and Carrizo phases.

Scrapers (8)

Side (5)

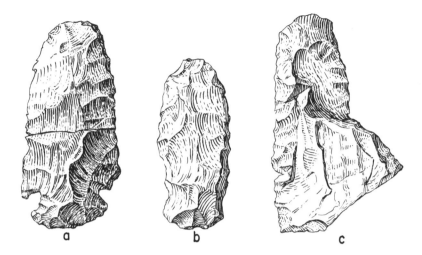

Figure 64. Knives. Length of *c* is 9.1 cm.

Chert and petrified wood; random thick flakes with one edge reworked. Lengths, 3.0–5.2 cm. Room 17, and general testing; expectable in all phases.

Ground edge (3; Fig. 63*c*)

Chert flakes, thick; a convex edge shows rounding by abrasion. Lengths, 2.8–3.7 cm. Unit Structure 1, Storage Pit 1, testing; Dry Valley phase.

Gravers (3; Fig. 63*e*)

Chert and chalcedony; small elongate flakes with finely retouched tip, either sharp-pointed or chisel-edged. Lengths, 2.8–4.2 cm. Room 15, testing; Carrizo phase, probably earlier.

Toothed tools (26; Fig. 63*f–i*)

Mostly chert but some petrified wood; thin, random flakes with regularly spaced, deep serrations. A few flakes show only one indentation, but majority have a series of indentations along one edge (*f, g*) or following the curve of the flake (*h*). Extremely fine serrations (*i*) also occur, but less commonly than coarse notching. Lengths, 1.8–9.0 cm. Proveniences about evenly divided between pit houses, storage pits, and pueblo rooms, hence Corduroy, Dry Valley, and Carrizo phases. It is noteworthy that the coarser serrations are in the Dry Valley or Carrizo contexts; the finer serrations are Corduroy or earlier (Part II: *Chipped Stone Tools, Flake Implements*; Part III: *Chipped Stone, Pressure, Flake Implements*).

Knives, bifacial chipping (4; Fig. 64)

Chert; three are side-notched for hafting (Fig. 64*a, b*); the fourth specimen was chipped from a large flake, producing the effect of a one-piece handle and blade tool. Lengths, 7.0-9.1 cm. Pit House 1, Rooms 14 and 17, Corduroy phase trash; probably all phases.

Projectile points (29; 2 fragments not classified; Fig. 65)

Unnotched (7)

1. Leaf-shaped, straight base (1; Fig. 65*a*)
   Chert. Length, 4.3 cm. Room 7, Carrizo phase.
2. Triangular (6; Fig. 65*b*)
   Original flakes triangular, limited chipping; chert, chalcedony. Lengths, 2.1-3.8 cm. Rooms 3 and 13, Storage Pit 1, testing; principally Carrizo and probably Dry Valley phase.

Notched (20)

1. Rudimentary stem (1; Fig. 65*c*)
   Shallow thinning of side toward base, typologically an earlier form; chert. Surface, phase association uncertain.
2. Lateral, broad and shallow (6; Fig. 65*d*)
   Stem about as wide as shoulder, base convex; chert and obsidian. Lengths, 1.4-4.8 cm. Room 3, general testing, and surface; probably occurs in all phases.
3. Lateral, broad and deep (6; Fig. 65*e, f*)
   Stem expanding, narrower than shoulder, straight base; chert. Lengths, 2.1-3.5+ cm. Pit House 1, Unit Structure 2, testing, and surface; probably Corduroy and Dry Valley phases.
4. Lateral, shallow, low on blade (4; Fig. 65*g*)
   Stem expanding, wider than shoulder, concave base; chert and petrified wood. Pit House 2, Storage Pit 12, surface; probably Corduroy and Dry Valley phases.
5. Lateral, shallow, high on blade (1; Fig. 65*h*)
   Deep basal chipping produced flaring extensions, edges serrated; chert. Length, 2.5 cm. Room 4; Carrizo phase, a typically late form.
6. Lateral and basal (1; Fig. 65*i*)
   Chert. Length, 2.4 cm. Surface; probably Carrizo phase.

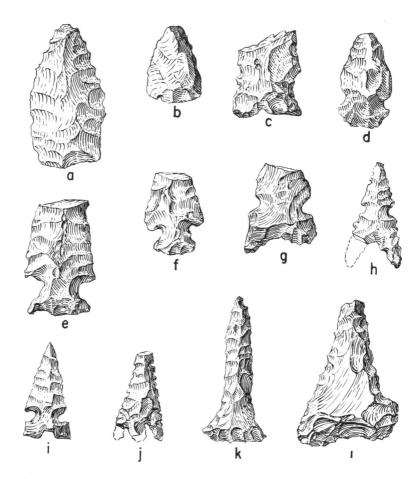

Figure 65. Projectile points and drills. Length of *a* is 4.3 cm.

7. Corner notched (1; Fig. 65*j*)
    Narrow triangular form with basal barbs separated
    by small rounded stem, edges finely serrated; gray
    chert. Pit House 1; Corduroy phase. This style of point
    is typical of the Hohokam of the Santa Cruz phase
    (Gladwin and others 1937, Pl. 91). The form and
    material of the above specimen indicate it was intru-
    sive in Tla Kii Ruin, and by ceramic chronology the
    Santa Cruz and Corduroy phases were broadly
    contemporaneous.

Drills (4; Fig. 65*k*, *l*)
    All are flanged at base; chert. Lengths, 4.1-4.4 cm. Pit
    House 1, Storage Structure 1, Room 18, testing; probably
    all phases.

PAINT MATERIALS

Pigment sources, roughly in the order of abundance, included
hematite (red and specular forms), limonite (yellow), azurite
(blue), malachite (green), and gypsum (white). Of the 16
occurrences of minerals, 11 were in storage pits containing Dry
Valley phase trash, and the remainder were from: Pit House 3,
Corduroy phase (1); pueblo Rooms 13 and 15, Corduroy phase
(3); and random testing (1). No occurrence of paints with
burials was noted.

MISCELLANEOUS STONES

Two iron concretions, derived from the nearby Coconino
sandstone, came from Room 13 and Burial 13. A single quartz
crystal was found on the floor of Room 8.

BONE AND HORN

Faunal bone and bone tools have been notably scarce in the
earliest phases of the Forestdale sequence. The Tla Kii sample
in both categories reflects a substantial increase, perhaps
indicating a greater dependence on animal protein after the
Corduroy phase than before, and a growing willingness to view
bone as a useful tool material.

Awls (29; Fig. 66)
    Broken shaft type (3; Fig. 66*a*, *b*,)
        Split end sharpened, articular end intact; rabbit leg
        bones. Lengths, 5.6-7.6 cm; Corduroy phase (1), Dry
        Valley phase (2).
    Whole bone (3; Fig. 66*c*)
        Shaft reduced to point, articular ends intact; deer meta-
        podial. Lengths, 9.3 cm to about 15.0 cm; Dry Valley
        phase (3).
    Split bone, articular end present (11; Fig. 66*d*, *e*)
        Bone split by sawing, cutting through articular end;
        protruding knobs may be worn down; one of the notched
        variety (Fig. 66*e*); mostly deer metapodial. Lengths, 7.9
        cm. to about 15.0 cm. Corduroy phase (4), Dry Valley
        phase (1), Carrizo phase (6).

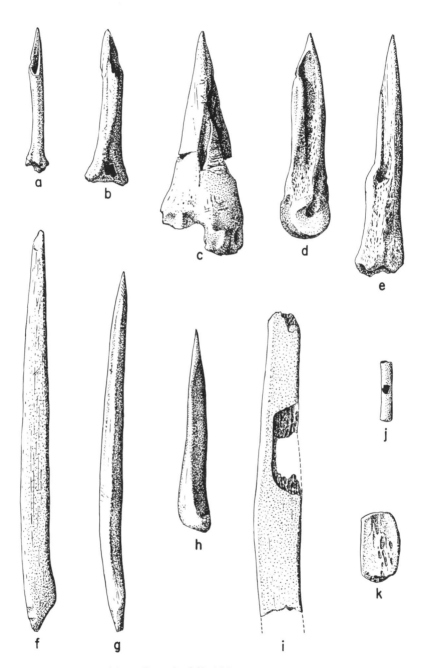

Figure 66. Bone objects. Length of *f* is 16.5 cm.

Split bone, without articular ends (12; Fig. 66*f–h*)

Bone slivers obtained by sawing, all edges and bases well worked down; generally thin and flat in section. Lengths, 8.4–16.6 cm. Corduroy phase (7), Dry Valley phase (2), Carrizo phase (3).

Rib Scrapers (4; Fig. 66*i*)

Deer ribs, naturally sharp edges worn from use; no intentional shaping. Corduroy phase (2), Dry Valley phase (2).

Perforated Tube (1; Fig. 66*j*)

Bird bone, joint ends removed, with central perforation. Length, 2.3 cm. Corduroy phase.

Die (1; Fig. 66*k*)

Oblate fragment of thick shaft bone; plano-convex, plain. Length, 3.0 cm. Corduroy phase.

Antler Flakers (2)

Antler tines, one with chisel-shaped end, other rounded. Carrizo phase.

SHELL

Marine shells from Forestdale Valley sites have been notably scarce. The Bluff Ruin produced none; the Bear Ruin contained a few whole *Olivella* and disc beads, *Glycymeris* bracelets, and an unworked shell of *Haliotis*. We have no record of shells in Corduroy phase contexts. The Tla Kii Ruin collection is listed in Table 7.

Although most of these shells came from Dry Valley phase trash, it would appear that no significant distinction between that phase and the Carrizo phase can be drawn. There was no apparent increase in number of species at these times over those present in the Forestdale phase. Later, however, in the Pinedale and Canyon Creek phases, *Conus*, *Turritella*, *Pecten*, and *Nassarius* have been noted, and the variety of jewelry was enlarged.

The child-size bracelet (Fig. 67*a*) has some interest because typologically it is the bulky kind with widened umbo, matching the Sedentary Period and later form in the Hohokam shell industry (Haury 1976: 313). The Tla Kii Ruin was roughly equivalent in age to the end of the Sedentary in the Hohokam sequence.

Although jewelry of stone, in the shape of pendants and beads mostly, was found with 7 of 19 burials, it seems strange that more shell was not present. I do not think the absence of shell is attributable to the acid soil of the region, because the specimens present do not show much attrition. The conclusion

Table 7
SHELL FROM TLA KII RUIN

Species	Artifact	Provenience	Quantity
Olivella sp.	Whole shell, unmodified	Surface	1
Glycymeris maculata	Bracelet, diameter 5.5 cm (Fig. 67a)	Room 14 fill	1
Glycymeris sp.	Bracelet, fragments	Room 14 fill, Storage Pits 1 and 2	3
Glycymeris sp.	Finger ring, diameter 1.9 cm (Fig. 67b)	Storage Pit 11	1
Haliotis sp.	Fragments of indeterminate ornament	Storage Pit 12	2
Laevicardium? elatum	Probable pendant fragment, open work (Fig. 67c)	Storage Pit 12	2
?	Disc bead, with turquoise and steatite beads	Burial 17	1

may be drawn that the Forestdale Valley was not in the main path of shell distributors, that the valley was something of a cul-de-sac, particularly with reference to the people south and west of it. This is further substantiated by the absence of widely diffused pottery types such as red-on-browns and black-on-whites from the Mimbres area, and the red-on-buffs from the Gila and Salt River valleys.

THE SIGNIFICANCE OF TLA KII RUIN

The annals of Southwestern excavations give us numerous examples of multiroomed stone or adobe houses resting on top of pit houses. The simple stratigraphic truth is that for many centuries the family was sheltered in structures of various shapes, the floor depressed below the surrounding ground surface, but always separated from other similar structures in the village. The pit house was common to all parts of the Southwest. In time, the architectural mode changed to the pueblo, wherein many families lived in close proximity in adjacent rooms. The actual origin of the pueblo, whether indigenous to the Southwest or an idea imported from Mexico, continues to be a problem of considerable interest. The Forestdale Valley record does not help us much in that respect, but the transition from one house form to the other is reasonably pinpointed as to time and character.

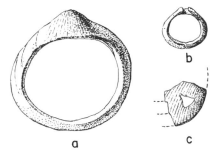

a   c

Figure 67. Shell jewelry, probably representative of both Dry Valley and Carrizo phases: *a*, *b*, *Glycymeris* bracelet and ring; *c*, fragment of possible pendant with cut-out design. Diameter of *a* is 5.5 cm.

Stripped of its overburden, Tla Kii Ruin, while not a stellar example of excellence of the pueblo architectural idiom, nevertheless occupies a significant place in Forestdale building history. While wholly typical for a pueblo in its episodic growth, a possible measure of the agglutinative social process of the time, it manifested a sharp departure from the centuries-long pattern of scattered family living in the valley. A community of that size was not unique in the valley up to that time, for both the Bluff and Bear villages must have been that large or even larger. The difference was in the amount of area needed to shelter that number of people. The openness of early villages was replaced by the compaction of houses into a small area, a ratio of at least 10 to 1. A change of that dimension suggests a shift in attitude and may well reflect a psychological factor as well. The willingness to endure tight cluster living impresses me as the result of a deeply based cultural inheritance. In short, close living—the pueblo mode—along with black-painted white pottery, stand out as the readily recognizable elements in the "Anasazization" of a Mogollon-rooted people. The residence clustering that began in Tla Kii Ruin thus was a forecast of what is seen later in Tundastusa and the many other large pueblos.

The Tla Kii Ruin findings, along with those from the Bear Ruin and Bluff Site that are reproduced in Parts II and III, provide us now with a cultural continuum from roughly A.D. 200 to the historic present. In part IV, bringing together the material from all three sites, the entire cultural history of the Forestdale Valley and its development through time is discussed.

PART II

Excavations in the Forestdale Valley, East-central Arizona

Emil W. Haury

With an Appendix
The Skeletal Remains of the Bear Ruin
Norman E. Gabel

Originally published as
University of Arizona Bulletin
Vol. XI, No. 4   October 1, 1940
Social Science Bulletin No. 12

Plate I.—a, The Forestdale Valley, looking west (infrared by E. T. Nichols, III). b, The Bear Ruin as seen from the hills on the southern edge of the valley.

PREFACE

This report[1] is the outgrowth of two seasons of archaeological work in the Forestdale Valley near the northern boundary of the Fort Apache Indian Reservation in east-central Arizona. It is the first installment of an intended series which will give the history of this little valley from the beginning of the human occupation in the seventh century A.D. to the present Apache inhabitants. During the two seasons of digging, June 15 to August 15 in 1939 and 1940, emphasis was placed on the Bear Ruin (Arizona P:16:1),[2] the oldest site in the valley, and secondarily, work was started in 1940 on a small pueblo (Arizona P:16:2) of early Pueblo III date and its environs which yielded refuse, burials, and houses of a somewhat earlier horizon. Owing to the incompleteness of the excavations in the latter, a discussion of the same will be postponed until more work will have been done. The bulk of this report, then, is concerned with the Bear Ruin, representing a single phase of occupation dating from the seventh century A.D.

These excavations were carried out under the auspices of the Arizona State Museum and the Department of Anthropology of the University of Arizona. The co-operation of institutions and individuals has largely been instrumental in making the study a success. It is a genuine pleasure to acknowledge the support given by the American Philosophical Society of Philadelphia through two grants from the Penrose Fund. Without this assistance field work could not have been begun. Generous financial assistance was also given by Mr. Burridge D. Butler, Mrs. E. B. Danson, and Mr. and Mrs. Wm. H. Kelly.

Special gratitude is due the Apache Indian Tribal Council for its unanimous assent to the proposal to conduct archaeological work on their land, and to Mr. William Donner, Superintendent of the Fort Apache Agency, who assisted in many ways to speed up the work. Through his kindly interest and approval, an allotment of CCC-ID funds made available the services of thirteen Apache Indian laborers for a month in the summer of 1940, thus enabling the party to dig far more extensively than would have been possible otherwise.

On March 29, 1939, Superintendent Donner and Dr. Byron Cummings met the writer on the site to discuss the proposed excavation from the standpoints of the Indian Service and

---

[1]For a preliminary report see E. W. Haury, 1940 b.
[2]Arizona State Museum Survey.

the archaeological work already in progress on the reservation at Kinishba. Both agreed to the timeliness and potential significance of the plan.

The help of the following persons is gratefully acknowledged: Dr. Ernst Antevs, who spent several days in studying and clarifying the terrace problem in the valley; Dr. F. W. Galbraith and Mr. R. E. S. Heineman of the University of Arizona for their identifications of geological specimens; Dr. W. H. Burt, Museum of Zoology, University of Michigan, for the identification of faunal material; Gordon C. Baldwin and Frederick H. Scantling for undertaking the study of tree-ring specimens; and Brigham Arnold who is responsible for all text figure work. During both seasons a number of students participated in the field work. Most of the digging and all the attendant tasks of mapping, washing, cataloguing, mending, and analyzing pottery were done by them on the spot. Assisting in this were Mrs. Gordon Lee, Florence Connolly, Albert Schroeder, and Arnold Withers, all graduates of the University of Arizona. It is certain that the interpretation of the materials recovered has benefited greatly from the helpful and often critical suggestions of the entire student group.

Finally, much was added to the pleasure of the camp in Forestdale Valley by the helpfulness of Mr. and Mrs. Thomas Jennings who operate the Forestdale Trading Post.

EXCAVATIONS IN THE FORESTDALE VALLEY, EAST-CENTRAL ARIZONA

INTRODUCTION

As a part of its widespread survey of the Southwest, Gila Pueblo became interested in 1931 in the archaeological aspects of the mountainous section of Arizona and New Mexico trending from the northwest to the southeast. This region comprises the southern part of the Colorado Plateau, the area to the south or below the Mogollon Rim and southeast through the White, Blue, and the Mogollon mountains of New Mexico and ultimately the Mimbres Valley north of Deming. Mr. Russell Hastings and the writer were assigned the task that year of conducting a reconnaissance which began at Showlow and was extended by stages in a southeasterly direction to the Mimbres Valley. During that survey these men first saw the Bear Ruin, the Mogollon Village (Mogollon 1:15),[3] and the Harris Ruin (New Mexico Q:1:14).[3] The latter two were subsequently excavated by Gila Pueblo,[4] and, although the original plans also included the Forestdale Valley site, circumstances arose which prevented this.

When it became evident that Gila Pueblo would not dig the site it was suggested in 1936 by Mr. Harold S. Gladwin, Director, to Mr. Earl H. Morris of the Carnegie Institution that he take over the study. This he proposed to do, pending the completion of work already in progress. In 1938 Morris was attracted to Basketmaker II cave sites near Durango, Colorado. The results of his first summer there proved to be of such interest and significance that plans were laid by him to continue the investigations in that area. At this point the writer, feeling that the study of the Bear Ruin was necessary to the understanding of what actually happened in the fringe of country mutually shared by the Basketmaker and the Mogollon peoples, was bold enough to suggest to Mr. Morris that this work be done under the auspices of the University of Arizona. To this Morris gave his cheerful assent.

The study of the survey material gathered in 1931 showed the Bear Ruin to be unlike anything seen up to that time and possibly representative of a culture which had not yet been segregated. This situation provided a real impetus to a study of the Forestdale area. Then, as the Mogollon and

---

[3]Gila Pueblo Survey.
[4]E. W. Haury, 1936, *a* and *b*.

Harris villages in New Mexico were dug, the relationship between these and the Forestdale Valley site became apparent; they were all a part of the same complex—the Mogollon Culture. The writer was further encouraged to continue studies on the Mogollon problem by the insistence of many of those who attended the 1938 Chaco Canyon Conference of the University of New Mexico. It was felt that knowledge of the Mogollon Culture had reached an impasse and that only further work could clear it up. The importance of excavating a site well toward the northern limits of the culture's distribution seemed to be twofold. First, being in juxtaposition to Basketmaker, it was supposed that the likes and unlikes and the degree of amalgamation between the two could be picked up easily; second, that if no amalgamation was indicated, the contrast between the Basketmaker and Mogollon would be all the greater in view of the frontier location. How right or how wrong these assumptions were can only be determined after the reader has gone through the pages of this report.

PREVIOUS WORK

The Forestdale Valley is in the approximate center of an area which has received intense archaeological attention. The largest ruin of the valley, known as Tundastusa, was first examined by Bandelier in 1883[5] and partially excavated by Hough in 1901, who in that year directed the Museum-Gates Expedition.[6] Hough's party visited fifty-five ruins during that field season within a radius of 100 miles of Holbrook and conducted excavations in eighteen. A few years later, in 1907, Hough returned to the Southwest to survey widely in the upper Gila River system of New Mexico, the Blue, White, and Gila rivers proper in Arizona.[7] It was primarily through these endeavors that ruins, now occupying prominent positions in southwestern archaeology, were first called to notice. Hough's description of the Forestdale area fails to mention the Bear Ruin (Arizona P: 16:1), an oversight which is not difficult to understand owing to the unobtrusiveness of the site, although he visited[8] the small pueblo (Arizona P: 16:2) which adjoins the former on the southern margin. In 1896 and 1897, Fewkes spent some time on the Colorado Plateau digging in a series of sites which included

---

[5] A. Bandelier, 1892, pt. 2, p. 400.
[6] W. Hough, 1903, pp. 289-97.
[7] W. Hough, 1907.
[8] *Ibid.*, p. 291.

the well-known Four-mile Ruin west of Taylor.[9] Considerably later followed Spier's admirable reconnaissance in the
Zuñi,[10] Little Colorado,[11] and the White Mountain[12] areas
which was the basis for the beginning of a historical reconstruction of the occupation of the area.

From this time on studies followed in rapid succession in
the southern margin of the plateau and below the Mogollon
Rim. These include the Third National Geographic Society
Beam Expedition,[13] further work by Hough,[14] and Roberts'
digging at Kiatuthlanna for the Smithsonian Institution.[15]
In the following year Roberts continued work in the region
with excavations near Zuñi in the Village of the Great
Kivas,[16] and Gila Pueblo began a 2-year survey program
including the Heber, Showlow, Whiteriver, and Reserve
regions, during which time a number of Mogollon sites, including the Bear Ruin, were visited. In 1931 Roberts under-
took a 3-year study of ruins in the Whitewater district along
the Puerco River,[17] and Cummings started the excavations of
Kinishba for the University of Arizona which have continued
to the present time.[18] Mera's survey for the Laboratory of
Anthropology of the Petrified Forest came in 1934,[19] and the
White Mound Village on the Puerco River was excavated in
1936 by Gila Pueblo.[20] Less is known of the area to the west
and southwest, this being a broken and rugged territory.
Some suggestion of the richness, however, of the archae-
ological resources is seen in Gila Pueblo's excavations of the
Canyon Creek Ruin in 1932 and the reconnaissance of the
Sierra Ancha region a few years earlier.[21]

Much of the foregoing work has been devoted to ruins
dating from Pueblo III and IV times, less to earlier horizons.
There is a recognizable tendency on the part of archaeologists
to work back in search of beginnings and to establish frame-
works on which the later and more spectacular developments
may be solidly placed. This paper is similarly directed and

---

[9]J. W. Fewkes, 1904.
[10]L. Spier, 1917.
[11]*Ibid.*, 1918.
[12]*Ibid.*, 1919.
[13]A. E. Douglass, 1929; E. W. Haury, and L. L. Hargrave, 1931.
[14]W. Hough, 1930.
[15]F. H. H. Roberts, Jr., 1931.
[16]*Ibid.*, 1932.
[17]*Ibid.*, 1939, 1940.
[18]B. Cummings, 1940.
[19]H. P. Mera, 1934.
[20]H. S. Gladwin, in preparation.
[21]E. W. Haury, 1934.

it follows that without the investigations already completed the results from the work in the Bear Ruin would be far less meaningful.

THE BEAR RUIN[22]

ENVIRONMENT

LOCATION

The Bear Ruin is situated on the Fort Apache Indian Reservation, Township 9 North, Range 21 East, Section 36, northwest quarter, approximately 8 miles in air line south of Showlow, Arizona. The principal part of the village occupies the highest of five terraces on the south bank of the Forestdale Creek about 4 miles above its confluence with Corduroy Creek, a tributary of Carrizo Creek (Fig. 1).

The village is at an elevation of 6,560 feet above sea level and is in the heart of the vast western yellow pine belt which runs diagonally across Arizona from the northwest to the southeast. The Mogollon Rim which separates the Colorado Plateau from the southern rugged mountainous country lies only 4 miles to the north.

The Forestdale Valley (Pl. I *a*) at the village site is roughly 300 meters in width, the creek having cut a channel along the northwest margin, exposing the valley fill of alternate bands of sand and sandy clays to a depth of 5 to 7 meters. To the east several hundred meters a small valley emerges from the neighboring hills forming a detrital fan, the lower margin of which determines the limits of the village in that direction. The main valley has been scoured out of cross-bedded Coconino sandstone of Permian age, a formation which is visible in the hills bordering the valley. The more recent volcanic activity, which was responsible for the formation of the White Mountains and the partial filling with lava of some of the valleys in the northern part of the Fort Apache Indian Reservation, had no effect on Forestdale Creek except in the lower part. The surroundings, although sandy, thus provided a much more habitable place than those valleys in which the lava occurs. The desirability of the Forestdale Valley, made so by an abundance of wood, water, and good farming land, is well shown by the numerous small ruins occurring along its axis and by the large, late ruin, Tundastusa, described by Hough.[23]

---

[22]A bear cub, frequent visitor in camp and later captured to become the camp mascot, gave the site its name.

[23]W. Hough, 1903, pp. 289-97.

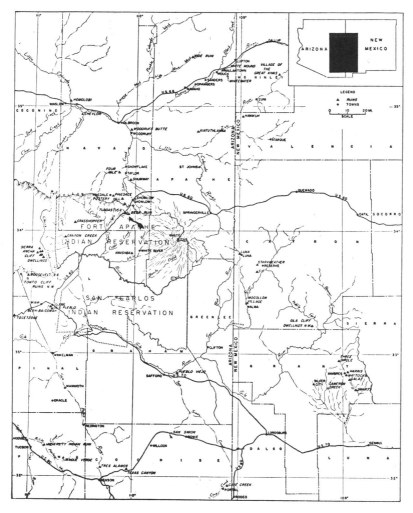

Figure 1.—Map of east-central Arizona and west-central New Mexico showing location of the Bear Ruin in relation to other sites in the area which are either well known or have been excavated. See Selected Bibliography.

TERRACES

Forestdale Creek, now running in a channel from 5 to 7 meters in depth, has frequently changed its course in the past and has been the instrument in the formation of the valley's terrace system. Dr. Ernst Antevs has recognized five, some of which can be approximately dated on the basis of archaeology. These are shown in Figure 2 as they occur near the Bear Ruin and the story of the terraces is briefly told by the following outline:

Terrace 1 (oldest)
  Age: Formed before 600 A.D.
  Justification: The Bear Ruin, with tree-ring dates of about 675, is on this terrace (Pl. I b). Antevs suggests this terrace may date from the Pluvial Period.

Terrace 2
  Age: Formed after 600 and before 1100 A.D.
  Justification: The Great Kiva of Arizona P:16:2, dating about 1100, was built into this terrace; no evidence of Bear Ruin level of occupation on second terrace.

Terrace 3
  Age: Formed after 1100 and before 1910.
  Justification: The Great Kiva of Arizona P:16:2 was partially washed away together with some of the second terrace after 1100 during an erosion cycle possibly datable to the drought of 1276-99 (Antevs). The channel thus formed (Fig. 2) was refilled by material of the third terrace; the stream subsequently flowed in a shallow channel which became willow-lined and apparently remained quite stable until about 1910.[24]

Terrace 4
  Age: After 1910; formed by lowering of channel by erosion and not by silting of old channel and recutting.
  Justification: This terrace supports young growth of pine and juniper.

Terrace 5
  Age: Very recent; formation similar to Terrace 4.
  Justification: Tree growth not established.

CLIMATE

There are no climatic records for the immediate Forestdale area, but both precipitation and temperature records exist for the neighboring places of Fort Apache, Cibicue, Lakeside, Pinedale, and Heber, stations which range in elevation from 5,300 to 6,500 feet above sea level. Since the elevation of the Bear Ruin is 6,560 feet, the climatic conditions may be approximated with the above named stations as a basis.

---

[24]Local informants state that up to about this time Forestdale Creek was perennial, that it could be crossed anywhere without difficulty, and that the banks were lined with willow. Short sections of this channel are still visible, the banks littered with dead and nearly dead willow.

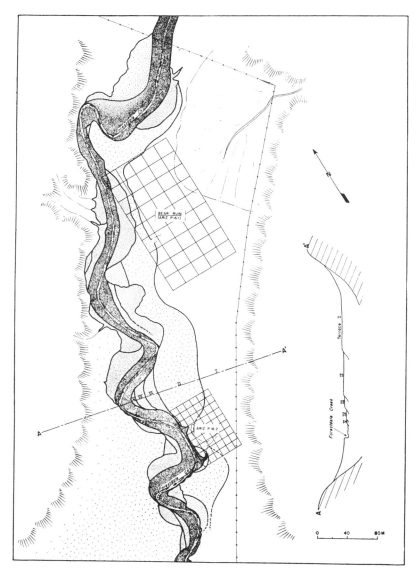

Figure 2.—Map of a small segment of the Forestdale Valley locating
the Bear Ruin and the adjoining pueblo (Arizona P: 16:2) in relation
to the terraces and the present stream.

The maximum and minimum temperatures at Lakeside, 5 miles from the Bear Ruin in air line, are 105 degrees (in July) and —23 degrees (in February). At Pinedale, which has the same elevation as Lakeside, the mean daily temperature range for January is 27.3 degrees and for June is 38.4 degrees.[25] Killing frosts at Pinedale are not expected much after May 29, and the first average frost in fall comes about October 10, making a growing season of 134 days.[26] The conditions at the Bear Ruin probably depart from these figures for Pinedale on the side of slightly milder temperatures, somewhat later killing frosts, and a slightly longer growing season, amounting to about 140 days. At the present time Apaches plant corn late in May and harvest the fully ripened crops in September.

The Bear Ruin lies just within the southern border of that portion of Arizona which receives on the average 20 or more inches of annual rainfall. The mean annual rainfall for Fort Apache is 18.27 inches[27] and 20.68 inches[28] for Pinedale. Local informants state that the snowfall may amount to 3 feet, but this is not an annual occurrence, nor does the snow lie on the ground very long as a rule. As elsewhere within the region of heavy rainfall the precipitation comes principally in the two seasons, midwinter and midsummer.

WATER SUPPLY

The residents of the Bear Ruin village either drew their water from Forestdale Creek which ran along the brink of the site or from numerous springs which come to life at the base of the sandstone outcrops. At the present time this stream is dry during much of the year, but there is abundant evidence that it was a flowing stream not many years ago. Local inhabitants say that 30 years ago the stream was permanent. The drying up of the stream is obviously connected with the general erosion which has taken place in the Southwest. Even so, one does not need to dig deep for a usable supply of water along the stream's course. In connection with establishing camp a well was dug just out of the stream channel, and water was encountered at a depth of 1 meter. Along the south margin of the valley, numerous grassy spots testify to the presence of springs. One of these developed a usable water supply after digging down less than a meter. Black-on-white and other sherds in and about this spring indicate its former use also.

[25]H. V. Smith, 1930, p. 377.
[26]*Ibid.*, p. 381.
[27]*Ibid.*, p. 390.
[28]*Ibid.*, p. 391.

FLORA AND FAUNA

By altitude and plant life, the Forestdale Valley lies in the Transitional Life Zone. The hill slopes carry a heavy growth of western yellow pine with some juniper and manzanita, while the valley floor is dotted with juniper, clumps of oak, and native walnut. Of these, both manzanita and walnut would offer seasonable native foods.[29]

Animal life, particularly the larger game, has been reduced to small numbers by both Apache and white hunters. Some deer were seen, as were black bear, coyote, porcupine, rabbits, and turkey. Elk were exterminated in early pioneering days and have since been re-established by the State Game Commission.

Animal bones in the debris scattered over the ruin indicate those which were living in the area during the seventh century and were used as a source of food: [30]

Mule deer (*Odocoileus hemionus*)
Bison (*Bison bison*)
Bear (*Ursus* sp.)
Gray fox (*Urocyon cinereoargenteus*)
Racoon (*Procyon* sp.)
Jack rabbit (*Lepus* sp.)
Cottontail rabbit (*Sylvilagus* sp.)
Prairie dog (*Cynomys* sp.)
Wood rat (*Neotoma* sp.)
Pocket gopher (*Thomomys* sp.)
Mud turtle (*Kinosternon* sp.)
Turkey (*Meleagris gallopavo*)
Horned owl (*Bubo virginianus*)
Hawk (sp. ?)

This list represents a relatively small number of animals sought by a people who apparently depended as heavily on hunting as they did on agriculture. But what they lacked in variety, they made up by capturing many larger animals, particularly deer. These were clearly the prizes, as elements of the mule deer outnumbered those of all other animals by a ratio of three to one. Of the smaller mammals, rabbits were most frequently represented in the bone collection. A noteworthy occurrence was bison, identified by a lower jaw. It does not seem probable that this part of the animal would have been brought in to the village from far away and the

---

[29]Evidence for the use of these foods during the fourteenth century was found in the Showlow Ruin. E. W. Haury and L. L. Hargrave, 1931, p. 20.

[30]Identifications by Dr. W. H. Burt, Museum of Zoology, University of Michigan.

evidence thus suggests that the bison ranged within striking distance of the Forestdale hunters.

The dog was not certainly identified as present, and a single element of a turkey would indicate that, although native to the area, this bird was not regarded as important, and certainly not domesticated at this time.

LAND

With a mean annual precipitation of approximately 20 inches in the Forestdale area, dry farming is quite possible today, and, while the arable land in the valley is not limitless, the natural conditions during the seventh century were probably such as to allow the residents of the Bear Ruin to carry on agriculture to an extent harmonious with their economic pattern. Their dependence upon this pursuit may be seen in part by the relatively numerous metates and manos. Nearly every house was equipped with one or more of these mills. Direct evidence for agricultural products was slim and limited to a single short segment of an eight-row corn cob, preserved by charring. Corn was doubtless the main crop.

Dry land farming is employed by white residents in the Lakeside-Showlow-Pinedale area and to some extent by the Apache on Forestdale Creek within a mile or two of the ruin.[31] Old Apache residents claim the tribe has had this land under cultivation for a century or more, harking back to the days of internecine warfare when it was necessary to work the fields by night and remain concealed during the day. In the late 1870's several Mormon families from Shumway and vicinity took advantage of the agricultural resources of Forestdale, establishing there a small community. The crops then grown were corn, beans, squash, and potatoes.[32]

APPEARANCE OF THE SITE

The Bear Ruin presented no striking surface features which would indicate it to be the location of a former village. There were no rock mounds or areas of heavy rubbish such

[31]Currently the Apache are cultivating from 30 to 50 acres of corn, broken down into small patches of several acres each. This represents a small percentage of the available land, and there is evidence that much more land has been under the plow in former years.

[32]Mrs. Sarah M. Mills of Showlow informed the writer that her family went to Forestdale from Shumway in 1880 to get corn from a white family already established there, and that in the same year all Mormon families were removed from the valley.

as mark the later sites of the region. A close inspection of the surface revealed only a thin scattering of broken pottery, chipped stone, and occasional metate and mano fragments. There were no depressions indicative of pit houses. A fine sand, shifting readily in a light breeze, alternately covers or exposes what little evidence of occupation there is.

The nature of the site demanded a systematic and economical form of testing to find what lay below the surface. The area which indicated the most intense occupation was marked off on a system of co-ordinates crossing at 20-meter intervals. The north-south lines were given alphabetical designations, the east-west lines were assigned numerals, each beginning in the northwest corner of the grid system (Fig. 3). The resulting squares were designated as blocks, the identifying number being the northwest stake of each. Excavations were begun by sinking test pits 0.75 by 1.5 meters at each block stake. This soon showed that the trash accumulation was thin, lying on top of a very dense and undisturbed clay bed (Fig. 4). Deep features as houses, if they existed, would have to be located by closely spaced test pits or trenches. In many instances the top rubbish-filled layer of sandy soil graded so imperceptibly into the clay that the only clue showing sterile native subsoil had been reached was the absence of charcoal and pottery. In this respect the Bear Ruin was considerably different from other sites of the Mogollon Culture, where the occupational debris and the native material were sharply separated.

It was learned early in the excavation that much could be gained by profile digging. This demanded going through some features, such as large hearths, well into the native soil and examining the profile of the trench to determine the exact limits of pits. Occupation apparently began on the upper of the five terraces recognized in this part of the valley when the surface approximately coincided with the upper level of the clay layer. Most of the sandy silt lying above this old surface has accumulated during and since the village's existence.

As will be recognized from the descriptions of cultural material from this site, the excavations did not result in the recovery of a large number of specimens. This is doubtless due in part to the poverty stricken nature of the village's residents and partly to the fact that the site was not occupied for a particularly long period of time. On the whole it represents a good example of a single phase site where the time was not long enough to allow for detectable advances in any of the cultural traits. This is fortunate since it does away

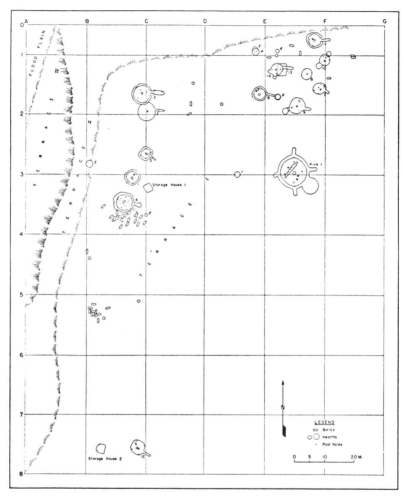

Figure 3.—Plan of the Bear Ruin showing grid system and chief
excavated features.

with the troublesome problem of late artifacts drifting downward into earlier horizons or items of early phases becoming
mixed with late materials, which so often happens in sites of
long occupation.

It should be mentioned in this connection that at the very
edge of the terrace at the western margin of the village there
was a rectangular slab-lined hearth with a few late sherds,

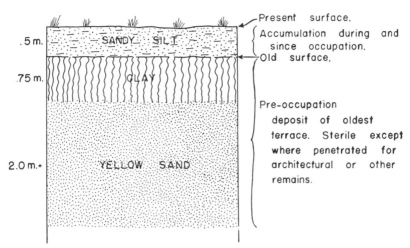

Figure 4.—Profile of the subsurface conditions at the Bear Ruin.

notably St. Johns Polychrome and corrugated pottery of the same age. The area covered by these was so small as to be negligible. The later occupation of this immediate part of the Forestdale Valley is seen in a small stone pueblo (Arizona P:16:2) which lies approximately 300 meters south or down valley and was partially dug in 1940. This was far enough away so that drift material from this horizon seems to have reached the area excavated in a very limited form only. There is every assurance therefore that the items that have been described herein belonged to the Forestdale Phase.

TRASH

In common with such sites as the Mogollon and Harris villages, rubbish occurred in sheet form. Over the whole occupied area the debris was generally thin, averaging 25 centimeters and rarely going below 50 centimeters, and so lacking in pottery that stratigraphic testing was futile. In addition to this the single period represented by the occupation was a further discouragement in attempting extensive controlled tests. Attempts at obtaining horizontal changes within the site were also unproductive.

HOUSE REMAINS

The absence of surface features revealing the locations of houses in the Bear Ruin was chiefly responsible for the fact that during the two seasons only seventeen pit structures of all types were uncovered. While this number is small and represents possibly 50 per cent or less of the original buildings in the village, a provocative architectural situation is seen in the presence of what appears to be two well-established forms of domestic buildings—rectangular and round pit houses. The significance of this will be examined after the descriptive details have been given.

The placement of the houses in the occupied area seems to have been controlled to a certain extent by the nature of the terrain, as the buildings were located more or less parallel to the edge of the terrace (Fig. 3), placing all of them within easy reach of the water supply. Each house was detached from its neighbors in a manner characteristic of pit house villages, evidencing no tendency toward the cellular arrangement of rooms characterizing later pueblos. All buildings, regardless of function, were semisubterranean, ranging in depth from 0.25 to 2.0 meters, the average being somewhat over a meter. None showed any use of stone in a structural capacity. The two instances of house overlapping or stratification due to a difference in ages (Houses 2 and 3, 13 and 14) should be pointed out as being potentially useful in determining sequence, but the associated material culture fails to reveal significant differences, and it would seem rather that the interval of time between the superpositions was too short to reflect changes in the culture. It is assumed then that all buildings belong to approximately the same time level, or the Forestdale Phase.

The classification and frequency of structures, based on function and form, is given below:

Domestic 14
    Rectangular (Nos. 1, 5, and 13) 3
    Round (Nos. 2, 3, 4, 6, 7, 8, 9, 10, 11, 12, and 14) 11
Storage 2
    Rectangular (Nos. 1 and 2) 2
Religious 1
    Round (No. 1) 1

DOMESTIC STRUCTURES

Rectangular
  House 1 (Fig. 5, Pl. II *a*).
    Shape.—Built on rectangular plan but corners rounded and sides slightly bowed out; dimensions, 4.0 by 4.5 m.
    Walls.—Plaster on native clay of bench; plaster 3.5 cm. thick, hand smoothed, turns over on flat part of bench.

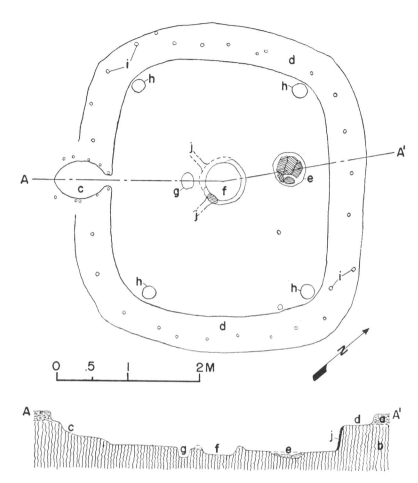

Figure 5.—Plan and sections of House 1: *a*, silt; *b*, undisturbed clay; *c*, ventilator duct; *d*, bench; *e*, floor pit filled with stones and clean sand; *f*, hearth with clay coping; *g*, ladder hole (?); *h*, main postholes; *i*, secondary postholes; *j*, remnants of floor ridges.

Floor.—Native clay, rough.

Hearth.—Basin with clay lining and coping, centrally located; clay ridge (poorly preserved) joining hearth coping continues toward room corners on vent side.

Deflector.—None set in floor but a large oval stone leaning against bench (see Pl. II *a*, lower right) apparently so used.

Ventilator.—To southwest, short, expanding back of

opening in house; duct opening in bench arched with
neatly made plaster framing, stick reinforced, 0.25
by 0.40 m.

Entrance.—Apparently through roof.

Pits.—One on ventilator side of hearth, possibly ash pit;
second north of hearth, filled with rocks and clean
sand, floored over with clay.

Postholes.—Four main holes, one in each corner; secondary and smaller holes on bench and surrounding
ventilator.

Roof.—Central portion flat, apparently with combined
entrance-smoke hole; sides closed by poles leaning
to meet roof from bench. Logs up to 0.12 m. in
diameter used, as seen in charred roof remnants
(Fig. 20 a).

Dates.—Two datable logs, sections of main roof beams,
gave the following dates: A.D. 636+x and 667+x.
Since on both specimens the true outside was missing, an indefinite number of years must be added to
obtain the construction date. This number is probably not large, as the specimen dating 667 has lost
relatively few rings through checking of the charcoal. A date of 675 is probably close to correct.

Comments.—House 1 is interesting because of the great
number of specimens (fifty-eight) found in it. It
clearly shows that the bench was a favored place for
tucking things away, enough of it projecting into the
room to make this possible. It should also be
pointed out that of all houses, this one resembles
most closely those of the Anasazi of the same time
level.

House 5 (Fig. 6, Pl. II b).

Shape.—Squarish in layout but corners markedly
rounded; dimensions, 4.2 by 4.2 m.

Walls.—Clay and sand, covered with thin (1.0 cm.)
plaster layer; slightly overhanging, resulting possibly from inward "squeezing" of clay when very
wet. Bench present and unusually wide.

Floor.—In yellow sand, rough.

Hearth.—Central; shallow oval excavation in sand, lacking clay lining and coping.

Deflector.—None.

Ventilator.—Long, narrow duct to southeast; has slight
steplike rise in floor outside of house line; charred
sticks indicated duct was roofed on level with bench.

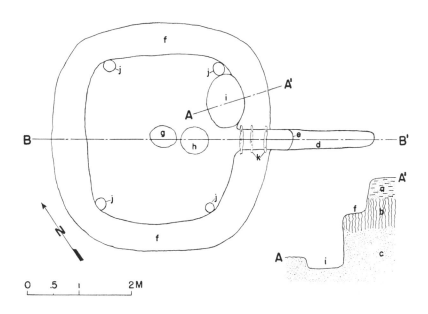

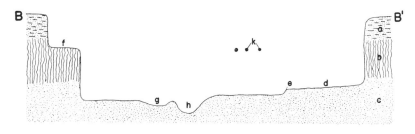

Figure 6.—Plan and sections of House 5: *a*, silt; *b*, undisturbed clay; *c*, sand; *d*, ventilator duct; *e*, step in duct; *f*, bench; *g*, hearth; *h*, ash pit; *i*, storage pit; *j*, main roof supports; *k*, charred sticks supporting cover for air duct at bench level.

Entrance.—Through roof; no evidence of construction.

Pits.—Ash pit between hearth and vent, and a storage pit in east corner.

Postholes.—Principal posts set in corners on four-post plan; no evidence of holes on bench.

Roof.—As in House 1.

Dates.—None.

Comments.—While not dated by tree rings, the occupation of this house, by type and material contents (fifty-three specimens), must parallel House 1 very closely. It is essentially a northern type.

Plate II.—*a*, House 1, showing ventilating duct, central hearth, bench, and numerous artifacts (slab for closing ventilator duct, lower right). Direction arrow, 1 meter long. *b*, House 5, a deep rectangular pit dwelling with wide bench and long ventilating duct. Direction arrow 1 meter long.

House 13 (Fig. 7, Pl. III *a*).

> Shape.—Straight-sided and nearly square-cornered; more pronouncedly rectangular than Houses 1 and 5; dimensions, 3.0 by 3.85 m.

> Walls.—Native clay, no evidence of plaster; bench absent.

> Floor.—In clay but not especially coated.

> Hearth.—Ashy area directly on floor, no depression; located slightly off-center toward probable entrance.

> Deflector.—None.

> Ventilator.—None evident in portion of house remaining.

> Entrance.—Lateral, with step, although evidence was not entirely satisfactory.

> Pits.—None.

> Postholes.—No indication of main roof supports; two holes flanking entrance.

> Roof.—No evidence.

> Dates.—None.

> Comments.—House 13 is significant because of its early stratigraphic relationship with House 14 which is of a different type. The straight sides, sharp corners, ash area instead of a pit, lack of bench and ventilator, and apparent side entrance with step tend to relate this structure to those of the San Francisco Phase of the Mogollon Culture[33] and to distinguish it from Houses 1 and 2 which manifest northern or Anasazi characteristics. Comparison of potsherds from Houses 13 and 14 show no significant differences, and apparently no great time elapsed between the construction of the two houses. (For a description of House 14 see p. 174.)

Round

> House 2 (Fig. 8; Pl. III *b*).

> Walls.—Clay, without plaster, not high because of shallow excavation for floor; bench absent; diameter, 6.0 m.

> Floor.—In clay, uneven.

> Hearth.—Irregular depression in floor.

> Deflector.—Metate fragment set on end at edge of hearth; has apparently been displaced as it does not line up with ventilator.

---

[33]E. W. Haury, 1936 b, p. 83.

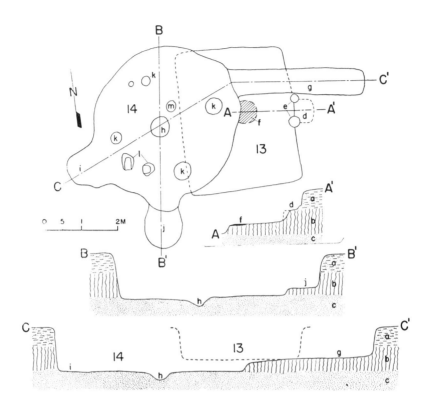

Figure 7.—Plan and sections of Houses 13 and 14: *a,* silt; *b,* undisturbed clay; *c,* sand; *d,* probable stepped entrance; *e,* postholes; *f,*
hearth area; *g,* entrance of House 14 running out over the floor and
beyond the east wall of House 13; *h,* hearth; *i, j,* lateral extensions,
possibly for storage (*j* may have been ventilator); *k,* main postholes;
l, metates on floor; *m,* floor pit.

Ventilator.—A long duct, extending eastward at an angle
from the radius of the house; clay of sides heavily
burned; duct evidently covered by sticks.

Entrance.—No evidence.

Pits.—None.

Postholes.—Only one found, near ventilator.

Roof.—No evidence.

Dates.—None.

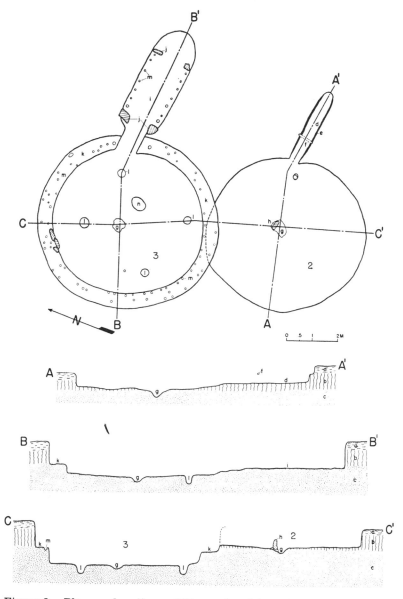

Figure 8.—Plans and sections of Houses 2 and 3: *a*, silt; *b*, undisturbed
clay; *c*, sand; *d*, ventilator passage of House 2; *e*, burnt sides; *f*, stick,
part of cover; *g*, hearths; *h*, deflector; *i*, entrance of House 3; *j*, angular
rocks; *k*, bench; *l*, main support postholes; *m*, secondary postholes; *n*,
floor pit; *o*, three stones arranged so as to support a weak spot in
bench.

House 3 (Fig. 8; Pl. III *b*).

Walls.—Badly broken up by gophers, no evidence of plaster; bench at sand level, the face braced at one point with three stones; diameter, 7.0 m.

Floor.—Not prepared, rough.

Hearth.—Irregular floor depression.

Deflector.—None.

Ventilator.—None. Function of one probably served by entrance.

Entrance.—Lateral, to east, at an angle to arc formed by perimeter of house; passage is long (4.0 m.) and widens out after leaving house; lined with postholes of entrance cover supports and four rocks, symmetrically placed, probably functionally related to roof structure; actual exit must have been up a short ladder through opening in passage end.

Pits.—One east of hearth.

Postholes.—Four main posts set in from bench on a square plan, northwest and northeast posts line up with axis of entrance; bench shows many secondary holes from leaning members of roof.

Roof.—Insufficient evidence to judge materials.

Dates.—None.

Comments.—Of these two houses, the deep one, No. 3, is clearly the later, although culturally there appears to be no difference. They contrast rather sharply in details but are analogous in size and in the curious skewing of the air duct and entrance.

House 4 (Fig. 9; Pl. IV *a*).

Walls.—Native soil with occasional patches of a sandy plaster; well-made bench is present; diameter, 6.85 m.

Floor.—In sand, rough, and broken up by features.

Hearth.—Centrally located; a large irregular pit filled with wood ash.

Deflector.—Metate fragment imbedded in floor near air duct opening in house.

Ventilator.—Long, narrow passage to southeast.

Entrance.--Pear-shaped lateral extension to east; enters house on bench level, floor does not slope upward; passage cover suggested by post holes in floor.

Pits.—Four variously placed about floor; a fifth pit near bench at west side had a log lying horizontally in bottom; the charred condition of this log suggests

a

b

Plate III.—*a*, Houses 13 (rectangular) and 14 (round). This was the most noteworthy instance of architectural stratification in the Bear Ruin, the rectangular house being the earlier of the two. It manifests distinctive Mogollon Culture architectural traits. Measuring stick 1 meter long. *b*, Houses 2 (right) and 3. The latter, with bench and long lateral entrance, is the later of the two. Measuring stick 1 meter long.

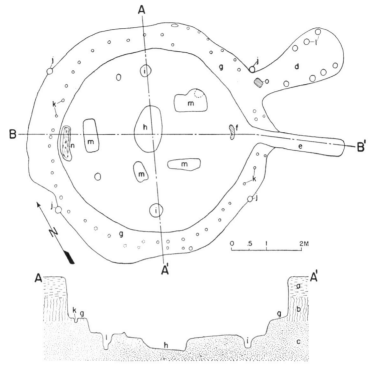

Figure 9.—Plan and sections of House 4: *a*, silt; *b*, undisturbed clay; *c*, sand; *d*, entrance; *e*, ventilating duct; *f*, metate deflector; *g*, bench; *h*, hearth; *i*, the two main postholes; *j*, secondary posts in edge of house; *k*, minor postholes in bench; *l*, posts for entrance hood; *m*, floor pits; *n*, floor pit with charred pine log; *o*, flat stone imbedded in floor of entrance.

pit was open at time house burned; purpose not known.

Postholes.—Two main holes on north-south axis in floor with four secondary support posts in perimeter of house provided chief structural elements; numerous small postholes on bench.

Roof.—Abundant charred remains; structural wood mostly juniper, covered with unidentified plants and pine needles before earth layer was placed on roof. (See reconstructions, Fig. 20 *b*.)

Dates.—None.

Comments.—This house is noteworthy for its great size and depth (2.15 m.), its unusual pattern of roof support posts, and in having both a ventilator and entrance passage. These features showed the burning which destroyed the house, and it is inferred that both were in simultaneous use.

House 6 (Fig. 10, Pl. IV *b*).

Walls.—House shallowly scooped into clay, hence walls must have been chiefly of wood; no bench or evidence of plaster; maximum diameter, 6.75 m.

Floor.—Native clay, smoothed; rises steeply at edges.

Hearth.—Deep circular pit, not clay-lined; centrally located; contained four stones.

Deflector.—Sandstone slab imbedded in floor immediately east of hearth.

Ventilator.—Suggestion of ventilator or entrance in east wall but feature not well preserved because of lack of depth.

Entrance.—See above. The shallow excavation for the floor suggests a lateral rather than a roof entrance.

Pits.—None.

Postholes.—Three placed along wall; the fourth hole may be inferred to complete the square plan.

Roof.—Some burnt clay but no timbers to give structural details.

Dates.—None.

Comments.—This house was both the smallest and the shallowest in the entire village. The roof plan is the same as in the others, but the side walls must have rested directly on the old surface. An unusually large number of metates (seven) was on the floor, several upside down.

House 7 (Fig. 11).

Walls.—Rough and irregular, preserving no evidence of plaster; lowest part in yellow sand curves in to meet floor; bench lacking; maximum diameter, 4.25 m.

Floor.—Yellow sand, rough.

Hearth.—Somewhat off-center; deep; not lined.

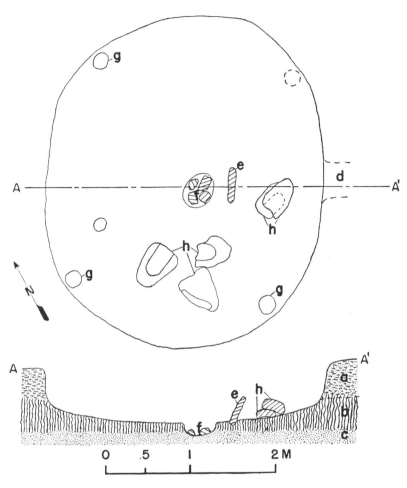

Figure 10.—Plan and section of House 6: *a*, silt; *b*, undisturbed clay; *c*, sand; *d*, problematical entrance or ventilator duct; *e*, deflector; *f*, hearth with stones; *g*, main postholes; *h*, five of seven metates.

Deflector.—None.

Ventilator.—None.

Entrance.—Short passage to east with rising floor, but actual exit must still have been with some form of ladder.

Pits.—Five: two near hearth; two near north wall, one being deep and undercut, containing four bone dice, one bone tube, two pottery scrapers, one *Olivella*

Plate IV.—*a*, House 4, a typical round dwelling with bench, ventilating duct, and deflector. The entrance passage (dotted lines) had not been found at the time this picture was taken. Stadia rod in metric system. *b*, House 6, a shallow round structure without bench. Note hearth stones. Direction arrow 1 meter long.

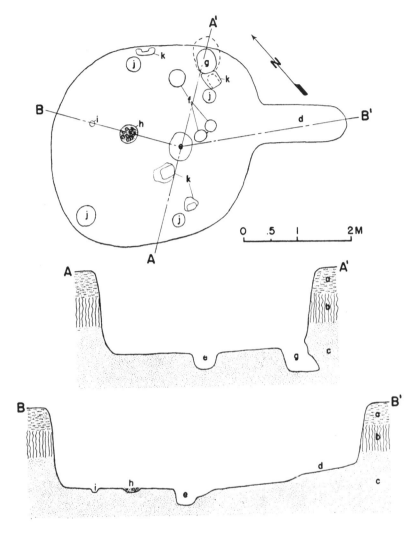

Figure 11.—Plan and sections of House 7: *a*, silt; *b*, undisturbed clay; *c*, sand; *d*, entrance; *e*, hearth; *f*, floor pits of uncertain use; *g*, floor cache pit; *h*, shallow pit filled with stones and sand; *i*, sipapu (?); *j*, main postholes; *k*, metates.

bead, a stone maul, and hammerstone; and one shallow pit west of hearth filled with angular fragments of sandstone and clean sand. There is also a small hole near west wall and approximately in line with hearth and entrance, occupying the right position for a sipapu.

Postholes.—Four-post plan; digging along margin of house on old surface level revealed no secondary holes.

Roof.—Little evidence except burned clay.

Dates.—None.

Comments.—The outstanding feature of this house is its depth and lack of bench, suggesting that the side members of the roof rested directly on the old ground surface as in House 6. The cache pit in the floor could definitely be identified as such on the basis of its contents.

House 8 (Fig. 12, Pl. V *a*).

Walls.—Native soil, rough, no indication of plaster; bench present; maximum diameter, 5.25 m.

Floor.—Saucer-shaped and very irregular; in sand.

Hearth.—Large and irregular, set well toward back of house.

Deflector.—None.

Ventilator.—None.

Entrance.—Long eastward passage beginning with step in house and gradually rising toward end. End cut through by Hearth 8, evidently after this house had fallen into disuse.

Pits.—None.

Bins.—Three along north wall: the westernmost apparently having been built by laying up massive coils of clay, leaving an opening which was closed by a flat slab; other two bins apparently made of wattle-and-daub construction.

Postholes.—Four main support posts, one set at edge of entrance skewing the flat part of the roof in relation to the entrance; secondary support posts on bench, and two in entrance to support roof extension forming passage cover.

Roof.—No evidence.

Dates.—None.

Comments.—Of special interest are the bins, built on, or slightly above floor level, found in no other houses of the site. The construction details of clay laid up in layers and wattle and daub, as surmised from the available evidence, suggest Basketmaker practices.

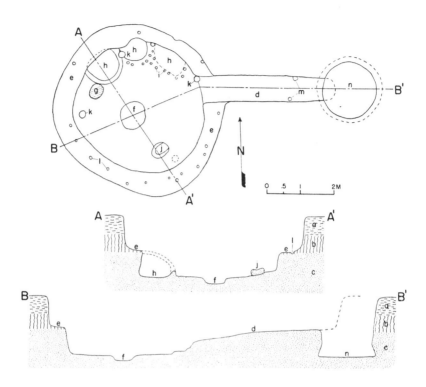

Figure 12.—Plan and sections of House 8: *a*, silt; *b*, undisturbed clay; *c*, sand; *d*, entrance; *e*, bench; *f*, hearth; *g*, sandstone slab probably used as cover for opening in bins *h*; *h*, storage bins; *i*, holes for wattle-and-daub construction of bins; *j*, metate; *k*, main roof supports; *l*, secondary roof supports; *m*, posts supporting entrance cover; *n*, Hearth 8.

House 9 (Fig. 13).

Walls.—Clay, unplastered; bench absent; maximum diameter, 5.0 m.

Floor.—On clay-sand contact; no prepared flooring.

Hearth.—Central; oval and shallow.

Deflector.—None.

Ventilator.—None.

Entrance.—To east, floor slightly rising toward end.

Pits.—Two: one west of hearth (may be enlarged post-hole) and the second north of hearth, 20.0 cm. deep, filled with angular sandstone and clean sand.

Postholes.—Three set well in from wall.

Roof.—No evidence.

Plate V.—*a*, House 8, showing bench, stepped entrance, and storage bins along north wall. Excavation at end of passageway is Hearth 8. *b*, House 12, a deep, round structure without bench. The trench coming in on the far side is the entrance passage. Measuring stick 1 meter long.

Dates.—None.

Comments.—If pit *f* (Fig. 13) is interpreted as a posthole, the roof had the same four-post plan as most of the

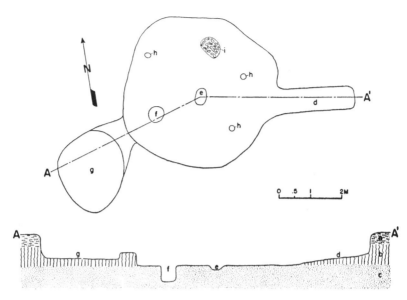

Figure 13.—Plan and section of House 9: *a*, silt; *b*, undisturbed clay; *c*, sand; *d*, entrance; *e*, hearth; *f*, pit, possibly posthole; *g*, annex (?); *h*, main postholes; *i*, floor pit filled with stones and sand.

other houses, but the posts were set much more closely together than was common. A possible annex (*g*) to House 9 should be noted, separated from the house by a sill of native clay. It was, however, impossible to determine with certainty that the pit was an integral part of the dwelling.

House 10 (Fig. 14).

    Walls.—Rough unplastered clay; bench absent; maximum diameter, 3.80 m.

    Floor.—In sand; uneven.

    Hearth.—Somewhat off-center; large and shallow.

    Deflector.—Flat stone, lying at edge of hearth.

    Ventilator.—Not found.

    Entrance.—Not found.

    Pits.—None.

    Postholes.—Five principal roof supports.

    Roof.—No evidence.

    Dates.—None.

    Comments.—The presence of a deflector suggests an entrance or ventilator, but persistent search failed to

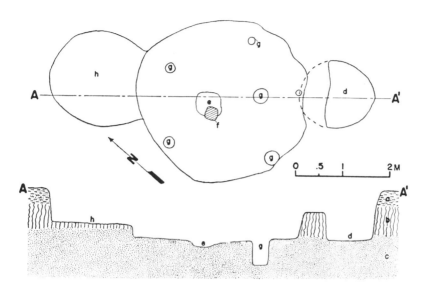

Figure 14.—Plan and section of House 10: *a*, silt; *b*, undisturbed clay; *c*, sand; *d*, storage pit (?) predating house; *e*, hearth; *f*, deflector of shaped sandstone, displaced; *g*, main roof support holes; *h*, annex.

reveal either. A large extension to the north (*h*, Fig. 14) appeared to be an integral part of the house, but it seems to be much too large an opening and in the wrong direction to be regarded as an entrance. The feature to the southeast (*d*) is a storage pit (?) which had fallen into disuse before the house was built.

House 11 (Fig. 15).

Walls.—Badly eroded; complete bench except where broken by entrance; maximum diameter, 6.0 m.

Floor.—Smoothed native sand.

Hearth.—Central, circular basin; no lining.

Deflector.—Shaped sandstone slab lying on floor northwest of hearth.

Ventilator.—None found.

Entrance.—Extends to east, with rising floor and slightly expanding toward outer end.

Pits.—One near southwest wall, 25.0 cm. deep, filled with stones and clean sand.

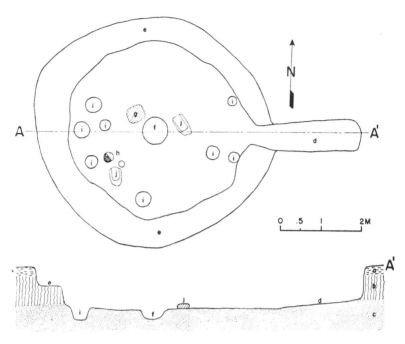

Figure 15.—Plan and section of House 11: *a*, silt; *b*, undisturbed clay; *c*, sand; *d*, entrance; *e*, bench; *f*, hearth; *g*, shaped sandstone deflector, displaced; *h*, floor pit filled with stone and clean yellow sand; *i*, postholes and possibly some floor pits; *j*, metates.

Postholes.—Many holes of the same general size in floor, some may be floor pits; holes in bench not determined.

Roof.—No evidence.

Dates.—None.

Comments.—A typical round structure with bench but evidence for plan of roof supports is somewhat confused.

House 12 (Fig. 16, Pl. V *b*).

Walls.—Badly eroded native soil, no evidence of plaster; bench absent; maximum diameter, 5.20 m.

Floor.—Uneven sand.

Hearth.—Deep oval pit, somewhat off-center toward entrance.

Deflector.—Sandstone slab set in edge of hearth.

Ventilator.—None found.

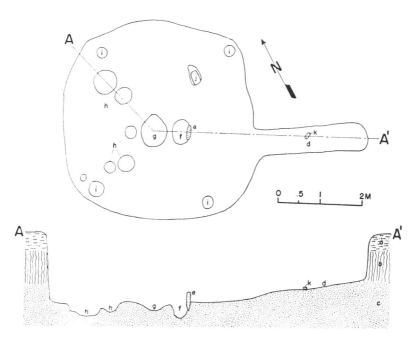

Figure 16.—Plan and section of House 12: *a*, silt; *b*, undisturbed clay; *c*, sand; *d*, entrance; *e*, deflector; *f*, hearth; *g, h*, floor pits; *i*, main roof-support posts; *j*, metate; *k*, mano.

Entrance.—Directed to southeast and not centrally placed in east side of dwelling; floor rises moderately but ends at a depth of 1 meter below surface; floor heavily trodden; mano on floor about halfway out.

Pits.—Six of varying size and depth in western part of house.

Postholes.—Four near wall at cardinal points.

Roof.—No evidence.

Dates.—None.

Comments.—This house is more or less transitional in shape between rectangular and round but somewhat closer to the latter. The timbers forming the sides of the roof must have been placed on the old ground level and leaned against the horizontal beams supported by the four main roof supports (Fig. 20 c).

House 14 (Fig. 7, Pl. III *a*).

> Walls.—Native clay, no indication of plaster; bench absent; broken at two points by extensions; maximum diameter, 4.25 m.
>
> Floor.—On sand.
>
> Hearth.—Central floor depression.
>
> Deflector.—None.
>
> Ventilator.—Evidence not clear, extension to south may be one.
>
> Entrance.—To east, long, not centrally placed; begins with step out of house and rises gradually toward end.
>
> Pits.—One north of hearth.
>
> Postholes.—Four set in from wall.
>
> Roof.—No evidence.
>
> Dates.—None.
>
> Comments.—House 14 was obviously cut through the earlier rectangular structure (No. 13), thereby providing a good case of architectural stratigraphy. It shared with Houses 3 and 8 the curious off-center position of the entry.

Storage Rooms

Rectangular

> No. 1 (Fig. 17).
>
> Walls.—Clay on wattle work; no evidence of plaster; dimensions, 2.5 by 2.5 m.
>
> Floor.—Clay; 20.0 cm. below old surface, 40.0 cm. below present surface.
>
> Entrance.—Probably on southwest side as indicated by stones.
>
> Postholes.—Four set approximately 0.5 m. towards center of room from corners.
>
> Roof.—Timbers with brush and clay cover.
>
> Dates.—None.
>
> Comments.—The location of this structure was such as to suggest that it was associated with House 1 in a way which was common among Anasazi villages of this period. Being very shallow, the outlines were determined mostly by the area burnt and by the spread of the artifacts and broken pottery. The usual house features as hearth, deflector, and bench were not present. Specimens from floor include manos, three jars, two clay jar covers, figurine, and fragments of a burnt basket.

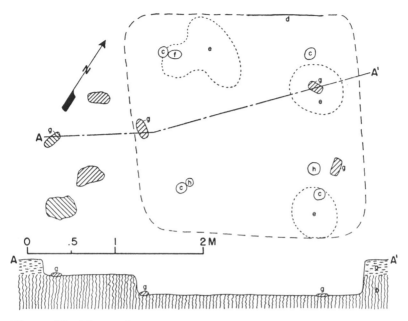

Figure 17.—Plan and section of Storage Room No. 1: *a*, silt; *b*, undisturbed clay; *c*, postholes for roof supports; *d*, plaster; *e*, areas of broken pottery; *f*, burnt basket; *g*, manos; *h*, clay pot cover.

No. 2 (Fig. 18).

 Walls.—Clay, no plaster in evidence; dimensions, 2.75 by 3.0 m.

 Floor.—Showed very little trampling, determined mainly by position of artifacts; 0.6 m. below present surface.

 Entrance.—None found; recess in southeast corner was too small to be considered an entrance.

 Postholes.—Three as in No. 1; fourth hole not found.

 Roof.—Burnt clay only evidence.

 Dates.—None.

 Comments.—The area about this structure was not fully explored for a possible adjoining house. Hearth and other features lacking as in No. 1, and the floor was liberally covered with an assortment of stone tools.

RELIGIOUS STRUCTURES

Kiva No. 1 (Fig. 19, Pl. VI *a*).

 Shape.—Round with directional recesses orientated almost exactly to the cardinal points, and a large oval

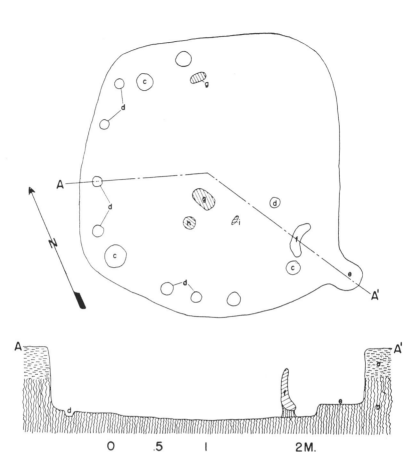

Figure 18.—Plan and section of Storage Room No. 2: *a*, silt; *b*, un-disturbed clay; *c*, main roof support posts; *d*, auxiliary roof supports; *e*, corner recess; *f*, metate in vertical position above floor; *g*, *h*, *i*, stone implements.

extension to the southeast; maximum diameter in-cluding main recess, 15.3 m.; greatest inside diameter to bench, 9.0 m.; depth 1.75 m.

Walls.—Plaster on sand and clay of bench, native clay and fill above bench level; bench completely en-circles room without break.

Floor.—Sand without clay veneer; even, except where broken up by rodent burrows.

Hearth.—Approximately central; basin dug into sand, without clay lining; partially filled with hearth stones.

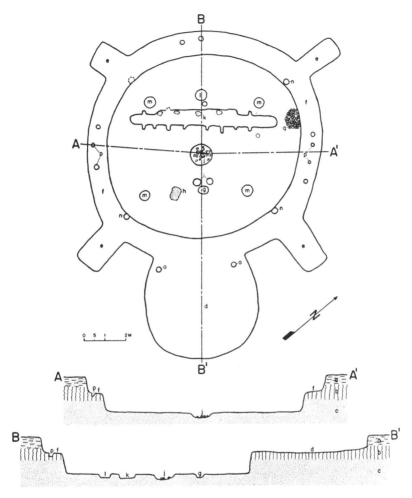

Figure 19.—Plan and sections of the Bear Ruin Kiva No. 1: *a*, silt; *b*, undisturbed clay; *c*, sand; *d*, large southeasterly recess, floor at bench level; *e*, four directional recesses, floors at bench level; *f*, bench; *g*, floor pit; *h*, flat rock; *i*, holes for ladder butts (?); *j*, hearth with stones; *k*, floor trench, possibly for loom anchorages; *l*, sipapu (?); *m*, main roof support posts; *n*, secondary roof supports in bench; *o*, support posts for roof over recess; *p*, side beams; *q*, pile of hearth stones.

Deflector.—None in position; flat stone south of hearth may have served as such.

Ventilator.—None.

Entrance.—Probably through roof, two holes in floor (*i*) southeast of hearth taken to be ladder holes; the

a

b

Plate VI.—a, A seventh century kiva in the Bear Ruin; diameter (not including recesses), 9.0 meters. b, Floor trench in a believed to have been used in fastening the lower beams of looms.

large southeastern recess may have been used as
entrance, but there was no evidence of a means to
gain bench and recess level.

Pits.—Two; (*g*) purpose unknown, (*l*) possibly the
sipapu.

Other floor features.—Pile of hearth stones (*q*) at base
of bench, north side, but no evidence of burning at
this spot other than general house burning; long,
shallow trench in floor (Pl. VI *b*) between hearth
and north and west roof supports has more or less
symmetrically placed notches mainly on southeastern margin and an offset on opposite side with
several stones on trench floor at regular intervals.

Postholes.—Four main supports (*m*) with secondary
posts opposite these in bench (*n*) and in line with
directional recesses (*e*); two posts in main recess
(*o*); and auxiliary poles imbedded in bench (*p*).

Roof.—Scattered charcoal and burnt clay only.

Dates.—667+x (one log).

Comments.—This building was situated well back from
the terrace and in the outskirts of the village. Looking at its plan, one is struck by the similarity of the
outline to that of a turtle. It is believed, however,
that the large recess and the four small recesses
which were directly in line with the roof supports
were purely functional and that no effigy was intended by the makers of the building.

The curious trench in the floor is not readily interpreted. It is suggested, however, that this feature
may have been the place of anchorage of the lower
beams of looms. Sticks laid transversely to the
trench in the grooves and plastered down might
have served as the tying points for the beams in the
same way as has been pointed out in later kivas.[34]
Such a view naturally presupposes that weaving was
done in early ceremonial rooms much as in more
recent ones, and also that the fiber was cotton.[35]
Two houses in the Whitewater district of eastern
Arizona showed similar but much shorter floor
features.[36]

---

[34]N. M. Judd, 1930, pp. 28-29.

[35]Large fabrics were apparently not woven by the Anasazi before they
acquired cotton in Pueblo I (S. J. Guernsey, 1931, p. 115) in the
seventh or eighth century. Obviously, the loom was not as long as
the trench, but if it was used as suggested, a series of small looms
could have been set up in line.

[36]F. H. H. Roberts, Jr., 1939, Figures 2 and 26.

Discussion

In reviewing the architecture of the Bear Ruin in a broad
and general light, it must be pointed out again that the lack
of differences in ceramics and artifacts from the various
houses and the limited number of tree-ring dates do not
permit a chronological grading of the dwellings. The one
good instance of stratigraphy, Houses 13 and 14 (Pl. III *a*),
while suggestive in showing that the rectangular structures
were earlier than the round, is hardly sufficient evidence on
which to build a case. Lacking better data it may be assumed
that houses of both forms were broadly in contemporaneous
use. A discussion of architectural development must consequently be postponed until further work has been done in
ruins in which a greater lapse of time will be involved.
But something may be said of the shapes and structural details of houses and of their possible meaning from a more
strictly cultural point of view.

It has become quite obvious in the literature of recent
years that pit houses of almost any shape may occur almost
anywhere at any time. In the Anasazi area both rectangular
and round structures may occur together in the same time
level. In the Mogollon territory, while round dwellings appear to be early generally, there are usually just enough
variations from the norm to prevent categorical statements.
Considered, however, with other architectural features, as
the position and type of entrance, bench, roof details, floor
features, and interior furnishings, affinities with houses of
adjoining areas may be detected. Houses 1 and 13 may be
offered as examples of this. While both are approximately
of the same size and depth, the former with its bench, southern ventilating duct, coping about the hearth, floor ridges,
postulated roof entrance, and four-post roof support plan,
and adjoining storage structure is essentially Anasazi in detail, indeed, more so than any other house in the village.
House 13, on the other hand, without bench, straight sides,
and square corners, side entrance framed with poles, and
hearth directly on floor bears clear resemblances to Mogollon
structures of the San Francisco Phase.[37] The finding of these
two houses, representing northern and southern building
styles respectively, suggests the coming together of two
cultural streams, a condition which is confirmed by other
elements of local culture also.

Houses of round form were strongly in the majority in
the Bear Ruin. Equipped as they often were with benches,

---

[37]Compare with House 4 and 5B of the Mogollon Village, E. W. Haury,
1936 *b*, p. 18.

central hearths, ventilating ducts, deflectors, floor pits, and bins, they manifest a direct link with the Anasazi among whom similar houses were in vogue at the same time. Round houses were in style in the Mogollon area too but at a somewhat earlier time than those of the Bear Ruin[38] and had largely been replaced by rectangular dwellings by the end of the seventh and eighth centuries.

Looking at the details of construction, a number of interesting situations may be pointed out. There is apparently no significance in the variability of the depth of houses. The subsoil of the site permitted any depth, and the extremes of 0.5 to 2.1 meters apparently depended upon the industry of the builders. House orientation displays some uniformity, since most entrances and ventilators were directed to the northeast, east, and southeast. The exception to this was House 1 in which the ventilator was on the south side, the common orientation in the Anasazi house of late Basketmaker III in the White Mound Ruin.[39]

The methods for gaining entrance to the houses varied. Houses 1 and 5, both rectangular, almost certainly were entered through the roof, generally considered a non-Mogollon form.[40] With the exception of a few (Houses 2, 6, and 10) in which the digging did not present a clear-cut picture, all others had lateral entrance passages. These should be viewed as representing two styles, the broad expanding type of Houses 3 and 4, and the narrow, parallel-sided type of the others. The former may be taken as a relative of the Anasazi type in which the passage is expanded into an antechamber,[41] whereas the latter is distinctly in the Mogollon tradition. The predominance of the narrow type suggests that the builders looked favorably on this form of exit and incorporated it in an essentially northern house type.

But these entries differ from the standard Mogollon style in two minor respects which give them local individuality: first, the failure to grade the passage floor towards the surface, thus forcing the use of some form of ladder and, second, the eccentric location of the passage as seen in Houses 3, 8, and 13.

---

[38]E. W. Haury, 1936 b, Figure 30; P. H. Nesbitt, 1938, pp. 86 ff.; P. S. Martin, J. Rinaldo, and M. Kelly, 1940, p. 85.

[39]Excavations by Gila Pueblo; in preparation.

[40]P. H. Nesbitt, 1938, pp. 88-89 and W. Hough, 1919, p. 415 both record roof-entered houses, possibly the southernmost extensions of the roof entrance idea.

[41]F. H. H. Roberts, Jr., 1929, Figures 5, 8, 9, 10, 13, and 14.

Nowhere were rocks used as masonry or in a true structural sense, although stones were employed individually as deflectors, in shoring up weak spots in benches (House 3), and as stepping stones. The rocks in the entrance of House 3 and in the floor trench of the kiva obviously served some definite purpose, but it can hardly be said that they foreshadow stone masonry. The practice in the north of lining house pits with stone slabs was wholly lacking. It is believed that stone masonry, when it appears in the area in a local Pueblo I horizon,[42] came in from the north where rock construction was already well understood. At that time Anasazi traits become strongly predominant in the Forestdale Valley, and inferentially one may believe that it marks a fresh increment of people. To the southeast in the Mogollon area proper, stone construction appears to be somewhat later than here, appearing for the first time in the Three Circle Phase.[43] Even there this coincides with an impressive outburst of Anasazi features which must be connected with the southward diffusion of this culture in about the tenth century.

The ventilator-deflector complex carries with it a decided northern flavor, but the lack of standardization in these features probably means that its southern limits of diffusion are being approached. These features occur only sporadically deeper into the Mogollon territory. In the Bear Ruin only Houses 1, 2, and 5 had a ventilator passage to the exclusion of an entrance, while House 4, curiously, had both. In most of those houses with side entrances, the deflector was carried over, doubtless serving as effectively with these as with true ventilator ducts, thus combining a predominantly northern with a predominantly southern trait.

On several occasions the side entrance of the Mogollon houses has been seriously questioned, the supposition being that they have been confused by excavators with ventilating ducts. A number of conditions argue against this view as, for example, the well-trodden floors in the passages, the steps occasionally seen at the beginnings or ends of passages (sometimes with stone treads), and the occurrences of vessels and artifacts on the entry floor. Another argument is in the position of the hearth. In roof-entered houses the entrance and smoke hole are combined as a rule, and the hearth occupies a central position. In side-entered houses, such as

---

[42]As shown by preliminary excavations in Arizona P:16:2, to be reported in another paper.
[43]E. W. Haury, 1936 *b*, Figures 25 and 30; P. H. Nesbitt, 1938, pp. 46-48.

those of the Hohokam and the Mogollon, presumably there was no special smoke vent, since the side entrance was thought sufficient to ventilate the room properly. In such cases the hearth position is toward the door, apparently a measure to compensate for the inadequacy of side ventilation. The hearths in Bear Ruin houses, for the most part, did not follow this pattern even though they had lateral entrances, and it must be assumed either that smoke holes were also present, or that side ventilation was considered adequate.

As further evidence that side passages and ventilators are not being confused, it should be pointed out that the opening of the duct in House 1 was neatly framed with a clay coping and that in Houses 2 and 5 there was evidence of a duct cover. These details are lacking in the houses which show side entrances. There is also the matter of size. Ducts were narrow, less than 0.5 meter in width, while passages were considerably in excess of this figure.

The roofs of houses in this village, irrespective of shape, more or less uniformly followed a support-post plan based on four timbers set near the corners in rectangular dwellings and at some little distance in from the bench in round rooms. The bench itself appears to have been directly linked structurally with the roof as a base on which the poles closing the sides of the houses rested. It was optional, moreover, since serviceable houses could be built without it. For this reason one is inclined to look at the bench as a matter of cultural preference and hence useful in appraising the degree of mixture. Through the Anasazi territory the bench is a common accompaniment of underground rooms together with a four-post roof support plan. In Bear Ruin, however, only six of the fourteen domestic structures revealed a bench. Farther to the south Nesbitt mentions but one in Starkweather Ruin,[44] and only one house with end benches was noted in the Mogollon Village.[45] This fading out of the bench to the south appears to be fairly conclusive evidence that the feature is northern. The same holds true for the roof style except that it appears to have been in somewhat more general use deeper into the Mogollon territory than the bench, in as much as it shows up rather strongly at Starkweather[46] in Georgetown and San Francisco Phase houses and not until the Three Circle Phase in the Mimbres.[47]

---

[44] P. H. Nesbitt, 1938, pp. 16-17.
[45] E. W. Haury, 1936 *b*, pp. 20-21.
[46] P. H. Nesbitt, 1938, p. 88.
[47] E. W. Haury, 1936 *b*, p. 83.

How the main types of Bear Ruin houses may have looked originally is illustrated in Figure 20. Although the roof reconstructions are based on available evidence, such features as the smoke hole and the type of ladder are purely theoretical.

Floor features of various sorts, as ridges, lines of slabs set on end, well-made hearths with coping, ash pits, sundry floor pits, and bins, are commonly seen in Basketmaker III houses of the Anasazi, while in the Mogollon area the houses are notoriously lacking in furnishings of these types. In this respect the present houses show a somewhat closer relationship with the north, although one senses again from certain absences and lack of standardization that work was being done in a transitional or marginal zone. Specifically Bear Ruin houses, except House 1, did not show the unexplained floor ridges nor the stone slab partitions as seen in the houses of Shabik'eshchee[48] of the Anasazi. Hearths scooped out of the floor and, except in House 1, lacking a coping are more reminiscent of the southern form, and the absence of ash pits shows a parallel condition, unless the floor depressions in Houses 1 and 5 may be regarded as such. The floor cache pits and particularly those filled with stones and clean sand are northern in flavor.[49] The use of bins in houses (House 8) was apparently unknown in orthodox Mogollon villages but was of fairly frequent occurrence in the Anasazi area. The same situation holds for annexes, as seen in Houses 9, 10, and 14.

Storage structures, occurring near pit houses and of which only two were found, have not been reported in the Mogollon villages excavated thus far, but they do appear with increasing frequency and complexity as one proceeds northward, culminating in the San Juan. Doubtless the two uncovered in the Bear Ruin are another manifestation of northern architectural elements.

The discovery of a large kiva in the Bear Ruin injects interesting angles into the architectural problems of the village. What was its origin and into what did it ultimately develop? A sufficient number of great kivas of early Anasazi periods

---

[48]F. H. H. Roberts, Jr., 1929, pp. 10-40.

[49]How general this stone- and sand-filled pit is may be debated, but such occurred in the White Mound Village (Gila Pueblo; in preparation) and at Shabik'eshchee (F. H. H. Roberts, Jr., 1929, pp. 48, 66) where they were interpreted as secondary hearths. While these pits in the Bear Ruin often held heat-fractured stones, they never contained ash nor did the sides show any signs of burning.

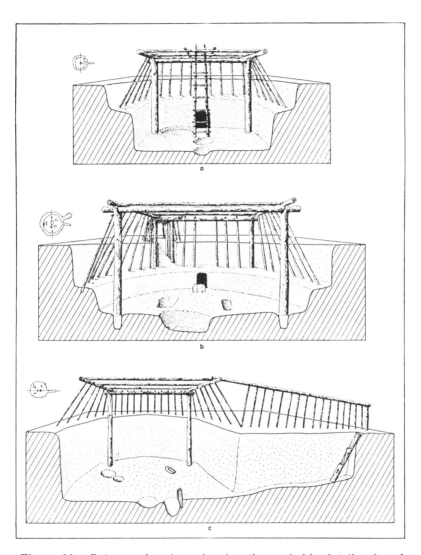

Figure 20.—Cutaway drawings showing the probable details of roof construction of: *a*, House 5, rectangular, with bench, ventilator, and roof entrance; *b*, House 4, round, with bench, ventilator, and side entrance; *c*, House 12, round, without bench and ventilator, side entrance.

have been discovered[50] to indicate a broad cultural relationship of the Bear Ruin kiva with those, particularly as the heavy stamp of Anasazi architecture is also seen in the domestic quarters. Although differing individually, all of the early Anasazi great kivas have enough features in common to be classed as the manifestation of a single idea. But even at that early date, there were already regional differences suggesting the possibility of a long ancestry. Whether the great kiva is attributable to the Anasazi, as has been implied in all writings, cannot be reviewed here, but at the present time the writer provisionally identifies the Bear Ruin kiva with those of the Anasazi.[51]

The persistence of the great kiva idea in the Forestdale area after the Forestdale Phase to fully developed Pueblo is shown by one of early twelfth century date located a few hundred meters southwest of the Bear Ruin kiva.[52] This suggests the possibility that the great kiva of the classic Anasazi did not emerge in a single locality, but rather that it arose more or less simultaneously in several areas from an earlier and apparently more widely spread prototype.

In concluding this discussion of architecture, it should be reiterated that Bear Ruin houses were the result of the mixture of two patterns of building, the one northern and Anasazi, the other southern and Mogollon. It seems that the impact of this meeting was great enough to cause an era of architectural unbalance as evidenced by the lack of standardization in details. These were combined and recombined rarely twice in the same way. As indicated in the tabulation below, Anasazi features were in the majority. This would appear to be argument enough to claim that here was an

[50]Cummings reports one (verbally) in Juniper Cove of the Kayenta area, Basketmaker III; Roberts (1929, pp. 73-81) describes one of the same period in Chaco Canyon; Martin uncovered two (1939, pp. 350-59) in southwestern Colorado dating from late Basketmaker times; and Morris (1939, pp. 82-84) describes one from the La Plata-Mancos area with a tree-ring date of 831±.

[51]The reluctance to accept without qualification a northern origin for the great kiva is the presence of a similar structure in what is believed to be an early horizon in the area of the Mogollon Culture (E. W. Haury, 1936 b, pp. 14-17, 56-57). Pit house A in the SU site (P. S. Martin, J. Rinaldo, and M. Kelly, 1940, pp. 14-17), while not specifically labeled as such, looks suspiciously like one and is almost certainly older than any uncovered to date. It seems to the writer that a full review of this problem should be undertaken.

[52]Reference is made to a great kiva, about 19.0 meters in diameter but partially washed away, which was excavated in the summer of 1940 in Arizona P:16:2 (report in preparation). A second great kiva in the valley, not excavated as yet, has also been recognized.

Plate VII.—*a*, Hearth stones scattered over old surface in the Bear Ruin. This concentration occurred near a large hearth. *b*, Burnt rock mound (arrow) exposed by the cutting of Forestdale Creek. A deep hearth was found a few meters back from the channel face (see Fig. 21 *e*).

essentially Anasazi group merely affected by the southern culture because of its geographic nearness. But with ceramics giving exactly the opposite picture, this question must be reopened for discussion later on.

Cultural Allocation of Architectural Features

Anasazi	Mogollon
Roof plan	
Roof entrance	
Expanding side entrance	Long, narrow side entrance
Central hearth	Hearth not lined and without coping
Ventilator-deflector	Lack of floor ridges
	Lack of stone in construction
Bench	
Bins	
Storage structures	
Kiva	

STORAGE PITS (?)

There is no sure way of assigning a use to several circular pits found in the site. Of the two cleared of fill, one had apparently fallen into disuse and was refilled when House 10 was built through it (see Fig. 14), and the other was situated in the northeast margin of the site. These pits measured approximately a meter in diameter and depth and did not show the undercutting of the sides as was the case in the pits of the Mogollon Village.[53] Their identification as storage pits must be held as provisional, and the uncovering of only two suggests that they played a rather minor role.

HEARTHS

The work of Gila Pueblo in the Cochise Culture of southeastern Arizona has called attention to a condition which, for the most part, has gone unrecognized in archaeological studies of the Southwest—namely, the presence of great numbers of hearth stones in and about old camps and village sites. Normally these stones are about the size of a fist or smaller and quite angular, made so by thermal fracturing from use in hearths. The evidence indicates that stones were used in connection with the preparation of food, beginning as sizable chunks and gradually being reduced to useless bits by continued heating.

It should be pointed out further that stones of this sort occur frequently in the sites of the Hohokam and Mogollon

---

[53]E. W. Haury, 1936 b, p. 22.

Plate VIII.—Deep hearth with undercut and heavily burned sides. Measuring stick 1 meter long.

cultures and are infrequent, if not absent, in Anasazi villages.[54] In the Bear Ruin, regardless of their location, test pits invariably disclosed hearth stones, showing that they were widely spread over the entire occupied area. For the most part they were scattered from hearths which were located in and about the houses at points convenient to the users (Pl. VII a). One exception to this was the concentration of hearth material on the north bank of Forestdale Creek, amounting to a small, burnt rock mound (Pl. VII b and Fig. 21 e). The use of rocks and large hearths in connection with preparing food was apparently firmly fixed in the daily routine, and this practice must have a significant bearing on one's notion of the culture pattern as a whole.

The hearths may be classified as follows:

1. Shallow basin pits (Fig. 21 a).. 9
    Generally circular in shape, ranging in diameter from 0.25 to 1.0 m., apparently excavated only slightly into surface existing at time of use; hearth area more or less completely filled with stones.

2. Pits with sloping sides (Fig. 21 b)................................... 2
    Up to 2.0 m. in diameter and excavated as much as 1.0 m. below old surface; contents of pits show an abundance of or dearth of hearth stones, depending upon extent to which these were raked out after last use; sides of pit not plastered but show some signs of burning.

3. Pits with vertical sides (Fig. 21 c)................................. 1
    Diameter and depth approximately 0.80 m.; no applied clay lining; shows moderately heavy firing; bottom somewhat rounded.

4. Pits with undercut sides (Fig. 21 d, Pl. VIII)................. 4
    Depths from 1.5 to 2.0 m.; average diameter at bottom, 1.75 m.; mouth constricted so diameter is approximately two thirds as great as maximum diameter; bottoms flat; the great depth put lower part of oven in yellow sand substratum, apparently responsible for application of clay plaster over bottom and sides up to bottom of native clay layer; pits of this type show very heavy burning, the color being brick red and the penetration as much as 5.0 cm.

---

[54]E. H. Morris informed the writer that in a Basketmaker II cave near Durango, Colorado, excavated by him in 1938, he encountered numerous burnt rocks but found no real clue as to their origin.

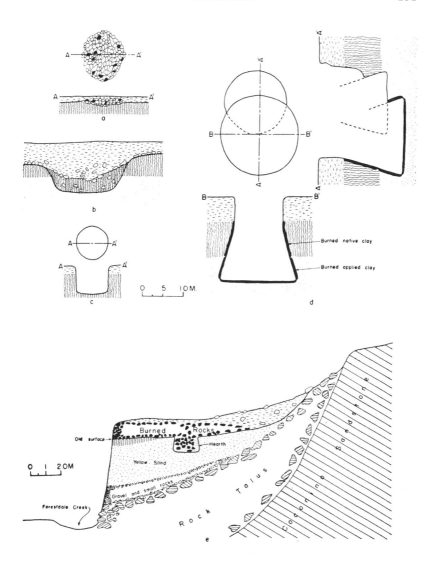

Figure 21.—*a-d*, Hearth types in the Bear Ruin (solid rocks in *a* indicate artifact fragments); profile of burned rock mound and Hearth 7 on the north bank of Forestdale Creek (*e*).

Discussion

Pit contents

Excluding the sand and clay which has washed into the pits since their use, hearth stones make up the bulk of the fill. Sherds occur rarely, and occasionally one finds fragments of calcined animal bones, assumed to be remnants of the type of food prepared therein. In no case were vegetal remains observed.

It was noted that implement fragments such as manos, metates, and hammerstones occurred frequently. The reason for this is not difficult to see, since such tools were normally made of tough crystalline and volcanic rocks which would withstand heat far more readily than the sandstone available locally. The latter breaks up easily under heat and soon forms such small stones that they are no longer usable. This gradual reduction of stones accounts for the large amount of wastage which goes with this type of economy.

To test the occurrence of materials, the contents of the pit shown in Figure 21 *a* were removed and sorted, yielding the following things:

    4 chert hammerstones
   19 lava metate fragments
   17 lava fragments, probably of metates
    1 sandstone metate fragment
    1 sandstone rubbing stone
   20 rounded quartzite pebbles
  235 angular sandstone fragments
    1 indurated sandstone maul fragment
    1 burnt clay lump

In this instance the weight of the hearth stones ranged from a few ounces to approximately 3 pounds.

Use

In attempting to visualize the specific use of these pits, it is not necessary to draw much upon the imagination. They were essentially earth ovens such as are still extensively employed by many peoples the world over and which have been found archaeologically in many other areas. The principle involved is evidently that of the fireless cooker in which stones are heated in order to provide the source of heat for the preparation of food. The procedure is generally to build a large fire in a pit, thereby heating a number of large rocks. After the fire has died down some of these rocks are raked out, the remaining stones and pit sides are then lined with green leaves or grass to act as a protective layer between the stones and the food. After the food is placed on the grass, there follows more insulating material, the already heated rocks, and finally earth. After allowing the time necessary to cook the food properly, the top materials are raked back, and the food is removed ready for consumption.

As already implied, the use of earth ovens must have been an almost daily occurrence, establishing this trait as an important one in the economy of the Forestdale people. The method of preparing food may, to some extent, be controlled by environment—that is, by the type of food available and by the abundance of stone and wood; but on the other hand, it must also be recognized that the availability of all the materials does not dictate such a method for preparing foods. Hence the cultural factor comes to the fore, leading one to assume that this practice was a matter of choice and probably a custom of long standing.

Reviewing the distribution of earth ovens in the Southwest, there is first of all in southeastern Arizona a specialization which may be indicative of long usage. Excavations by Trischka[55] and the Amerind Foundation[56] have shown undercut pits sometimes up to 2.0 m. in depth with curious pit and trench patterns in the bottoms. These are associated with sites attributable to a culture showing a blending of Mogollon and Hohokam elements. In time they are apparently not much older than 1000 A.D., but in all probability the trait may be pushed backwards into more remote horizons so as to connect ultimately with the late stage of the Cochise Culture.

The prime example known to the writer where the earth oven idea was carried to an extreme is a site situated at La Playa in northern Sonora.[57] At this village, now undergoing heavy erosion, one may see scores of earth ovens filled with hearth stones. These stones are so abundant that they literally form a pavement over several hundred acres of the occupied area in the silt-filled flat adjoining the Boquillas River. Here the pits do not seem to have exceeded a meter in depth or diameter. The sides were undercut, and frequently one finds animal bones in the contents. Cultural affiliations of this village appear to be predominantly with the Mogollon and to a minor extent with the Hohokam cultures.

Among the Hohokam, large earth ovens were also employed.[58] Hohokam pits are usually straight-sided or con-

[55]C. Trischka, 1933, pp. 427-31.
[56]W. S. Fulton and C. Tuthill, 1940, pp. 20-25.
[57]C. Sauer and D. Brand, 1931, pp. 93-94.
[58]A. Woodward, 1931, p. 15; E. W. Haury, 1932, pp. 57-61; A. Schroeder, 1940, pp. 76-78.

verging toward the bottom and may be over a meter in depth; a maximum diameter of almost 4.0 meters has been recorded. The sides, more than in any other region, show a very heavy layer of carbonized material and the contents, as at Forestdale, are principally angular stones many of which are implement fragments. So far the pits unearthed in Hohokam sites have been associated principally with Colonial and Sedentary Period horizons, and there is no good evidence yet to assume that the trait was used much earlier.

In the Anasazi territory during Basketmaker II times large undercut cists were known,[59] but the evidence tends to show that the primary use of these was storage and not the preparation of food. Later the pigummi oven was apparently in considerable use among the pueblos,[60] a trait which has survived to the present day. There are two notable differences between these ovens and the pits occurring all through southern New Mexico and Arizona. The first is the presence of a flue or vent and the second is an absence of cooking stones in and about the ovens. These are undoubtedly due to the fact that the pueblo oven was primarily used for preparing corn mush as opposed to the baking of animal foods.

Patayan Culture[61] hearth stones are said to occur in abundance, generally as concentrations over small areas near habitations.[62]

In recent times Apaches have made extensive use of large sunken hearths in the preparation of mescal, and the Navaho use the same device for roasting corn. One of the distinguishing features of the mescal pit is the surrounding ring of angular hearth stones resulting from the raking back of the stones after each use.

This rapid survey will bring out the wide tribal and time distribution of the earth oven idea. The striking fact is that the trait seems to have been lacking among the Basketmakers as opposed to its early and extensive use in the south. This must be considered as having some weight when one tries to formulate an opinion as to the individualities of the Basketmakers and the Mogollon.

Although the earth oven itself has not yet been found in the covered sites of the Cochise Culture, hearth stones are plentiful,[63] and there may be in this occurrence the source from which to draw the later practice.

---

[59]S. J. Guernsey and A. V. Kidder, 1921, p. 20.
[60]F. H. H. Roberts, Jr., 1939, p. 55; 1932, pp. 44-46.
[61]H. S. Colton, 1939 b.
[62]Verbal communication from L. L. Hargrave.
[63]E. B. Sayles. In preparation.

Plate IX.—*a*, Mortuary offerings with infant burial of which few traces remain. Note bone tube under inverted bowl (lower right). *b*, The normal burial position showing also the poor condition of the skeletons.

DISPOSAL OF THE DEAD

Earth burial was the usual procedure followed by the occupants of the Bear Ruin in disposing of the dead. Of the forty burials uncovered, approximately one fourth were scattered indiscriminately through the village, the remainder occurring in two areas of concentration south of House 4 (Fig. 3). While there was thus some choice in location, this was by no means uniform, and disposition here largely paralleled the scattered form found in other Mogollon villages.[64] For the most part Anasazi villages of the same age show a more pronounced development of burial areas. All graves were dug as shallow pits, never more than 0.75 meter in depth and just large enough to accommodate the body. Graves were not lined, and no indications were seen to suggest the use of pole covers. In no case was a burial found below the floor of a house or in the fill of a house, hearth, or any other feature originally used for another purpose. Either these were avoided in selecting the grave site, a precaution not usually taken in the Southwest, or it may mean that, with few exceptions, houses were simultaneously occupied and that the time span of the village was relatively short. No preference of location is seen for persons of different ages, young and old having been buried side by side.

As most of the graves were dug into the clay layer where there was practically no subterranean drainage, the bones were in a very poor state of preservation. In a few small graves of youths, the bones had entirely disappeared, leaving behind only the few burial accompaniments to mark the spot (Pl. IX *a*). Adult burials were likewise often quite incomplete from advanced decay. A serious loss has thus been suffered when it comes to a study of the racial traits of the people (see pp. 132 ff.). In Figure 22 the salient points of Forestdale Phase burials as seen in the Bear Ruin are given. From this it is easy to establish the normal burial details and the degree of departure from the same where the standard practice was not adhered to.

The preferred orientation of the head was to the northeast, and only occasionally to the north or east. This predominance is also seen in burials to the south[65] in ruins of approximately the same age, and the northeasterly orientation became the rule in the Puerco drainage during the Developmental Pueblo Period, although in earlier times there appears to have been no preference.[66]

---

[64]E. W. Haury, 1936 *b*, pp. 24, 64, 91-92.
[65]E. W. Haury, 1936 *b*, pp. 24, 64.
[66]F. H. H. Roberts, Jr., 1940, p. 133.

NUMBER	BODY																		OFFERINGS								
	AGE			SEX		HEAD DIRECTION						POSITION				ARMS			KIND						WHERE		
NUMBER	INFANT	YOUTH	ADULT	MALE	FEMALE	NORTH	NORTH-EAST	EAST	SOUTH-EAST	WEST	NORTH-WEST	TIGHT FLEX	SEMI-FLEX	ON BACK	ON SIDE	AT SIDE	FOLDED	MIXED	POTTERY	STONE	TURQUOISE	PAINT	BONE	SHELL	AT HEAD	AT SHOULDER	AT SIDE
1		X																	X							X	
2			X	X		X							X	X		X			X	X						X	
3	X																		X			X					
4		X						X				X		X				X									
5		X						X				X		X				X				X			X		
6	X							X					X		X				X								X
7		X				X							X	X				X	X		X						X
8	X																		X						X		
9		X																	X								
10		X					X						X	X			X		X						X	X	
11		X						X											X						X		
12			X				X						X	X			X		X	X	X				X		
13			X	X		X							X	X			X										
14		X																	X								
15		X					X						X	X				X	X					X		X	
16		X					X						X	X					X					X		X	
17			X	X		X							X			X			X						X		X
18		X									X		X	X					X						X	X	X
19		X								X			X		X				X								X
20	X																		X								
21			X	X		X							X	X					X							X	
22			X		X		X						X	X		X			X		X		X			X	
23																			X								
24			X				X						X	X		X			X		X					X	
25			X				X							X	X				X								
26			X						X				X	X												X	
27			X								X		X	X		X			X						X		X
28			X					X					X	X		X			X		X	X			X		X
29			X					X					X						X						X		
30			X		X		X						X	X		X			X			X	X		X	X	X
31			X										X	X					X							X	
32			X																		X	X			X		
33			X				X						X	X		X			X			X	X		X	X	
34			X				X						X	X		X			X							X	X
35																			X								
36			X					X				X		X		X			X			X	X	X	X	X	X
37			X					X					X						X							X	
38			X				X						X			X			X							X	
39			X										X		X				X		X						X
40																			X								
TOT.	4	12	21	4	2	5	11	8	1	1	2	3	24	22	4	11	3	4	35	2	6	7	4	3	15	17	10

Figure 22.—A table giving the significant data on the Bear Ruin burials.

The standard body position was semiflexure, on the back, the knees drawn to one or the other side so the thighs formed a right angle with the spinal column, and the arms straight down the sides (Pl. IX b). Some variation from this is evident, as in the case of tight or complete flexion (three instances, Pl. X a), or where the body was placed on its side.

Thirty-six of the forty burials had mortuary offerings, and pottery was present in every instance except one, making it the most frequently recurring material. The range in the number of pieces was from one to seventeen, this high number occurring with the remains of a child (Burial 18, Pl. X b). Nine vessels of this number were miniatures and doubtless the child's toys. The usual position of pottery in the grave was at the head or at the shoulders of the body. Vessels were often nested, and in upright position. One exception to this was a bowl with Burial 3 which had been inverted over an incised bone tube (Pl. IX a). Breakage of pottery through earth pressure was frequent, and there was no sure evidence of the custom of "killing" pottery at the time of burial. Shell and turquoise jewelry was not common, which, together with the dearth of such materials in the excavations generally, shows a rather mild emphasis on personal ornamentation. Attention should be called to "jewels" found in a small jar with Burial 2. These consisted of four small garnets, a chip each of olivine and quartz. Other offerings of bone and stone implements and pigments were infrequent.

No evidence was seen of cremation, multiple or fractional burial, or willful disturbance of graves in early times.

In summing up the burial custom during the Forestdale Phase, characteristic was the semiflexed body, placed on its back, head to the northeast, in a shallow grave located anywhere within the inhabited area or in areas where burials were concentrated. A moderate amount of offerings, notably pottery, was customary. In these details there appear no significant differences between the pit house dwellers of the Foresdale Valley and those of adjoining areas. Both the Anasazi and the Mogollon people buried their dead and, on the whole, about in the same way. The latter, it seems, in the early horizons had not developed the habit of burying in specified areas, a feature which is reflected to some extent in the Bear Ruin. As a rule Mogollon burials are infrequently accompanied by offerings. The Anasazi were somewhat more liberal in this respect, a characteristic also noted in the Bear Ruin burials.

Plate X.—*a*, Tightly flexed burials.   *b*, Infant burial (No. 18) with seventeen crushed vessels.

POTTERY

The making of pottery was a well-established art among the residents of the Bear Ruin. They occupied a rather unique position, however, with respect to other pottery-producing tribes of their day because they produced no painted pottery whatsoever. Yet their plain, red, and smoke-blackened wares were excellent from a technical standpoint, and had they so desired they could no doubt have produced good painted ware too. This lack is the more surprising since they were getting by trade the very dissimilar painted products of three neighboring tribes, the Hohokam to the southwest, the Mogollon to the southeast, and the Anasazi to the north. These trade wares could have served both as a stimulus and as copy material.

Most of the whole or restorable vessels found in the Bear Ruin were associated with burials, a few coming from houses. Potsherds were widely and thinly spread through the sheet rubbish which covered the site, usually occurring in somewhat greater concentrations in surface depressions existing at the time of occupation. This study of pottery is based on a sherd sample of over 22,000 pieces and 126 whole or restorable vessels. The whole vessels have been identified as to type as follows:

Native
  Forestdale Smudged.. 47
  Alma Plain.. 43
  Forestdale Plain.. 11
  Forestdale Red... 7
  Miniatures (not identified as to type)..................... 10
Foreign
  Woodruff Smudged.. 4
  Lino Gray.. 2
  Woodruff Red... 1
  Alma Neck Banded... 1

The relative importance of the types believed to be truly indigenous, and therefore diagnostic of the Forestdale Phase, may be derived from the sherd sample rather than from the whole vessels found mainly with burials where the element of selection strongly entered in. Frequencies expressed in percentages are as follows:

  Alma Plain.. 78.4
  Forestdale Smudged.. 15.3
  Forestdale Plain.. 4.2
  Forestdale Red... 2.1

All other types, intrusives and those whose status is doubtful, will be duly evaluated under their respective sections.

The coil-scrape manufacturing method was employed for all local wares. As a rule vessel surfaces were well polished inside and out and firing was habitually in an oxidizing atmosphere. However, when heavy smudging was desired, a reducing atmosphere was used. The high incidence of lustrous smudged pottery in this early site is probably one of the more significant ceramic features. The firing process and the liberal iron content in the clay coupled to give a dark-toned ceramic fabric—reds, browns, and deep grays—contrasting sharply with the white and light gray wares characterizing the reducing atmosphere products of the Anasazi to the north.

ALMA PLAIN

The basic type of pottery of the Mogollon Culture, known as Alma Plain, has already been described for the San Francisco River-Mimbres River areas.[67] In the Bear Ruin this type was strongly in the majority (78 per cent) and differed so slightly from the southern Alma Plain that it seems inadvisable to recognize a new type. The following description therefore repeats in part what has already been given, but at the same time points out the differences which may be useful in its identification.

Paste

    Color.—Variable from black to gray (LIII, Neutral Gray, k)[68] to light brown (XL, 17‴, b), occasionally zoned from dark gray (interior surface) to gray or brown (outside surface); if zoned, the lighter outer color always appears as a thin veneer not exceeding one third of vessel wall thickness.

    Inclusions.—Coarse, angular, white grains of quartz.

    Texture.—Granular and friable; heavily tempered with quartz grains frequently exceeding 1.0 mm. in diameter.

    Fracture.—Irregular, oblique to vessel surface; broken surface very rough and granular.

Surface features

    Color.—Exterior gray-brown (XLVI, 13⁗, k) predominant, with extremes from dark gray (LIII, Carbon Gray, *2) to brown (XL, 17‴, b); mottling due to firing common. Interiors normally dark gray to black, occasionally light gray if heavily fired.

---

[67]E. W. Haury, 1936 a, pp. 32-34.
[68]Symbols refer to plate, color, and tone in R. Ridgway, 1912, *Color Standards and Color Nomenclature.*

Hardness.—4.0 to 5.0 (Mohs' scale).

Evenness.—Uneven and bumpy, sometimes slight ridging from polishing.

Texture.—Smooth, temper particles conspicuous but do not protrude; all surfaces lightly polished with stone, occasionally hand smoothed. There is one instance of faint incising about the neck of a small jar, possibly a copy of Alma Incised.

Luster.—Dull.

Slip.—None.

Defects.—Slight basal abrasion; crazing in heavily burnt areas and particularly noticeable on some jar interiors.

Thickness of vessel walls

Range 4.0 to 8.0 mm., average 6.0 mm.

Forms

Bowls.—Very rare, about 1 per cent of all Alma Plain produced; hemispherical (Fig. 23 a) and incurved with flared rim (Fig. 23 b); a specialized form has constriction below rim producing a groove on the outside and a sharp shoulder on the inside (Fig. 23 c); rim rounded; diameters 15.0 to 20.0 cm.

Jars.—Predominant (about 99 per cent); bodies spherical; necks may be short (Fig. 23 d) but commonly elongated with flaring rims (Fig. 23 e-g); constricted neck jars (Fig 23 h) and jars without necks (Fig. 23 i) rare and tend to have vertically compressed bodies; neck shoulder (Fig. 23 j, k) fairly common; handled and lugged jars (Fig. 23 l-n) occur in a ratio of about 1:6.

Handles.—Attached to rim and upper part of body; rod and strap types prevail (Fig. 24 a, b), composite form of two rods welded together (Fig. 24 c) also present; one case of decoration by incising (Fig. 24 d).

Lugs.—Fastened well up on body as prominent projectives, axes either vertical or horizontal and perforated vertically (Fig. 24 e-h).

Type sites

The Mogollon Village[69] and the Bear Ruin.

Range

Northern Chihuahua to the Mogollon Rim, western New Mexico south of Quemado and east-central and southeastern Arizona.

Comments

Alma Plain was the principal culinary product of the Mogollon Culture. The form of Alma Plain here

[69]E. W. Haury, 1936 a, b.

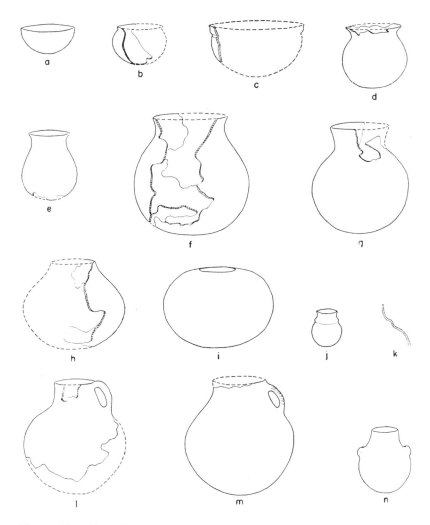

Figure 23.—Alma Plain vessel forms.

described, constituting about 78 per cent of all the
pottery produced in the Bear Ruin, differs in only
minor ways from that occurring in the heart of the
Mogollon territory. These differences are accountable
by environment and a somewhat more intense contact
with the Anasazi by the people living in the Forestdale

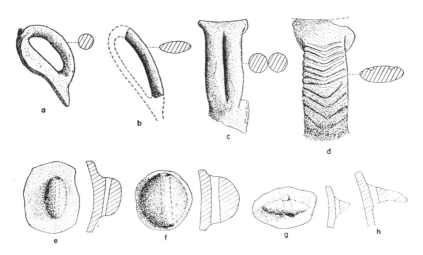

Figure 24.--Alma Plain handle and lug types.

arca than by those much farther to the south. Summarizing, the Forestdale variant of Alma Plain differs from the southern form in the following ways: the temper is coarser, more angular, and more uniform as to size; the color tends to be somewhat lighter and, on the whole, the surface is well polished; the bowl-jar ratio is approximately 1 to 100 as compared with 1 to 4. In shape, neck treatment, and sizes there are no appreciable differences, but the northern form made much greater use of handles and lugs than did the southern type. In this respect the influence of Anasazi pottery is clearly seen, and it is noticeable that in many cases in which handles or lugs were employed the vessel form is also suggestive of Anasazi pottery. While the impact of Anasazi ceramic art was considerable at Forestdale, it did not succeed in making over Alma Plain. The real tangible result was the emergence, in small amounts, of Forestdale Plain (see p. 75), a hybridization of Alma Plain and Lino Gray.

The relationship of Alma Plain to Adamana and Woodruff Browns[70] still needs to be determined, although there can be no doubt that they are fundamentally related.

_____

[70]H. P. Mera, 1934, pp. 4-6.

FORESTDALE SMUDGED

Paste

Color.—Solid gray (LIII, Carbon Gray, m) if section is examined at point in vessel where exterior is fire clouded; when exterior is red, wall shows zoning, gray, as above, merging gradually (sometimes sharply) through brown (XL, 17''', b) to red (XXVIII, 7'', i). Gray zone usually two thirds to three fourths of vessel wall thickness.

Texture.—Granular and friable; heavily tempered with fine, rounded quartz grains.

Fracture.—Irregular and ragged, often oblique to surface; fractured surface rough.

Surface features

Color.—Interiors uniformly black up to and usually including rim. Exteriors heavily clouded black, especially about rim where tongues may extend toward bottom, suggesting vessels were fired inverted; isolated clouds occur occasionally toward bottom from contact with fuel; unclouded areas range from brown (XL, 13''', i) to red-brown (XXVIII, 7'', i) which predominates and was apparently the color desired.

Hardness.—3.0 to 4.0 (Mohs' scale).

Evenness.—Interiors smoothly planed; exteriors often somewhat bumpy from imperfect planing.

Texture.—Smooth, temper rarely shows on surfaces; interior highly polished, the marks showing only faintly; exteriors, polishing not as complete as in interiors, leaving conspicuous marks; no regularity in direction of polishing.

Luster.—Lustrous.

Slip.—None; fine particles of clay brought to surface by polishing.

Defects.—Abrasion on bottoms and exteriors often lightly eroded leaving a sandy surface.

Thickness of vessel walls

Range 4.0 to 8.0 mm., average 5.0 mm.

Forms

Bowls only;[71] mainly hemispherical (Fig. 25 a) sometimes running to deep forms (Fig. 25 b); bowls of outcurved (Fig. 25 c), flared (Fig. 25 d), and recurved (Fig. 25 e) forms rare, the latter occurring in small (7.0 to 10.0 cm.) vessels only. Rounded rims are

---

[71]That jars were occasionally made is suggested by one found in the White Mound Village, Gila Pueblo collection.

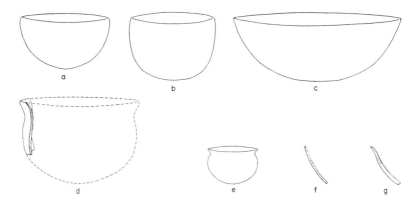

Figure 25.—Forestdale Smudged bowl and rim forms.

standard with slight thinning of vessel wall (Fig. 25 *f*),
tapered rims infrequent (Fig. 25 *g*). Diameter range:
7.0 to 22.0 cm., average 15.0 cm.
Type site
　　　　Bear Ruin (Arizona P: 16: 1).
Range
　　　　The Forestdale area with a strong showing in the
White Mound Village.[72] Intrusively it occurs widely
in late Basketmaker III sites and at Snaketown in Gila
Butte Phase and later deposits.[73]
Comments
　　　　Approximately 15 per cent of all pottery produced in
the Bear Ruin was of this type, being second in prominence. In all particulars except firing it is the same
as Forestdale Red. It was fired mouth down, probably
in green fuel, thus creating a reducing atmosphere on
the vessels' interiors to allow the carbon to be depos-
ited. The exteriors tend to be somewhat redder in
color than the Forestdale Smudged type recovered by
Gila Pueblo in the White Mound Village. Compared
with Mera's Woodruff Smudged,[74] apparently an older
and probably the ancestral type, Forestdale Smudged
is thinner, much finer in paste, and more varied as to
shape.
　　　　These two types undoubtedly represent the oldest

---

[72]Gila Pueblo collection.
[73]H. S. Gladwin *et al.*, 1937, pp. 214-15.
[74]H. P. Mera, 1934, pp. 6-7.

smudged wares in the Southwest, created by the northern contingent of the Mogollon Culture.

Forestdale Smudged persisted locally into later phases in diminishing amounts and was finally transformed into a corrugated type with white outside decoration known as McDonald Corrugated,[75] the smudging technique of the Mogollon thus leaving its heavy imprint on the later Anasazi pottery.

FORESTDALE PLAIN

Paste
   Color.—Highly irregular, ranging from dark gray (LIII, Neutral Gray, *m*) to brown (XL, 13''', *b*); zoning occasionally seen, widths variable, gray toward interior and brown toward exterior of vessel wall.
   Texture.—Granular, somewhat friable; heavily tempered with coarse angular quartz grains (up to 1.0 mm. in diameter); temper visible on surface.
   Fracture.—Irregular and ragged, often oblique to surface; fractured surface very granular.
Surface features
   Color.—Commonly gray (LIII, Neutral Gray, *k*) ranging to light brown (XL, 17''', *b*); variable on individual specimens, depending on extent of fire clouding.
   Hardness.—4.0 (Mohs' scale).
   Evenness.—Very uneven, marked undulations on both surfaces from imperfect scraping.
   Texture.—Interiors usually show closely spaced but prominent wiping marks; occasionally lightly smoothed with hand. Exteriors rough and pebbly, hand smoothing marks sometimes visible, but pebble polishing never seen.
   Luster.—Dull.
   Slip.—None.
   Defects.—None evident.
Thickness of vessel walls
         3.0 to 8.0 mm.; average 5.0 mm.
Forms
         Mostly small vessels. Largest in collection of ten whole specimens is 15.0 cm. in diameter; average 10.0 cm.
   Bowls.—Rare, but both outcurved and incurved types occur (Fig. 26 *a*, *b*); rims rounded and irregular.

---

[75] H. S. Colton and L. L. Hargrave, 1937, p. 61.

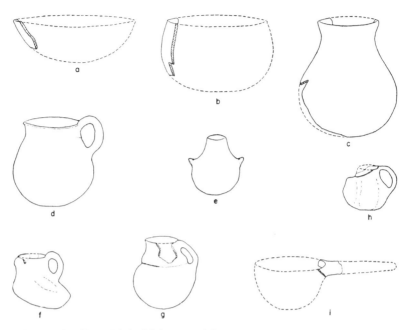

Figure 26.—Forestdale Plain vessel forms.

Jars.—Bodies spherical with elongated necks tending
   toward small mouths (Fig. 26 c), occasionally with
   handles (Fig. 26 d).
Eccentric.—Vessels of odd form common, usually with
   handles or lugs (Fig. 25 e-h); handles usually single
   rod but may be composite (two rod); lugs vertically
   perforated; bowl-and-handle variety of ladle (Fig. 25
   i) present but rare.
Type site
      Bear Ruin (Arizona P: 16: 1).
Range
      Forestdale area; a few sherds have been seen north
   as far as Woodruff.
Comments
      Forestdale Plain, while constituting only approxi-
   mately 4 per cent of all the pottery produced in the
   Bear Ruin, is very illuminating in that it clearly represents a fusion of two ceramic styles, Lino Gray of the
   Anasazi and Alma Plain of the Mogollon group. This
   hybridization in pottery assists materially, along with
   other elements, in arriving at the conclusion that a

blending of two cultural streams in the Bear Ruin must be recognized. Specifically, Forestdale Plain is somewhat stronger in its Anasazi characters than in the elements of the other contributing culture. The scoring of vessel interiors, the gritty quartz temper, lack of polishing, smallness of vessel size and shapes, often with handles,[76] are all attributable to the northern ceramic tradition, while the dark paste and oxidized firing atmosphere used in the manufacturing process bring in elements seen in Alma Plain.

FORESTDALE RED

Paste

Color.—Vessel walls in cross section normally show zoning; inner zone gray to black changing abruptly to red-brown (XXVIII, 7″, *i*) toward surfaces giving the false impression of a thick slip. Red zones somewhat variable in width, depending on firing intensity, but usually these are one third or less the thickness of vessel wall.

Texture.—Granular, friable, heavily tempered with very fine, angular quartz grains.

Fracture.—Irregular, often oblique to surface; fractured surface rough.

Surface features

Color.—Normally red-brown (XXVIII, 7″, *i*), ranging through brown (XLVI, 13‴′, *i*) to black in fire-clouded areas; clouds always present on exteriors where vessel rested in normal position on fuel.

Hardness.—3.0 to 4.0 (Mohs' scale).

Evenness.—Bowl interiors evenly planed, exteriors sometimes slightly ridged from imperfect polishing. Jar interiors and exteriors even. Dimpling lacking.

Texture.—Smooth; temper not conspicuous on surface; all surfaces polished in both bowls and jars; polishing striations faintly visible, indiscriminate.

Luster.—Lustrous.

Slip.—None. Clay contained unusually heavy pigment content to give paste rich color.[77]

Defects.—Abrasion on bottoms common.

----

[76]H. S. Colton and L. L. Hargrave, 1937, pp. 191-92; E. H. Morris, 1927, Figs. 16 and 17.

[77]Fragments of an unfired Forestdale Red vessel, found in House 5, when softened produced a paste which readily stained the fingers.

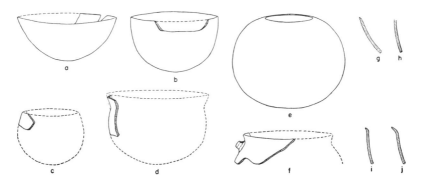

Figure 27.—Forestdale Red vessel and rim forms.

Thickness of vessel walls
    Range 3.0 to 5.0 mm., average 4.0 mm.
Forms
    Bowls.—Outcurved and hemispherical types predominate
        (Fig. 27 a, b); incurved and flared forms rare (Fig. 27
        c, d); diameters from 5.0 to 25.0 cm.; rims slightly
        tapered or rounded as a rule (Fig. 27 g, h) but lips and
        flares occasionally showing (Fig. 27 i, j).
    Jars.—Spherical rimless and rimmed forms (Fig. 27 e, f).
        Lugs used occasionally; consist of clay pellets stuck to
        vessel walls and perforated vertically.
    Bowl-jar ratio.—50 to 1.
Type Site
    Bear Ruin (Arizona P: 16:1).
Range
    Currently known chiefly from the Forestdale area.
    Sporadic examples have been seen in White Mound Phase
    contexts on the Puerco and in Gila Butte Phase associations
    of the Hohokam near Globe.[78]
Comments
    This type appears to be basically related to San Francisco
    Red[79] which was not only in existence longer but had a
    much wider distribution to the south. It differs from San
    Francisco Red in having a much softer, finer tempered
    paste, in lacking a slip, finger dimpling, and in being a
    somewhat lighter shade of red. Similarities, on the other
    hand, are seen in an almost identical range in shapes, sizes,
    and in the degree of polishing.
        Woodruff Red, of the Petrified Forest area,[80] a very close

[78]I. Vickrey, in preparation.
[79]E. W. Haury, 1936 a, pp. 28-31.
[80]H. P. Mera, 1934, p. 6.

and possibly somewhat earlier relative, is slipped, less polished, and coarser tempered, characteristics which allow ready segregation from Forestdale Red.

Forestdale Red is identical with Forestdale Smudged in paste and shape, differing only in the lack of the smudging and in the amount produced. Approximately 2 per cent of all Bear Ruin pottery was of this type.

INTRUSIVE POTTERY

The foregoing types are all considered to have been native products of the Bear Ruin. In addition there were found sherds and a few whole pieces representing pottery made elsewhere which eventually reached the village through exchange. Since one important means of determining contact between cultural groups is on the basis of intrusive pottery, it becomes clear that such material is highly significant. This is particularly true in the Bear Ruin. Because of its early date, the foreign pottery not only shows that other groups, distinct at least in their ceramic arts, were in existence in the seventh century but also that the Forestdale people were in more or less direct contact with them. The following types, assigned to their respective cultural authors, were present:

	Sherds	Restorable vessels
Mogollon Culture		
Woodruff Smudged	90	4
Woodruff Red	23	1
Adamana Brown	9	..
Alma Scored	19	..
Alma Incised	17	..
Alma Neck Banded	2	1
San Francisco Red	8	..
Mogollon Red-on-brown	9	..
Anasazi Culture		
Lino Gray	205	2
Lino Black-on-gray	4	..
White Mound Black-on-white	67	..
Lino Smudged	2	..
Late types (Pueblo I to III)	115	..
Hohokam Culture		
Gila Plain	36	..
Gila Butte Red-on-buff	6	..
Patayan Culture		
Acquarius Brown	3	..

Mogollon Culture

Woodruff Smudged and Woodruff Red.[81]—These two types have tentatively been regarded as intrusives, since Mera has shown them to be at home in the Petrified Forest area near Holbrook. On the other hand they are related through technology to Forestdale Smudged and Forestdale Red which appear to be somewhat more evolved forms. It is quite possible that in the Bear Ruin there was an early occupation level, characterized by the Woodruff types, thus accounting for the sherds recovered, but excavations failed to produce evidence to support this view. Because the Forestdale types can be directly linked with Mogollon ceramics and the Woodruff forms, there is some indication that the Mogollon pottery complex had spread at least by 700 well into the Anasazi domain. Whether the Woodruff types were directly ancestral to the Forestdale forms or whether they represent a collateral development, being retarded technologically because of their marginal position, remains to be shown.

Adamana Brown.[82]—This type, also at home in the Petrified Forest region, was not strongly represented in the Bear Ruin. Its painted ware associate in that area was Lino Black-on-gray. There can be no doubt that Adamana Brown is an early type, and its occurrence in the Forestdale Valley may be taken as added evidence for the age of the first occupation there.

Alma Scored and Alma Incised.[83]—These two Mogollon types (Pl. XI *a-d*), derivatives of Alma Plain, occur well to the south in Mogollon villages.

Alma Neck Banded.[84]—Alma Neck Banded is represented in the Bear Ruin by a few sherds and one small pot (Pl. XI *i*). This type raises the interesting question as to the priority of the neck banding technique exemplified so well in Kana-a Gray[85]—that is, whether this treatment is older in Anasazi or in Mogollon ceramics. In the Mimbres Branch it was strongly present in the San Francisco Phase[86] of the Harris Village and present to a lesser extent in the Georgetown Phase of the same site. It must also be considered as

[81]H. P. Mera, 1934, pp. 6-7. Bear Ruin sherds identified by Mera. See also H. S. Colton and L. L. Hargrave, 1937, pp. 58-60.
[82]*Ibid.*, pp. 4-5.
[83]E. W. Haury, 1936 *a*, pp. 38, 40.
[84]*Ibid.*, p. 35.
[85]H. S. Colton and L. L. Hargrave, 1937, pp. 195-96.
[86]E. W. Haury, 1936 *b*, p. 99.

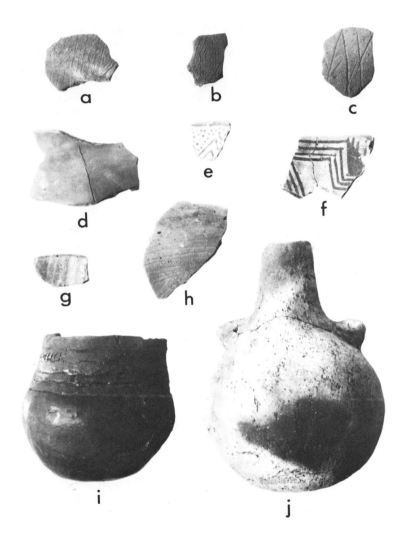

Plate XI.—Intrusive pottery found in the Bear Ruin: *a, b,* Alma Scored; *c, d,* Alma Incised; *e,* Lino Black-on-gray; *f,* White Mound Black-on-white; *g, h,* Gila Butte Red-on-buff; *i,* Alma Neck Banded; *j,* Lino Gray. Diameter of *j,* 12.5 cm.

present in the postulated San Lorenzo Phase[87] which falls chronologically between the Georgetown and San Francisco

---

[87]Confirmed by E. B. Sayles in recent excavations for Gila Pueblo.

phases.   Sayles' excavations in the Cave Creek site[88] in
southeastern Arizona have also shown what appears to be
the beginning of the neck banding idea in a phase which is
almost certainly ancestral to the Georgetown Phase and
probably contemporary with the SU site.

In the Anasazi area, neck banding is usually considered to
be a Pueblo I diagnostic, although Morris[89] finds it occasionally present in late La Plata Basketmaker III.   In the Whitewater district of eastern Arizona, Roberts[90] finds neck banding in the Developmental Pueblo or Pueblo I stage, and in
the White Mound Ruin of late Basketmaker III date only a
few sherds of this type were found.   The time for this type is
generally given as from 700 to 900, based on tree-ring
calculations.

The northern and southern chronologies must now be
brought together.   To do this the evidence of tree-rings and
cross-finds of pottery may be relied on.   The presence of
Mogollon Red-on-brown in the Bear Ruin suggests that the
Forestdale Phase was contemporary with the San Francisco
Phase, but since the beginning of this phase is put at 700
and the Bear Ruin dates are in the late 600's, it is a safe assumption that the Forestdale Phase also overlapped the end
of the San Lorenzo Phase.   Tree-ring dates for the San
Francisco Phase tell only a part of the story, as those available appear to represent the end of the phase,[91] about 900.
Yet the presence of White Mound Black-on-white in the San
Francisco Phase deposits of the Mogollon Village and also
in the Bear Ruin, in spite of its seventh century tree-ring
dates, shows that these two coexisted in part.   Further, the
White Mound Phase may be assigned to a period contemporary with the Forestdale Phase because of a mutual interchange of pottery and general agreement in dates in the late
600's.[92]   The White Mound Phase was apparently a late
southern variant of the Basketmaker complex.   Putting this
together in the form of a chart and superimposing thereon
wedges representing the introduction and rise of the neck
banding technique (Fig. 28), it will readily be seen where
the priority lies.   Even allowing for some errors in the correlation, there seems to be no other alternative but to look

---

[88]In preparation.
[89]E. H. Morris, 1939, Pl. 183.
[90]F. H. H. Roberts, Jr., 1940, pp. 19-21.
[91]E. W. Haury, 1936 b, p. 116.
[92]Many of the White Mound Ruin dates fell in the 700's and as late as
802 (Haury, 1938, p. 3).

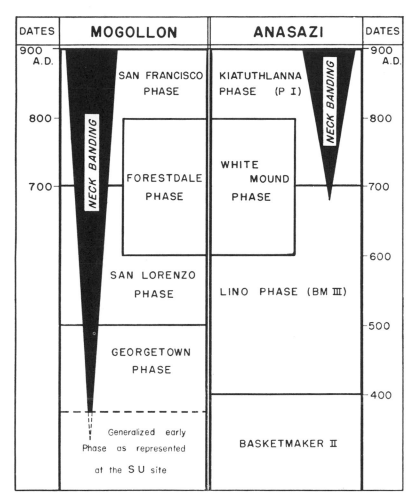

DATES	MOGOLLON	ANASAZI	DATES

Figure 28.—A chart showing the relative time of appearance of neck banding in the Mogollon (Mimbres Branch) and Anasazi cultures.

upon the Mogollon Culture as the originator of neck banding whence it eventually spread to the Anasazi. That other pottery treatments also spread is highly likely, as will be discussed later (p. 93).

San Francisco Red.[93]—Because of its very long life, San Francisco Red is not a good medium for establishing cross-

---

[93]E. W. Haury, 1936 *a*, pp. 28-31.

dates. Sherds of this type in the Bear Ruin, some showing the characteristic dimpling of the exterior, may be taken as further evidence of the contact maintained between Forest-dale and more southerly Mogollon territories.

Mogollon Red-on-brown.[94]—A few of the sherds of this type conform in every way to the Mogollon Red-on-brown of the Mogollon Village, while some others are strongly sug-gestive of San Lorenzo Red-on-brown.[95] Precise identifica-tion is not possible because of the small size and eroded con-dition of the sherds.

Anasazi Culture

Lino Gray.[96]—In sherd form this type was the most abun-dant of all intrusives, and there are also two complete vessels in the collection. Its age on the whole may be given as be-fore 750 A.D., agreeing with the tree-ring dates from the Bear Ruin. The abundance of this material is indicative of the close contact that was maintained with the Anasazi, a rela-tionship borne out further by the emergence in the Forest-dale Valley of Forestdale Plain which was a hybridization of Lino Gray and Alma Plain. It is interesting to note here that Kana-a Gray with neck banding was not found.

Lino Black-on-gray.[97]—This type (Pl. XI *e*) is a criterion for Basketmaker III and an associate of Lino Gray. It prob-ably did not survive as late as the type listed below, White Mound Black-on-white. If this is true, then there may be some indication that in the Bear Ruin there was a phase whose ceramic components were Lino Black-on-gray and Woodruff Smudged and Red, a combination which existed in the Petrified Forest as previously suggested. It must be pointed out again that investigation failed to produce con-crete evidence of this.

White Mound Black-on-white.[98]—White Mound Black-on-white (Pl. XI *f*) is well represented as an intrusive type in the Bear Ruin. This might be anticipated from the abun-dance of Lino Gray. The type site, the White Mound Village on the Puerco River, yielded tree-ring dates from the late 600's to 800 A.D., the latter appearing to be associated with Pueblo I remains.

Lino Smudged.[99]—This type was apparently never very

---

[94]*Ibid.,* **pp.** 10-17.
[95]*Ibid.,* pp. 6-9.
[96]H. S. Colton and L. L. Hargrave, 1937, pp. 191-92.
[97]*Ibid.,* pp. 194-95.
[98]H. S. Gladwin, in preparation.
[99]F. Connolly, 1940, p. 130.

common. Some geographic spread for it may be recognized however, as sherds have been seen in a Basketmaker III site in the Jeddito Valley. The paste is that of Lino Gray but the interiors of bowls were both polished and smudged in the characteristic Forestdale Smudged fashion. The significance of this lies in the fact that here is further evidence of the fusion of two ceramic traditions.

Late Anasazi types.—It is clear that the majority of the sherds representing types dating from Pueblo I to Pueblo III did not reach the Bear Ruin during its occupancy. They may be considered as having come from later occupations adjoining this village. A Pueblo I site lies just across the creek to the northwest and a few hundred meters to the southwest is a combined pit house and pueblo site (Arizona P: 16: 2) occupied from Pueblo I to III times. These sherds may therefore be eliminated as having any bearing on the problem at hand.

Hohokam Culture

Gila Plain.[100]—The Gila Plain sherds recovered in the Bear Ruin are typical in every way of the paddle-and-anvil-made wares of the Hohokam. They may have come from either the Gila Basin or the Globe area where similar material has been recovered in Colonial Period Hohokam sites.[101] Because Gila Plain varied so little from phase to phase, it is not possible to allocate the Bear Ruin intrusives to any one phase.

Gila Butte Red-on-buff.[102]—The six sherds of this type occurred in unmistakable Forestdale Phase contexts. They are typical in every way of Gila Basin material (Pl. XI *g, h*), several showing the specific form of scoring seen on the painted pottery of the Gila Butte Phase.

This pottery is of more than passing interest. It is evidence on the one hand that the occupants of the Bear Ruin were in contact with the Hohokam during Forestdale Phase times, a fact which goes a long way toward explaining the strong Hohokam flavor in the designs of the first indigenous black-on-white of the area in the succeeding phase;[103] and on the other hand it has provided much needed evidence corroborating the dating of the Gila Butte Phase at Snaketown.

In its studies at Snaketown, Gila Pueblo judged the age of the Gila Butte Phase to be about from 500 to 700 A.D. and roughly contemporary with Basketmaker III of the An-

---

[100]H. S. Gladwin *et al.*, 1937, pp. 205-11.
[101]I. Vickrey, in preparation.
[102]H. S. Gladwin *et al.*, 1937, pp. 185-89.
[103]E. W. Haury, in preparation.

asazi.[104] This assignment, together with the dating of phases earlier than Gila Butte, has been questioned for several reasons. one being the failure of excavators to find Hohokam sherds in early northern sites. The Hohokam material from the Bear Ruin seems now effectively to answer that question insofar as the Gila Butte Phase is concerned. Both the presence of dated Anasazi intrusives in this site and the local tree-ring dates themselves in every way substantiate the 500 to 700 dating of the Gila Butte Phase. This means further that while the Anasazi were still in the first stage of making fired pottery, the ceramic history of the Hohokam had already passed through four stages of development.

Patayan Culture

Acquarius Brown.[105]—The Patayan Culture of northwestern Arizona is, as yet, not very well known. Acquarius Brown is one of the ceramic components of the Cerbat Branch of this culture and is believed to have been made from before 750 to about 950 A.D. It is found in the region of the Acquarius Cliffs in Mohave County, Arizona. Little may be said about this type except that it provides evidence of contact between the Forestdale area and northwestern Arizona.

Discussion

The absence of painted pottery in the Bear Ruin and no manifest internal changes in the types present during the occupancy of the site combine to make a simple ceramic picture for the Forestdale Phase. Yet simplicity in no way implies inferior products as has been seen in the foregoing description of the the types.

On its objective characters, this pottery must be accepted as a relative of the oxidized brown and red ceramics of southern New Mexico and Arizona, assignable in the main to Mogollon authorship. Shape analogies and technological treatments such as polishing and the production of red pottery as a companion of brown ware are all southern characteristics in early horizons. Two significant departures, however, are to be noted. The first of these is the absence of painted pottery, placing the Forestdale area in the unique position of being an island within a vast area where at least three basic types of painted pottery were being made, Lino Black-on-gray of the Anasazi, San Lorenzo and Mogollon

[104]H. S. Gladwin *et al.*, 1937, p. 216.
[105]H. S. Colton, 1939 *a*, p. 10; 1939 b, p. 24.

Red-on-browns of the Mogollon, and Gila Butte Red-on-buff of the Hohokam. It seems highly improbable that this lack is to be explained on the basis of a lag owing to the marginal position of the Forestdale people. It is much more likely to have been a matter of cultural preference. The second is the emphasis on smudging bowl interiors, a process used nowhere else in the Southwest so extensively as here during the seventh and eighth centuries.

It is appropriate here to discuss several aspects of southwestern ceramics on which the excavations in the Bear Ruin have shed some light. Listed in the order of presentation these are: (1) the status of smudging, (2) the individualities of Anasazi and Mogollon ceramics, (3) the influence of Mogollon on Anasazi ceramics, and (4) what intrusive pottery tells.

The status of smudging.—Forestdale Smudged brings to the fore the interesting problem of the origin and genesis of smudging in the Southwest. In early horizons from the Anasazi to the Hohokam, occasional highly polished, lustrous black vessels and sherds have been found.[106] These occurrences were never satisfactorily explained. In some instances the material was recognized as foreign, but the exact source was unknown. In other instances it was interpreted as an indigenous product of the site or sites where it was found without wholly accounting for the tremendous technological difference which separated it from its associated and more prevalent types. It now begins to appear certain that this technique of smudging, coupled with the high polishing of pottery, occurred most abundantly in the mountainous area below the Mogollon Rim, ranging from the Forestdale region southeast to some undetermined point, and that it was present at a time comparable to Basketmaker III when neither the Anasazi nor the contemporary Hohokam was producing pottery which in any way resembled the smudged black.

Reviewing the evidence for the time of origin, one may resort to indications coming from both within the area where it was supposed to be at home and from the sites lying outside of this area where it occurs as an intrusive. The dates from the Bear Ruin establish a seventh century occupation which doubtless lasted also into the eighth century. In the Harris and Mogollon villages, smudging on the basic Alma Plain type was very rare, but its occurrence there, possibly as an accidental or borrowed feature, was as early as the

---

[106]E. H. Morris, 1927, p. 186; F. H. H. Roberts, Jr., 1929, pp. 108, 117-18; 1931, pp. 117-18; 1940, pp. 14-15; H. S. Gladwin *et al.*, 1937, p. 215.

Georgetown Phase.   In the Reserve section of New Mexico, smudging appears to have come in rather strongly during Pueblo II or the Reserve Phase[107] and was well established by Pueblo III in Nesbitt's Reserve Plain.[108]   At the White Mound site on the Puerco River, Gila Pueblo found Forest-dale Smudged occurring as companion ware of Lino Gray and White Mound Black-on-white, dating principally from the eighth century.   This suggests that smudging did not appear in Basketmaker III of the Puerco region until shortly prior to or just after the beginning of the occupation of the White Mound Village, probably in the late 600's or early 700's.   In the Petrified Forest area Mera recognized several complementary types known as Woodruff Brown, Woodruff Red. and Woodruff Smudged.[109]   The latter is said to be rather uncommon, but the complex is placed chronologically before 800 A.D.   From all appearances one must recognize a generic relationship between the White Mound and Petrified Forest smudged types.   Mera's work has shown further that Wood-ruff Smudged was preceded by Adamana Brown,[110] which dates apparently from before 700 and which did not have a smudged companion ware.   Once again it seems as though the smudging technique in that area did not occur much before 700.

To the west in the vicinity of Flagstaff smudging was common, but on the whole the types were fairly late, the oldest being Rio de Flag Smudged dating in the ninth to eleventh centuries.[111]

In the Hohokam area, although intrusive pottery types occurred in all phases defined by Gila Pueblo at Snaketown, smudged pottery of an alien source appears for the first time in Gila Butte Phase contexts, the first phase in the Colonial Period.[112]   The dates of this phase were estimated to have extended roughly from 500 to 700 A.D.   On the whole this harmonizes once more with the evidence for the age of smudging so far derived from northern sources.

In the timber belt along the southern edge of the Colorado Plateau, smudging was so strong in early sites that one may regard this area as the actual homeland of the technique. From this center it is possible to recognize a series of radia-tions of the smudging method which resulted in the produc-

---

[107]W. and H. S. Gladwin, 1934, Fig. 3.
[108]P. H. Nesbitt, 1938, p. 139.
[109]H. P. Mera, 1934, p. 6.
[110]*Ibid.*, pp. 4-6.
[111]H. S. Colton and L. L. Hargrave, 1937, p. 162.
[112]H. S. Gladwin *et al.*, 1937, p. 214.

tion of many well-known kinds of pottery. Pueblo II and Pueblo III ruins in the Puerco (west) and Chaco Canyon areas produced small amounts of a rather thick pottery with smudged interiors and mottled brown-red to red exteriors. In the main the clearest red exteriors were the latest.[113] These forms must be regarded as certain derivatives from the parent type, Forestdale Smudged.

At Flagstaff a host of types developed after the initial type, Rio de Flag Smudged, made its appearance,[114] and below the Mogollon Rim in the Tonto Basin, Tonto and Salado Reds evolved in the twelfth and thirteenth centuries.[115] Gila Red,[116] apparently an offshoot of this complex, became dominant somewhat later and after 1200 A.D. spread south and west just prior to the Salado invasion of the desert country to become a very common brand of pottery through a large part of the region occupied by the Hohokam.

East in the Rio Grande drainage, roughly from Albuquerque south to San Marcial, there was another derivative, Los Lunas Smudged, dating from Pueblo II times.[117]

Whether the polished black of Chihuahua, Ramos Black,[118] is to be considered as a part of this same pattern may be a debatable point, but since Mogollon Culture traits have been recognized as extending into Chihuahua,[119] and in the absence of contradictory evidence this may be assumed.

A historic survival of the smudging technique may be represented in Kapo Black of the Rio Grande.[120]

This is in no way intended to be a complete catalogue of smudged pottery or an effort to trace all the genealogical links of smudged types.[121] Reference to the maps in Figure 29 will portray graphically the ever widening distribution of the smudging technique centering originally in the east-central Arizona and west-central New Mexico focus. It needs to be pointed out again that smudging was not habitually employed over the whole of the Mogollon domain, since in the southern part an all-over red seems to have been preferred. If the northern group of Mogollon people is to be

[113]F. H. H. Roberts, Jr., 1931, p. 118.
[114]H. S. Colton and L. L. Hargrave, 1937, pp. 52-53, 63-64, 162-65.
[115]*Ibid.*, pp. 65, 166.
[116]W. and H. S. Gladwin, 1930, p. 12; H. S. Colton and L. L. Hargrave, 1937, pp. 176-77.
[117]H. P. Mera, 1935, pp. 28-29.
[118]E. B. Sayles, 1936 *a*, pp. 43-44.
[119]E. B. Sayles, 1936 *b*.
[120]H. P. Mera, 1939, pp. 14-15.
[121]This has been fully covered by F. Connolly, 1940.

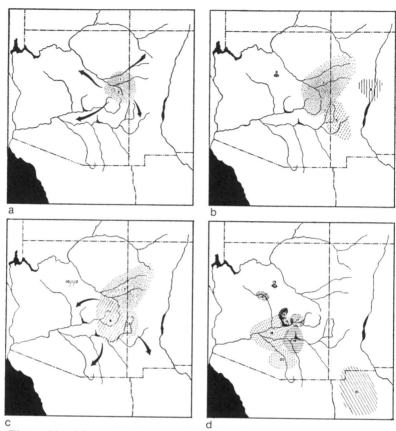

Figure 29.—Maps of Arizona and neighboring states showing approximately the point of origin and the subsequent spread of the smudging
technique as represented by the more significant pottery types during:
a, 600-800 A.D.—Types: *1,* Woodruff Smudged; *2,* Forestdale Smudged.
Intrusions to adjoining areas, notably Flagstaff, Chaco, upper Gila,
and Gila Basin.   *b,* 800-1000 A.D.—Types: *3,* Forestdale Smudged
derivatives including corrugated forms; *4,* Rio de Flag Smudged; *5,*
Reserve Smudged; *6,* Los Lunas Smudged.   *c,* 1000-1200 A.D.—Types:
7, Forestdale Smudged derivatives; *8,* McDonald Corrugated; *9,* Reserve Fillet Rim; *10,* Winona Red; *11,* Sunset Red; *12,* Elden Corrugated.   Intrusions primarily south and west.   *d,* 1200-1400 A.D.—Types:
13, Turkey Hill Red; *14,* Tuzigoot Red; *15,* Tonto Red; *16,* Salado Red;
17, Cibecue Polychrome; *18,* Gila Red; *19,* San Carlos Red-on-brown;
20, Tanque Verde Red-on-brown; *21,* Ramos Black.   Note shift to
south.

credited with a specific contribution to southwestern ceramics, it is the technique of smudging.

Individualities of Anasazi and Mogollon ceramics.—Even those who have been most reluctant to accept the Mogollon Culture per se have been willing to recognize that pottery of the Mogollon area was different from that of the adjoining area to the north. The outline below summarizes these differences at a date of about 700 A.D. Hohokam pottery has been included by way of adding another point for comparison.

	Anasazi	Mogollon	Hohokam
Firing	reducing	oxidizing	oxidizing
Manufacture	coil-scrape	coil-scrape	paddle-and-anvil
Temper	rounded quartz	volcanics, feldspar (crushed)	granites, mica schist, volcanics
Texturing	rare	common	on painted ware only
Neck banding	not common	common	absent
Smudging	absent	common in northern part	absent
Polishing	rare to absent	prevalent	uncommon
Slip	none	yes	wash[122] (slight use)
Paint color	black	red	red
Paint material	mineral and carbon	iron	iron
Paint treatment	not polished over decoration	polished over decoration	not polished over decoration
Decoration	unit designs, open fields	all-over	all-over
Shapes	large- & small-mouth vessels	mostly large-mouth vessels	large-mouth vessels
Eccentric forms	common	rare to absent	present
Handles and lugs	common	few	rare to absent

Apart from these more obvious differences something may also be learned from the distributions of certain seventh to ninth century types. In the following brief survey four sites have been selected, all of which have been excavated within the past few years. They are located in a general north-south line running from northeastern Arizona to southwestern New Mexico. The results of this analysis have been combined in Figure 30.[123]

Beginning with the White Mound site, located in the Puerco drainage of the west, there is basically a late Basketmaker III horizon with Lino Gray and White Mound Black-

---

[122]An arbitrary distinction between a slip and a wash is drawn on the basis of subsequent treatment. A slip is polished, a wash is not.

[123]It will be interesting to add here Peabody Museum's Site 264 (J. O. Brew, 1941, pp. 42-44) in the Jeddito Valley when the report on this ruin has been completed.

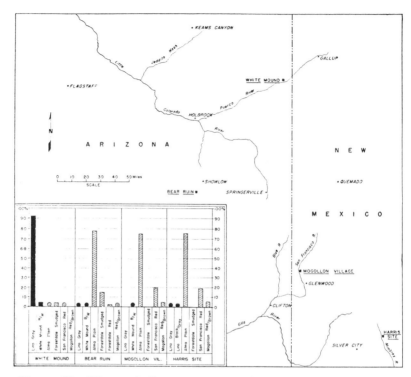

Figure 30.—Map and diagram of approximate percentages showing changes in pottery types of four sites ranging from nearly pure Basketmaker of the Anasazi to pure San Francisco Phase horizons of the Mogollon. Solid percentage columns represent Anasazi types; hatched percentage columns represent Mogollon types; dots indicate presence or less than 1 per cent.

on-white as the native pottery types. Almost as abundant as the latter, however, is Forestdale Smudged[124] which quite certainly represents a sharp increase of this type over what one would expect to find in ruins of the same time level still farther to the north. The process of finishing, the color, and paste of Forestdale Smudged in the White Mound Village are so completely at variance with the native wares that it is recognized as having been produced elsewhere.

Moving southwest 80 miles into the Forestdale Valley to the Bear Ruin, White Mound Black-on-white and Lino Gray occur very weakly as intrusives with native pottery consist-

---

[124]Information kindly supplied by Gila Pueblo.

ing of Forestdale Smudged and Alma Plain. Jogging back southeast for 100 miles is the Mogollon Village where Alma Plain occurs dominantly with the polished San Francisco Red as a companion form. Here White Mound Black-on-white occurs as a very rare intrusive. The final step, 65 miles to the southeast, carries one into the Mimbres Valley to the Harris site where orthodox White Mound Black-on-white was completely lacking.

Thus one passes from a region in the north where Basketmaker is pure with few foreign types present to an intermediate area where there is an obvious mixture of Basketmaker with non-Basketmaker, and finally to the south where Basketmaker pottery is intrusive, all but disappearing in the extreme south. In reversing the situation it will be necessary first of all to recognize the fact that San Francisco Red and Forestdale Smudged are genetically related, the former being southern, the latter northern, in the Mogollon territory. The principal difference lies in the fact that one has a red, the other a black interior—an achievement brought about by a rather simple trick in firing. This relationship is supported by the presence of Forestdale Red in the timber area which is the local equivalent of the southern San Francisco Red.

Now, in tracing these types south to north, there is a progressive diminution in their frequency of occurrence. The types are strong as far north as the Mogollon Rim, representing approximately 15 to 20 per cent of the whole ceramic output. This value is reduced appreciably by the time one reaches the Puerco River where the types already occur in a foreign complex; and then there is rapid reduction as one moves north to the Jeddito and Lukachukai areas, where one finds only an occasional sherd. This may be taken to mean that there were two centers from which ceramic elements radiated toward each other, losing themselves in alien cultures as their own centers were left behind.

Influence of Mogollon on Anasazi ceramics.—In the discussion of Alma Neck Banded (p.212) it was implied that certain technological treatments originally known to Mogollon potters may have been adopted by the Anasazi. The acceptance of such a possibility must, first of all, be preceded by the recognition that there were several ceramic traditions. An effort to strengthen this contention has just been made. Secondly, it must also be recognized that the history of Mogollon and Hohokam pottery is longer than that of the Anasazi—i.e., that fired pottery was well established among the former two groups and had passed through several developmental stages before the Anasazi began producing

fired pottery about 400 A.D.   That this was the case seems
clear from recent work in Hohokam and Mogollon sites.   The
Hohokam may be eliminated from this discussion on the
grounds that the effect of their pottery was not felt to any
extent until after 700 A.D. and that a far greater intimacy of
contact is shown between the pottery of the Mogollon and the
Anasazi.

One of the transitions in Anasazi pottery which has always
been difficult to explain lies between Basketmaker III and
Pueblo I.   Basketmaker III pottery types, wherever they
occur, both painted and plain, are characterized by a rough-
ness of surface.   Mogollon types, on the other hand, even
including Alma Plain, habitually show a well-polished
surface which reaches its greatest excellence in such specific
types as Forestdale Smudged and San Francisco Red.   Polishing, in other words, is the dominant theme in Mogollon pottery which before 700 A.D. was not shared by either the
Anasazi or Hohokam.   One of the striking additions to the
Anasazi ceramic complex at the beginning of Pueblo I is the
adoption of a polishing technique.   This is so marked that
one is inclined to doubt the genetic evolution of Pueblo I
painted ware from Basketmaker III.   Slipping and smudging may also be added to the list.

If these traits are placed on a chart (Fig. 31), showing their
time of emergence in the Mimbres Branch of the Mogollon
Culture and in the Anasazi Culture, it will be seen that all

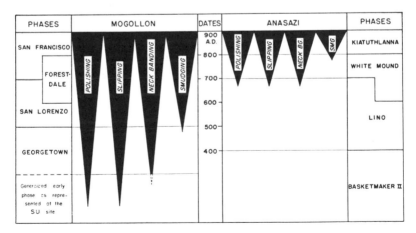

Figure 31.—Chart showing the priority of certain ceramic traits in
the Mogollon Culture (Mimbres Branch), which appeared later in
the Anasazi Culture.

were a part and parcel of Mogollon pottery before they were adopted by the Anasazi. It is suggested therefore that the shift in treatment of pottery between Basketmaker III and Pueblo I may well have been stimulated from the south, resulting in the rapid development from a crude, rough ware in the seventh century to more sophisticated and varied wares of a few centuries later.

Along with this the possibility may be pointed out of south to north design migrations as well. Basketmaker III painted pottery, on broad lines, may be identified on the basis of two types, exemplified by Lino Black-on-gray and White Mound Black-on-white. The former, as a rule, shows a few elements of design spotted independently of each other within the decorative field. In the latter this tradition is replaced by a prevalent use of small solid triangles, often with lined extensions from the apexes, the solids being framed with sets of parallel lines. This style is undoubtedly Mogollon as will be seen in any San Lorenzo or Mogollon Red-on-brown.

Since these two styles are so incompatible and since the geometric Basketmaker style lies in the southern portion of the Basketmaker area, one cannot escape the conclusion that there has been some interchange. It remains to determine whether the White Mound Black-on-white form or the Mogollon form is the older. The answer to this is not wholly clear as yet, but, adopting the stand that the ceramic complex of Mogollon is more ancient than that of the Anasazi and recognizing the fact that there is reasonably good evidence that neck banding, polishing, slipping, and smudging moved north, one may infer that designs should be included.

What intrusive pottery tells.—While tree rings and stratigraphy have been useful controls in establishing the approximate time levels of culture periods and phases, a valuable check on the correctness of these determinations is to be had in the occurrences of sherds in one area which represent wares of known horizons indigenous to other sections. The accompanying chart (Fig. 32) is an attempt to represent instances of this sort which are known to the writer in phases of the three principal southwestern cultures between the dates of 500 to 900 A.D.

The phases shown have been placed in their respective places either by tree-ring dating or by their stratigraphic relationship to each other where a direct development is indicated. Obviously it is impossible to express correctly the exact duration of any phase, and the time limits should therefore be considered approximations.[125]

---

[125]For footnote see pages 97 and 98.

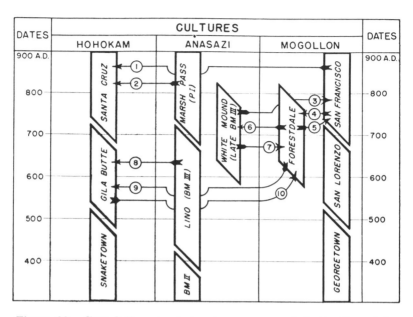

Figure 32.—Correlation chart showing source and destination of intrusive pottery between 500 and 900 A.D. The numbered arrows are explained thus: *1*, Mogollon Red-on-brown at Snaketown (H. S. Gladwin *et al.*, 1937, Fig. 105). *2*, Kana-a Black-on-white at Snaketown (*ibid.*). *3*, White Mound Black-on-white at the Mogollon Village (E. W. Haury, 1936 *b*, p. 26). *4*, Mogollon Red-on-brown at the Bear Ruin (see p.216 herein). *5*, Smudged ware at the Mogollon Village. (At the time that the Mogollon and Harris villages were excavated little was known about the early smudging of pottery. Smudging was recognized as present, but the types were not specifically identified. E. W. Haury, 1936 *a*, p.216) *6*, Forestdale Smudged at the White Mound Village (H. S. Gladwin, in preparation). *7*, White Mound Black-on-white and Lino Gray at the Bear Ruin (see p. 84 herein). *8*, Lino Black-on-gray at Snaketown (H. S. Gladwin *et al.*, 1937, Fig. 105). *9*, Forestdale Smudged at Snaketown (*ibid.*). *10*, Gila Butte Red-on-buff and Gila Plain at the Bear Ruin (see p.216 herein).

The interchange of wares in the phases as outlined is a strong confirmation of contemporaneity and should establish a common denominator from which correlations for both earlier and later horizons may be made.

STONEWORK

The number of ground stone tools collected in the Bear Ruin during the two field seasons probably does not express the full degree to which the occupants of the village relied on stone as a material for implements. The reason for this is bound up with the use of stone in the process of preparing food carried on in the large earth ovens.   The local supply of stone was Coconino sandstone which readily goes to pieces on heating and is inferior for the manufacture of such implements as metates because of its softness.   On that account tough crystalline rocks were brought in from some distance to replace the locally available materials. A discarded metate then became desirable as a cooking stone and usually was used as such until it was reduced to small bits.   Hence, on examining collections of thermally fractured rocks a substantial number of artifact fragments appears, but owing to their reduction to small bits they become useless in any analysis.   In spite of this situation, however, it is believed that the stone tools described are reasonably representative.

A ready supply of chert in the vicinity of the Bear Ruin was apparently responsible for a stronger showing of chipped implements than is usually found in southwestern ruins. Chert occurs in the form of nodules on the ridges flanking the Forestdale Valley, remnants of the Kaibab limestone formation which once capped the local sandstone.

While chert was most generally employed, a few other materials were also used on occasion.   A study of a sample of 1,021 pieces of chipping wastage collected at random over the site shows the following distribution of materials:

Chert	780
Chalcedony	93
Quartzite	71
Fine-grain lava	43
Petrified wood	31
Obsidian	3
Total	1,021

A similar ratio is maintained by the complete specimens.

---

[125]Substantiation for phase placements is to be found as follows:

Snaketown Phase: earlier than Gila Butte Phase, H. S. Gladwin *et al.*, 1937, pp. 29-34; intrusives other than Mogollon absent, *ibid.*, pp. 212-20.

Gila Butte Phase: see above references, first Anasazi intrusives.

Santa Cruz Phase: see above references, Anasazi intrusives fairly abundant.

Basketmaker II: stratigraphically early; tree-ring dating not yet fully established, but probably before 400 A.D.

Lino Phase (Basketmaker III): H. S. Colton, 1939 *b*, p. 53.

Marsh Pass Phase: H. S. Colton, 1939 *b*, pp. 54-55.

White Mound Phase: H. S. Gladwin, in preparation; tree-ring dates from White Mound Village $671+x$ to 802.

Forestdale Phase: tree-ring dates, *ca.* 675 (see pp. 120-21 herein).

Georgetown Phase: stratigraphic position early (E. W. Haury, 1936 *a* and *b*) but position as indicated inferential. (*Cont.* p.230)

Excluding the pressure flaked projectiles and blades, there is a rather large variety of standard but poorly executed flake types. Some of these do not appear to be tools until a close examination has been made revealing the intentional trimming or changes brought about in the flake through use. Either rough core percussion-made tools were decidedly unpopular or economy did not call for their use.

GROUND STONE TOOLS

Metates (75) [126]

Type I, basin (Fig. 33 a).. 10

Indurated sandstone blocks, unshaped, usually thick and irregular; grinding surface oval and shallow, placed off-center so area extends to one edge of stone; grinding stroke free and semirotary. Average length: 35.0 cm. Type I, II, and III manos suitable for use with these.

Type II, troughed (Fig. 33 b).. 34

Sandstone (8), vesicular lava (26); mostly waterworn boulders and blocks of lava, unshaped, hence variable in size (range: 35.0 to 55.0 cm. in length); grinding surface troughed, parallel sides, and deeply concave; trough open at far end,[127] and floor rises sharply at near end well forward in stone leaving a shelflike projection; grinding stroke lineal, with mano completely filling lateral axis of trough. A few metates in both classes of material show troughs on both faces of the stone. Type IV and V manos used herewith.

Type III ,"Utah" type (Fig. 33 c)... 30

Sandstone (4), vesicular lava (26); similar to Type II except that these have a slight basinlike depression on the near-end shelf, commonly known as the "Utah" type;[128] this depression usually exhibits wearing by grinding. Type I and II manos would be usable on this surface, while wearing in main trough must be attributed to Type IV and V manos. Metates of Types II and III

San Lorenzo Phase: postulated on the basis of a pottery type (E. W. Haury, 1936 b, p. 9) and since verified by E. B. Sayles, excavating for Gila Pueblo at the San Simon site, near Willcox, Arizona.

San Francisco Phase: stratigraphy and tree-ring dates which fell at end of phase, E. W. Haury, 1936 a, pp. 116-18.

[126]Metate frequencies were derived from whole specimens and fragments of sufficient size to determine the type.

[127]The closed part of the metate is considered to have been near the person using same and the open end would then be away from user.

[128]N. M. Judd, 1926, p. 74; J. H. Steward, 1933, pp. 9-10.

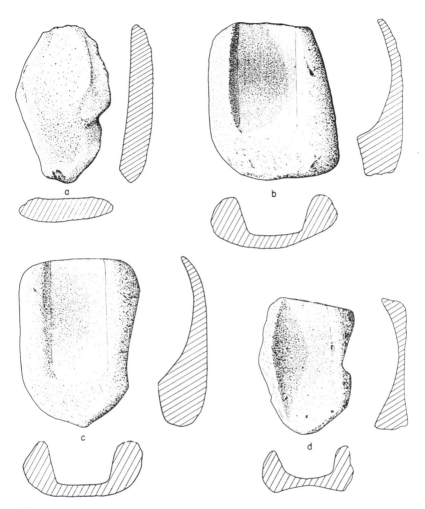

Figure 33.—Metate types. Length of d, 40.0 cm.

occasionally show "killing" by having a round hole
broken through the thinnest part of the trough.
Type IV, full trough (Fig. 33 d) 1
    Vesicular lava, unshaped; full trough with deepest
part about midway between center and far end; reverse
side has Type II grinding surface. Length: 40.0 cm.
Manos (76)
    Type I (Fig. 34 a) 22

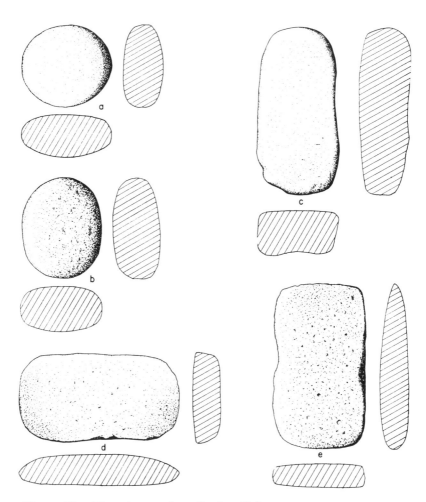

Figure 34.—Mano types. Length of e, 21.0 cm.

Indurated sandstone and vesicular lava; oval to
elongate in form, showing slight abrading around edge
to produce symmetry; single grinding face; suitable for
use on Type I metates or on small grinding surface at
near end of some Type III metates. Average maximum
diameter: 12.0 cm.

Type II (Fig. 34 b) 9
   Identical with Type I in all details except that these
have grinding faces on both flat surfaces of stone.

Type III (Fig. 34 c).. 3
Indurated sandstone; stream boulders of convenient size and form, not shaped; single grinding surface slightly convex on both axes suggesting use on slab metate. Average dimensions: length, 20.0 cm.; width, 9.0 cm.; thickness, 5.0 cm.

Type IV (Fig. 34 d)... 31
Indurated sandstone and vesicular lava; sides approximately straight and parallel, ends rounded; worn on one face only which is flat along lateral axis, slightly convex longitudinally becoming acute near ends, indicating mano fits snugly in trough of metate; edges somewhat trimmed; five specimens have finger grooves. Used with Types II, III, and IV metates. Average dimensions: length, 20.0 cm.; width, 11.0 cm.; thickness, 4.0 cm.

Type V (Fig. 34 e).. 11
Materials as in Type IV; bifacial grinding surfaces, one face consistently showing heavy wear, otherwise the same as Type IV; three specimens have finger grooves. Used with Types II, III, and IV metates.

Small metates (6) (Fig. 35 a, b)
Lava and sandstone; two specimens made of convenient stone without shaping (a), remainder shaped about margin by pecking (b); grinding surface oval and shallow, occasionally used on both sides; one example represents a mano reused for this purpose; a clue as to use seen in pulverized pigment stain in two instances. Average dimensions: length, 20.0 cm.; width, 15.0 cm.; thickness, 6.0 cm.

Pestles (3) (Fig. 35 c, d)
Indurated sandstone and lava; both unshaped and shaped; used end rounded and scarred; two examples slightly employed also as manos. Average dimensions: length, 15.0 cm.; diameter, 8.0 cm.

Mortars (6) (Fig. 35 e, f)
One lava, remainder sandstone; all are metates secondarily used as mortars; both Type I (e) and Type II (f) metates employed; mortar depressions worn in deepest part of metate troughs.

Abraders (4)
Irregular pieces of soft sandstone, no shaping, with a single flat abrading surface. Average diameter, 8.0 cm.

Abrading slabs (2)
Hard, tabular sandstone slabs; form roughly rectangular; abrading surface flat, extending to edge of implement; both examples fragmentary but probably did not exceed 15.0 cm. in greatest dimension, thickness 1.5 cm.

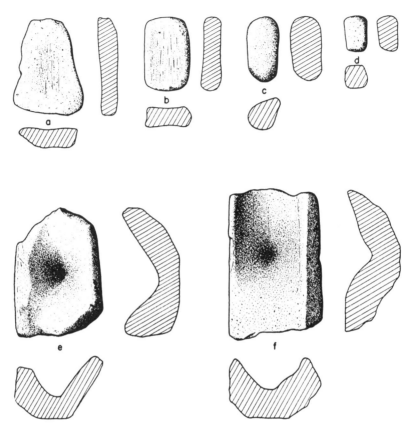

Figure 35.--Small grinding slabs, pestles, and mortars. Length of *f*,
44.0 cm.

Polishers (10)
     Fine-grained waterworn pebbles; unmodified except
from use, probably for polishing pottery; worn surfaces
convex on both axes. Length range from 5.0 to 9.0 cm.
Hammerstones (92)
  Type I (Fig. 36 *a*) 41
     Angular to rounded chunks of chert and petrified
wood; shape depending upon amount of use. Diameters:
from 4.0 to 8.0 cm.
  Type II (Fig. 36 *b*) 50
     Waterworn pebbles, usually somewhat flat and elon-
gated; pecked surface limited to ends and thin edges.

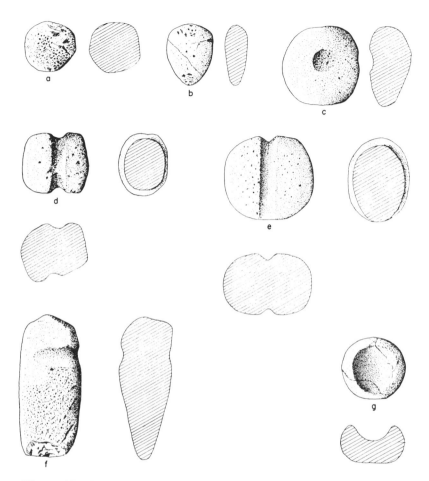

Figure 36.—Stone implements. Length of *f*, 19.0 cm.

On the whole these are light in weight and small as
compared with Type I. Diameters: from 3.0 to 10.0 cm.
Type III (Fig. 36 c) 1
Discoidal quartzite pebble, centrally pitted on one side.
Diameter: 11.0 cm.
Mauls (8) (Fig. 36 *d, e*)
Lava (4) and quartzite (4) ; mostly well shaped, oval to
round in transverse section; heads extensively flattened
from use; three specimens show traces of potter's clay on
heads, probably from pulverizing this material; grooves

medially placed and usually well polished; groove types occur as follows:

Three quarter 4
Full groove 2
Intermediate .... 2[129]

Average length: 11.0 cm.

Axes (1) (Fig. 36 *f*)

Fine-grained crystalline stone; a waterworn pebble in process of shaping; bit was intended to be long and groove of three-quarter type. Length: 19.0 cm.

Vessels (1) (Fig. 36 *g*)

Limestone; convex sides, lacking in decoration. Diameter: 8.5 cm.; depth of depression: 1.8 cm.

Balls (10)

Natural concretions (5) and shaped by pecking from sandstone and lava (5). Diameters: from 1.0 to 6.5 cm.

Cooking stones (7)

Stream pebbles 4.0 to 6.0 cm. in diameter; three found inside a cooking jar; remainder in a cluster.

Ornaments (8)

Pendants (Fig. 37 *a, b*) 4

Pale turquoise; all occurred with burials either at wrist as though worn on arm or near head as though worn in ear. Lengths: 1.1 to 1.9 cm.

Beads (Fig. 37 *c, d*) 4

Pale turquoise; three large and thick; average diameter 0.7 cm. All found with burials; one small, 0.3 cm. in diameter, found in fill of House 4.

Gems 6

Four garnets (0.5 cm. in diameter), one chip olivine, one chip quartz crystal, found with adult burial (No. 2).

CHIPPED STONE TOOLS

Core implements (20) (percussion)

Cores 9

Chert and petrified wood nuclei from which flakes have been struck.

Blanks 6

Rough, leaf-shaped blades of chert; probably unfinished projectiles. Average length: 4.0 cm.

Choppers (Fig. 37 *e*) 5

Chert and dioritic material; trimmed down on one or both sides to make a ragged working edge; part of orig-

---

[129]On these two examples the groove originally appears to have been of the three-quarter type, the groove being completed at some later time in a shallow fashion.

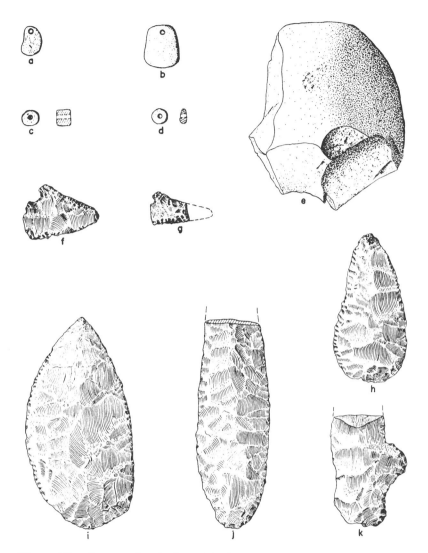

Figure 37.—Ornaments; single notched and unnotched blades. Length of c, 9.5 cm.

inal crust of nodule visible on all specimens. Maximum
diameters: 6.5 to 9.0 cm.
Flake implements (75) (fully worked by pressure)
Blades 7

a)   Single notch (2) (Fig. 37 *f, g*)
Chert; shallow notch oblique to cutting edge.
Lengths: 1.6 and 3.3 cm.
b)   Unnotched (4) (Fig. 37 *h-j*)
Fossiliferous chert and igneous stone; length
range: 5.5 to 9.5 cm.
c)   With lateral projection (1) (Fig. 37 *k*)
Chert; fragmentary. Length: 5.0 cm.

Projectile points.. 59
a)   Unnotched (23)
Triangular (21) (Fig. 38 *a-d*)
Mainly chert, a few obsidian; slight differences
seen in treatment of base: straight (12), convex
(7), concave (2). Length range: 1.6 to 4.7 cm.,
average, 2.7 cm.
Straight base, convex edges (2) (Fig. 38 *e, f*)
Chert; both thick-bladed in proportion to size;
note serrations (*f*). Lengths: 3.5 and 4.7 cm.
b)   Stemmed (8) (Fig. 38 *g-j*)
Chert and crystalline rock; tangs well developed.
Length range: 1.6 to 6.0 cm., average, 3.4 cm.
c)   Notched (28)
Diagonal, expanding stem (18) (Fig. 38 *k-n, s*)
Mostly chert, a few obsidian, the latter all small;
edges rarely serrated; length range: 1.8 to 8.3 cm.,
average, 2.8 cm.
Lateral (10) (Fig. 38 *o-r*)
Stem as wide or wider than broadest part of
blade; base straight or slightly convex, in one case
(*r*) notched; example *o* with serrations and long,
slender blade suggests Hohokam type of point.
Length range: 1.8 to 4.8 cm., average, 2.6 cm.

Drills (Fig. 38) 9
Chert; range in type from a retouched chip (*t*) to
flanged (*u, v*) to notched with broad base form (*w*).
Average length, 3.6 cm.

Flake implements (133) (lightly worked by pressure)
Knives 81
a)   Unmodified flakes (52) (Fig. 39 *a-c*)
Chert, a few petrified wood; any suitable thin
flake, edges slightly chipped through use. Maximum dimensions: 2.0 to 6.0 cm.
b)   Flakes modified by serrating (29) (Fig. 39 *d, e*)
Chance flakes of chert; one edge, usually straight
or convex, serrated by regularly placed pressure

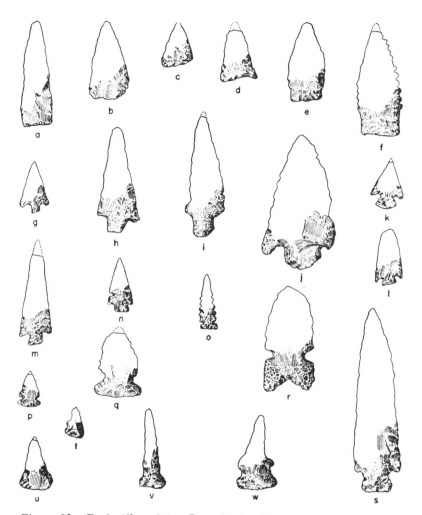

Figure 38.—Projectile points. Length of s, 8.3 cm.

flaking all directed from one side. Maximum
dimensions: 2.5 to 5.0 cm.

Scrapers 38

   a) End (2) (Fig. 39 f)

       Thick flakes of chert; end steeply and irregu-
larly retouched. Lengths: 3.0 and 4.0 cm.

   b) Rough flake (15) (Fig. 39 g)

       Chert, petrified wood; any convenient thick (0.5

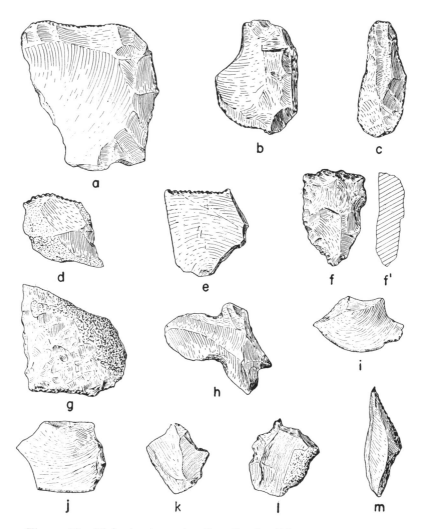

Figure 39.—Flake implements. Length of *a*, 7.5 cm.

to 1.0 cm.) flake, 3.0 to 4.5 cm. long, one edge
trimmed with steep and poorly directed retouch;
no uniformity as to shape or character of scraping edge.
c)   Hollow (10) (Fig. 39 *h*)
Chert; any convenient thick flake; dented deeply
on one edge. Lengths: 3.0 to 6.0 cm.

d) Ground edge (11) (Fig. 39 *i, j*)
Chert and diorite; edge convex, ground smooth as if from drawing across abrasive surface; type of flake selected usually shows hinge fracture. Lengths: 2.5 to 4.0 cm.

Gravers 11
a) Double-faced point (2) (Fig. 39 *k*)
Thin chert flakes with small projections, finely and sharply retouched on both faces. Lengths: 2.7 to 3.0 cm.
b) Single-faced (9) (Fig. 39 *l*)
Thick chert flakes, usually showing crust of nodule; edge or corner notched at two places to produce and throw graving point into prominence; all chipping directed toward outer surface of flake; retouch steep and carried around point which is usually somewhat blunt. Flake lengths: 3.0 to 5.2 cm.

Scraper-gravers (Fig. 39 *m*).. 3
Prismatic chert flakes; scraping edge concavo-convex, ending in sharp graving point. Lengths: 2.8 to 4.5 cm.

Minerals[130]

Not plentiful, occurred generally with burials; used mostly for deriving pigments; clay mixed with ground ores in a few cases to add body. Samples represent the following minerals and colors, roughly listed in order of abundance:

Hematite (sesquioxide of iron) black, red, and specular forms
Limonite (hydrous iron oxide) yellow, brown
Gypsum (hydrous calcium sulphate) white
Pyrolusite (manganese dioxide) black
Azurite (copper carbonate) blue
Malachite (copper carbonate) green
Chrysocolla (copper silicate) blue
Jarosite (potassium iron sulphate) yellow
Cinnabar (sulphide of mercury) red
Realgar (sulphide of arsenic) red
Galena (lead sulphide)

All of these minerals, excepting the first four which probably occurred locally, were acquired through trade from some distance, and deposits of all except realgar are known

---

[130]Other than those used in toolmaking. Identifications by Mr. R. E. S. Heineman, Mineralogist, Arizona Bureau of Mines, University of Arizona.

within the state. Cinnabar probably came from the Mazatzal
Mountains, 90 miles west of Forestdale, where deposits
have been worked commercially. That cinnabar was at a
premium is suggested by the fact that in two cases it had
been mixed with red hematite, occurring only in very small
amounts. Realgar, an arsenic derivative, is unknown in
Arizona, but deposits are known at Mercur, Utah, Man-
hattan, Nevada, and in Yellowstone Park.

DISCUSSION

Since there has not yet been gathered enough data to
evaluate the lithic products of the Bear Ruin from the standpoint of their full meaning in the local evolution of stone
tools, a more general discussion must be given, pointing out
relationships with other areas and comparisons with the
products of other cultures.

First, since the Bear Ruin is situated in an area marginal
to the fully blown Anasazi and Mogollon cultures and since
it had also established some contact with the Hohokam, it
should be decided to which of these three groups the stonework is most closely related. As an aid in this determina-
tion, reference is made to the accompanying table in which
all stone traits of the Bear Ruin are listed, and the presence
or absence of comparable traits in the three comparative
groups are indicated. To be valid such a tabulation should
be based on contemporaneous material as much as possible.
As the Forestdale Phase material is dated by tree rings in
the late 600's and to allow some leeway in assigning a time
level for the phase, the span from 600 to 800 has been selected.
Comparative material from the Anasazi can then be drawn
from the Basketmaker III-Pueblo I levels, preferably of the
San Juan because of its greater "purity," from the San Lor-
enzo-San Francisco phases of the Mogollon, and from the
Colonial Period of the Hohokam.

What this table shows may be briefly outlined: out of
forty-three traits listed for the Forestdale Phase, eleven or
approximately 25 per cent were peculiar to that phase, mostly
in the class of flake implements; eleven traits, or approximately 25 per cent were common to all; and with each of the
three groups Forestdale Phase materials have parallels in
about half of the elements listed. While there are therefore
a certain number of recognizable distinctions in the Forestdale Phase materials, the figures do not allow the establishment of relationship. But by evaluating some elements
more than others based on frequency or dominance and especially those which were more directly related to economy,

COMPARISON OF FORESTDALE PHASE STONE TRAITS WITH
ANASAZI, MOGOLLON, AND HOHOKAM MATERIALS
OF COMPARABLE AGE, 600-800 A.D.

	Anasazi	Mogollon	Hohokam
Basin metate (Type I)		x*	x
Trough metate (Type II)	x	x	
"Utah" type (Type III)		x	
Full trough metate (Type IV)	x		**x**
Manos: Type I (rubbing)	x	x	x
Type II	x	x	
Type III			
Type IV	**x**	**x**	x
Type V	x	x	**x**
Small metates			x
Pestles		x	x
Mortars (in metate)			
Abraders	x	x	x
Abrading slabs	x		x
Polishers (pottery)	**x**	x	x
Hammerstones: Type I (core)	**x**	x	**x**
Type II (pebble)			x
Type III (pitted)	x		x
Mauls: three-quarter groove	x	x	
Full groove	**x**	**x**	
Axes: three-quarter groove			**x**
Stone vessels	x	x	**x**
Balls			
Pendants (turquoise)	x		x
Beads (turquoise)	x		x
Choppers		x	x
Single notch blades			
Unnotched blades			x
Blade with lateral projection			
Triangular projectile point		x	
Stemmed projectile point	**x**	x	x
Diagonal notched projectile point	**x**	x	x
Lateral notched projectile point		x	x
Drills	x	x	x
Flake knives	x	x	x
Flake knives, serrated			
End scrapers		x	
Rough flake scrapers			
Hollow scrapers			
Ground-edge scrapers			
Double-faced gravers			
Single-faced gravers			
Scraper-gravers			
Totals 43	20	22	24

*x = present; **x** = predominant.

as the open ended trough and "Utah" type metates, mauls, pottery polishers, stemmed and diagonal notched projectiles, the opinion may be expressed that on the whole the pattern of Forestdale stonework is nearer the Anasazi-Mogollon combination than Hohokam. The inability to show more marked differences between Anasazi and Mogollon may be simply explained by the fact that by Forestdale Phase times the interplay of these two groups had been in operation long enough to blot them out. A few specific analogies with Hohokam stone elements, as the three-quarter grooved ax, small metates, and a long-bladed serrated point (Fig. 38 *o*), suggest direct influence through contact, known by ceramic evidence to have been established.

In milling stones, parallels are found both to the south and to the north. The basin metates (Type I) occurred in direct association with the other types thus suggesting that their significance was functional rather than chronological. It should be pointed out that the basin metate is a diagnostic for the earlier Mogollon Culture levels and that the sporadic occurrence of the same in later periods may indicate the survival of the earlier form.

The sandstone troughed variety with single open end is essentially the same as the type occurring in Basketmaker sites. Metates of the same basic type, although differing in material—namely lava, occur predominantly to the south. The noteworthy difference lies in the possession of the latter of a secondary depression in the near end of the stone suggesting a double function—i.e., it is possible to employ all mano types as described herein on the same milling base. This suggests the possibility that two different food products, certainly corn and possibly native seeds, were prepared on the same metate. This use would help to explain the presence of numerous Type I manos and so few basin metates with which they are normally associated. The distribution of this particular type of metate is not confined to the Mogollon area, as it ranges well up into western Utah.

Barring the difference of material explainable by environment, the open-end trough (Type II) metate is essentially the same in Basketmaker III and in the Forestdale Phase. In the "killing" of metates, the Forestdale examples have analogies to the south.[131]

It is impossible to assign the milling stones of the Bear Ruin solely to a Mogollon or Anasazi source, because by Forestdale Phase times features of both cultures were already incorporated. While the mortar principle of grinding was

---

[131]E. W. Haury, 1936 *b*, Plate XII *a*.

known, it appears to have been of relatively small importance in the Forestdale Phase, as the present excavations produced none of the more common boulder mortar types.

Pebbles identified provisionally as cooking stones on the
evidence of their occurrence in a jar and by thermal fracturing introduce a trait which is not common in the Southwest.
Further support of this should be found before much is made
of it. Turquoise, from all appearances, was at a premium as
suggested by its scarcity and by the apparent use of individual beads as pendants.

It has already been pointed out that the Forestdale Phase
is characterized by an unusually large complement of small
flake and chipped tools. Excluding projectile points, such
are certainly not associated with the Hohokam, and while it
seems that more should occur with Anasazi, they have not
been reported. In the Mogollon Culture a tendency in the
direction of using these tools is recognized. Of interest are
the two single notched blades, both small, which are reminiscent of the corner tang implements of Texas[132] but which
are not to be confused with them. Serration of projectile
point edges is on the whole a southern trait, particularly
among the Hohokam.

Flake scrapers with ground edges, the result of drawing
them over an abrasive surface, are numerous enough to
claim them as a distinctive type. The only parallel type in
the Southwest is the ground edge scraper from the Chiricahua
Stage of the Cochise Culture.[133] The tubular stone pipe or-
dinarily represented in Anasazi and Mogollon collections did
not occur in the Bear Ruin.

BONE AND ANTLER

In all, sixty-six objects of bone and antler, fashioned for
specific purposes, were found. For a people who apparently
relied rather heavily on the hunt and who thus had
a constant supply of bone for shaping into tools, this number
may seem small. Yet, compared with the totals of all other
kinds of specimens, and in view of the range of types of the
bone material at hand, it is believed that a fairly complete
cross-section of this phase of the material culture may be
given. Except the smaller tubes which were made of bird
bones, all identifiable bones represent the mule deer.

Awls (30)
 a) Splinter (Fig. 40 *a-c*) 3

---

[132]J. T. Patterson, 1936.
[133]E. B. Sayles, 1941.

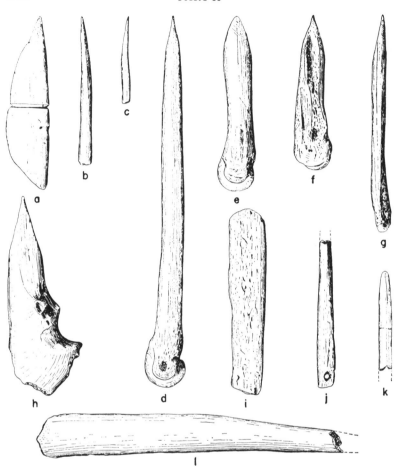

Figure 40.—Bone tools. Length of *d*, 19.5 cm.

Made of any convenient splinter; little attention paid to removing fracture irregularities. Lengths: 4.8 to 9.0 cm.

b)   Split bone (Fig. 40 *d-g*) 25

Fashioned chiefly of deer metapodials split down the middle of the shaft by sawing; when made from distal end, condyles were not modified (*d-f*); when made from proximal end, articular surface worn down (*g*); points usually stubby and blunt. Lengths: 8.5 to 19.8 cm., average, 10.0 cm.

c)   Whole bone (Fig. 40 *h*) 2

Deer ulnae made usable by sharpening shaft; articular end may or may not be reduced. Lengths: 10.5 and 15.7 cm.

Spatulates (2) (Fig. 40 *i*)

Sections of rib and large mammal leg bone; ends flattened and sharpened. Lengths: 9.0 and 10.0 cm.

Needles (2) (Fig. 40 *j, k*)

Both fragmentary, representing point and butt ends; latter has eyelet drilled from both sides; point fragment is broad and thin, well polished, measuring 0.7 cm. in width and 0.2 cm. in thickness.

Rib scrapers (2) (Fig. 40 *l*)

Sections of deer ribs; sharpest edge used for scraping, and tool held so that concave side of rib was toward user. Lengths: 16.0 and 16.8 cm.

Tubes (6)

a) Large mammal leg bone (Fig. 41 *a*) 4

All specimens plain except one which has incised geometric design, too badly eroded to be reconstructed. Lengths: 6.8 to 9.0 cm.; average diameter, 2.5 cm.

b) Turkey leg bone with spur (Fig. 41 *b, c*) 2

Spur may fall centrally or near one end of shaft. Lengths: 5.5 and 9.8 cm.

Whistles (7) (Fig. 41 *d, e*)

All made of bird bone, ends neatly trimmed and shafts perforated centrally with oval or slightly irregular hole. Lengths: 4.0 to 7.2 cm.

Dice (10) (Fig. 41 *f-i*)

Small pieces of bone worked to oval form; five examples are concavo-convex, others are biconvex; one shows criss-cross incised design on one face (*i*). Lengths: 1.6 to 2.5 cm.

Bead (1) (Fig. 41 *j*)

Small bird bone, perforated centrally on four sides. Length: 1.8 cm.

Disc (1) (Fig. 41 *k*)

Plano-convex; flat side centrally drilled and has radial incisions (*k*); convex side well polished (*k'*). Diameter: 1.1 cm.

Cylinder (1) (Fig. 41 *l*)

Nearly round in section; ends slightly tapered. Length: 2.8 cm.

Antler flakers (2) (Fig. 41 *m*)

Antler tine fragments; worn on one and both sides of tip.

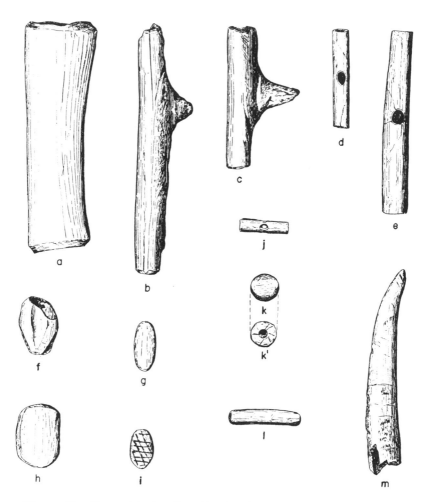

Figure 41.—Bone objects. Length of *a*, 9.0 cm.

Discussion

Little significant information appears in a review of the bone implements from the Bear Ruin. The awl type agrees with that of the Basketmakers, and the notched awl[134] heretofore identified chiefly with Mogollon sites was not present. Rib scrapers appear to be a new trait for the area, and the

[134]E. W. Haury, 1936 *b*, pp. 110-11.

needles or bodkins seem to be fairly general[135] in early horizons. Bone tubes likewise were widely used, but the incised type is somewhat suggestive of the early Hohokam form.[136] Dice were present in the early time levels of both the Anasazi and Mogollon, the only apparent difference being that those of the former tend to show more often the incising of one face.

SHELL

Shellwork was rare in the village, and the range of objects was notably limited. The absence of shell wastage would make it appear as though objects of this material were obtained in finished form by trade. Nearly all specimens were found with burials, but very few (three of forty) were thus supplied. The species represented are *Glycymeris* sp., *Olivella* sp., *Haliotis* sp., and *Cardium elatum*.

Beads (36)

Whole shell... 2

    Olivella, spires removed by grinding.

Disc 34

    Made of thick-walled unidentified shell. Average diameter: 0.8 cm.; thickness: 0.4 cm. Found in *Haliotis* shell on left shoulder of Burial 22 (female).

Bracelets (18)

    Glycymeris, very thin, beak portions almost entirely worn away. Average diameter: 5.0 cm. These occurred in lots of six and twelve in two graves, worn on the lower arms by youths.

Whole shell container (1)

    Badly distintegrated *Haliotis* on left shoulder of Burial 22.

CLAY OBJECTS AND WORKED POTSHERDS

Pipes (5) (Fig. 42 *a*)

    All of "cloud blower" type, conical; finely tempered brown clay, lightly polished, unslipped and undecorated. The only whole specimen measures 7.5 cm. in length.

Figurines (7)

Animal 1

    Fragmentary, fired brown clay; animal unidentifiable. Length: 3.1 cm.

Human (Fig. 42 *b-d*) 6

    Finely tempered brown clay, fired; bodies flattened, little attention paid to anatomical details; arms lacking

---

[135]F. H. H. Roberts, Jr., 1931, p. 152; P. S. Martin, J. Rinaldo, and M. Kelly, 1940, p. 70.
[136]H. S. Gladwin *et al.*, 1937, p. 155.

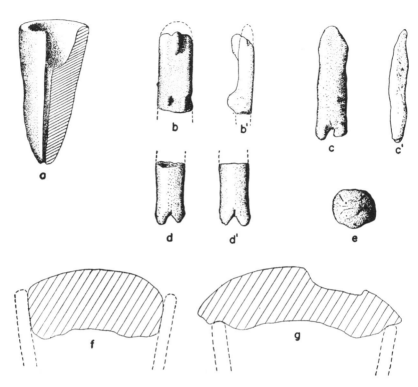

Figure 42.—Clay objects. Length of *a*, 7.5 cm.

and legs merely suggested. Length of only complete
specimen: 5.5 cm.

Ball (1) (Fig. 42 *e*)

Fine clay, fired, brown; surface irregular. Diameter:
2.3 cm.

Jar stoppers (4)

Thick clay discoidals, originally not fired; made to fit
either into or over mouths of jars (Fig. 42 *f, g*). Diameters: 7.3 to 18.4 cm.; average thickness: 5.0 cm.

Discs (119)

a)   Perforated (Fig. 43 *a*) 25

Cut imperfectly out of sherds; perforations made
by drilling from both sides, not always centrally
placed. Diameters: 3.0 to 6.0 cm.

b)   Unperforated (Fig. 43 *b-d*) 94

Made of any local pottery type but Forestdale
Smudged preferred; precision occasionally shown in

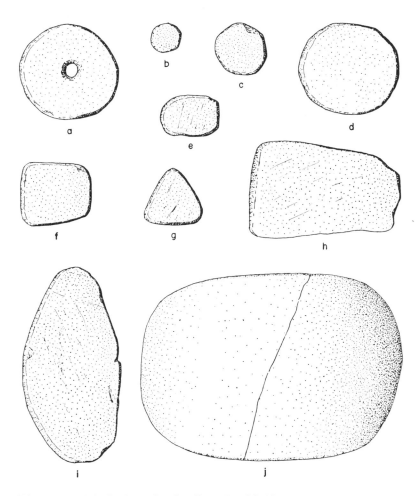

Figure 43.—Worked potsherds. Length of *j*, 11.0 cm.

grinding of disc edges. Diameters: 1.3 to 6.5 cm. One disc shows red paint on concave surface as though used for a palette.

Ovals (3) (Fig. 43 *e*)
Quadrilateral (8) (Fig. 43 *f*)
Triangular (2) (Fig. 43 *g*)
Scraping spoons (39)

a) Quadrilateral (Fig. 43 *h*) 9
b) Oval (Fig. 43 *i, j*) 30

Made either of Forestdale Smudged or Forestdale Red—types best suited for this purpose because of finely tempered paste. Several still have potter's clay adhering to surfaces from the scraping process. Maximum dimensions: 6.0 to 11.5 cm.

PERISHABLE MATERIAL

The sole objects in this category were two occurrences of charred basketry, one in living quarters and the other in a storage room (No. 1). Both examples represent coiled basketry with a two-rod-and-bundle foundation, measuring an average of three coils and seven stitches per centimeter. In technique these are no different than the coiled baskets of the Anasazi of the same age.

DATING THE BEAR RUIN

The problem of chronology is usually foremost in archaeological work but not always one of the easiest to establish. To determine the age of the Bear Ruin, several lines of evidence must be brought into play, all complementing each other to the extent that the age of the site may be confidently stated. The most reliable dating medium, as southwesternists have learned, is dendrochronology. This system is used here also, but the evidence is not abundant. Situated deep in the timber country, one would expect those pit houses of the Bear Ruin which had burned to be well filled with usable charcoal, but this was not the case. In only three structures, Houses 1, 4, and the large kiva (No. 1), was wood at all plentiful, and much of this was juniper which materially reduced dating possibilities. For two of these, House 1 and the kiva, dates were ultimately obtained.[137] In the former, two different pine logs, originally a part of the roof but unfortunately not preserving the outermost ring to give a cutting date, were assignable to the following places in the chronology:

No. 15b—580 A.D. (center) to $636+x$
No. 18 —586 A.D. (center) to $667+x$

The kiva provided but a single datable log:

No. 67 —611 A.D. (center) to $667+x$[138]

These three dates can in no way be interpreted as delimiting the span of occupation of the Bear Ruin, but they must obviously fall somewhere in that span, whether early or late.

---

[137]The author is indebted to Gordon C. Baldwin and F. H. Scantling for assisting in the analysis of the charcoal and to Dr. A. E. Douglass for checking the same.
[138]For complete record see E. W. Haury, 1940 *a*.

It is not possible to judge accurately the number of rings lost on these specimens through crumbling of the charcoal, but the number is probably not very great, and the stand may be adopted that construction was in progress in the final decades of the 600's. As the dates from the two structures are rather close together and the pottery from all structures shows no appreciable difference, it may be inferred that the building of the village was compressed into a relatively short span of time, perhaps several generations.

Turning to other lines for determining the age, there is first, the evidence of intrusive pottery for which dates have been established elsewhere, and second, cross-finds dated by stratigraphy. Starting with the former, White Mound Black-on-white and its companion ware, Lino Gray, were the most abundant of all foreign pottery (see p. 211). These have been dated in at least two sites where they were indigenous— at the White Mound site near Allantown, with a span of dates from $671+x$ to 802, and at Site 4A in the Jeddito recently excavated by the Peabody Museum Expedition with tree-ring dates in the eighth century.[139] The dates from these two villages and those of the Bear Ruin all fall within the same general segment of time, thus providing the necessary confirmation of the purely internal evidence from the Bear Ruin.

Cross-finds of pottery placed stratigraphically and dated indirectly by tree rings in that region where the type was at home was Gila Butte Red-on-buff. This type was the painted ware diagnostic of the Gila Butte Phase of the Colonial Period at Snaketown, dated at 500 to 700 on the strength of associated Basketmaker III pottery and by its stratigraphically earlier position in relation to the Santa Cruz Phase, reliably dated at 700 to 900. As every one of the painted sherds of Hohokam origin in the Bear Ruin was of the Gila Butte Red-on-buff type, the case is much stronger for direct equation with Hohokam than had there been a mixture of Hohokam types representing several phases.

There are also certain inferential points which may be advanced to bear out the dating evidence already cited, such as the inherent early nature of much of the material culture, the type of architecture, the long succession of developmental stages following the Forestdale Phase which will be taken up in a later report, and the absence of traits known to be late.

Subject to revision, the limiting dates for the Forestdale Phase as represented in the Bear Ruin may be given as from 600 to 800 A.D.

---

[139]Information kindly supplied by the Peabody Museum.

GENERAL DISCUSSION AND CONCLUSIONS

In concluding this report on two seasons' study of the Bear Ruin, there arises the need to view the culture as a whole and to see just where it can be fitted into the southwestern archaeological picture.

Inability to determine chronological steps or phases in these remains forces one to regard the material as falling within a given segment of time in the stream of development when no appreciable cultural change took place. The time has been designated as from about 600 to 800 A.D., and the name applied to this particular development is the Forestdale Phase, a name suggested by the Gladwins,[140] based on the survey of the Bear Ruin in 1931. The criteria of this phase are presented below in synoptic form, summarizing the essential data of this report:

Synopsis of Forestdale Phase

Area.—Known only from the Forestdale Valley, east-central
    Arizona.
Age.—Dated by the tree rings to the late seventh century.
    Estimated inclusive dates 600 to 800 A.D.
Excavated sites.—Bear Ruin (Arizona P:16:1).
Unexcavated sites.—Arizona P:16:9.
Environment.—Timbered country, elevation 6,000 to 7,000
    feet.
Determinants
  Pottery
      a) Indigenous decorated types
            None
      b) Indigenous utility types
            Alma Plain
            Forestdale Plain
            Forestdale Smudged
            Forestdale Red
      c) Intrusive decorated types
            Lino Black-on-gray
            White Mound Black-on-white
            Gila Butte Red-on-buff
            Mogollon Red-on-brown
      d) Intrusive utility types
            Lino Gray
            Gila Plain
            Acquarius Brown
            Woodruff Smudged

---

[140]W. and H. S. Gladwin, 1934, chart.

Woodruff Red
Adamana Brown
San Francisco Red
Alma Scored, incised, and neck banded

Architecture
- a) Round pit houses: central hearth, with or without bench, deflector-ventilator complex, or lateral entrance and deflector, or both; usually four-post roof support plan.
- b) Rectangular pit houses: central hearth, with or without bench, deflector-ventilator may or may not be present, both roof and lateral entries; generally four-post roof support plan.
- c) Kiva, with bench, directional recesses and large recess to southeast, no deflector or ventilator, four-post roof support plan.
- d) Shallow rectangular storage structures.

Economy
- a) Hunting and agriculture on an approximately equal basis.
- b) Food: corn, large game animals.
- c) Large earth ovens, stones used in cooking process.
- d) Storage pits (?).

Stone
- a) Ground: troughed metates, open one end, mostly lava with secondary grinding basin at near end. Oval and parallel-sided manos; mortars (converted metates); three-quarter and full-grooved mauls; stone vessels.
- b) Chipped: blades; triangular, lateral, and obliquely notched projectile points; flanged drills, flake knives; serrated and ground-edge scrapers; gravers.
- c) Ornaments: turquoise pendants and beads.

Bone.—Stubby awls, needles, rib scrapers, tubes, whistles, dice.

Shell.—Beads: whole shell *Olivella*. Bracelets: thin *Glycymeris* type.

Clay.—Conical pipes, human figurines, potsherd discs, pottery scraping spoons.

Basketry.—Coiled, two-rod-and-bundle foundation.

Disposal of dead.—Semiflexed burials, in concentrated groups or scattered; graves shallow, usually with offerings.

Physical type.—Mixed long and round heads, latter sometimes deformed.

The significance of the Bear Ruin, apart from being the basis for the establishment of the Forestdale Phase, lies in the nature of the criteria. These manifest a blending and hybridizing of elements which are assignable either to the Mogollon or to the Anasazi Culture. The problem is therefore one of assimilation and of determining the extent of the impact of these two groups on coming together. This can be shown best in the form of a chart (Fig. 44) indicating the alignments of the more important Forestdale Phase traits with Anasazi on the one hand and fullfledged Mogollon on the other hand at a time of about 700 A.D. A good many traits are indecisive because they were so generally used, but pottery, architecture, some phases of the economy, and physical types do show significant differences. Pottery is clearly allied with the Mogollon, whereas house building is preponderantly in the Anasazi tradition. Which one of these two groups was dominant from the start is not an easy question to settle, but it is the writer's view that the Mogollon factor was basic for reasons given below:

1.   The Bear Ruin is located outside of the area of distribution of early Anasazi and in the northern part of the Mogollon territory.

2.   The use of the earth oven and stone cooking is a southern link which was more likely to have been carried north by southern people than to have been borrowed by northern people at the early date of the Bear Ruin.

3.   Pottery technique and types were southern. Only in Forestdale Plain can one recognize any tendency at all for actual blending of southern and northern styles, and this might well have been the output of Anasazi who had taken up residence in the Bear Ruin and were affected by Mogollon potters. Technically the Anasazi potters had nothing to contribute to the Mogollon except painting and a greater variety of vessel forms, which, for some reason, the latter were loath to adopt. In architecture the situation was reversed, for Anasazi pit houses characteristically incorporated more features than Mogollon houses. The adoption of these implied no deep-seated alteration for the Mogollon but merely the incorporation of details in their own pit houses. Hence, it appears that the architecture was the more fluid—the more likely to be changed, while conservatism ruled for pottery which consequently would tend to identify the group.

4.   Racial types, while obviously mixed, show a prevalance of round heads.

5.   Considering the later history of the valley, it is clear that the Mogollon pattern was largely blotted out within a

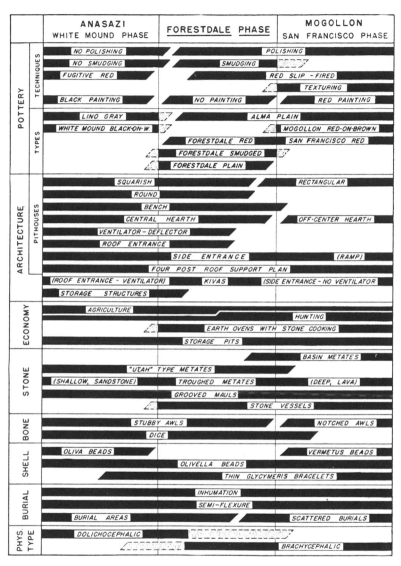

Figure 44.—A chart showing how the chief Forestdale Phase traits are related to the Anasazi or Mogollon cultures.

few centuries after the Forestdale Phase by the rise of the Anasazi. This early submergence of the Mogollon is in keeping with the fate of this group in other parts of its territory.

Generalizing, it therefore seems that the Bear Ruin was a local and marginal aspect of the Mogollon Culture, its individuality having been intensified by hybridization with the Anasazi. It is difficult to see any other way to account for this particular pattern of culture. Certainly it could not have been only an extension of the Anasazi which, because of its marginal position, was being altered by the force of environment alone.

It is unfortunate that the author and his staff were unable to identify a level of occupation earlier than the Forestdale Phase, supposedly characterized ceramically by such types as Woodruff Brown, Woodruff Smudged, and Woodruff Red, and an absence of painted pottery. The existence of such a phase, presumably much freer of Anasazi elements and therefore more purely Mogollon, would strengthen the present findings and at the same time provide the basis for breaking the Mogollon Culture down into northern and southern branches, the course of the former being altered by contact with the Anasazi and the latter by assimilation with Hohokam.

The influence of the Mogollon pattern of the Bear Ruin in the Anasazi area appears to have been strongest in the cosmopolitan region of Flagstaff. Here it was evident at least by 900 A.D.[141] and became somewhat intensified in later times[142] when Hohokam influence was also felt to produce a triple merger of cultures. On the evidence available it appears that another penetrating arm of Mogollon went north approximately along the Arizona-New Mexico state line, through the Chuska Mountain section, carrying at least certain Mogollon characteristics of pottery into the Basketmaker III sites of the Four Corners area. It is interesting to note that in each case these expansions followed a timber environment, the kind of surroundings to which the Mogollon Culture appears to have been attached.

————————

Throughout this report, by reference and recognition, the writer has clearly indicated his position with respect to the Mogollon Culture. There are those, however, who have doubted its validity or have attacked it vigorously from various angles. This skepticism is welcome because it will eventually lead to a better understanding of the Mogollon problem, either by establishing it once and for all or by showing the necessity of realigning the existing cultures so as to accommodate the material in question. It will be recalled

————————

[141]H. S. Colton, 1939 b, p. 24.
[142]J. C. McGregor, 1937, pp. 42-51.

that the Hohokam Culture experienced a similar precarious period before it was finally established to stand as a real and significant cultural unit. Whatever the outcome of the Mogollon Culture, the case should be fairly tested, and any opinion formulated as to its real or imaginary status should be based on all the evidence which has accumulated from a wide geographic area and which is representative of a period of development comparable in its time span to the histories of the existing southwestern groups. Furthermore, it should be borne in mind that the Mogollon Culture as an entity was being submerged at an early time by the Hohokam and Anasazi groups, which were then coming into their own. Any appraisal of it, therefore, must be made on material dating from before extensive blending took place. The author has in mind specifically such places as Sayles'[143] Cave Creek and San Simon sites in southeastern Arizona and Martin's SU Village[144] near Reserve, New Mexico, as the best sources for the earliest and possibly the purest Mogollon remains.

In a recent report on work in the Mogollon area its author commented rather critically on the affiliative aspects of the Mogollon Culture, subjecting this complex to a very close scrutiny.[145] In some points the author agrees with the statements made in this criticism. In other respects certain statements are either misleading or based on misinterpreted facts which impels one to consider them in some detail.

The principal objections voiced by Nesbitt, and in which Dr. Kidder concurs,[146] revolve around the following points. First, the view is taken that the Mogollon Culture is due to a mixture of Hohokam and Anasazi and that it was receptive rather than radiating; second, that it lacked individuality; and third, that because San Francisco Red was found as an intrusive in the early phases at Snaketown, alleged to be older than the oldest Mogollon, it is suggested that this type of pottery reached both the Mogollon and Hohokam from some unidentified source.

The author's answer to these objections can be put as follows: In determining whether or not the Mogollon Culture had the hall marks of a peripheral borrowing people who contributed nothing, it is necessary to look at that complex temporally in terms of two stages. The first and early stage was when it was radiating a limited number of fundamental traits, notably in pottery technology, which the other people

---

[143]E. B. Sayles, in preparation.
[144]P. S. Martin, J. Rinaldo, and M. Kelly, 1940.
[145]P. H. Nesbitt, 1938.
[146]A. V. Kidder, 1939, pp. 314-16.

wanted, as has been suggested in previous pages. It stands to reason that a culture which was not very far along according to standards set by the later Hohokam and Anasazi could not contribute much. Hence, in this light, to brand the Mogollon Culture without qualification as receptors only seems to misrepresent what actually took place. In the second and later stage, comparable in time to the San Francisco-Three Circle phases, the Mogollon people were obviously yielding to their stronger and more virile neighbors who, in the meantime, had passed through an accelerated development. It is hardly necessary here to recount the physical evidences of this hybridization, but it is well worth pointing out that in the whole of that region lying south of the Little Colorado River, the pottery of the late Anasazi phases (Pueblo III and Pueblo IV) was indelibly stamped by Mogollon techniques.

That the Mogollon complex was peripheral to contributing cultures in late times is true, but the connotation of the word "peripheral" as a culturally backward people in early times need not be so. It would seem to be just as proper to say that in some respects the Anasazi were peripheral to Mogollon.

It is not difficult to see how the second criticism comes about, arising in part from the inadequacy of the written word in portraying accurately what one encounters in a ruin. Nevertheless, enough tangible elements are evident which tend to justify the stand that Mogollon must be viewed as a separate entity. Not the least of these is in the physical make-up of the people themselves. Contrasting with the predominantly long-headed Basketmakers are the Mogollon brachycephals, undeformed for the most part. It may be countered that the evidence is too slight on which to base any conclusion, but the sixteen skulls from the Mogollon and Harris villages, others from the SU site, and the apparent predominance of this type from the Bear Ruin which fit this classification cannot be brushed aside lightly.

In architecture it is true that all three of the main southwestern cultures in early days were accustomed to lowering their house floors below ground level, and broadly, similarities occur. This is probably to be ascribed to a much wider sphere of influence than that which any one of these groups exerted upon another, witness the broad parallel in architecture from the midwestern part of the United States through the Great Basin and northwestward into Asia. In details and in the manner of furnishing dwellings, variations do occur in southwestern pit houses. Taken collectively, these variations were greater than those which existed in the houses of any one of the groups, thereby providing distinctive features for cultural identification. As shown in the description of the architecture of the Bear Ruin, certain non-Anasazi features were present, and these, while of a minor nature. nevertheless support the point under discussion.

The economy offers what seems to be one of the strongest individualizing traits. Meat, one of the chief sources of food, was apparently regularly cooked by heated stones in large earth ovens. This practice was probably inherited from the late stage (San Pedro) of the Cochise Culture when pit cooking appears to have been regularly employed. That this custom was a matter of cultural choice is suggested by distribution. In the Anasazi area such pits are rare to absent, although they are quite general throughout the Mogollon and Hohokam areas.

Without going into a detailed evaluation of material culture, the case of pottery will demonstrate what may be anticipated also in some other traits. Contrasted at the time of 700 A.D. or before, one finds that a wide gulf separated the ceramic achievements of the southwestern cultures. That the basis for these differences is inherent in the groups is hardly to be doubted, and in consideration of the long ceramic history of the Mogollon people, it is not surprising to find that they had made certain technological advances before they were known by their neighbors.

The third objection, having to do with San Francisco Red as a type not indigenous either to Hohokam or Mogollon, is most difficult to comprehend. The weaknesses in the reasoning of such a view are first, that it does not admit the possibility of phases in the Mogollon development older than the Georgetown; yet the excellence of pottery, notably San Francisco Red, at this time presupposes an antecedent phase or phases. One already suspects on the basis of Sayles' work, that one such phase does exist at Cave Creek, and even then the polished red pottery which was known, though less abundant than later, was of a superior type. Allowing for possible errors in computing the contemporaneity of Mogollon and Hohokam phases, there still seems to be ample opportunity that an indigenous Mogollon redware was made early enough even to be present in the Vahki Phase at Snaketown. Secondly, this view wholly ignores the petrographic evidence established by Nora Gladwin.[147] The parallel in constituents of the San Francisco Red included in

---

[147]H. S., Gladwin, E. W. Haury, E. B. Sayles, and N. Gladwin, 1937, pp. 230-32.

Snaketown and that of the Mimbres area obviously means a direct connection. This does not entirely overcome the objection raised by Nesbitt and Kidder, but coupled with the following it assumes real significance.

Thirdly, if the statement is valid that some unidentified area was the fountain from which San Francisco Red flowed to both Hohokam and Mogollon, then one must assume that 20 per cent of all the pottery of the San Francisco Phase was foreign to the Mogollon people, and even a greater percentage was foreign in the Georgetown Phase. Under any other circumstances such high percentages of a pottery so in keeping technologically with indigenous Mogollon types would be admitted at once to be nothing else but a local product. Mexico was suggested as the unknown source for all this red. That generically related reds to the south occur is not to be doubted. But so far nothing has come from Chihuahua or Sonora or even farther south which could be interpreted as the source for all Mogollon redware.

While it is a temptation to judge southwestern cultures purely on a trait basis, it is believed that there are other considerations which carry almost equal weight. Much has been heard of late of early man in the southern part of the Southwest—the Cochise Culture—together with the types of cultures from other parts of the United States. Practically all of these share the absence of a connection with the later and higher culture groups in the areas where they are found. In the Southwest neither the Hohokam nor the Anasazi offers clues which in any way would connect them with the Cochise Culture or any other preceramic people, whereas one does see this relationship strongly suggested in the case of the Mogollon. Early Mogollon material not only occurs in the Cochise Culture area, but as Sayles has pointed out,[148] if one adds pottery, house building, earth burial, agriculture, and a few minor traits to the San Pedro Stage, the result is the beginning of the Mogollon Culture. This, of course, has not been proved, but the terminal date of the San Pedro Stage, based on geological evidence as given by Antevs,[149] falls closely to the estimated beginning of the Mogollon Culture. It is quite possible, therefore, that before long this connection can reasonably be claimed, thereby pushing the Mogollon Culture roots far into antiquity. By comparison, the high attainments of both Hohokam and Anasazi will appear as a late veneer.

---

[148]E. B. Sayles and E. Antevs, 1941.
[149]*Ibid.*

Another argument, to follow this same general line of reasoning, is that the Mogollon Culture had a chronology in its own right before it faded away in favor of the Hohokam and Anasazi. There was, most definitely, a series of related phases which cannot be directly associated with either of these two cultures as they are now known.

All of this adds up to the view that the Mogollon Culture held roughly the same position in the Southwest which the Archaic Culture held in Mexico and Middle America. It was the underpinning for the later and higher cultural groups. In fact, it may be, without actually having been recognized, a northern expression of a very early and widely distributed group, now known in the south as the Archaic Culture.

There remains much to be told about the people inhabiting the Forestdale Valley after 800 A.D.—the rise of architecture from pit houses to large pueblos, the local development of the kiva, the enrichment of the material culture, the replacement of Anasazi by the Apache, and other equally provocative problems—the solution of which must await further field studies when it is hoped that a phase-by-phase account can be given.

APPENDIX

THE SKELETAL REMAINS OF THE BEAR RUIN

By Norman E. Gabel

The skeletal remains of the Bear Ruin are represented by forty burials, none of which are in a good state of preservation. In some instances the merest traces of bones remain; at best the skeletons are broken and incomplete. The discussion which follows includes morphological and metrical descriptions in various degrees of incompleteness of the relatively few burials that could be examined.

CRANIA

Burial 5 (0-513)

This cranium (Pl. XII *a*, *a'*) lacks adjoining portions of the parietal, temporal, sphenoid, and coronal bones on the left side; parts of the right sphenoid and maxillary as well as most of the skull base are also lacking. On the mandible the left ascending ramus and the right condyle are broken off.

This is the skull of a young adult male. The bony relief suggests a moderately muscled individual. A certain amount of posthumous lateral compression exaggerates the contours, but it is clearly apparent that the normal outline of the brain case viewed from above was relatively long. From the *Norma verticalis* the brain case approaches an elongated oval. The forehead is moderate in slope and height. The breadth of the frontal area is submedium, and the median sagittal line is clearly elevated. Brow ridges show but slight development and are of the median type, while the glabella is medium.

Conspicuous in the parietal region is a pronounced sagittal elevation which is continuous with a similar crested condition of the frontal bone. Anterior to the parietal foramina, however, the sagittal crest is abruptly ended by a flattening of the same axis; in other words, the median sagittal crest is interrupted by a small degree of lambdoidal deformation. The parietal bosses are moderately developed. In harmony with the long, narrow brain case is the submedium fullness of the temporal region. The temporal and supramastoid crests are both moderately expressed. The occipital bone is well curved and little affected by the small amount of lambdoidal deformation. The nuchal area is marked by a pronounced torus of the mound type.

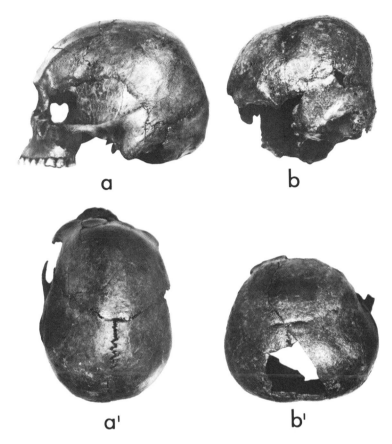

a

b

a'

b'

Plate XII.—Skulls of Burials 5 and 12 representing dolichocephalic and deformed brachycephalic types.

All of the vault sutures show simple serration, and none of them has begun to close. Two medium sized wormian bones occur on the lambdoidal suture on either side of the lambda. The left pterion approximates a K form; the right is missing.

Most of the skull base is lacking. The remaining portions indicate styloids of submedium size, moderate glenoid fossae, and no postglenoid processes. The tympanic plates are thick, and the external auditory meatuses are oval in shape.

On the face only the rims of the eye orbits are preserved and these assume the shape of a rhomboid with medium inclination. Suborbital fossae are present to a slight degree. The malars are moderate in size as well as lateral and anterior projection. The nasal architecture is somewhat primitive in several features. The nasal bones are but slightly elevated both at the root and bridge. In profile the nose is concavo-convex. The nasal aperture is noticeably broad relative to the height, and the sills are pronouncedly rounded. Small subnasal grooves underlie the aperture.

A little total and midfacial prognathism is in evidence, while the alveolar projection is increased to a moderate extent. The alveolar borders of the upper jaw are well preserved and show no absorption. The palatine bones are missing, but the remaining maxillary portions of the palate indicate a greater than usual height of that structure. In form the palate is elliptical.

The mandible is of average male size; the chin form is median and moderately projecting. No alveolar prognathism is present in the lower jaw, and muscular relief is moderate except the submedium geneal tubercles. There is no gonial eversion. The teeth are of excellent quality. Wear is moderate, and there are no caries, abscesses, or other pathological indications. The only abnormality of the teeth is the suppression of the third lower left molar. The corresponding molar on the right side was lost before death. The cusp pattern is 4-4-3 in the upper and 5-5-4 in the lower molars. The teeth show no crowding and the bite is edge to edge. The upper medial incisors are slightly shovel-shaped.

Measurements on this skull indicate hyperdolichocephaly, although the low value of 64.36 is doubtless somewhat exaggerated by posthumous lateral flattening. The length-auricular height index, which is the only expression of relative height possible on this specimen, places it in the hypsicranial class. Although the minimum frontal breath is 90 millimeters, a rather low absolute value, the forehead is broad relative to the narrow maximum cranial breadth. The pronounced leptoprosopic face is also accentuated by postmortem distortion, but there is little doubt that the original cranial proportions were long and narrow. Nasal diameters result in a moderate length-breadth ratio, as do those of the eye orbit. Compared as a whole with established cranial types of the Southwest, this skull conforms closest to the Basketmaker type of Hooton's series.[150]

---

[150]E. A. Hooton, 1930, pp. 231-47.

Burial 12 (0-516)

This skull (Pl. XII *b*, *b'*) lacks the entire upper face and the cranial base. The remaining parts, especially the vault, strongly suggest a different morphological type.

This individual is a middle-aged adult male. The muscularity and weight of the skull as a whole are comparable with that of Burial 5, but the contours show a marked departure. Where the first specimen is a scaphoid ultradolichocephal with a slight amount of lambdoidal deformation, the second vault is just as conspicuously broad, with the broadness accentuated by pronounced occipital deformation.

The frontal region of Burial 12 differs mostly in its greater breadth. The supraorbitals are of the same median type but more developed in size. Forehead height is much the same, but the frontal slope is noticeably less, as is the postorbital constriction. There is no suggestion of a median crest either on the frontal or parietal area. The parietal bosses of this deformed broad head are much more prominent than its contemporary, and the fullness of the temporal region is conspicuously greater. The temporal crests are moderately developed, and the supramastoids are pronounced. The occipital curve is sudmedium as well as the inion. A submedium torus of the mound type completes the available occipital features of note.

Suture serration of Burial 12 is simple, and their occlusion is fairly advanced on the coronal but not begun on the lambdoidal. Most of the sagittal suture is destroyed. Two small wormian bones on the lambdoidal suture are the only island bones on the vault. None of skull base remains except parts of the petrous portions. These show a large glenoid fossa, a medium thick tympanic plate, an elliptical auditory meatus, and no postglenoid process.

The mandible is of medium size; the chin is median in form and moderately projecting. No alveolar prognathism is shown. The geneal tubercles and mylohyoid ridge are submedium in size. Although the gonial angles are broken, enough remains to indicate moderate pterygoid attachment and lack of eversion. The teeth are represented by the lower jaw only. Eruption is complete; there is no tooth loss, and wear is moderate. The quality of the dentition is good. Only one caries occurs; there are no abscesses, but a small degree of absorption of the investing dental tissues is present. The lower lateral incisors are slightly shovel-shaped. The cusps of the lower molars show a 5-5-4 formula.

Measurements on this skull are necessarily few. The maximum cranial length and breadth are nearly the same;

in fact, the breadth is slightly superior, resulting in a cranial index of 102.60. The auricular height of this skull is less than that of Burial 5, but the height-length ratio is considerably higher because of much less cranial length. The incomplete condition does not permit further vault measurements and allows no upper facial diameters whatever.

The mandible lacks the gonial angles and condyles, but visual comparison shows the lower jaw as markedly broader in these posterior regions. In anterior parts the jaw is not unlike that of Burial 5. As far as the morphological type of this skull can be determined, it is quite certainly allied to the common deformed brachycephalic Pueblo type, or to what Hooton calls the "Pseudo-Alpine."[151]

BURIAL 13 (0-517)

This skull fragment is of an old adult male. It consists of the calva, parts of the petrous area of the temporal, incomplete maxillae including the palate, alveolar borders and nasal sills, and the body of the mandible. The musculature and weight of this individual are submedium. The skull is undeformed and oval in outline. Brow ridges are small and median in type, and the forehead tends to lowness with moderate slope. Medium also are the frontal breadth, the bosses, and postorbital constriction. There is a moderate sagittal elevation in the parietal area, and the parietal bosses are medium. Temporal fullness is average, and the crests are submedium. The occipital relief is also quite ordinary. The occipital curves moderately and the torus is a medium crest. The vault sutures are nearly all closed, so there is little indication of their former serration. The petrous fragments indicate a large glenoid fossa and no postglenoid process. The tympanic plate is thick, and the meatus is oval. The lower parts of the nasal skeleton show rounded sills, a medium spine, and suggestions of subnasal grooves. Moderate alveolar prognathism is shown in the upper jaw. There is a slight amount of absorption of the alveolar borders, although the teeth are in good condition. The palate is elliptical in shape and high. A submedium palatine torus of the ridge type occurs.

The lower jaw is medium in size; the chin is bilateral in form and quite projecting. No prognathism is exhibited by the mandible. Muscular relief in this area is variable: the geneal tubercles are medium, the mylohyoid ridge submedium, and the pterygoid attachments are pronounced. There is also pronounced eversion of the gonia.

---

[151]E. A. Hooton, 1930, pp. 277-82.

Eruption of the dentition is complete, and three teeth were lost before death. Attrition is pronounced. The generally good quality of the teeth is reflected by the total lack of caries, although there are two abscesses in the alveolar borders. The upper medial incisors are slightly shovel-shaped. The upper molar cusp formula is 4-4-3; the lower pattern is 5-5-4. Slight crowding of the teeth is present and the bite is edge to edge.

The only accurate measurements obtainable on Burial 13 are cranial length, breadth, and the least frontal diameter. The diameters are not remarkable, and the cranial index is 75.85. The frontoparietal ratio identifies the skull as eurymetopic.

The available remains of this cranium are insufficient to definitely establish its morphological type. Clearly, however, the skull cap more closely resembles the Basketmaker type of Burial 5.

The remaining skulls of this horizon are so fragmentary that only regional details can be observed and a few general impressions conveyed. These details and impressions in several instances tend to bear out certain conditions exhibited by the more complete skulls just described. There are further indications of a mixture of cranial types, especially in the vault region. Some of the cranial fragments clearly indicate occipital deformation coupled with brachycephaly. Others are obviously undeformed. The positive correlation shown by Burial 12 of innate broad-headedness with occipital deformation cannot be certainly substantiated by the more fragmentary specimens, but the impression remains that the Forestdale skeletons represent individuals who are divided between dolichocephaly, brachycephaly, and intermediate forms. Another tendency is in the direction of sub-medium forehead height associated with more than average frontal slope. The musculature of most of the skulls is sub-medium to medium. Suture serration in nearly every instance is simple. Little more can be added to the upper face appearance, although it may be significant that out of three fragments of upper maxillae, two show the same rounded nasal sills exhibited by Burial 5. Nothing unusual is noted in the remains of two mandibles.

LONG BONES

No complete specimens of long bones occur in this series, although several shafts permit some examination. The most noteworthy conditions of the leg bones are a high frequency of platymeria and platycnemia; both of these conditions are

well developed in most of the remains. Otherwise the long
bones are not unusual.

SUMMARY

Notwithstanding the meager nature of the Bear Ruin
skeletal material, it seems clear that one is dealing with a
mixed population. The two best preserved crania illustrate
a scaphoid ultradolicocephalic leptorrhine Basketmaker on
the one hand and a hyperbrachycephalic, artificially deformed Pueblo type on the other. The remainder of the
cranial material supports the probability of very considerable
variation in head form.[152]

---

[152]Some effort was made to observe head form while the skulls were
still in the ground, particularly those which were so fragile that
salvage was next to impossible. The impression gained was that the
majority of the skulls thus observed fell in the brachycephalic group
(E. W. H.).

BIBLIOGRAPHY

Anonymous
  1936.—"University Ruin," *The Kiva*, vol. 1, no. 8. Arizona Archaeological and Historical Society. Tucson.

Antevs, E.
  (See Sayles, E. B., and Antevs, E.).

Baldwin, G. C.
  1935.—"Dates from Kinishba Pueblo," *Tree-Ring Bulletin*, vol. 1, no. 4, p. 30. Flagstaff.
  1937.—"The Pottery of Kinishba," *The Kiva*, vol. 3, no. 1. Arizona Archaeological and Historical Society. Tucson.

Bandelier, A. F.
  1892.—"Final Report of the Investigations among the Indians of the Southwestern United States, Part II," *Papers of the Archaeological Institute of America*, American Series, no. 4. Cambridge.

Bradfield, W.
  1931.—*Cameron Creek Village, a Site in the Mimbres Area in Grant County, New Mexico.* The School of American Research. Santa Fe.
  Unpublished field notes, Museum of New Mexico. Santa Fe.

Brand, D.
  (See Sauer, C., and Brand, D.)

Brew, J. O.
  1941.—Preliminary Report of the Peabody Museum Awatovi Expedition of 1939," *Plateau*, Northern Arizona Society of Science and Art, Museum of Northern Arizona, vol. 13, no. 3, pp. 37-48. Flagstaff.

Bryan, B.
  1927.—"The Galaz Ruin in the Mimbres Valley," *El Palacio*, vol. 23, no. 12, pp. 323-37. Santa Fe.
  1931.—"Excavation of the Galaz Ruin," *The Master Key*, vol. 4, no. 6, pp. 179-89; vol. 4, no. 7, pp. 221-26. Southwest Museum. Los Angeles.

Connolly, F. M.
  1940.—*The Origin and Development of Smudged Pottery in the Southwest.* Master's thesis, Department of Anthropology, University of Arizona. Tucson.

Colton, H. S.
  1939 a.—*An Archaeological Survey of Northwestern Arizona, Including the Descriptions of Fifteen New Pottery Types.* Museum of Northern Arizona, Bull. 16. Flagstaff.
  1939 b.—*Prehistoric Culture Units and Their Relationships in Northern Arizona.* Museum of Northern Arizona, Bull. 17. Flagstaff.

Colton, H. S., and Hargrave, L. L.
  1937.—*Handbook of Northern Arizona Pottery Wares.* Museum of Northern Arizona, Bull. 11. Flagstaff.

Cosgrove, H. S., and C. B.
1932.—"The Swarts Ruin, a Typical Mimbres Site in Southwestern New Mexico, Report of the Mimbres Valley Expedition, Seasons of 1924-1927," *Papers of the Peabody Museum of American Archaeology and Ethnology*, Harvard University, vol. 15, no. 1. Cambridge.

Cummings, B.
1940.—*Kinishba, a Prehistoric Pueblo of the Great Pueblo Period.* Hohokam Museums Association and the University of Arizona. Phoenix.

Douglass, A. E.
1929.—"The Secret of the Southwest Solved by Talkative Tree Rings," *National Geographic Magazine*, vol. 56, no. 6, pp. 737-70. Washington.

Duffen, W. A.
1937.—"Tonto Ruins Stabilization, May 27 to June 30, 1937," *Southwestern Monuments Monthy Report*, July, 1937, pp. 43-54. Department of Interior, National Park Service. Coolidge.

Fewkes, J. W.
1904.—"Two Summers' Work in Pueblo Ruins," *Twenty-second Report of the Bureau of American Ethnology*, pt. 1, pp. 3-195. Washington.

Fraps, C. L.
1935.—"Tanque Verde Ruins," *The Kiva*, vol. 1, no. 4. Arizona Archaeological and Historical Society. Tucson.

Fulton, W. S.
1933.—"Archaeological Notes on Texas Canyon, Arizona," *Contributions from the Museum of the American Indian*, Heye Foundation, vol. 12, no. 1. New York.
1934.—"Archaeological Notes on Texas Canyon, Arizona," *Contributions from the Museum of the American Indian*, Heye Foundation, vol. 12, no. 2. New York.
1938.—"Archaeological Notes on Texas Canyon, Arizona," *Contributions from the Museum of the American Indian*, Heye Foundation, vol. 12, no. 3. New York.

Fulton, W. S., and Tuthill, C.
1940.—*An Archaeological Site near Gleeson, Arizona.* The Amerind Foundation, Inc., no. 1. Dragoon.
Reports on Tres Alamos in preparation.

Gavan, J. A.
1940.—"Physical Anthropology of Besh-ba-gowah." *The Kiva*, vol. 6, no. 3. Arizona Archaeological and Historical Society. Tucson.

Gladwin, N.
(See Gladwin, H. S., Haury, E. W., Sayles, E. B., and Gladwin, N.)

Gladwin, W., and H. S.
1930.—"Some Southwestern Pottery Types, Series I," *Medallion Papers*, no. 8. Gila Pueblo. Globe.
1934.—"A Method for Designation of Cultures and Their Variations," *Medallion Papers*, no. 15. Gila Pueblo. Globe.
Report on White Mound in preparation.

Gladwin, H. S., Haury, E. W., Sayles, E. B., and Gladwin, N.
1937.—"Excavations at Snaketown, Material Culture," *Medallion Papers*, no. 25. Gila Pueblo. Globe.

Gordon, G. H.
1935.—"A Visit to the Gila Cliff Ruins," *Southwestern Monuments Monthly Report*, March, 1935, p. 161. Department of the Interior, National Park Service. Coolidge.

Guernsey, S. J.
1931.—"Explorations in Northeastern Arizona: Report on the Archaeological Fieldwork of 1920-23," *Papers of the Peabody Museum of American Archaeology and Ethnology*, Harvard University, vol. 12, no. 1. Cambridge.

Guernsey, S. J., and Kidder, A. V.
1921.—"Basket Maker Caves of Northeastern Arizona," *Papers of the Peabody Museum of American Archaeology and Ethnology*, Harvard University, vol. 8, no. 2. Cambridge.

Hargrave, L. L.
(See Colton, H. S., and Hargrave, L. L.; Haury, E. W., and Hargrave, L. L.)

Haury, E. W.
1928.—*The Succession of House Types in the Pueblo Area.* Master's thesis, University of Arizona, pp. 38-58. Tucson.
1932.—"Roosevelt 9:6, a Hohokam Site of the Colonial Period," *Medallion Papers*, no. 11. Gila Pueblo. Globe.
1934.—"The Canyon Creek Ruin and Cliff Dwellings of the Sierra Ancha," *Medallion Papers*, no. 11. Gila Pueblo, Globe.
1936 a.—"Some Southwestern Pottery Types, Series IV," *Medallion Papers*, no. 19. Gila Pueblo. Globe.
1936 b.—"The Mogollon Culture of Southwestern New Mexico," *Medallion Papers*, no. 20. Gila Pueblo. Globe.
1938.—"Southwestern Dated Ruins: II," *Tree-Ring Bulletin*, vol. 4, no. 3, pp. 3-4. Tucson.
1940 a.—"New Tree-Ring Dates from the Forestdale Valley, East-Central Arizona," *Tree-Ring Bulletin*, vol. 7, no. 2, pp. 14-16. Tucson.
1940 b.—"Excavations at Forestdale," *The Kiva*, vol. 6, no. 2. Arizona Archaeological and Historical Society. Tucson.
(See also Gladwin, H. S., Haury, E. W., Sayles, E. B., and Gladwin, N.)

Haury, E. W., and Hargrave, L. L.
1931.—"Recently Dated Pueblo Ruins in Arizona," *Smithsonian Miscellaneous Collections*, vol. 82, no. 11. Washington.

Hayden, J.
Report on University Indian Ruin in preparation.

Hodge, F. W.
1920.—"Hawikuh Bonework," *Indian Notes and Monographs*, *Museum of the American Indian*, Heye Foundation, vol. 3, no. 3. New York.
1921.—"Turquoise Work of Hawikuh, New Mexico," *Leaflets of the Museum of the American Indian*, Heye Foundation, no. 2. New York.
1937.—"History of Hawikuh, New Mexico, One of the So-called Cities of Cibola," *Publications of the Frederick Webb Hodge Anniversary Publications Fund*, vol. 1. Los Angeles.

Hooton, E. A.
    1930.—*The Indians of Pecos, a Study of Their Skeletal Remains.* Department of Archaeology, Phillips Academy. Cambridge.

Hough, W.
    1903.—"Archaeological Field-work in Northeastern Arizona, the Museum-Gates Expedition of 1901," *Annual Report of the U.S. National Museum for 1901,* pp. 279-358. Washington.
    1907.—*Antiquities of the Upper Gila and Salt River Valleys in Arizona and New Mexico.* Bureau of American Ethnology, Bull. 35. Washington.
    1919.—"Exploration of a Pit House Village at Luna, New Mexico," *Proceedings of the U.S. National Museum,* vol. 55, pp. 409-31. Washington.
    1930.—"Exploration of Ruins in the White Mountain Apache Indian Reservation, Arizona," *Proceedings of the U.S. National Museum,* vol. 78, art. 13, pp. 1-21. Washington.

Jenks, A. E.
    1928.—*The Mimbres Valley Expedition.* Bulletin of the Minneapolis Institute of Art, bull. 17, no. 31. Minneapolis.

Judd, N. M.
    1926.—*Archaeological Observations North of the Rio Colorado.* Bureau of American Ethnology, Bull. 82. Washington.
    1930.—"The Excavation and Repair of Betatakin," *Proceedings of the U.S. National Museum,* vol. 77, pp. 1-77. Washington.

Kelly, I.
    Report on Hodge's Ruin in preparation.

Kelly, M.
    (See Martin, P. S., Rinaldo, J., and Kelly, M.)

Kidder, A. V.
    1939.—"Review of Nesbitt, P. H., Starkweather Ruin, a Mogollon-Pueblo Site in the Upper Gila Area of New Mexico and Affiliative Aspects of the Mogollon Culture," *American Anthropologist,* n.s., vol. 41, no. 2, pp. 314-16. Menasha.
    (See also Guernsey, S. J., and Kidder, A. V.)

Martin, P. S., and Rinaldo, J.
    1939.—*Modified Basketmaker Sites, Ackmen-Lowry Area, Southwestern Colorado, 1938.* Anthropological Series, vol. 23, no. 3, Field Museum of Natural History. Chicago.

Martin, P. S., Rinaldo, J., and Kelly, M.
    1940.—*The SU Site: Excavations at a Mogollon Village, Western New Mexico, 1939.* Anthropological Series, vol. 32, no. 1, Field Museum of Natural History. Chicago.

Mera, H. P.
    1934.—*Observations on the Archaeology of the Petrified Forest National Monument.* Technical Series, Bull. no. 7, Archaeological Survey, Laboratory of Anthropology. Santa Fe.
    1935.—*Ceramic Clues to the Prehistory of North Central New Mexico.* Technical Series, Bull. no. 8, Laboratory of Anthropology. Santa Fe.
    1939.—"Style Trends of Pueblo Pottery in the Rio Grande and Little Colorado Cultural Areas from the Sixteenth to the Nineteenth Century," *Memoirs of the Laboratory of Anthropology,* vol. 3. Santa Fe.

Mindeleff, V.
1891.—"A Study of Pueblo Architecture, Tusayan and Cibola," *Eighth Annual Report of the Bureau of Ethnology.* Washington.

Morris, E. H.
1927.—"The Beginnings of Pottery Making in the San Juan Area: Unfired Prototypes and the Wares of the Earliest Ceramic Period," *Anthropological Papers of the American Museum of Natural History,* vol. 28, pt. 2. New York.
1939.—"Archaeological Studies in the La Plata District, Southwestern Colorado and Northwestern New Mexico," *Carnegie Institution of Washington Publication,* no. 519. Washington.

McGregor, J. C.
1937.—*Winona Village: A XIIth Century Settlement with a Ball Court Near Flagstaff, Arizona.* Museum of Northern Arizona, Bull. 12. Flagstaff.

Nesbitt, P. H.
1931.—*The Ancient Mimbreños.* Logan Museum, Beloit College, Bull. 4. Beloit.
1938.—"Starkweather Ruin: A Mogollon-Pueblo Site in the Upper Gila Area of New Mexico, and Affiliative Aspects of the Mogollon Culture," *Logan Museum Publications in Anthropology,* Bull. 6. Beloit.

Patterson, J. T.
1936.—*The Corner-Tang Flint Artifacts of Texas.* University of Texas Bull. no. 3618, Anthropological Papers, vol. 1, no. 4. Austin.

Ridgway, R.
1912.—*Color Standards and Color Nomenclature.* Washington.

Rinaldo, J.
(See Martin, P. S., and Rinaldo, J.)

Roberts, F. H. H., Jr.
1929.—*Shabik'eshchee Village: A Late Basket Maker Site in the Chaco Canyon, New Mexico.* Bureau of American Ethnology, Bull. 92. Washington.
1931.—*The Ruins at Kiatuthlanna, Eastern Arizona.* Bureau of American Ethnology, Bull. 100. Washington.
1932.—*The Village of the Great Kivas on the Zuni Reservation, New Mexico.* Bureau of American Ethnology, Bull. 111. Washington.
1939.—*Archeological Remains in the Whitewater District, Eastern Arizona. Part I. House Types.* Bureau of American Ethnology, Bull. 121. Washington.
1940.—*Archeological Remains in the Whitewater District, Eastern Arizona. Part II. Artifacts and Burials.* Bureau of American Ethnology, Bull. 126. Washington.

Sauer, C., and Brand, D.
1931.—"Prehistoric Settlements of Sonora with Specific Reference to Cerros de Trincheras," *University of California Publications in Geography,* vol. 5, no. 3, pp. 67-148. Berkeley.

Sayles, E. B.
1936 *a.*—"Some Southwestern Pottery Types, Series V," *Medallion Papers*, no. 21. Gila Pueblo. Globe.
1936 *b.*—"An Archaeological Survey of Chihuahua, Mexico," *Medallion Papers*, no. 22. Gila Pueblo. Globe.
Report on Cave Creek and San Simon sites in preparation. (See also Gladwin, H. S., Haury, E. W., Sayles, E. B., and Gladwin, N.)

Sayles, E. B., and Antevs, E.
1941.—"The Cochise Culture," *Medallion Papers,* no. 29. Gila Pueblo. Globe.

Schmidt, E. F.
1927.—"The Mrs. William Boyce Thompson Expedition," *Natural History Magazine*, American Museum of Natural History, vol. 26, no. 6, pp. 635-44. New York.
1928.—"Time Relations of Prehistoric Pottery Types in Southern Arizona," *Anthropological Papers of the American Museum of Natural History*, vol 30, pt. 5, pp. 247-302. New York.

Schroeder, A. H.
1940.—*A Stratigraphic Survey of Pre-Spanish Trash Mounds of the Salt River Valley, Arizona.* Master's thesis, Department of Anthropology, University of Arizona. Tucson.

Smith, H. V.
1930.—*The Climate of Arizona.* College of Agriculture, Agricultural Experiment Station, University of Arizona Bull. no. 130. Tucson.

Spier, L.
1917.—"An Outline for a Chronology of Zuni Ruins," *Anthropological Papers of the American Museum of Natural History*, vol. 18, pt. 3. New York.
1918.—"Notes on Some Little Colorado Ruins," *Anthropological Papers of the American Museum of Natural History*, vol 18, pt. 4. New York.
1919.—"Ruins in the White Mountains, Arizona," *Anthropological Papers of the American Museum of Natural History*, vol. 18, pt. 5. New York.

Steen, C. R.
1941.—"The Upper Tonto Ruins," *The Kiva*, vol. 6, no. 5. Arizona Archaeological and Historical Society. Tucson.

Steward, J. H.
1933.—*Archaeological Problems of the Northern Periphery of the Southwest.* Museum of Northern Arizona, Bull. 5. Flagstaff.

Stoner, V. A.
1936.—"A Reconnaissance of Tonto Cliff Dwellings," *Southwestern Monuments Monthly Report*, April, 1936, pp. 304-12. Department of Interior, National Park Service. Coolidge.

Tuthill, C.
(See Fulton, W. S., and Tuthill, C.)

Trischka, C.
1933.—"Hohokam: A Chapter in the History of Red-on-Buff Culture of Arizona," *Scientific Monthly*, vol. 37, pp. 417-33. Lancaster.

Vickrey, I.
1937.—"Besh-ba-gowah," *The Kiva,* vol. 4, no. 5. Arizona Archaeological and Historical Society. Tucson.

Woodward, A.
1931.—"The Grewe Site," *Los Angeles Museum of History, Science
and Art, Occasional Papers,* no. 1. Los Angeles.

SELECTED BIBLIOGRAPHY FOR SITES SHOWN IN FIGURE 1

Bear Ruin
Haury, E. W., 1940 *a;* 1940 *b;* this report.

Besh-ba-gowah
Gavan, J. A., 1940.
Vickrey, I., 1939.

Cameron Creek
Bradfield, W., 1931.

Canyon Creek
Haury, E. W., 1934, pp. 23-148.

Cave Creek
Sayles, E. B. In preparation.

Chevlon
Fewkes, J. W., 1904, pp. 30-32.

Four-mile
Fewkes, J. W., 1904, pp. 136-64.

Galaz
Bryan, B., 1927; 1931.
Jenks, A. E., 1928.

Gila Cliff Dwellings National Monument
Bandelier, A. F., 1892, pp. 360-62.
Gordon, G. H., 1935, p. 161.
Hough, W., 1907, pp. 30-32.

Gila Pueblo
In Preparation.

Grasshopper
Hough, W., 1930, pp. 3-6, 10-20.

Harris
Haury, E. W., 1936 *a;* 1936 *b,* pp. 49-78.

Hawikuh
Hodge, F. W., 1920; 1921; 1937.

Hodge's Ruin
Kelly, I. In preparation.

Homolobi
Fewkes, J. W., 1904, pp. 23-30.

Kiatuthlanna
Roberts, F. H. H., Jr., 1931.

Kinishba
Baldwin, G. C., 1935; 1937.
Cummings, B., 1940.

Luna
  Hough, W., 1919.
Mattocks
  Nesbitt, P. H., 1931.
Mogollon Village
  Haury, E. W., 1936 *a;* 1936 *b,* pp. 5-48.
Pinedale
  Fewkes, J. W., 1904, pp. 164-67.
  Haury, E. W. and Hargrave, L. L., 1931, pp. 44-71.
Pottery Hill
  Hough, W., 1903, pp. 297-301.
Pueblo Viejo
  Fewkes, J. W., 1904, pp. 171-87.
Roosevelt 9:6
  Haury, E. W., 1932.
San Simon Village
  Sayles, E. B. In preparation.
Showlow (also Huning Ruin)
  Douglass, A. E., 1929.
  Haury, E. W., and Hargrave, L. L., 1931, pp. 7-44.
  Hough, W., 1903, p. 301.
Shumway
  Hough, W., 1903, p. 302.
Sierra Ancha Cliff Ruins
  Haury, E. W., 1934, pp. 1-21.
Starkweather
  Nesbitt, P. H., 1938.
SU
  Martin, P. S., Rinaldo, J., and Kelly, M., 1940.
Swarts
  Cosgrove, H. S., and C. B., 1932.
Tanque Verde
  Fraps, C. L., 1935.
  Haury, E. W., 1928, pp. 39-58.
Texas Canyon
  Fulton, W. S., 1933; 1934; 1938.
Three Circle
  Bradfield, W. Unpublished field notes, Museum of New Mexico,
  Santa Fe.
Togetzoge
  Schmidt, E. F., 1927; 1928.
Tonto Cliff Ruins National Monument
  Duffen, W. A., 1937, pp. 43-54.
  Steen, C. R., 1941.
  Stoner, V. A., 1936, pp. 304-10.
Tres Alamos
  Fulton, W. S., and Tuthill, C. In preparation.

Tundastusa
Hough, W., 1903, pp. 289-97.

University Indian Ruin
Anonymous, 1936.
Hayden, J. In preparation.

Village of the Great Kivas
Roberts, F. H. H., Jr., 1932.

White Mound
Gladwin, H. S. In preparation.

Whitewater
Roberts, F. H. H., Jr., 1939; 1940.

Wide Ruin (Kin Tiel)
Fewkes, J. W., 1904, pp. 124-34.
Hargrave, L. L. (in Haury, E. W., and Hargrave, L. L.), 1931, pp. 80-95.
Mindeleff, V., 1891.

Woodruff Butte
Hough, W., 1903, pp. 318-19.
Mera, H. P., 1934, p. 5.

PART III

An Early Pit House Village
of the
Mogollon Culture
Forestdale Valley, Arizona

Emil W. Haury and E. B. Sayles

Originally published as
University of Arizona Bulletin
Vol. XVIII, No. 4   October, 1947
Social Science Bulletin No. 16

Plate I.—*a*, Northern face of the bluff from the valley floor. The village is situated towards the left end of the ridge. *b*, Eastern slope, showing shallow depressions. Figures mark locations of Houses 1 and 2. The Forestdale Valley lies beyond.

ACKNOWLEDGMENTS

The archaeological work in the Forestdale Valley, east-central Arizona, which forms the basis of this report, was carried out as follows: In 1941 the excavations were conducted as a summer school project by the Department of Anthropology, University of Arizona, with sixteen students enrolled. To these registrants go my thanks for enthusiastically sharing the work and participating in lively discussions stimulated by the problems at hand. Mr. Ralph Patton and Mrs. Florence Connolly Shipek served efficiently as field and laboratory assistants respectively.

Financial aid was received from the following sources: A grant from the Penrose Fund, American Philosophical Society, Philadelphia; an allotment for Apache labor from the Indian Division of the Civilian Conservation Corps through the assistance of Mr. William Donner, Superintendent of the Fort Apache Indian Reservation; and further assistance from Mr. B. D. Butler and Mrs. E. B. Danson.

The digging during this season was extended to two ruins, the first a small stone pueblo (Ariz. P:16:2) located near the Bear Ruin (Ariz. P:16:1), and the second the Bluff Site (Ariz. P:16:20), with which this report is concerned. Excavations in the latter were begun on July 2 and continued through August 17.

As in previous years of our investigations in this area, we were aided in countless ways by Mr. and Mrs. Thomas Jennings, who operated the Forestdale Trading Post. The untimely death of Mr. Jennings on March 22, 1944, has brought this pleasant relationship to an end.

During the summer of 1944, from June 1 to July 12, the study of the Bluff Site was resumed. Camp personnel was limited to staff, as wartime restrictions made the maintenance of a field school inadvisable. Generous financial assistance was received in the form of a grant-in-aid from the Viking Fund, Inc., New York. Grateful acknowledgment is made to that organization for furthering this study, both in the field and in supporting the publication of the results.

Mr. E. B. Sayles, Curator of the Arizona State Museum, was directly in charge of the excavations. Because of the poverty of the culture with which we were dealing and the particularly difficult physical conditions presented by the site, Sayles is deserving of my unstinted admiration for his keenness of observation and perception of problems. Mrs. Frances T. Slutes, secretary to the Department of Anthropology and the Arizona State Museum, assisted with the clerical work.

Workmen were recruited from the local Apache population. During both seasons the studies were carried out under permits from the U.S. Department of the Interior and with the unanimous approval of the Apache Tribal Council.

EMIL W. HAURY
Tucson, Arizona
May 2, 1946

AN EARLY PIT HOUSE VILLAGE OF THE MOGOLLON CULTURE FORESTDALE VALLEY, ARIZONA

INTRODUCTION

One of the currently debated questions in southwestern archaeology concerns the identification, if not the reality, of the Mogollon Culture. It was the intention of the Arizona State Museum and the Department of Anthropology of the University of Arizona to bring new evidence to bear on this problem when, in 1939, investigations were begun in the Forestdale Valley, Fort Apache Indian Reservation, Arizona.

The results of the first two seasons of excavation in the Bear Ruin have already been published.[1] This ruin, a pit house village dating about A.D. 700, evidenced what was regarded to be a blend of Mogollon and Anasazi stocks. It provided the basis for the delineation of the Forestdale Phase, which in 1939-40 was considered the oldest horizon of a long sequence of human occupation recognizable in the numerous sites in the valley.

The present report covers the work in a still older ruin, the Bluff Site. This was first seen by us in 1939, but its cultural status was not realized until 1941, when excavation was started. The over-all significance of this ruin is twofold: (a) it has given us data on two early horizons, with pottery, called the Hilltop and Cottonwood Phases, respectively, both antecedent to the Forestdale Phase, and inaugurating the valley's history as we now know it; and (b) it has, we believe, further sharpened the evidence in support of an early non-Anasazi stock which falls within the as yet imperfectly defined label of Mogollon Culture.

THE BLUFF SITE[2]

While searching for archaeological remains in the Forestdale Valley, evidence of occupation was found on top of a sandstone bluff along the southern margin of the drainage at a point approximately 1.5 miles southwest and downstream from the Bear Ruin.[3] Directly north across the valley lies Tundastusa, the largest and latest pueblo ruin in the immediate area, studied by Hough in 1901 (Fig. 1).[4]

The bluff, formed by block-faulted Coconino sandstone of Permian age, rises some 50 meters above the valley and commands an excellent view of the chief agricultural land available in the area (Pl. I a).

[1]E. W. Haury, "Excavations in the Forestdale Valley, East-Central Arizona," Soc. Sc. Bull., No. 12, University of Arizona, 1940.
[2]Ariz. P:16:20, Arizona State Museum Survey.
[3]Township 8 North, Range 21 East, Section 2, northwest quarter.
[4]W. Hough, 1903, pp. 290 et seq.

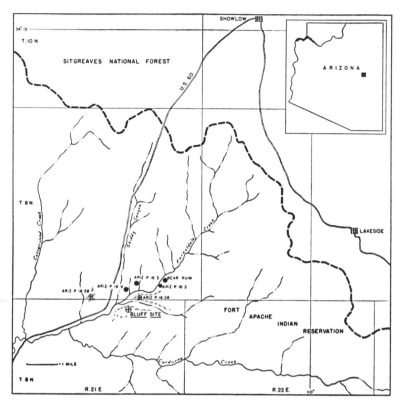

Figure 1.—Map of the Forestdale Valley and adjoining drainages, showing the location of the Bluff Site (Ariz. P:16:20) in relation to other key sites of the area. Ruins marked by crossed circles, namely Ariz. P:16:28 and Ariz. P:16:58 (Red Hill Site), belong to the same general horizon as the Bluff Site, or before A.D. 600. In the Bear Ruin (Ariz. P:16:1) and the others shown, the consecutive occupation of the valley from about A.D. 600 to 1400 can be traced. Insert locates area in Arizona.

The north face is nearly vertical and can be scaled only with difficulty. Easier approaches occur both to the east and west along apparently old and well-worn trails. To the south the country rises in a series of higher ridges.

There is no need here to recount the details of the local environment, as this has already been given previously,[5] but a few comments on the site itself are appropriate.

The crest of the bluff is highest along its northern face, whence it slopes gently to the east, south, and west (Fig. 2). The flattest area,

---

[5]E. W. Haury, 1940, pp. 10 *et seq.*

some 110 m. east-west by 90 m. north-south was best suited for occupancy, and it was here that practically all evidence of culture was found.

The present vegetative cover is heavy. This consists of a variety of grasses, dense manzanita clumps, live oaks, juniper, and pine trees. The latter, with the exception of a few growing around the lower margin of the occupied area, are only from forty to fifty years old. Stumps and snags of much older pine trees, scarred by fire, testify to a burning of the area, perhaps a half-century ago.

To the inexperienced eye, little was to be seen on the surface suggestive of human use. Chipped stone and pottery could be found only by diligent search. More important, however, was the unnatural contouring of the surface. There were a few slight depressions on the flatter part of the hill, and on the southern and eastern slopes, shelf-like terraces were quite distinct (Pl. I *b*). In evidence, too, were low mounds of burnt rock (Pl. II *a*), obviously hearth material. These clues were indicative of prolonged occupancy, and excavation was considered worthwhile.

It was felt at first that the area was the site of an early Apache encampment. The scarcity of pottery and the similarity to Apache pottery of such few sherds as were found, fit well with what is known of Apache endeavors along this line. The absence of iron, china, and glass and other objects of white manufacture suggested that, if Apache, it was a site of late prehistoric or early historic times, and any data on this tribe during these horizons was sorely needed. This possibility seemed all the more plausible with Hough's[6] identification of the bluff as an Apache fortification, presumably based on information obtained from Apaches working for him at the time. We also learned from a native informant, a woman of ninety odd years, that she had lived on the bluff as a little girl with her own and several other families.

It did not require much digging to show that this assumption was wrong and that the problem was not as simple as at first believed. While there were meager traces of Apache use of the bluff (see p. 289), these capped a much more extensive and much older occupation, the identity and chronologic position of which is here set forth.

NATURE OF TRASH

It is to be supposed that before the founding of this village the bluff top supported some vegetation and that the bedrock was covered with a veneer of varying depth of sand derived from the disintegrated bedrock. In a few places this original light gray material was detected. The trash, on the other hand, was black, heavily impregnated with pulverized charcoal and humic matter. Most everywhere this rested directly on bedrock, creating the impression that the hilltop was quite barren when houses were first built. The probability is, however, that

---

[6]W. Hough, 1903, Plate II.

Plate II.—*a*, Starting excavations. Tree-covered mounds in background are burnt-rock middens. *b*, General view towards southwest. Houses 8 and 9 in foreground.

the original accumulation has been discolored by the overlying trash, and because of the meagerness of the cultural remains, the separation cannot be made. On this account most of the house drawings show the trash directly on the bedrock.

The trash, black, sandy, and rocky, but with little culture per cubic meter, was scattered over the site sheetwise. It ranged in depth from a few centimeters to approximately 1.25 m. south of House 11. Even in the area of deepest trash there was no visible stratification of the debris. Root and rodent action, plus the porosity of the soil, have apparently combined to destroy such traces, if ever present.

APACHE USE OF THE BLUFF

That the Apache have camped on the bluff, as reported by one informant, is doubtless true, but we have seen very little tangible proof of this. There was one probable wickiup site, indicated by a few charred saplings near the surface (Figs. 2 and 18). Unlike pit houses, these leave few traces once the superstructure has collapsed and disintegrated. There have been no recent camps, with the usual wastage of tin cans, bottles, etc. Hence, any shelters that were there must be from seventy-five to a hundred years or more old.

Cow bones, found in a few places near the surface, are the residue of Apache activities. But among the stone tools and the pottery fragments nothing was seen which could be assigned to them with certainty. Yet it is only fair to state that the patterns of Apache culture a century ago had much in common with the fourth-century culture which lay below and that the task of segregating the two would be difficult if the mixture were appreciable. This situation we do not believe to have been the case.

Within the past twenty to thirty years an Apache burial was made northwest of House 5, simply marked by a pile of stone. At the same time it appears that a horse belonging to the deceased was killed, and its bones subsequently became scattered over the site. Horse bones, presumably of the same animal, were also exhumed from just below the surface in the center of the large depression marking House 5.

All told, these clues of Apache occupation are negligible, and further consideration of the tribe in the general problems of the site does not seem to be warranted.

ADDITIONAL SITES

Before proceeding with the analysis of the culture of the two phases, called the Hilltop and Cottonwood, respectively, it should be pointed out that other ruins of this same general level of attainment and age occur in the area. Our survey is by no means complete, but of about sixty sites two should be mentioned. The first, Ariz. P:16:28, lies atop another bluff a short distance northeast of the ruin described here, and the second, Ariz. P:16:58, is a little more than a mile to the northwest, situated on a cone-shaped hill about 75 m. high (Fig. 1, Pl. IX *b*).

From its color, this has been named the Red Hill Site. A dozen or so houses were closely arranged in the available space, and occupation was of some duration, as the trash is extensive and relatively deep. In both places mentioned the scarcity of pottery and other culture parallels the condition noted for the Bluff Site.

Significantly, all traces of the early horizon in question have so far been found on high eminences, in contrast to the villages of later times, which are located along the margin of the valley floor. Three instances of this may be taken to mean that our work on the Bluff Site sheds light on a well-established pattern for the selection of village sites and that it was not an isolated and, therefore, atypical case.

Just why hilltops were chosen for settlement is not wholly clear. All offered good defensive qualities, suggesting an actual or imagined threat of unfriendly people, but no proof in support of this idea has been found. An equally logical explanation is that these land heights were warmer in winter than the valley, through which the cold air from the higher regions drained at night. This nightly movement of air was very perceptible during our stay and even in summertime often brought down a bone-chilling breeze.

FAUNA

A dearth of animal bones in the refuse of the site presents a paradoxical situation which, in the final analysis, may be more apparent than real. The discrepancy comes in with the logical assumption that a people, presumably in the throes of becoming fully agricultural, would still be leaning heavily on animal food. Previous appraisals of Mogollon Culture economy have considered hunting as perhaps the main subsistence activity. The small amount of bones does not bear out this claim for the Bluff Site.

It is possible, of course, that soil conditions may have eliminated much of the bone. With this in mind, soil samples were given to Dr. T. F. Buehrer of the Department of Agricultural Chemistry of the University of Arizona, whose report is appended hereto.

His conclusions that the trash does not contain the chemical properties it should have if there had been any appreciable destruction of bone, together with the fact that the few bones recovered are quite well preserved and show no signs of chemical leaching, is basis for the belief that the evidence can be accepted without qualification. The conclusion, therefore, is that hunting for the people of this village was practically of no importance whatever. It may be remarked that a heavy timber environment such as that of the Forestdale Valley is far less attractive as a hunting area than an open grassland environment, offering a natural explanation of the situation noted. One might be inclined to regard this more seriously if it were not for the fact that in the large late pueblos of the valley animal bones are extremely abundant, showing that game was to be had if the inclination to take it were there.

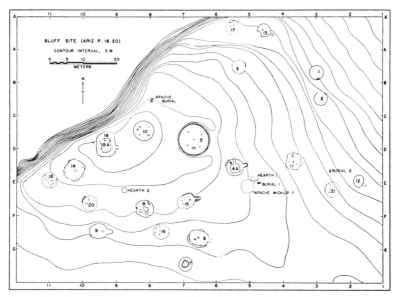

Figure 2.—Topographic map of the Bluff Site, showing distribution of houses and grid system.

Excluding a handful of shattered bone fragments, the identifiable elements numbered only twenty-three, and three of these were cow bones, attributable to the Apache occupation. The remaining twenty occurrences may be tabulated as follows:[7]

Deer	13
Pronghorn antelope	4
Gopher	2
Coyote	1

FLORA

Traces of vegetal food were not found, with the exception of charred hulls of black walnuts (*Juglans major*). Inferentially, on the basis of metate types, it may be stated that corn was grown, but no charred cobs or kernels have survived.

ARCHITECTURE

During the two seasons, twenty-three houses were entirely or partially cleared. These were well distributed over the highest part of the bluff, ranging from the very edge of the northern precipice to well down on the eastern slope of the ridges (Fig. 2). The houses located account for about two thirds of those originally comprising the village, judging from the space remaining which was not fully tested. We have

[7]Identification by Dr. Barbara Lawrence, Museum of Comparative Zoology, Harvard University, Cambridge, Mass.

Plate III.—*a*, Bedrock projecting into House 7, the face of which has been dressed by fracturing and pecking. *b*, House 1 partially cleared. Note bedrock overlain by trash on high side. Pine tree is 200 years old.

every reason to believe that the structures described in the following pages are representative of the architectural types present.

Shallow depressions marked the locations for about half of those uncovered. This situation was particularly true of the units on the flatter crest of the ridge, while the house pits on the slopes were generally well filled with washed-in debris. Since the bluff itself is a sandstone mass with only a thin veneer of loose rubble covering the solid stone, it stands to reason that builders of pit houses had two choices, either to go only through the loose top layer, in which event the structures would not have been over .25 m. deep on the average, or to penetrate the more resistant bedrock. In most cases the latter alternative was resorted to.

The bedrock, Coconino sandstone, is extensively jointed and fractured, so that by prying, sizable chunks can be lifted out. But with the tools available to a primitive people, as wooden bars, the task of excavating a meter into bedrock represents no mean undertaking. Large blocks of stone, free of joints, did offer insurmountable obstacles, and in a few cases, as in House 13 (Fig. 13), such rocks were left to form what must have been bothersome projections in the room. In other instances, smaller projecting rocks were broken off by force, and, as in House 7 (Pl. III *a*), the face was dressed down by pecking.

The nature of the rock prohibited the construction of a trim-appearing house, even though the people may have been capable of building them that way. Outlines were ragged and floors very uneven, as the photographs show. Needless to say, this enormously complicated the task of excavation, but at the same time it did not detract from the forceful impression gained during the work that a pit house-building people were not to be deterred from constructing houses according to the dictates of tradition, in spite of heavy obstacles. No clearer example is needed to illustrate the tenacity with which a people cling to certain age-old customs.

HOUSES

House 1 (Fig. 3, Pl. III *b*).

Shape.—Circular.

Size.—Diameter, 4.3 m.; depth, .7 to 1.3 m.

Walls.—Bedrock; sandy clay plaster, burned red, preserved in a few spots, rising .2 m. above floor.

Floor.—Bedrock; very rough; probably originally covered with clay, preserved in limited areas.

Hearth.—None located.

Lateral entrance.—None located.

Pits.—One, near south margin, irregular, .7 m. long by .3 m. deep.

Postholes.—None.

Roof.—No data.

Pottery.—Alma Plain, Bluff *var.,* 39.2 per cent; Forestdale *var.,* 45.0 per cent. Fine Paste Brown, 5.9 per cent; Woodruff Smudged, 3.9 per cent; Adamana Brown, 5.9 per cent.

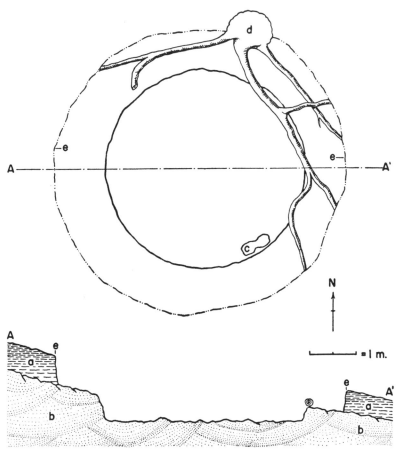

Figure 3.—Plan and section of House 1: *a,* trash;   *b,* bedrock; *c,* floor pit; *d,* 200-year-old pine tree; *e,* limits of excavation.

Dates.—A.D. 310 ± 15 (one tree).

Phase.—Hilltop.

Comments.—A typical featureless bedrock house, early for the site. Floor and walls burned.

House 2 (Pl. IV *a*).

Shape.—Circular.

Size.—Diameter, 4.1 m.; depth, 1.0-1.5 m.

Walls, floor, hearth, and lateral entrance.—As in House 1.

Pits.—One, northwest margin; .35 m. in diameter, .25 m. deep; contained one mano.

Postholes.—None.

Roof.—No data.

Plate IV.—*a,* House 2, penetrating bedrock to a depth of 1.3 m. on the high side, shown by meter stick resting against wall. Excavations here have been carried beyond periphery of house to locate possible exterior features. *b,* House 3, during excavation. The metates rest on the rough floor. Note bedrock rising towards surface to left of shovel and deep trash to right.

Pottery.—Alma Plain, Bluff *var.,* 59.3 per cent; Forestdale *var.,* 29.6 per cent. Fine Paste Brown, 9.3 per cent; Gila Plain, 1.9 per cent.

Dates.—306 + x (one tree).

Phase.—Hilltop.

Comments.—One of the deeper structures of the site, House 2 is a good example of the rock-cut type. It was heavily burned, and a Type II metate lay on the floor.

House 3 (Pl. IV *b*).

Shape.—Vague, probably circular, judging by burned area.

Size.—Approximately 4.0 m. in diameter; depth, about 1.0 m. at deepest point, but excavation into bedrock was cut in excess of .5 m.

Walls.—Low and very irregular.

Floor.—Uneven, with large blocks of bedrock projecting well above floor level. One of these was used as an anvil.

Hearth, lateral entrance, pits, postholes.—None located.

Roof.—No data.

Pottery.—Alma Plain, Bluff *var.,* 38.2 per cent; Forestdale *var.,* 54.4 per cent. Fine Paste Brown, 6.2 per cent; Alma Scored, 1.2 per cent.

Dates.—288 + x (one tree).

Phase.—Hilltop.

Comments.—Two metates and numerous manos, together with the burning and the obvious but irregular removal of bedrock certainly makes this a habitation site. Its importance is in the fact that a layer of trash, deep for the site, lay over the house, indicating that it was relatively early in the life of the village. This is supported by the ceramic content of the trash, too.

House 4 (Fig. 4; Pl. V *a*).

Shape.—Circular.

Size.—Diameter, 4.9 m.; depth, .7 m. to floor.

Walls.—Bedrock, no evidence of plaster; short rubble wall along northwest side, where original excavation was carried too far into the sandstone.

Floor.—Rough, with no trace of clay flooring; partly torn out by construction of House 4A.

Hearth.—None located.

Lateral entrance.—Parallel-sided extension to east; cut into bedrock with slightly rising floor towards end; trough about .2 m. deep and of same width in floor follows entrance contour.

Pits, postholes, and roof.—No evidence.

Pottery.—See 4A.

Dates.—None.

Phase.—Hilltop.

Comments.—See 4A.

Plate V.—*a*, Houses 4 and 4A, the former being the older. The extension in the foreground is the entry to House 4. *b*, House 5, western half. Note the depth of penetration into bedrock and trench at edge of floor.

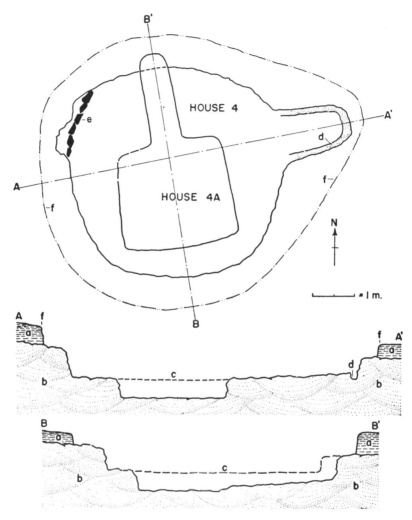

Figure 4.—Plans and sections of Houses 4 and 4A: *a*, trash; *b*, bedrock; *c*, projected floor of House 4; *d*, trough; *e*, rubble wall; *f*, limits of excavation.

House 4A (Fig. 4; Pl. V *a*).

    Shape.—Rectangular.

    Size.—2.5 by 2.7 m.; depth, floor approximately .5 m. below floor of House 4, and a maximum of 1.6 m. below surface at deepest point.

    Walls.—Probably rubble, as much rock was removed from within 4A.

Floor.—Bedrock.

Hearth.—None.

Lateral entrance.—Long, parallel-sided, to north; end carried into bedrock forming north wall of House 4; floor rises perceptibly; trough absent.

Pits, postholes, roof.—No evidence.

Pottery.—Since House 4A was not recognized until excavations were nearly completed, a sherd separation for the two structures was not made. The total sample is much like that of the other Hilltop Phase houses: Alma Plain, Bluff *var.,* 56.5 per cent; Forestdale *var.,* 36.2 per cent. Fine Paste Brown, 5.8 per cent; Gila Plain, 1.5 per cent.

Dates.—None.

Phase.—Although different in shape from most other Hilltop Phase houses and later than House 4, 4A probably belongs to that horizon.

Comments.—While this is a clear-cut case of stratigraphy, House 4A being the later of the two, and at the same time showing a shape difference, nothing was found to indicate an appreciable lapse of time between the two constructions. It is worth calling attention here to a case of house superposition in the Bear Ruin[8] (Forestdale Phase), where an older rectangular house was partly destroyed in the building of a round house, just the reverse of the situation here. It is undoubtedly possible to detect norms of house types for any given site or period, but it is also clear that almost anything can happen architecturally to cloud the evolutionary side of the problem.

House 5 (Fig. 5; Pl. V *b*).

Shape.—Circular.

Size.—Diameter, 10.3 m.; depth, 1.1 to 1.45 m.

Walls.—Bedrock, clay plaster preserved at one point to a height of .7 m. above floor.

Floor.—Bedrock, but originally covered with thick layer of clay. Floor at perimeter has trench .25 m. wide and .15 m. in depth on the average.

Hearth.—About midway between center and south wall; a declivity in bedrock, rimmed on north side with stones.

Lateral entrance.—Persistent search failed to produce any evidence of a side entrance. If present, it was on bedrock level and considerably above floor.

Pits.—None.

Postholes.—Five; one central and four set well in from wall as at the corners of a square; up to .4 m. in depth, made by prying out chunks of sandstone.

Roof.—No data, but posthole plan suggests squarish central portion with sloping roof to ground level over rest of structure.

---

[8]E. W. Haury, 1940, Fig. 7, p. 48.

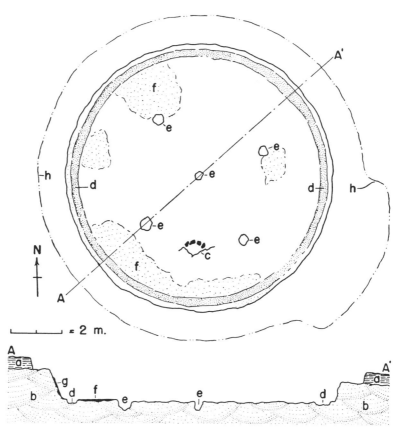

Figure 5.—Plan and section of House 5: *a*, trash; *b*, bedrock; *c*, hearth, partly bedrock and placed rocks; *d*, floor trench; *e*, postholes; *f*, clay flooring; *g*, clay plaster on bedrock; *h*, limits of excavation.

Pottery.—Alma Plain, Bluff *var.*, 39.2 per cent; Forestdale *var.*, 55 per cent. Fine Paste Brown, 2.6 per cent; Woodruff Red .7 per cent; Woodruff Smudged, 1.9 per cent; Gila Plain, .7 per cent.

Dates.—320 ± 5 (two trees) and 318 (bark date, one tree).

Phase.—Hilltop.

Comments.—This structure commands attention notably for its size, being about three times larger than any of the other houses. This characteristic, coupled with its more or less central location in the village, suggests community use. Its floor plan, posthole arrangement, and position of the hearth, are about the same as found in a structure of similar size labelled Kiva No. 1 in

Plate VI.—*a*, House 6. Displaced rough stone wall used as a facing against trash. Viewed from inside the house. *b*, House 7. A round bedrock structure with circular sill on floor.

the Bear Ruin,[9] but it differs in not having had a bench, directional or other recesses. House 5 may well be the prototype of Kiva 1 in the Bear Ruin.

The purpose of the trench running about the edge of the floor is not known. As plaster was applied to the bedrock face of the wall, it is not likely that the butt ends of poles or brush making the siding were set in this trench.

There is good indication that this building was not in use throughout the period of village occupancy, for some time after it fell into disuse a burned rock midden formed to the southeast, which grew to such proportions that it eventually overlapped the partly filled pit of House 5. This, together with the tree-ring dates and the pottery, is the justification for placing the structure in the Hilltop Phase.

House 6 (Fig. 6; Pl. VI *a*).
   Shape.—Oval.
   Size.—Diameters, 4.0 by 5.7 m.; depth, .9 to 1.25 m.
   Walls.—Bedrock on northern or high side; rough rubble wall laid up against trash on south side. This apparently represented remodeling of a former larger house with bedrock wall on south (see plan).
   Floor.—Central area shows clay veneer on bedrock, burned red. Projecting bedrock west of hearth used as anvil.
   Hearth.—Centrally located, more or less circular and basin shaped; diameter, .45 m., depth, .25 m.
   Lateral entrance.—Probably to east where bedrock slopes up, but evidence not conclusive.
   Pits, postholes, and roof.—No certain evidence.
   Pottery.—Alma Plain, Bluff *var.,* 42.0 per cent; Forestdale *var.,* 47.0 per cent. Fine Paste Brown, 1.0 per cent; Alma Scored, 8.0 per cent; Woodruff Red, 1.0 per cent; Woodruff Smudged, 1.0 per cent.
Dates.—303 + x and 287 + x (two trees).
   Phase.—Hilltop.
   Comments.—The new feature in House 6 over those previously described is the use of a very crude stone wall, probably laid up without mortar as a facing against standing trash. This has some significance from the chronological point of view, for it means that houses with this type of construction could only have been built after considerable trash had accumulated, and hence well along in the life of the village. But while House 6, and others to be mentioned later, is not the oldest house, it nevertheless can still be placed in the Hilltop Phase on the associated ceramics, thus hinting that this phase was of some duration.

---

[9]E. W. Haury, 1940, pp. 43-47.

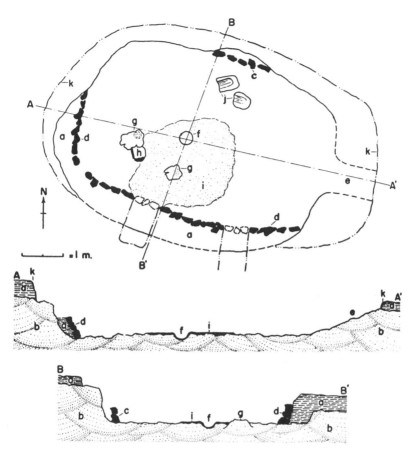

Figure 6.—Plan and sections of House 6: *a,* trash; *b,* bedrock; *c,* rubble wall straightening out irregularity in bedrock; *d,* rubble wall remodeling southern contour of house; *e,* probable sloped entrance; *f,* hearth; *g,* bedrock projections used as anvils; *h,* subfloor pit; *i,* clay flooring; *j,* metates; *k,* limits of excavation.

House 7 (Fig. 7; Pl. VI *b*).
    Shape.—Circular.
    Size.—Diameter, 4.3 m.; depth, 1.05 to 1.4 m.
    Walls.—Bedrock; plaster preserved to a height of .6 m.
    Floor.—Thickly clayed over and well preserved. An added feature
       is a clay sill, roughly circular and 2.6 m. in diameter, constructed
       on the floor. This sill sloped outward and rose to a maximum
       height of .28 m.
    Hearth, lateral entrance, pits, postholes.—None.
    Roof.—No data.

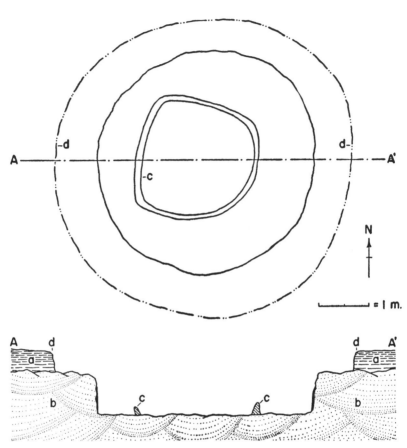

Figure 7.—Plan and section of House 7: *a*, trash; *b*, bedrock; *c*, clay sill; *d*, limits of excavation.

Pottery.—Alma Plain, Bluff *var.*, 47.3 per cent; Forestdale *var.*, 47.3 per cent. Fine Paste Brown, 5.3 per cent.

Dates.—None.

Phase.—Hilltop.

Comments.—House 7 is a duplicate of Houses 1 and 2 except for the circular floor sill. An almost identical feature was found in the Harris Village in New Mexico,[10] where the evidence was clear that the sill marked the outline of a later smaller house built within an older, larger structure. Here the evidence is not so convincing, and if the sill in House 7 does represent a house, it was very small.

[10]E. W. Haury, 1936, Pl. XXIII, Fig. 20.

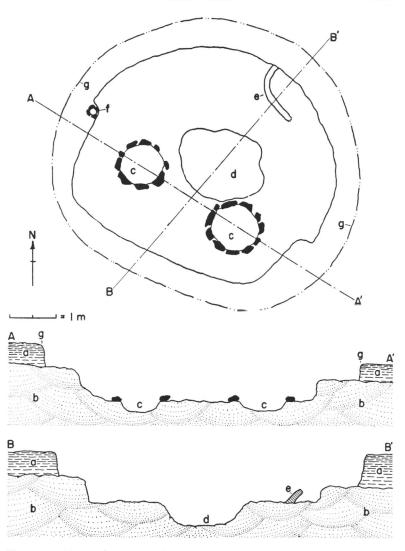

Figure 8.—Plan and sections of House 8: *a*, trash; *b*, bedrock; *c*, floor pits, ringed with stones on floor level; *d*, irregular floor pit; *e*, clay wall, probably remnant of a bin; *f*, post support, on bedrock; *g*, limits of excavation.

House 8 (Fig. 8; Pl. II *b*).

    Shape.—Roughly circular, but south side straight and jogs in outline on northwestern and southeastern sides.

    Size.—Diameter, 5.5 m. by 5.0 m.; depth, 1.0 to 1.5 m.

    Walls.—Bedrock.

Floor.—Very rough and cut up by pits; level areas originally plastered. Fragmentary clay wall of bin (?) on floor preserved in northeast section.

Hearth.—Evidence not clear, probably one of the rock-rimmed basins.

Lateral entrance.—No data.

Pits.—Three: two rock-rimmed in southern part, about .60 and .90 m. in diameter and .30 m. deep; one irregular pit in center, 1.7 m. in diameter and .6 m. deep.

Postholes.—One, at northwest jog, rock-lined.

Roof.—No convincing data.

Pottery.—Alma Plain, Bluff *var.,* 35.6 per cent; Forestdale *var.,* 59.2 per cent. Woodruff Smudged, 3.9 per cent; Gila Plain, 1.3 per cent.

Dates.—None.

Phase.—Hilltop.

Comments.—This house is unique for the site in the offsets of the outline, undoubtedly related in some way to the type of roof, in the rock-rimmed pits, and in the problematical storage bins. It was elaborately equipped as compared to the rest.

House 9 (Fig. 9; Pl. VII *a*).

Shape.—Oval.

Size.—Approximately 4.0 by 5.0 m.; depth, .65 to .95 m.

Walls and floor.—Bedrock; no evidence of plaster on either.

Hearth.—Towards eastern end of room near entrance; partly ringed with rocks; vitrified material found at east edge.

Lateral entrance.—Wide and short, not expanding, east side.

Pits, postholes, roof.—No clear evidence.

Pottery.—Alma Plain, Bluff *var.,* 29.6 per cent; Forestdale *var.,* 59.3 per cent. Woodruff Smudged, 3.7 per cent; Gila Plain, 7.4 per cent.

Dates.—None.

Phase.—Hilltop.

Comments.—A good example of a shallow bedrock house with side entry.

House 10 (Fig. 10).

Shape.—Circular.

Size.—Diameter, 6.1 m. (maximum); depth, .8 to 1.0 m.

Walls and floor.—Bedrock, plastered.

Hearth.—Shallow basin towards western side.

Lateral entrance.—No evidence.

Pits.—None.

Postholes.—Four, set in from wall; two were rock-lined.

Roof.—Central section evidently flat; rest of roof probably sloped down to ground level.

Pottery.—Alma Plain, Bluff *var.,* 5.4 per cent; Forestdale *var.,* 94.6 per cent.

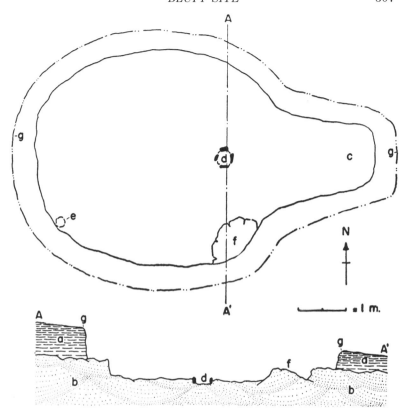

Figure 9.—Plan and section of House 9: *a*, trash; *b*, bedrock; *c*, entrance, not sloping; *d*, rock-lined hearth; *e*, posthole (?); *f*, bedrock projection in room; *g*, limits of excavation.

 Dates.—None.

 Phase.—Hilltop.

 Comments.—Excepting Houses 11 and 14 of the Cottonwood Phase, House 10 is the only domestic structure of the Hilltop Phase with a clear-cut four-post roof support plan.

House 11 (Fig. 11; Pl. VII *b*).

 Shape.—Subrectangular.

 Size.—4.3 by 5.0 m.; depth, .5 to 1.20 m.

 Walls.—Stone slabs, set on end, with some rocks laid flat on top of slabs.

 Floor.—Bedrock, but not excavated into it as in previously described houses.

 Hearth.—Shallow central pit, lined with clay.

 Lateral entrance.—Probably to east, but evidence not clear.

 Pits.—One; irregular, .45 m. deep.

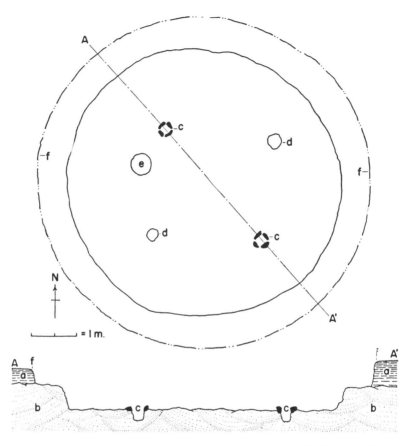

Figure 10.—Plan and section of House 10: *a*, trash; *b*, bedrock; *c*, postholes, ringed with stones; *d*, postholes; *e*, hearth; *f*, limits of excavation.

Postholes.—Three; two at probable entrance position; one in western side of room.

Roof.—Probably flat central part with sloping sides.

Pottery.—Alma Plain, Bluff *var.*, 50.5 per cent; Forestdale *var.*, 44.4 per cent. Fine Paste Brown, 1.8 per cent; Alma Scored, 1.1 per cent; Gila Plain, .5 per cent; Adamana Brown, 1.8 per cent.

Dates.—None.

Phase.—Cottonwood.

Comments.—This house contrasts sharply with those previously listed in its shape, slab lining, and because it was built entirely in trash, which is indicative of relative lateness in the occupation. Its resemblance to the orthodox Basketmaker house is

Plate VII.—*a*, House 9, shallowly excavated into bedrock with short side entrance. *b*, House 11. A Basketmaker type of slab house entirely built in trash.

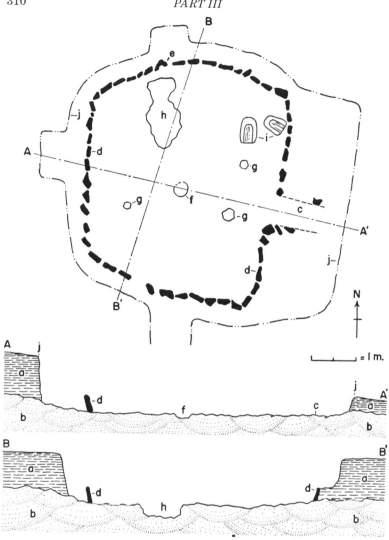

Figure 11.—Plan and sections of House 11: *a*, trash; *b*, bedrock; *c*, probable entrance; *d*, slab lining, set against trash; *e*, metate in wall (early type); *f*, hearth; *g*, postholes; *h*, floor pit; *i*, Basketmaker type metate; *j*, limits of excavation.

clear, a fact which injects an interesting cultural angle to the local problem.

A discarded deep trough metate was built into the wall (Pl. VIII *a*), while two metates on the floor were of the shallow troughed Basketmaker type.

Plate VIII.—*a,* House 11. Early metate built into wall with tumbled rocks from wall above slabs shown to left of metate. *b,* House 14, predominantly slab-lined, with corner posts.

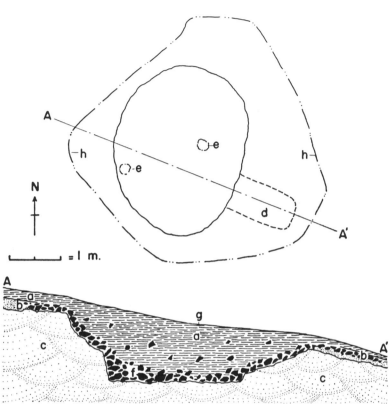

Figure 12.—Plan and profile of trash fill in House 12: *a*, trash; *b*, native soil; *c*, bedrock; *d*, probable location of entry; *e*, burnt areas, possibly hearths; *f*, rocks from surface, representing original excavated bedrock; *g*, surface; *h*, limits of excavation.

House 12 (Fig. 12).

Shape.—Oval.

Size.—Diameters, 2.6 by 3.25 m.; depth, 1.1 to 1.4 m. In all other particulars this structure was like Houses 1 and 2.

Pottery.—Alma Plain, Bluff *var.*, 46.8 per cent; Forestdale *var.*, 43.8 per cent. Fine Paste Brown, 9.4 per cent.

Dates.—None.

Phase.—Hilltop.

Comments.—This house shows better than all others the piling of rock taken from the original excavation about the edge of the house. Much of this rubble was later washed back into the pit.

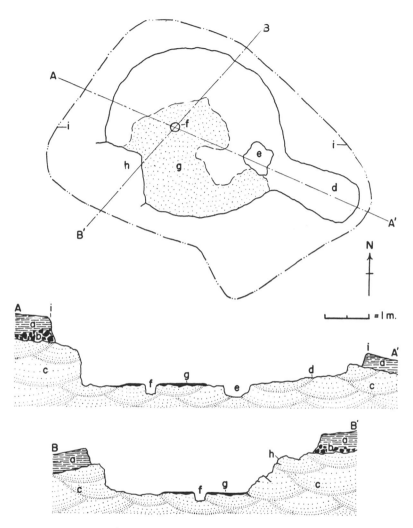

Figure 13.—Plan and sections of House 13: *a*, trash; *b*, rocks thrown out of original excavation; *c*, bedrock; *d*, entrance; *e*, floor pit; *f*, posthole (?); *g*, burnt clay flooring; *h*, bedrock projection; *i*, limits of excavation.

House 13 (Fig. 13).

    Shape.—Circular.

    Size.—Diameter, 4.0 m.; depth, 1.0 to 1.5 m.

    Walls.—Bedrock, with a large section projecting into room on west side which was too resistant to be removed.

Floor.—Heavy layer of clay preserved on a sizable portion; burned brick red.

Hearth.—No evidence.

Lateral entrance.—To southeast; a long (1.9 m.), slightly expanding passage scooped into bedrock.

Pits.—One, near inner end of entrance; an awkward place for a pit.

Postholes.—One, near center.

Roof.—Heavy clay layer, burned, on floor, with some rock inclusions.

Pottery.—Alma Plain, Bluff *var.*, 36.7 per cent; Forestdale *var.*, 57.5 per cent. Fine Paste Brown, 1.5 per cent; Adamana Brown, 4.3 per cent.

Dates.—None.

Phase.—Hilltop.

Comments.—House 13 was built on an easterly slope, and the entrance was oriented towards the most sloping area, eliminating the necessity for a deep excavation of the passage. This structure also showed the disposition of rubble around the perimeter, and it was the only one of the type to yield convincing proof that roofs were covered with earth.

House 14 (Fig. 14; Pl. VIII *b*).

Shape.—Subrectangular.

Size.—5.6 by 6.0 m.; depth, .3 to .7 m.

Walls.—Mostly sandstone slabs set against trash and into a shallow trough in floor; north wall largely bedrock.

Floor.—Bedrock, very rough.

Hearth.—Slightly southeast of center; shallow (.15 m. deep), rock-rimmed depression.

Lateral entrance.—Possible to southeast; burned roofing lay outside of slabs here as though from hood over entry; but if entrance was on this side, it was necessary to step over slabs to gain access to the room.

Pits.—None.

Postholes.—Three, near corners; fourth post probably rested on rock floor.

Roof.—Probably flat over major part of house; steeply sloping sides; much burned clay roofing bearing pole and brush impressions.

Pottery.—Alma Plain, Bluff *var.*, 2.2 per cent; Forestdale *var.*, 90.7 per cent. Fine Paste Brown, 2.1 per cent; Forestdale Plain, .4 per cent; Woodruff Red, 1.5 per cent; Forestdale Smudged, 2.2 per cent; Adamana Brown, .6 per cent; Lino Gray, .2 per cent. Approximately one third of all the sherds from the site were recovered in this house.

Dates.—None.

Phase.—Cottonwood.

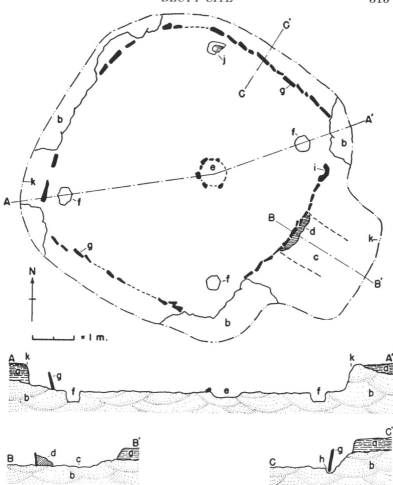

Figure 14.—Plan and sections of House 14: *a*, trash; *b*, bedrock; *c*, problematical entrance; *d*, clay, packed against slabs; *e*, hearth; *f*, postholes; *g*, sandstone slabs, set on ends; *h*, groove in bedrock for slabs; *i*, metate (old type) set in wall; *j*, metate; *k*, limits of excavation.

Comments.—This is a companion structure to House 11, bearing obvious kinship to Basketmaker architecture. It was large, shallow, and only enough bedrock was removed in construction to level off the floor and bring some symmetry to the walls. Again an old-style deep trough metate was built into the wall, whereas the metate on the floor was of the shallow northern type.

House 15 (Fig. 15).

Shape.—Oval.

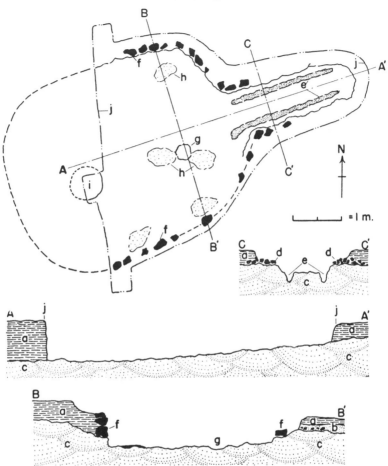

Figure 15.—Plan and sections of House 15: *a*, trash; *b*, native soil; *c*, bedrock; *d*, rocks from original excavation; *e*, grooves in entry; *f*, rubble wall; *g*, hearth; *h*, clay flooring, burnt; *i*, floor pit; *j*, limits of excavation.

Size.—Length, about 4.5 m. (incompletely excavated).

Walls.—Bedrock on north side; rubble wall against deep trash, south side.

Floor.—Bedrock some plaster.

Hearth.—Evidence uncertain.

Lateral entrance.—Long, parallel sides; to northeast; floor slopes upward and edged with a groove about .15 m. wide and .25 m. deep; groove does not curve around end of passage and was probably used to secure the butt ends of reeds or grass siding of the entrance hood.

Pits, postholes, roof.—No data.

Pottery.—Alma Plain, Bluff *var.*, 28.8 per cent; Forestdale *var.*, 64.4 per cent. Fine Paste Brown, 3.4 per cent; Woodruff Red, 1.7 per cent; Woodruff Smudged, 1.7 per cent.

Dates.—None.

Phase.—Hilltop.

Comments.—A bedrock-rubble wall structure much like House 6. Houses 16, 17, and 18 were circular bedrock structures, as revealed in limited tests. By architecture and pottery they belong to the Hilltop Phase.

House 19 (Fig. 16).

Shape.—Subrectangular.

Size.—6.0 by 7.4 m.; depth, .4 m.

Walls.—A combination of bedrock, rubble, and slabs; originally covered with hand-smoothed plaster.

Floor.—Bedrock; partially destroyed in construction of House 19A.

Hearth.—No data.

Lateral entrance.—A break in east wall suggested position of entry, but roots from clump of oaks at this point had extensively disarranged rocks.

Pits, postholes, roof.—No data.

Pottery.—Alma Plain, Bluff *var.*, 1.7 per cent; Forestdale *var.*, 77.0 per cent. Fine Paste Brown, 5.9 per cent; Forestdale Smudged, 11.0 per cent; Adamana Brown, 2.5 per cent; Pueblo I Black-on-White, .9 per cent; Pueblo I neck-banded, .9 per cent.

Dates.—None.

Phase.—Probably Cottonwood.

Comments.—(See under House 19A.)

House 19A (Fig. 16).

Shape.—Subrectangular.

Size.—3.0 by 4.3 m.; depth, .75 m.

Walls.—Lower portion bedrock where excavation was carried below floor level of House 19; rubble wall above.

Hearth.—None found.

Lateral entrance.—Probably off east wall near south end.

Pits.—One, small and shallow, north end.

Postholes and roof.—No data.

Pottery.—Alma Plain, Bluff *var.*, 2.1 per cent; Forestdale *var.*, 87.2 per cent. Pueblo I Black-on-White, 1.1 per cent; Pueblo I neck-banded, 3.2 per cent; Forestdale Smudged, 5.3 per cent; Lino Gray, 1.1 per cent.

Dates.—None.

Phase.—Probably Corduroy[11] (Pueblo I).

---

[11]Determined at Ariz. P:16:2, to be described in a later report.

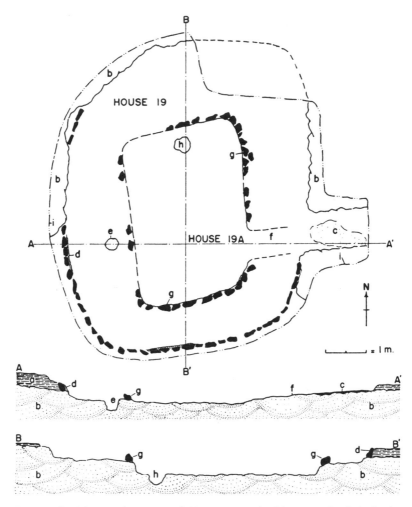

Figure 16.—Plans and sections of Houses 19 and 19A: *a*, trash; *b*, bedrock; *c*, clay on floor of entry, House 19; *d*, stones of varying thickness set against trash and imbedded in clay; *e*, postholes (?); *f*, probable location of entrance to House 19A; *g*, rubble wall; *h*, floor pit; *i*, limits of excavation.

Comments.—Here is another case of house superposition with ceramics indicating some time lapse between the two units. House 19A probably represents the reoccupation of the site for a short time by at least one family some centuries after the village's abandonment.

House 20.—Bedrock and rubble wall house (tested only).

House 21.—Bedrock structure (tested only).
    Dates.—312 + 10 (one tree).
    Phase.—Hilltop.

DISCUSSION

The impressive feature of Bluff Site architecture was its simplicity and crudeness. The latter condition is doubtless heightened to some extent by the difficulty of excavating a symmetrical and trim pit in shattered bedrock. But this does not account for the failure to build interior features which might have made life more comfortable, or which would indicate, at any rate, a somewhat more formalized attitude towards housebuilding. From the evidence we have, these houses did provide the minimum requirement of shelter, but they hardly went beyond that. Yet the prodigious task of scooping out the bedrock and of bringing up clay from the valley below for floors, plaster, and roof topping belies any feeling one may have that the people were content to find the easiest way out to build a home. Pit house construction was long known to them.

In the description above, houses have been assigned to phases, indicating differences in age. Architectural type, ceramic content, and whether or not they were built in trash, lie at the bottom of this ranking. In using penetration of the house pit into trash as a criterion of relative age we do not intend to imply that late houses could not have been built entirely in bedrock in trash-free areas, but it is certain that early houses could not have been built in trash before it accumulated. To that extent relative age can be appraised.

The houses fall logically into three broad types, eliminating House 19A from consideration, as it represents a late (Pueblo I) reoccupation. First, the oldest structures, a few of which have yielded tree-ring dates in the early fourth century, may be characterized as follows: round to oval house pits excavated into bedrock to a depth of .5 to 1.3 m., average diameter 4.0 m.; with or without lateral entrance, parallel-sided, oriented in an easterly direction when present; postholes generally absent, but basically a four-post plan was probably used (House 10); hearths not specialized and near center when present; floor pits sometimes present; other furnishings, as bins, rare. Typical examples are: Houses 1, 2, 4, 7, 8, 9, 10, 12, and 13. Phase: Hilltop, although some may have been occupied later as well.

The second type, numerically much smaller, includes houses partly cut into bedrock on the high side and walled with rubble masonry against trash on the low side. Otherwise they are much like those of the preceding group. The implication of the construction in trash is that some time had elapsed before they were built and that they represent an architectural modification occasioned by changing conditions. While thus later than perhaps the majority of the rock-cut houses, the material goods from them show no differences whatever, suggesting that the elapsed time was not great enough for cultural

progression. For that reason these houses have been placed in the Hilltop Phase with the first group. Examples of this type are Houses 6
and 15.

Finally, the third house type departs radically from the foregoing in
both character and time. These are the houses of subrectangular shape,
lined with slabs and built entirely or partly in the accumulated trash
of prior inhabitants. The latter circumstance, together with the pottery
from them, which was both more abundant and later as to types, allows
their placement in another phase called Cottonwood. Regrettably,
Houses 11, 14, and 19, which represent the type, produced no datable
wood to confirm this placement. Further discussion of the cultural
angles of this architectural type follow shortly.

In Figure 17, the essential data on the preceding types have been
assembled for ready access and to recapitulate the earlier house-by-
house description.

Purposely omitted from the above discussion are Houses 3, 4A, and
5, and those not completely excavated. House 3, while certainly a
living quarter, was too vague in its details to be included. House 4A,
a rectangular structure built inside of House 4, is anomalous. While
the dating evidence is insecure, it is considered to belong to the Hilltop Phase and is of interest only in showing that departure from the
normal house type may occur.

House 5 poses quite a different problem because of its probable
use as a communal center, perhaps for religious observances. The point
of immediate interest is in the fact that a structure of this sort should
occur in an early horizon (Hilltop Phase) of what is believed to be
a pure manifestation of the Mogollon Culture, when the general opinion
holds that kivas, or their prototypes, are one of the prominent diagnostics of the Anasazi. Kivas were certainly the norm for the Anasazi
during their heyday, but we feel certain that the last word on kiva
origin and development has not been written, and that the units suggestive of a kiva-in-the-making, seen in some early Mogollon Culture
sites, must be taken into consideration. Reference is again made to
the one in the Bear Ruin,[12] which, though dating about 700, does
not strictly follow the Anasazi pattern and may be considered as an
evolved descendant of House 5. Also, attention is called to Pit House
A of the SU Site, which may have been similar in function to House
5, although Martin[13] does not consider it to have been a ceremonial
structure. The situation in early Mogollon sites to the south and therefore farther away from the Anasazi will obviously have a bearing on
this problem. It is only fair to say that the excavation by Gila Pueblo
in the Cave Creek and San Simon[14] villages did not produce analogous
structures.

---

[12]E. W. Haury, 1940, pp. 52-54.
[13]P. S. Martin, 1943, p. 133.
[14]E. B. Sayles, 1945.

PHASE	TYPE	HOUSE	SHAPE			WALLS			ENTRANCE				FLOOR PITS	POSTHOLES		
														4-POST PLAN		
			CIRCULAR	OVAL	SUB-RECTANGULAR	BEDROCK	BEDROCK-RUBBLE	SLAB	PARALLEL-SIDED	EXPANDING	GROOVE IN FLOOR	NONE OR UNCERTAIN		SET FAR FROM WALL	SET NEAR WALL	NONE OR INCOMPLETE DATA
HILLTOP	BEDROCK	1	X			X						X	1			X
		2	X			X						X	1			X
		4	X			X			X							X
		7	X			X						X	3			X
		8	X[1]			X			X							X
		9		X		X						X				X
		10	X			X						X		X		
		12		X		X						X				X
		13	X			X					X		1			X
	BEDROCK & RUBBLE	6	X			X			?							X
		15	X			X			X	X						X
COTTONWOOD	SLAB	11			X			X				X	1			X
		14			X			X				X			X	
		19			X			X[2]				X				

1-WITH JOGS   2-PLUS BEDROCK & RUBBLE

Figure 17.—Table summarizing essential features of the three house types of the Bluff Ruin.

Anyone familiar with early Anasazi architecture will quickly see marked differences between the rock-hewn houses of the Bluff Site and the pit structures of the north. For example, ventilating ducts, deflectors, benches, antechambers, partition walls, and standardized hearths are absent. Evidence on the roof plan is too meager to attempt comparisons. The simplicity of the style of Hilltop Phase houses, on the other hand, strongly favors the houses of the SU Village[15] and the Georgetown Phase houses of the Harris Site[16] to establish what

[15]P. S. Martin, J. Rinaldo, and M. Kelly, 1940, pp. 14-30; P. S. Martin, 1943, pp. 150-69.

[16]E. W. Haury, 1936, pp. 54-57.

appears to be at least one regional variety of Mogollon architecture. Anasazi house features were being assimilated in the Mogollon area by perhaps 700, a fact which has been noted for the Bear Ruin,[17] long after the first northern influences were felt, if we are correct in assigning Houses 11, 14, and 19 of the Bluff Site to Basketmaker inspiration, if not authorship. The important fact to be recognized is that the Bluff Site possessed houses segregable into two types or groups, each stemming from a different architectural tradition, the rock-cut houses being Mogollon and the slab-sided houses being Basketmaker. The latter, however, in spite of its early introduction, does not appear to have persisted locally into the Forestdale or later phases.

The mere presence of Basketmaker architecture has some interesting implications. For one, it is the earliest tangible evidence we have of contact between them and the Mogollon people, and in this case it would appear that it was actual fraternization rather than an arm of influence. The Basketmaker metate type came in with the house. This helps to explain the hybridization of northern and southern architectural features by 700 in the Forestdale Phase, as well as the mixing of other traits of material culture. Strangely enough, Basketmaker pottery was represented by only a few sherds, which arouses the suspicion that actual contact may have been established on the Basketmaker level before this group had pottery. Meetings at this time between the pottery-making Mogollon and the Basketmaker, who lacked it, may have provided the spark which set off the ceramic art among them.

Also we may find in this contact the answer to the rather puzzling situation seen in some Basketmaker III sites in the Four Corners area, where a good quality brown and red ware sometimes appears as an intrusive in an undeveloped ceramic horizon. There can be little doubt of the fact that the people south of the Mogollon Rim were well ahead of their northern neighbors in ceramic technology.

The foregoing comments have been oriented from the point of view that the architectural differences between Houses 11, 14, and 19 and the others were culturally determined. A second approach to the problem, not to be overlooked, is considering the slab-house as a local evolutionary advancement from the earlier and more primitive structures. The relative lateness of the slab houses suggests this as a possibility. But what stands in the way of accepting the idea is the fact that during the Forestdale Phase, succeeding the Cottonwood Phase in which the slab-houses of the Bluff Site have been placed, this Basketmaker trait of housebuilding was not present at all, although the opportunities for employing it were present.

HEARTHS

The hearths in houses, as already noted, did not follow a standard form or a uniform location on the floor. In some structures the fire pits could not even be located. Cooking in houses was obviously

[17]E. W. Haury, 1940, pp. 54-56.

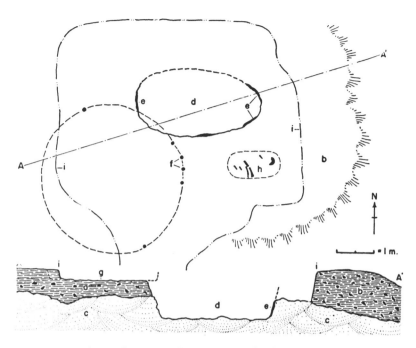

Figure 18.—Plan and section of Hearth 1 and adjoining features: *a*, trash, with considerable rock; *b*, the same as *a*, but heaped up as a midden; *c*, bedrock; *d*, Hearth 1; *e*, burnt clay sides; *f*, pole butts of an Apache wickiup (?); *g*, floor of wickiup; *h*, Burial 1; *i*, limits of excavation.

practiced, but it is also true that much preparation of food was done outside of the house. Occasional hearth accumulations were found in the testing between houses, and of particular interest were two large pits of the earth oven class (see Fig. 2 for locations).

Hearth 1, scooped into the bedrock, was oval in form and approximately 3.0 m. in greatest diameter (Fig. 18). In its shape and in the outward sloping sides, it differed from the better examples of the Bear Ruin, which were circular and had inward sloping sides.[18] The pit was clay-lined and heavily burned. Adjoining it to the southeast was one of the more conspicuous burned rock middens seen on the site, obviously the residue of disintegrated rock, all sandstone, used in cooking. While we cannot be sure as to the age, it probably is to be assigned to the Hilltop Phase, judging from the pit and midden contents. Its location near Houses 4 and 4A offers a possible clue that ovens of this sort were a part of each domestic unit.

Hearth 2 was circular, somewhat smaller, being 1.6 m. in diameter by .9 m. deep, and irregularly carved into the sandstone layer for half

---

[18]E. W. Haury, 1940, pp. 56-59.

its depth. This pit did not have an associated midden, and its contents, the black-on-white pottery scraper shown in Figure 24, together with a few other sherds of the Pueblo I horizon, lead to the conclusion that it postdates the main occupation and was used by the occupants of House 19A near by, the best proof of a limited reoccupation of the village during this period.

The practice of earth oven cooking has been linked with the Mogollon people along with other groups to the south and west of them. The presence of other pits in the Bluff Site pushes their use in this culture into an earlier horizon than has been known heretofore.

BURIALS

The excavations netted only two burials, both very fragmentary and rather badly disarranged by rodents. These were found in the occupational area without respect, it appears, to any fixed village features (Fig. 2). Enough of the bones remained to show that bodies were semiflexed (Pl. IX *a*), No. 1 with head directed to the east and facing south and No. 2 with head to the south. The skulls were too incomplete to make measurements or even reliable observations, except that No. 1 showed slight occipital deformation of a probable meso- or brachycranial type. Both individuals were adults.

The graves were dug down to bedrock, and as found the skeletons rested .5 m. below the present surface. Burial offerings were lacking.

Although the above clues as to physical type are vague, such as there are indicate similarity to the people of the SU Site,[19] with which cultural parallels are also pronounced.

MATERIAL CULTURE

The imperishable culture of the Bluff Site was meager to the extreme, both as to the range of artifact types and the quantity of any one type. Such basic utilitarian tools as metates and manos and even pottery were not overly abundant. Some classes of materials were absent altogether. With an evident long occupation and considerable depth of trash, this scarcity was all the more perplexing. Extensive screening of both house and general trash, a tedious process in rocky soil, was resorted to without appreciable results. Charred remains of any description, except some architectural wood, were not encountered.

It is a temptation to judge the entire level of cultural development on the basis of the indestructible goods, usually the evidence on which the archaeologist must rely. But in spite of the poor showing which this makes in the Bluff Site, it is not beyond possibility that, had we access to the perishable culture, an altogether different picture would appear. Woodworking, basketry, and leather work may have flourished, but without the evidence no such claim can be made. Nevertheless,

---

[19]P. S. Martin, J. Rinaldo, and M. Kelly, 1940, p. 91.

a

b

Plate IX.—*a,* Burial 1, made through trash to bedrock. *b,* Telephoto view from the Bluff Ruin across the valley to the Red Hill Site, Ariz. P:16:58 (center). Flat lands below, adjoining Forestdale Creek, are sporadically farmed by the **Apache.**

the poverty of the imperishable remains, taken with the early date of the village, undoubtedly carries its own significance. Relative to later horizons, the culture was undeveloped and simple.

Some 390 specimens have been analyzed in the following pages, the total number of classifiable objects collected during the two seasons of digging. Most of these are stone.

POTTERY

One of the marked characteristics of the Bluff Site is the scarcity of pottery. During the two seasons an aggregate of only 2,900 sherds and no whole or restorable vessels were recovered. To anyone accustomed to digging in late ruins where a day's work might net hundreds or even thousands of sherds, the recovery of only a dozen or so sherds a day was a constant source of astonishment. Under these conditions one wakes up to the realization of how much southwestern archaeology has depended on this trait and how little is left for analysis when the ceramic picture is simple.

The rudimentary character of the pottery is well demonstrated by the presence of only a few types, by simplicity of form, by the absence of painting or the development of other means of decoration, and by the small quantity.

The method of manufacture appears to have been by coiling and scraping, and there was some use of the polishing stone, although none of the pottery can be described as highly polished. Firing was done in an oxidizing atmosphere, and poor control of the same is seen in the clouded and blotched vessel surface.

In analyzing this pottery we have not felt justified in establishing new types. Some of the material can be accommodated in existing forms with, of course, departures in details. It is our feeling that much more work needs to be done in this general horizon and cultural complex before attempts are made at final categorization.

ALMA PLAIN

Approximately 95 per cent of all pottery recovered was a plain brown ware conforming in a broad way to the description of Alma Plain from the Bear Ruin.[20] But a close inspection of the sherds shows two varieties, recognizable in the extremes but frequently sharing characteristics. Since some temporal difference is apparent in these two forms, they are here provisionally described separately as variants of . Alma Plain, pending the time when more will be known about them. For the sake of convenience, the one is called the Bluff variety, the other the Forestdale variety, the latter agreeing with the type described as Alma Plain in the Bear Ruin report.[21]

---

[20]E. W. Haury, 1940, pp. 69-72.
[21]*Ibid.*

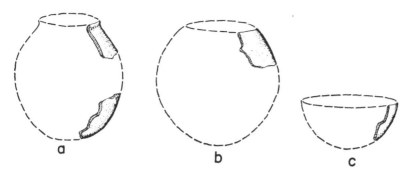

Figure 19.—Alma Plain, Bluff variety, vessel forms.

Alma Plain, Bluff variety:
   Paste
      Color.—Predominantly chocolate brown, usually uniform, but
         sometimes showing a gray core equaling about one-third the
         thickness of the vessel wall.
      Inclusions.—Some rounded quartz grains, but conspicuously an
         abundance of soft opaque white angular particles.
      Texture.—Granular and friable.
      Fracture.—Very ragged and irregular. Little tensile strength.
   Surface features
      Color.—Dark gray through light gray to warm brown, the latter
         predominating. No appreciable difference between interior and
         exterior. Some mottling from firing, but no sharply defined fir-
         ing clouds.
      Hardness.—3.0 to 3.5 (Mohs' scale).
      Evenness.—Somewhat bumpy and often showing finger depres-
         sions.
      Texture.—Moderately smoothed, apparently by hand, as clear-cut
         polishing marks do not show. Exteriors generally better finished
         than interior. Interiors show faint scraping marks. White tem-
         per particles usually show on surface but do not protrude. No
         scoring, incising, or appliqué decoration.
      Luster.—Dull.
      Slip.—None.
      Defects.—Excessive exfoliation of interiors, particularly near bot-
         tom of vessel.
   Thickness of vessel walls
      Range 5.0 to 10.0 mm., average 6.0 mm.
   Forms
      Jars.—Neckless, spherical to vertically elongated jars predominate
         (Fig. 19, *a*), rims rounded and slightly everted; also "seed"

jar type (Fig. 19, *b*). All jars small, probably not exceeding 20 cm. in diameter. Orifices equal about one half maximum diameter. Bottoms rounded.

Bowls.—Rare, generally hemispherical (Fig. 19, *c*) and small, 12 to 18 cm. in diameter.

Handles and lugs.—None.

Type site
Bluff Site (Ariz. P:16:20).

Range
At present known only from the Forestdale Valley.

Comments

This variant of Alma Plain constituted 26 per cent of the brown wares from the site. What attracts attention to it are its simplicity of form and its evident early chronological position in relation to the second variety described below. In fact, it is believed that this type of brown ware represents the earliest known ceramic product in the northern fringes of the Mogollon area. A further word in support of this acknowledged early position is in order. In the bedrock houses it occurred in about equal proportions with the Forestdale variety of Alma Plain, but in the late slab houses it was almost nonexistent. As an example, of the 966 sherds from House 14, only 21, or 2.18 per cent were of the Bluff variety, and in a test south of House 11, in the deep trash, which therefore was old, relatively at least, of twelve sherds,[22] ten were of this variety and only two of the Forestdale variety were present. This would make it look as though there were a possibility of the existence of this variant in pure form. However, since we have no direct stratigraphic proof of this, it is offered only as a possibility. We may be certain, however, that the Bluff and Forestdale varieties coexisted and that the former was lost in favor of the latter before the occupation of the site came to an end.

The simple forms, a neckless jar with slightly everted rim, "seed" jar and few bowls, are even more rudimentary than the forms of the Forestdale variety. The vertical neck jar, for example, is not represented at all. There is also a noticeable difference in size, all vessels of this variety being smaller on the average than the Forestdale variety. The age of this variety may be ascribed to the fourth century, although how much earlier its history may go and how much later it survived are problematical.

Alma Plain, Forestdale variety:

This variant form agrees in almost every detail with the published description.[23] Without repeating the same, only the noteworthy differ-

---

[22]This sample came from 1.5 cubic meters of trash, and although small it cannot be dismissed. In the older trash deposits of the site, sherd frequencies averaged only 6 to 10 per cubic meter.
[23]E. W. Haury, 1940, pp. 69-72.

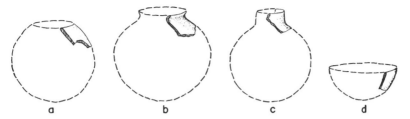

Figure 20.—Alma Plain, Forestdale variety, vessel forms.

ences need to be pointed out. These are principally in form. The "seed" jar type (Fig. 20, *a*), prevailed, and there are a few examples of low-necked jars with everted rims (Fig. 20, *b*) and vertical-necked jars (Fig. 20, *c*). Bowls are of hemispherical form (Fig. 20, *d*), and there are none of the flare-rimmed type as reported for the Bear Ruin.[24]

Handles and lugs were not employed, and there is one instance of appliqué decoration (Fig. 21, *a*) in the form of a raised, scalloped ridge around the orifice of a neckless jar.

Compared with the Bluff variety, the Forestdale variety shows the following differences: it is generally grayer in surface color; quartz sand tempered; thinner (range 3.0 to 7.0 mm., average 5.0 mm.); harder (4.0 to 5.0); greater tensile strength; greater form range; and somewhat larger vessels (maximum about 35 cm. in diameter).

Comments

The Forestdale variety of Alma Plain from the Bluff Site makes up 71.5 per cent of the brown ware sample. As already noted, it was present in the fill of the oldest bedrock houses, but not until sometime later did it predominate, eclipsing the Bluff variety. How much later is a question, but possibly by A.D. 500 it prevailed. In a developmental sense, it was directly antecedent to the almost indistinguishable Alma Plain of the Forestdale Phase (Bear Ruin), thereby giv-

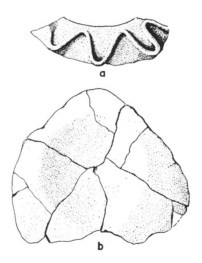

Figure 21.—Jar rim sherd with raised decoration (*a*); potsherd tray (*b*). Length of *a*, 15.0 cm.

[24] E. W. Haury, 1940, Fig. 23 *c*.

ing us a desirable earlier step in the sequence. This introductory position is borne out by the greater simplicity of form, including the lack of handles and lugs,[25] together with the reduced frequency with which sherds occurred.

FINE PASTE BROWN WARE

The sherd sample of this type includes seventy-six fragments, or about 2.5 per cent of the brown wares, differing from the foregoing varieties in both paste and finish. But because both the amount and the sherds are small, it is described without benefit of a specific name.

Paste
> Color.—Tan to brown, usually showing a gray to black core. In cases of extreme firing, color is reddish brown and quite uniform through vessel wall.
> Inclusions.—Very fine rounded quartz grains.
> Texture.—Granular, friable, sandy to the touch.
> Fractures.—Highly irregular and ragged; edges tend to flake; readily broken by hand.

Surface features
> Color.—Gray, red-brown to tan, latter predominating. Little difference between exterior and interior.
> Hardness.—2.5 to 3.5 (Mohs' scale).
> Texture.—Somewhat bumpy and in a few cases slightly ridged. Polishing marks visible; bowl interiors more highly polished than exteriors.
> Luster.—Dull.
> Slip.—None.
> Defects.—None apparent.

Thickness of vessel walls
> Range, 2.5 to 10.0 mm., average 5.0 mm.

Forms
> Chiefly small (diameter up to 16.0 cm.), hemispherical bowls, "seed" type jars rare. Rims rounded or slightly tapered. No handles or lugs.

Type site
> Bluff Site (Ariz. P:16:20).

Range
> Known only from the above site.

Comments
This class of pottery occurred in small quantities in association with the two varieties of Alma Plain in all houses. The chief significance we can attach to it is that by paste, quality, form, and the more highly polished surfaces, it represents the basic fabric which, during the Forestdale Phase, by control of the fire, was converted to Forestdale Smudged

---

[25]Compare Figure 20 of this report with Figure 24 in E. W. Haury, 1940, p. 71.

or Forestdale Red.[26] Were it not for the fact that the weak representation of Forestdale Smudged from the Bluff Site was restricted to the late houses, one might suspect the above described pottery to be Forestdale Smudged but with the smudge burned out. Refinements in paste and finish were evidently achieved before the potters experimented to achieve a satisfactory smudged or red surface.

FORESTDALE PLAIN

In addition to the foregoing, there are three sherds of brown ware which conform to the description of Forestdale Plain.[27] This type was considered to be the result of a fusion of Lino Gray of the Anasazi and Alma Plain of the Mogollon Culture and one of the ceramic diagnostics of the Forestdale Phase, although the type was never very abundant. The three sherds from the Bluff Site were all found in House 14, a slab house, which, as already pointed out, was occupied towards the end of the village's history, bringing the time element roughly in agreement with the beginning of the occupation of the Bear Ruin.

ALMA SCORED

There were five occurrences of Alma Scored[28] coming from houses of all architectural types. Several fragments of one pot came from House 6. This type is more abundant in the San Francisco and Mimbres valleys of New Mexico, and the few sherds of it which were found in the Bear Ruin were regarded as intrusives. This may be the case with the Bluff Site sherds also, but short of a petrographic analysis, we cannot be sure about this.

SMUDGED POTTERY

Smudged vessels, that is, pottery with polished and blackened interiors, the latter achieved in the firing process by causing a deposit of carbon to be put on the vessel wall, were not very plentiful. Some sixty-five sherds were recovered, and their distribution in the site has considerable significance.

Broadly speaking, two qualities of smudged are recognizable, a rather rough, poorly finished variety and a well-executed smudged pottery of the same kind found in the Bear Ruin and called Forestdale Smudged.[29] The former kind agrees on the whole with Woodruff Smudged[30] and is classed as such. Tracing these back to their sources

---

[26]See description of these types, E. W. Haury, 1940, pp. 73-75; 77-79.
[27]E. W. Haury, 1940, pp. 75-77.
[28]E. W. Haury, 1936a, p. 38.
[29]E. W. Haury, 1940, pp. 73-75.
[30]H. P. Mera, 1934, pp. 6-7.

in the site and using only those sherds found in houses, we have the following:

Woodruff Smudged:
    House 1 2
    House 5 3
    House 6 1
    House 9 1
    House 15 1
Forestdale Smudged:
    House 8 1
    House 14 22
    House 18 12
    House 19A 19

Woodruff Smudged occurred in small amounts only in the bedrock and bedrock-and-rubble-wall houses. From this may be deduced the fact that it was the oldest type of smudging in the valley and that the technique was just being learned, either locally if this pottery was indigenous, or elsewhere if intrusive.

Disregarding the lone Forestdale Smudged sherd from House 8, apparently an accidental association, all Forestdale Smudged came from late structures, and in considerably increased quantities over Woodruff Smudged. Houses 14 and 18 by type and sherd content have been identified as coeval with Basketmaker III, and House 19A appears to have been later, or Pueblo I, when, from other work we have done in the valley (Ariz. P:16:2), Forestdale Smudged was still in vogue.

To repeat, while the evidence is not absolutely definitive, Woodruff Smudged appears to be ancestral to Forestdale Smudged, and its beginnings can probably be put in the fourth century.[31]

RED WARE

Red ware was achieved by adding a red slip to the paste employed in the Forestdale variety of Alma Plain. It is the only pottery from the ruin in which a slip was used. Shapes were limited to small bowls with interiors slipped only and lightly polished. Exteriors are rough. It is similar but not like Woodruff Red.[32]

This class of pottery was never very abundant and is represented in the collection by only seventeen sherds. Fourteen of these came from the late House 14 and one each from Houses 5, 6, and 15.

The chief points to be noted are:

1. That the older bedrock houses did not produce red ware (excepting the one sherd, probably late, from House 5), indicating a ceramic horizon without red ware.

---

[31]For a general discussion of the smudging technique, see E. W. Haury, 1940, pp. 87-90.
[32]H. P. Mera, 1934, p. 6.

2. What red ware there was belonged to a later ceramic period.

3. The absence of Forestdale Red[33] shows this type to have evolved still later and evidently not until the Forestdale Phase, or probably after A.D. 600.

4. In a sense this reflects the marginal position of the Bluff Site to the center of the Mogollon development somewhere to the south and east, where all early ruins, like SU and Cave Creek and the Harris Site, explored to date, have produced higher quantities of red ware on approximately the same time level.

INTRUSIVE POTTERY

Adamana Brown.—Adamana Brown was first singled out by Mera in 1934 in the course of reconnaissance in the Petrified Forest area,[34] and in the ensuing years little fresh information about it has been added. One of its obvious paste characters is mica. This is also the case with Gila Plain, but the two types are easily segregated by the amount of mica, Gila Plain having much more of it, and on other details as well.

In all, thirty-four sherds of Adamana Brown were found in the Bluff Site, much more abundantly than any other intrusive pottery type.[35] Well over half of these sherds were associated with Hilltop Phase houses or trash, the rest coming from Cottonwood Phase contexts. Considerable significance is to be attached to this in the light of Mera's previous observations. He points out[36] that Adamana Brown was found pure on some sites with no intrusives of any kind and that occasional sherds of it were found associated with Woodruff Brown, representing an horizon when Basketmaker intrusives were also present.

Putting the evidence of his and our work together, it may be concluded that his pure Adamana Brown sites are roughly contemporary with the Hilltop Phase, which lacked Basketmaker pottery of any description and that its lesser occurrence in Petrified Forest sites with a predominance of Woodruff Brown and related wares, some of Basketmaker origin, can be equated with the Cottonwood Phase, also tinted by Basketmaker elements. This correlation, of course, needs further confirmation, but accepting it provisionally, we see well within the Anasazi area a ceramic pattern of non-Anasazi character prior to the emergence of the Anasazi wares. This does not yet account for the genesis of Adamana Brown. Venturing a guess, both Adamana Brown and the Bluff variety of Alma Plain may be regional variants of the brown ware complex basic to the southeastern quarter of Arizona and

[33]E. W. Haury, 1940, pp. 77-79.
[34]H. P. Mera, 1934, pp. 4-5; see also H. S. Colton and L. L. Hargrave, 1937, pp. 159-160.
[35]A sample lot from the Bluff Site was submitted to Mera, who has verified the identification.
[36]H. P. Mera, 1934, p. 5; letter, July 24, 1944.

the southwestern quarter of New Mexico, in short, roughly the area of the Mogollon Culture.

Anasazi

Lino Gray var.—There are three sherds of gray ware whose source must have been somewhere to the north in the Anasazi territory. The paste is quartz sand tempered, plus some angular soft white particles in which they depart from the standard form of Lino Gray.[37] Two of these sherds were found in House 14 and one in House 19A, both structures being late.

Considerable importance is to be attached to their presence and to the absence of others like them in the bedrock houses and early trash deposits. Since the Bluff Site was located near the southern periphery of the Basketmaker domain, there was every opportunity for ceramic interchange. That this took place is evident, both in the Bear Ruin[38] on a late Basketmaker III horizon and here towards the end of the occupation in Basketmaker III. But the absence of Basketmaker pottery in the earlier houses we believe to be highly significant. The appearance of pottery-making among the Basketmakers is generally put at about A.D. 400. Dates from northern ruins in the 200's are suggestive of a nonpottery level of culture,[39] and the inference which can be drawn is the fact that although the early residents of the Bluff Site were making pottery, their northern neighbors were not.

Hohokam

Gila Plain.—Seven sherds with very heavy mica content and made by the paddle-and-anvil method are easily identified as Gila Plain[40] of the Hohokam Culture.

The distribution in the site was as follows:

House 2	1
House 4	1
House 5	1
House 8	1
House 9	2
House 11	1

It is known that Gila Plain was a pottery with a long life and that changes within its history were not marked. Generally speaking, the Gila Plain of the Pioneer Period was more micaceous than in later periods, but specific assignment to phase is impossible. All that can

[37] H. S. Colton and L. L. Hargrave, 1937, pp. 191-92.
[38] E. W. Haury, 1940, pp. 84-85.
[39] E. W. Haury, 1942, p. 8.
[40] H. S. Gladwin, E. W. Haury, E. B. Sayles, and N. Gladwin, 1937, pp. 205-11.

be said of the Gila Plain of the Bluff Site is that it is heavily micaceous and that it therefore conforms to the earlier rather than the later form.

Houses 2 and 5 yielded tree-ring dates in the fourth century, and by type the other houses where Gila Plain occurred, excepting House 11, were probably of about the same age. It would look as though Gila Plain reached the Bluff Site quite early in its life.

Red-on-buff.—Apart from the Pueblo I and later Anasazi sherds discussed below, there is a single red-on-buff fragment which completes the list of painted wares from the site. While unmistakably red-on-buff, the design has been almost entirely lost through time, and, unfortunately, it cannot be identified to phase. It retains enough characters to permit one to say that it was neither very late nor very early in the Hohokam painted ware sequence. This sherd was removed in the first 25.0 cm. of trash in House 3. To say when it reached the site would be guesswork, but its presence with Gila Plain strengthens the idea that this was early rather than late in the life of the village. The inference may be drawn that while Bluff Site pottery was still in an early developmental stage, Hohokam pottery arrived via trade channels which itself was by no means the earliest pottery produced by that tribe.

Pueblo I Pottery

In the discussion of architecture it was pointed out that House 19A, constructed inside House 19, yielded several types of pottery classed as local Pueblo I, which gave rise to the belief that a single family lived briefly on the bluff, perhaps in the neighborhood of A.D. 900, and therefore considerably after the main occupation had come to an end. Neither the pottery nor the architecture of the local Pueblo I (Corduroy Phase) have been described, although this is projected for a future report. Familiarity with the material, however, gives us some assurance that the identifications here are correct.

Represented are sherds of at least two neck-banded jars made of a brown, sandy paste and a fragment from the bottom of a black-on-white jar, displaying typical local Pueblo I paste and finish characteristics. Also the Forestdale Smudged from this house, mentioned above, tends to be slightly heavier walled, on the whole, and with redder exteriors than this type does from the Forestdale Phase.

The pottery scraper (Fig. 24) made of Pueblo I black-on-white pottery, from Hearth 2 near House 19A, also probably was left by the occupants of this dwelling.

Pueblo III Pottery

It has long been recognized that almost any early ruin may produce some sherds which are far out of horizon, much in the same way that one can occasionally pick up glass on pre-Spanish sites, left by more recent Indians or white settlers. The fifty-odd ruins we have seen in the Forestdale area are proof enough not only of a long but of an intense occupation during some periods. Under these conditions, some mixtures of early and late material is bound to occur. While these circumstances can be disturbing, they are no cause for assuming that a weakness exists in the ceramic chronology as a whole. This is particularly true where sequence has been determined through stratigraphy and the full ceramic complement of any horizon has been determined through excavation.

There are a dozen or so sherds from the Bluff Site which can be allocated to Pueblo III. These were found at random, usually in the surface debris, and apparently do not stem from a Pueblo III reoccupation of the bluff. They are mentioned here to complete the list of what was found, but it should be obvious that they have no bearing on the main problem.

APACHE POTTERY

Some use of the bluff by the Apache was pointed out earlier in this report. Presumably this was more than fifty to seventy-five years ago, when the Apaches were still producing a small amount of pottery. Judging from undoubted Apache pottery which we have found in a village of stone house rings[41] in the Carrizo Valley, it was so much like the oldest Bluff Site pottery that, if mixed with it, there is some doubt as to whether or not it could be segregated. If any Apache pottery existed on the bluff, we did not detect it.

DISCUSSION

The Bluff Site departs from most southwestern pottery producing ruins in the meagerness of this trait. There were but few types, simple as to form, unpainted, and generally unsophisticated. Some inequality in the amount of pottery from the various houses was detected. These conditions call for further discussion, which can be framed around the broad question: What does the sparseness of pottery mean?

By way of comparison, it might be well to point out the situation in other ruins. At Snaketown some of the test blocks in Sedentary Period trash of one half cubic meter volume produced as many or even more sherds than accrued from all the work in the Bluff Site, and one stratigraphic test alone yielded 170,000 sherds.[42] Anasazi ruins of Pueblo III times are also highly productive, although possibly not to the same degree as Snaketown.

Earlier ruins than the foregoing, which probably bear some tribal

---

[41]Arizona P:15:7, located on a high, defensive hill. The house rings are superimposed on a demolished stone pueblo, and the sherds were collected from a deposit of Apache trash.

[42]H. S. Gladwin, E. W. Haury, E. B. Sayles, and N. Gladwin, 1937, p. 25, footnote 3.

relationship to the Bluff Site, have been somewhat more productive of pottery. For example, the Bear Ruin in the Forestdale Valley, dating about A.D. 700, yielded 22,000 sherds,[43] with seventeen houses excavated. The SU Site in New Mexico, of undoubted earlier date than the Bear Ruin, netted 30,000 sherds with eighteen houses cleared.[44] The Mogollon and Harris villages yielded 13,000 (eleven houses) and 45,000 (thirty-four houses) sherds, respectively.[45] The Cave Creek Site of southeastern Arizona, of undetermined but obviously early date, excavated by Sayles for Gila Pueblo, produced somewhat less than 2,000 sherds from eight houses and general testing, which roughly parallels the conditions at the Bluff Site.

The point involved here is the fact that we believe the relative amount of pottery a site yields, a marked scarcity in the case of the Bluff Site, is not without its meaning. There are two likely explanations for this situation: (1) that although pottery was fixed in the culture pattern, it was not important, as with the Apache and Navajo in recent times, and (2) that pottery was a new acquisition and had not yet fully risen to the indispensable place it held in later times. In consideration of the quantitative increase exhibited by the ruins in the Forestdale Valley, early to late, and the increase seen in the late houses of the Bluff Site itself over the older houses, it is our belief that the latter alternative is nearer the truth. In short, the paucity of pottery in this case is regarded as an indication that the occupants of the village had only recently learned the art of making earthenware vessels.

The tree-ring dates in the fourth century fit the general situation quite well, for to the north the Basketmakers appear to have acquired pottery in the neighborhood of 400. In Ventana Cave, where the dating is much more tenuous, the introduction of ceramics has been put at about A.D. 1, and it should be added that here, too, after its introduction, there was a steady increase in the amount produced.

The varying amounts of pottery yielded by the trash-filled houses is considered significant, and particularly so when correlated with architectural differences. Of the total 2,900 sherds recovered, 2,292 came from houses. If the structures which were completely cleared are arranged in accordance with the architectural categories outlined earlier in this report, and sherd frequencies tabulated accordingly, we have the following:

---

[43]E. W. Haury, 1940, p. 68.
[44]P. S. Martin, 1943, p. 109.
[45]E. W. Haury, 1936, pp. 26, 66.

Bedrock houses

No.	Sherds
1	52
2	54
3	81
4 and 4A	69
5	155
7	19
8	76
9	28
10	38
12	32
13	144[46]
	748

Bedrock and rubble wall houses

No.	Sherds
6	100
15	59
	159

Slab or late houses

No.	Sherds
11	215
14	958
19A	212
	1,385
Grand total	2,292

The bedrock houses and those partially dug into bedrock with low sides built up of rubble masonry as a lining against the trash show no appreciable differences. The latter may, on the whole, be somewhat later than the former, but ceramics do not reflect this. The real change comes in with the slab Houses 11 and 14 and the late structure (19A) built inside an earlier house. Expressed percentagewise, three houses produced approximately 51 per cent of the pottery and 49 per cent of the sherds came from fifteen houses. One house alone (14) yielded about 42 per cent of all pottery from houses.

When next the types of pottery are considered, it becomes apparent that the situation as outlined was not accidental but that the real explanation is a temporal one. Bedrock houses produced about equal amounts of the two varieties of Alma Plain, a few fine sand-tempered sherds, and a handful of Woodruff Smudged. The trash fill of Houses 11, 14, and 19A, on the other hand, contained almost exclusively the sand-tempered variety of Alma Plain, showing a greater shape range than the other varieties, plus small quantities of red ware, Forestdale Smudged, and the only sherds of Lino Gray *var.* Thus, by quantity

---

[46]This includes sherds from rather extensive digging outside of the house pit.

and type of pottery, as well as architecturally, these houses may be regarded as late in the occupation. But what is more pertinent to the discussion here is the fact that the late houses reflect a greater ceramic output among the potters of the day than do the early houses. This suggests that pottery was coming to be a fixed and important attribute of the culture. Conversely, it may be argued that the bedrock houses with little pottery represent a time when the culture had just received pottery.

The information bearing on differences in kinds of pottery from the architectural units should now be assimilated in another way so as to crystalize the ceramic horizons. These, in fact, constitute an important, but not an exclusive criterion of the phases ascribed to the ruin. As stated in the introduction, we recognized a Hilltop Phase, the oldest, followed by the Cottonwood Phase. Both of these were antecedent to the Forestdale Phase seen in the Bear Ruin, but which appears not to have been present in the Bluff Site. Then follows the Corduroy Phase (Pueblo I), represented by House 19A, which yielded clues of a brief reoccupation. With the rest of the sequence in the Forestdale Valley we are not now concerned. These phases, assigned to certain ceramic associations, are outlined in Figure 22.

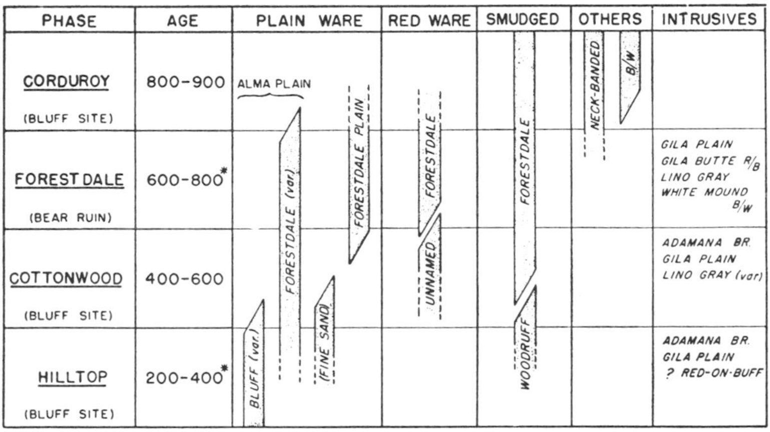

PHASE	AGE	PLAIN WARE	RED WARE	SMUDGED	OTHERS	INTRUSIVES
CORDUROY (BLUFF SITE)	800-900	ALMA PLAIN			NECK-BANDED B/W	
FORESTDALE (BEAR RUIN)	600-800*	FORESTDALE (var) FORESTDALE PLAIN	FORESTDALE	FORESTDALE		GILA PLAIN GILA BUTTE R/B LINO GRAY WHITE MOUND B/W
COTTONWOOD (BLUFF SITE)	400-600	FINE SAND	UNNAMED			ADAMANA BR. GILA PLAIN LINO GRAY (var)
HILLTOP (BLUFF SITE)	200-400*	BLUFF (var) FINE SAND		WOODRUFF		ADAMANA BR. GILA PLAIN ? RED-ON-BUFF

Figure 22.—The phase scheme of the Bluff and Bear Ruins, showing ceramic components. These constitute the oldest horizons of the Forestdale Valley chronology. Asterisk indicates that there are tree-ring dates within the range of years shown.

In the light of the limited evidence now at our disposal, it may be too early even to speculate on the beginnings of southwestern pottery. But we would like to offer the following as an hypothesis for further studies to prove or disprove.

In the minds of a few southwestern archaeologists, the notion has been fermenting for some time that pottery came to both Hohokam

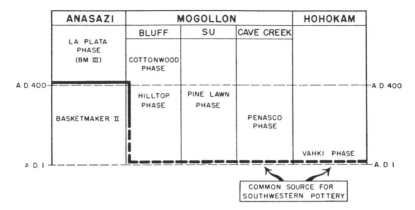

Figure 23.—Schematic drawings suggesting the relative time of appearance of pottery in the Anasazi, Mogollon, and Hohokam cultures, shown by the heavy line. The solid portion of the pottery line denotes dating by tree-rings the broken portion is an estimate only. The early plain ware phases for both Mogollon and Hohokam are represented as approximately coeval to express a generally uniform level of attainment. Obviously, time differences, probably of a minor order, can be expected, but the data necessary to express these are lacking.

and Mogollon before it reached the Anasazi.[47] The oldest Hohokam and Mogollon pottery had much in common, superficially at least, and it has been suggested[48] that pottery plus agriculture was adopted by people in southern Arizona on the San Pedro Stage level of the Cochise Culture and because of environmental influences, together with possible ethnic factors, evolved along different lines.

The idea which we wish to propose is best expressed schematically (Fig. 23). Using A.D. 400 as a convenient datum, approximately the time of pottery acquisition by the Basketmakers, and accepting the tree-ring dates for the Bluff Site as well as the cross-finds, or lack of them, in other early Mogollon and Hohokam horizons, it looks as though the ceramic art was well established among the latter two cultures well before 400. The actual beginnings for pottery in the Southwest are placed at about A.D. 1, frankly a guess. By "beginnings" we mean introduction, rather than invention, from some source outside the Southwest, most likely Mexico.

Before leaving the discussion of pottery, one further observation should be made. The Bluff Site is not only an early village of the Mogollon Culture with tree-ring dates, but the only ruin in the Southwest with fourth-century dates and an established, though rudimentary, ceramic complex excavated so far.

[47]H. S. Gladwin, E. W. Haury, E. B. Sayles, and N. Gladwin, 1937, pp. 217-18, 229.
[48]E. W. Haury, 1943, pp. 260-63; E. B. Sayles, 1945, p. 65.

Bearing this fact in mind, pottery intrusives from other areas become doubly significant: Adamana Brown as an early offshoot of the Mogollon complex within the Anasazi area and prior to the development of Anasazi ceramics; Gila Plain as evidence of contact with the Hohokam, possessing well-established ceramics, and Lino Gray, appearing later than either of the above types, as evidence of the relative lateness of the characteristic Anasazi gray paste pottery.

WORKED POTSHERDS AND CLAY OBJECTS

Containers (three) (Fig. 21 *b*)
> Sherds of both the Bluff and Forestdale varieties of Alma Plain; irregular in outline; edges ground. Diameters: 7.5 to 20.5 cm. From Houses 8 and 10. Hilltop Phase.

Discs (nine)
> a) Perforated (five)
>> Broken and ground out of sherds of both varieties of Alma Plain; edges irregular to smooth; perforations biconical and central, or nearly so. Diameters: 3.2 to 5.5 cm. From Houses 3, 6, and 15. Hilltop Phase.
> b) Unperforated (four)
>> As above, but not pierced. Diameters: 4.0 to 7.6 cm. From Houses 3, 6, and 13. Hilltop Phase.

Pottery scraper (one) (Fig 24)
> Large rim sherd from bowl of local Pueblo I black-on-white pottery.[49] Length, 11.2 cm. From Hearth 2. Corduroy Phase.

Figure 24.—Pueblo I pottery scraper from Hearth 2.

Figurines (three)
> a) Heads (two) (Fig. 25, *a, b*)
>> Brown, sandy paste, fired; both heads almost identical, with flat backs, pinched up noses, coffee bean eyes, of which only one remains; eye slits extend across eye pellet and back to edge of head; largest specimen shows shoulder prominence but no arms. Length, 3.4 cm. From Houses 3 and 8. Hilltop Phase.
> b) Leg (one) (Fig. 25, *c*)
>> Paste as above, fired; peglike; faint incisions mark toes; probably animal. Length, 2.9 cm. From House 14. Cottonwood Phase (?).

---

[49]A systematic study of this type is projected for the future. At present it bears no name.

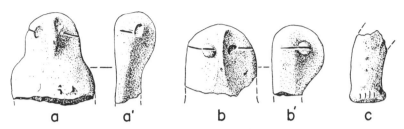

Figure 25.—Clay figurine fragments.   Length of *a,* 3.5 cm.

DISCUSSION

The rough sherd containers, or trays, the nearest thing to whole vessels from the ruin, probably have little significance. If it were not for the fact that they also occur in later horizons when pottery was abundant, one might be tempted to regard them as evidence of a premium on pottery. Sherd discs are no different than those from local later horizons and appear to be as old as pottery itself. Worked sherds of other geometric forms were not found.

The black-on-white pottery scraper has special interest. Its Pueblo I derivation places it later than the main occupation by perhaps 500 years. Hearth 2, in which it was found, was evidently used by the occupants of House 19A, dating from the same horizon.

The figurines bear superficial resemblances to those of the Hohokam, particularly before Sedentary times, but it is impossible to try to place them stylistically on the basis of the Snaketown series.

STONEWORK

The immediate locality provided the occupants of the Bluff village with needed raw stone for tools. Sandstone for metates lay underfoot, and lava for the same implement could be had a mile or two down the valley. The bed of Forestdale Creek is strewn with quartzite boulders for manos, hammerstones, and choppers; and chert, weathering from remnants of Kaibab limestone nearby, supplied the chief material used in pressure flaking. Some petrified wood, also found locally, was used. Except for one projectile point, obsidian was lacking.

Stone objects intentionally shaped by grinding and polishing number only six, indicating a lack of emphasis on this process. Ground tools resulting from use are, of course, relatively plentiful. Percussion and pressure flaking were approximately of equal importance.

GROUND STONE
SHAPED BY USE

Metates (sixteen)
    Type I, basin (four) (Fig. 26, *a*)
        Sandstone (three) and lava (one) blocks; unshaped except for
           occasional breaking away of projections; grinding surface oval

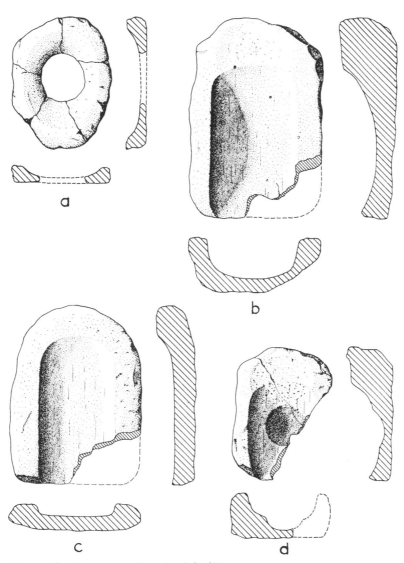

Figure 26.—Metate types. Length of *b,* 60.0 cm.

and shallow, placed centrally or somewhat off center on stone; grinding stroke free but not rotary; sharpening by pecking; one specimen has bottom intentionally broken out. Size range: lengths, 34.0-48.0 cm.; width, 30.0-43.0 cm.; thickness, 7.0-14.0 cm. Type I Manos usable in these. From Houses 5, 8, and

14 (latter built into house wall). Hilltop Phase.

Type II, troughed (nine) (Fig. 26, *b*)

   Predominantly indurated sandstone, but also some lava; thick, irregular, unshaped blocks; grinding trough parallel-sided, deep in worn examples, and strongly concave both axes; trough open at far end; near end shelflike, sometimes slightly worn, evidently intended to receive mano when not in use;[50] mano length equals width of trough, grinding stroke restricted to one axis; two specimens used as mortars (Fig. 26, *d*); sharpening by pecking. Size range: lengths, 43.0-60.0 cm.; widths, 30.0-38.0 cm.; thickness, 8.0-21.0 cm. Type I and II manos fit these metates, possibly also Type III in some. From Houses 3, 5, 8, 9, and 11 (latter built into house wall). Hilltop Phase.

Type III, troughed (three) (Fig. 26, *c*)

   Sandstone only; fairly thin slabs, some shaping of edges by breaking off projections; grinding trough open at far end, parallel-sided, shallow, and relatively wider than in Type II metates; floor of trough quite flat in both axes; grinding stroke restricted. Size range: lengths, 40.0-62.0 cm.; widths, 40 cm.; thickness, 12.0-15.0 cm. Type III manos used with these. From Houses 11 and 14. Cottonwood Phase.

Manos (fifty-two)

Type I, unshaped pebbles (twenty-seven) (Fig. 27, *a*)

   Generally quartzite or indurated sandstone stream pebbles (one limestone); oval to elongated in outline, following natural form of rock; usually unifacial, sometimes bifacial; finger grips on one specimen; grinding face convex on long axis and quite nearly flat on short axis. Size range: lengths, 10.0-19.0 cm.; widths, 8.0-12.0 cm.; thickness, 3.0-6.0 cm. Oval examples fit Type I metates, longer manos fit both Types II and III metates. From Houses 1, 3, 4, 6, 8, 13, 14, 15, 19A. Chiefly Hilltop Phase but probably also Cottonwood Phase.

Type II, shaped (twenty-two) (Fig. 27, *b-d*)

   Quartzite, indurated sandstone, rarely lava; shaped by pecking and brought either to oval or subrectangular form; about equally divided between uni- and bifacial forms; shallow finger grips pecked into edges on about half of the lot; grinding face convex on long axis and extends around on ends of the longer examples, and nearly flat on short axis; two specimens show a pitted upper surface (Fig. 27, *e*). Size range: lengths, 12.0-17.0 cm.; widths, 8.0-11.0 cm.; thickness, 3.5-6.0 cm. Used chiefly in Type II metate, although longer specimens could be used in Type III metates. From Houses 1, 2, 3, 6, 8, and 11. Chiefly Hilltop Phase, also Cottonwood Phase.

---

[50]This resembles the so-called "Utah" type of metate, but the local examples are not so well developed and do not show this feature even as well as those from the Bear Ruin (E. W. Haury, 1940, pp. 98-99).

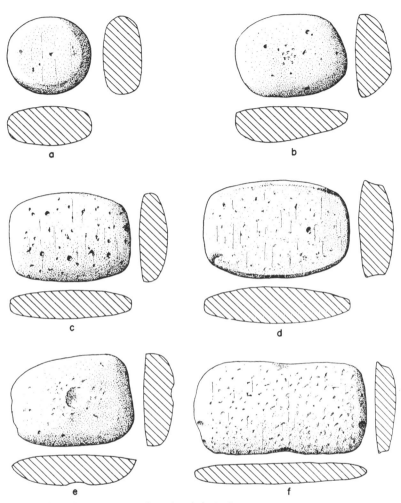

Figure 27.—Mano types. Length of *f*, 21.0 cm.

Type III, shaped, long (three) (Fig. 27, *f*)
    Indurated sandstone (two), lava (one); subrectangular, shaped
    by pecking; wearing faces single or double; all have finger grips;
    grinding faces nearly flat on both axes and on long axis, curv-
    ing onto ends. Size range: lengths, 18.0-21.0 cm.; widths, 10.0-
    11.0 cm.; thickness, 3.0-4.0 cm. Fits Type III metate best, but
    probably usable in some Type II metates also. From Houses
    3, 5, and 19. Chiefly Cottonwood Phase.[51]

---

[51]For footnote see next page.

Small mortarlike stones (seven)
  Type I, thick (four) (Fig. 28, *a*)
    Vesicular basalt or compact igneous rock; thick in proportion to size, unshaped; oval grinding depression not exceeding 2.0 cm. in depth and extending well over upper surface of stone. Size range: lengths, 14.0-24.0 cm.; widths, 11.0-20.0 cm.; thickness, 8.0-13.0 cm. From Houses 4, 5, and 6. Hilltop Phase.
  Type II, thin (three) (Fig. 28, *b*)
    Materials as above; thin in proportion to size and extensively shaped to give oval form; oval depression framed by a pronounced rim, which itself has been smoothed. Only complete specimen measures: length, 22.5 cm.; width, 16.0 cm.; thickness, 7.0 cm.; depth of depression, 2.5 cm. From Houses 4 and 8. Hilltop Phase.

Flat grinding slabs (five) (not illustrated)
  Thin sandstone slabs of variable size and shape, one surface showing some abrasion. From Houses 5, 6, 13, and 14. Hilltop and Cottonwood Phases.

Rubbing stones (twelve)
  Type I, pebble (eight) (Fig. 28, *c*)
    Quartzite stream-worn pebbles, unshaped; used one or more sides; could be used on grinding slabs (above) or metates; some also employed as hammerstones and pitted from use as anvils. Size range: lengths, 8.0-11.0 cm.; widths, 6.0-8.0 cm.; thickness, 2.5-4.5 cm. From Houses 3, 4, 6, and 11. Hilltop and Cottonwood Phases.
  Type II, tabular (four) (Fig. 28, *d*)
    Sandstone; thin, more or less rectangular; one face only; worn surface flat. Size range: lengths, 7.0-9.5 cm.; width, 5.0-7.5 cm.; thickness, 1.5-3.0 cm. From House 11 and Block 3E, Test 2 (outside of House 11). Cottonwood Phase.

Mortars (three)
  Type I, converted metate (two) (Fig. 26, *d*)
    Depression within deepest part of grinding trough. Houses 8 and 11 (latter built into house wall). Hilltop Phase, probably also Cottonwood Phase.
  Type II, pebble (one) (Fig. 28, *e*)
    Quartzite pebble with symmetrically placed and formed depression. Maximum diameter, 10.9 cm.; thickness, 5.4 cm.; depth of depression, 2.2 cm. From House 5. Hilltop Phase.

Pestles (four) (Fig. 28, *f*)
  Quartzite and lava; short chunky waterworn boulders, adapted for use without shaping; both ends occasionally show wear. From

---

[51]The associations do not show this to be the case, but Type III metates were limited to this phase. Type III manos might have been used on newly made Type II metates, but with use the long axis would have become strongly convex.

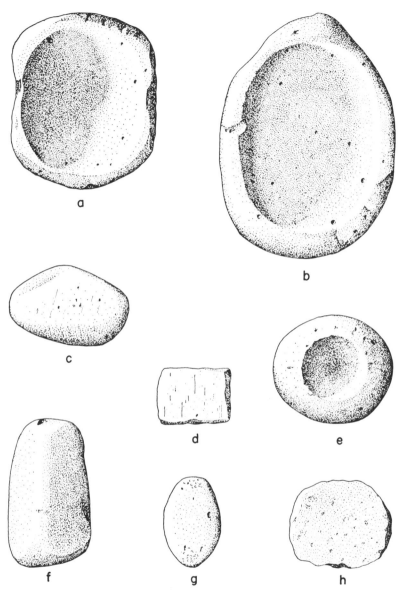

Figure 28.—Stone implements. Length of *b,* 22.5 cm.

  Houses 6, 13, and Hearth 2. Hilltop Phase, probably continuous through Corduroy Phase.
Hammerstones (forty-seven)
  Type I, angular (forty) (not illustrated)

Chunks of basalt, quartzite, and chert; some originally stream pebbles, broken to form sharp edges; worn specimens nearly round. Diameters, 5.0-11.0 cm. From general digging and nearly all houses. Hilltop and Cottonwood Phases.

Type II, pebble (six) (Fig. 28, *g*)
Smooth, egg-shaped pebble, not fractured; pecked surface generally restricted to flat surface near ends. Greatest diameter, 3.5-7.0 cm. From Houses 3, 6, 14, and 15. Probably both Hilltop and Cottonwood Phases.

Type III, pitted (one) (not illustrated)
More or less discoidal quartzite pebble, originally used as rubbing stone; both faces centrally pitted. Diameter, 7.5 cm. From House 7. Probably Hilltop Phase.

Rough discs (two) (Fig. 28, *h*)
Sandstone; thin, roughly broken to circular form. Diameters: 10.0-14.0 cm.; thickness, 1.5 cm. Probably used as jar covers. From Houses 6 and 7. Hilltop Phase.

Polishing stones (six) (not illustrated)
Small stream pebbles showing worn facets, probably from polishing pottery. Diameters: 2.7-7.3 cm. From Houses 5, 11, and 14. Hilltop and Cottonwood Phases.

Rasps (two) (Fig. 29, *a*)
Highly abrasive, fine-grained sandstone; elongated; show abrasive facets. Lengths: 9.6 and 13.1 cm. From Houses 11 and 13. Probably Hilltop and Cottonwood Phases.

STONE OBJECTS INTENTIONALLY POLISHED

Discs (one) (Fig. 29, *b*)
Indurated sandstone; appreciably thinned towards edge. Diameter: 5.2 cm.; thickness, .9 cm. From House 14. Cottonwood Phase.

Pipes (three) (Fig. 29, *c*)
All vesicular lava; short, tubular; good workmanship; little differentiation between bowl and mouthpiece ends; one bowl and fragment blackened; bore drilled from both ends. Dimensions of complete specimen: length, 6.9 cm.; diameters, 2.7 cm. (max.), 2.1 cm. (min.); diameter of bore, 1.5 cm. (bowl), 1.2 cm. (mouthpiece). From Houses 5, 7, and test in Block C4. Probably Hilltop Phase.

"Medicine" stone (one) (Fig. 29, *d*)
Chalcedony; ground and polished cylinder, tapered towards one end, other end flat; pronounced longitudinal polishing facets. Length, 3.6 cm.; greatest diameter, 1.0 cm. From House 14. Cottonwood Phase.

ORNAMENTS

Bead (one) (Fig. 29, *e*)
Gray argillaceous stone; irregular outline showing scored polishing

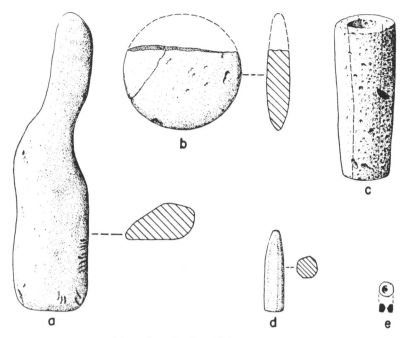

Figure 29.—Stone objects. Length of *a*, 13.0 cm.

facets; perforation biconical. Diameter, 6.5 mm.; thickness, 4.0 mm. From House 19A. Corduroy Phase.

CHIPPED STONE

PERCUSSION

Core implements (twenty-one)
  Choppers (twenty-one) (Fig. 30, *a, b*)
    Mostly quartzite stream pebbles; fractured from one face to give a wedge-shaped, ragged cutting edge. Diameter range: 6.0-17.0 cm. From Houses 3, 5, 6, 8, 11, 13, 15, 19, and general testing. Predominantly Hilltop Phase, but also Cottonwood Phase.
Flake implements (twenty)
  Primary flake scrapers (four) (Fig. 30, *c*)
    Large quartzite flakes; little retouching; irregular outline. Lengths: 7.2-9.3 cm. From Houses 3, 5, and 6. Hilltop Phase.
  Side and end scrapers (sixteen) (Fig. 30, *d, e*)
    Predominantly chert, some quartzite; thick flakes, very irregular; one edge steeply retoucheed. Lengths: 3.2-7.5 cm. From Houses 3, 4, 5, 6, 11, 13, 14, 19, and general digging. Hilltop and Cottonwood Phases.

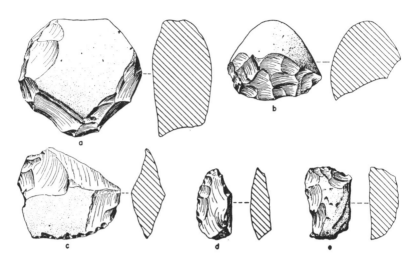

Figure 30.—Percussion flaked tools.   Diameter of *a*, 9.5 cm.

Flake implements (sixty-two)
  Knives (thirty-eight) (Fig. 31, *a, b*)
    Chert and petrified wood; thin, sharp, fortuitous flakes; mostly
    chipped by use rather than for use; no regularity of outline.
    Length range: 2.7-5.9 cm. From practically all houses and
    general digging. Hilltop and Cottonwood Phases.
  Scrapers (twenty-four)
    a) Side (seven) (Fig. 31, *c, d*)
        Chert; generally elongated flakes; one edge retouched on one
        side. Length range: 2.8-4.8 cm. From Houses 2, 3, 4, and
        11. Hilltop and Cottonwood Phases.
    b) Hollow (seven) (Fig. 31, *e, f*)
        Chert and petrified wood; fortuitous flakes, with chipped con-
        cavity. Length range: 2.4-4.8 cm. From Houses 3, 5, 6, 13,
        and 19. Predominantly Hilltop Phase.
    c) Serrate (one) (Fig. 31, *g*)
        Triangular chert flake; thin edge finely serrated. Length: 4.8
        cm. From House 19A. Corduroy Phase.
    d) Ground edge scrapers (nine) (Fig. 31, *h, i*)
        Chert and quartzite, convenient flakes with convex edges, some-
        times slightly chipped; edges ground smooth from drawing
        across abrasive surface. Length range: 2.9-7.8 cm. From
        Houses 4, 12, 13, 14, and 19. Hilltop and Cottonwood
        Phases.

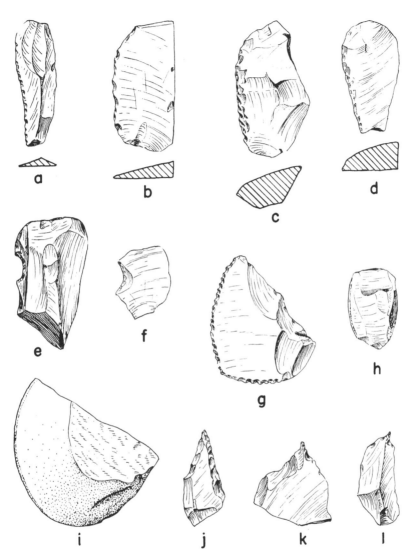

Figure 31.—Pressure flaked and ground edge tools. Length of *a,* 4.6 cm.

Gravers (twenty-three) (Fig. 31, *j-l*)

Chert and petrified wood; generally triangular flakes; sharpest point finely retouched on one or both faces of flake; points rounded from use. Length range: 2.9-5.6 cm. From Houses 3, 8, 9, 11, 12, and 13. Predominantly Hilltop Phase.

Knives and projectile points[52] (forty-seven)
  A. Unnotched, leaf-shaped (twenty-four)
      1. Pointed base (two) (Fig. 32, *a*)
          Chert; base shows slight drawing in on both sides. Lengths:
          3.6 and 5.2 cm. From Houses 7 and 11. Probably Hilltop and
          Cottonwood Phases.
      2. Round base (five) (Fig. 32, *b*)
          Chert, jasper, petrified wood. Lengths: 3.5 to 7.0 cm. (esti-
          mate). From Houses 3, 6, 11, and 14. Probably Hilltop and
          Cottonwood Phases.
      3. Straight base (seventeen)
          a) Without rudimentary stem (nine) (Fig. 32, *c, d*).
              Chert; widest part at about mid-point on blade. Lengths:
              2.1 to 7.0 cm. (estimate). From Houses 3, 14, and 18.
              Hilltop and Cottonwood Phases.
          b) With rudimentary stem (ten) (Fig. 32, *e-g*)
              Chert; edges slightly reduced from one-third to one-half
              the length of blade above base. Lengths: 2.6-4.5 cm.
              From Houses 2, 6, 8, 9, 10, 11, and 14. Predominantly
              Hilltop Phase.
  B. Notched (twenty-three)
      1. Lateral (fourteen)
          a) Broad and shallow (ten) (Fig. 32, *h, i*)
              Chert, jasper, and petrified wood; base convex to straight.
              Lengths: 2.6-5.0 cm. From Houses 3, 4, 6, and 13. Hill-
              top Phase.
          b) Broad and deep (two) (Fig. 32, *j, k*)
              Variant of above. Lengths: 3.3-3.6 cm. From House 11.
              Cottonwood Phase.
          c) Narrow and deep (two) (Fig. 32, *l, m*)
              Chert and basalt; concave base, stem wide; one has extra
              notch at mid-point on blade. Lengths: 2.4 and 2.8 cm.
              Both from surface. Probably late, as they agree in type
              with points from the large local pueblos.
      2. Diagonal (nine) (Fig. 32, *n-r*)
          Predominantly chert, one each of chalcedony, obsidian, and
          basalt; stem expanding, sharp tang; base convex to straight;
          one serrated. Lengths: 2.3 to 6.8 cm. From Houses 2, 4,
          5, 11, and 14, trash and surface. Probably Hilltop and Cotton-
          wood Phases.
Drills (six) (Fig. 33)
  Chert; plain-shafted (three), *a,* and flanged (three), *b-d.* Lengths:
  3.6-5.1 cm. From Houses 11 and 14, general digging and surface.
  Probably Hilltop and Cottonwood Phases.

---

[52]Large and small chipped blades have been put together because of the
impossibility of telling when a blade was used as a knife or as a projectile
point.

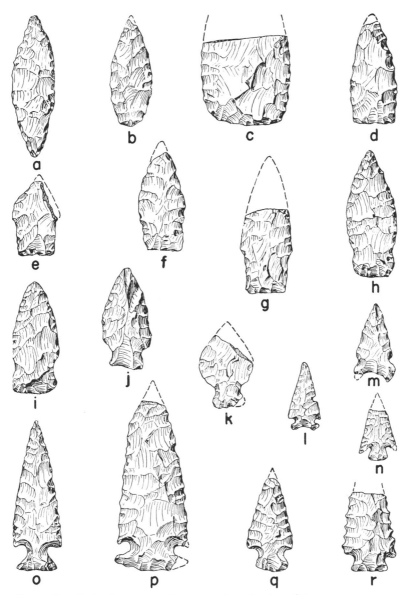

Figure 32.—Projectile points and knives. Length of *o*, 6.2 cm.

MINERALS

Very rare; only two lumps of hematite found, one of which has been rubbed for deriving paint.

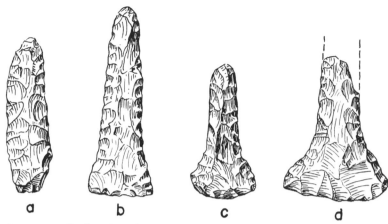

Figure 33.—Drills. Actual size.

DISCUSSION

The lithic products of the Bluff Site, like the pottery, are characterized by scarcity and simplicity. There were few formalized types in all categories of stone processing. This further heightens the general impression gained from the analysis of other aspects of culture, namely, that it was incipient.

In the foregoing pages more or less specific phase assignments of the various traits have been made. This has been done on the basis of associations with houses, or trash related to them. There may be some objection to this, particularly since many of the associations were not repeated often enough to be convincing. But in defense of our procedure, it is worth pointing out that there appears to have been relatively little mixture of early with late rubbish and that most Hilltop Phase house pits were filled or nearly so before the Cottonwood Phase structures were put up.

As examples, supporting the validity of the associations, may be pointed out the tabular rubbing stones (Type II) of the Cottonwood Phase. The four recovered were either in or just outside of House 11, a slab-lined structure. None came from elsewhere in the site. The thin trough metates of Basketmaker linkage (Type III) were only found on the floor of slab houses, while in two cases Type II metates, the predominant and Hilltop Phase form, were built into the wall of slab-houses, having been salvaged from the older horizon. It is to be hoped, of course, that future excavations will add strength to the assignments made here.

Some of the stone elements require a further word. The predominant metate (Type II) was reported also as characteristic of the Forestdale Phase,[53] which makes the Basketmaker metate (Type III)

---

[53]E. W. Haury, 1940, pp. 98-99.

look all the more like an intrusive element which was not accepted locally. Basin metates (Type I) were in the minority and may be reminders of their relationship to, or survival from, a still earlier horizon without pottery and agriculture when basin metates were the normal type.[54] Perhaps the most significant feature of the deep trough metate of the Bluff Site is the fact that they are more like those from such sites as SU, the Harris and Mogollon villages, than they are like those from San Juan Basketmaker ruins.[55]

The smaller mortarlike stones are, strictly speaking, neither metates nor mortars. Manos could not be operated in them, and pestles were not used in them in the normal fashion, although a pestle might have been rubbed over the surface in a more or less rotary fashion. They are manifestly early in the Bluff Site and are similar but not identical with the pebble mortars illustrated from the SU Site.[56]

Metates later used as mortars occur also in the Forestdale Phase locally.[57] Evidently a true boulder mortar was not used. The converted metate apparently ranges south and east, as it is also seen at SU.[58]

The small pebble mortar, of which only one was found in the Bluff Site, survived into the Forestdale Phase in the local chronology[59] and appears with greater frequency in Mogollon sites to the southeast.

As more and more sites of the Mogollon Culture are excavated, it becomes clear that the tubular stone pipe, in contrast to the short clay "cloud blower" type of the Anasazi,[60] is a strong characteristic of them. The two forms are not strictly mutually exclusive in the respective areas, but predominances are becoming marked.

Stone ornaments were lacking, with the exception of a single stone bead from a late (Corduroy Phase) house. Turquoise, almost always present in southwestern sites, was not even represented by waste scraps. What may have been used in the way of perishable ornaments we cannot say, but it is clear that little or nothing was made of durable materials for personal decoration.

Among the percussion chipped tools, the pebble chopper is noteworthy. In the local cultural scheme it was most prevalent in the

---

[54]The San Pedro Stage of the Cochise Culture or its equivalent. Mera reports the basin metate to be characteristic in the Petrified Forest Site, showing Adamana Brown and the presumed later ruins with Woodruff types. (1934, pp. 2-5.)

[55]Compare with Plate 147, E. H. Morris, 1939; see also F. H. H. Roberts, Jr. 1929, Plate 26.

[56]P. S. Martin, J. Rinaldo, and M. Kelly, 1940, Figs. 21, 22.

[57]E. W. Haury, 1940, p. 101.

[58]P. S. Martin, 1943, Fig. 64.

[59]E. W. Haury, 1940, p. 104, perhaps erroneously called a stone vessel.

[60]F. H. H. Roberts, Jr., 1929, pp. 124-25; S. J. Guernsey, 1931, Table, p. 118.

Hilltop Phase, weakly represented some centuries later in the Forestdale Phase,[61] and in still later phases our excavations have produced none at all. This increase from late to early probably means the type was in general use in the preceramic horizons.[62]

For smaller chipped tools, much dependence was placed on fortuitous flakes which could be put directly to work with little or no modification. Especially to be singled out are the serrate and ground edge scrapers. The former, represented by only one example from House 19A (Corduroy Phase), is of the same type that appeared strongly in the Forestdale Phase[63] but probably not much earlier. Ground edge scrapers, too, were found in the Forestdale Phase,[64] imparting a considerable length of time to this trait in the local prehistory. In southern Arizona, the ground edge scraper has been reported in the Cochise Culture[65] and in Ventana Cave.[66]

The liberal number of gravers suggests this to have been an important tool. But nothing was found to indicate what was done with them. It is possible that these keenly chipped implements were used in connection with wood working.

Leaf-shaped projectile points, slightly reduced along the edges towards the base to make a rudimentary stem, and the shallow lateral notched variety, characterize the Hilltop Phase. These were in the minority during the Forestdale Phase.[67] Martin shows similar points from SU,[68] but there they were secondary to diagonal notched projectiles. Points of the latter type in the Bluff Site, while early, or in Hilltop Phase contexts, were numerically stronger in Cottonwood Phase trash, and they agree, on the whole, with the standard point of Basketmaker III[69] with which they were roughly contemporary.

Notably absent in the implement typology were axes and mauls. This is surprising, since they have invariably been present in numbers in other early Mogollon Culture sites, as the Bear Ruin,[70] SU,[71]

---

[61]E. W. Haury, 1940, pp. 104-05.
[62]E. B. Sayles and E. Antevs, 1941, the "plano-convex axe," Fig. 10, p. 27.
[63]E. W. Haury, 1940, pp. 106-07.
[64]*Ibid.,* p. 109.
[65]E. B. Sayles and E. Antevs, 1941, p. 27, Fig. 10.
[66]E. W. Haury, in preparation.
[67]E. W. Haury, 1940, p. 106.
[68]P. S. Martin, 1941, Fig. 73, D.
[69]E. H. Morris, 1939, p. 127.
[70]E. W. Haury, 1940, pp. 103-04.
[71]P. S. Martin, J. Rinaldo, and M. Kelly, 1940, p. 56; P. S. Martin, 1943, p. 202.

the Mogollon and Harris villages.[72] With mauls present in the Bear Ruin by A.D. 700 but absent in the Bluff Site during the fourth century, we gain some notion as to the possible time of introduction of this widespread hafted tool.

Without endeavoring at this time to present a detailed comparative analysis of the above listed stone tools, we would like to present the following observations, whose merits must be tested against the results of future studies:

1. That some Bluff Site stone tools, notably basin metates, pebble choppers, and ground edge scrapers, stem directly from the Cochise Culture.

2. That the over-all pattern of the lithic products of the Bluff Site is in a southern (Mogollon) rather than in a northern (Anasazi) tradition.

BONE

It is difficult to explain why no bone implements were recovered. The collection contains only two small fragments, which have been worked but are too incomplete to identify the type of tool. While animal bones were not abundant, such as came to light were well preserved, and these indicated, furthermore, that large animals like deer and antelope, whose leg bones were ideal for awl manufacture, were occasionally hunted. Dr. Buehrer's analysis of the soil (see Appendix) dispels the feeling that most of the bone remains have been disintegrated by chemical action in the soil. The conclusion is inevitable that bone was of little importance as a raw material for tools, as a corollary of the fact that little emphasis was put on hunting itself. Bone may have been largely replaced by wood in the production of certain tools.

Whether this situation was peculiar only to the occupants of the Bluff Village, or whether it reflects a widespread condition, only future work can tell. The SU Site in New Mexico, culturally the nearest to the Bluff Site of any ruin yet excavated, produced a relatively small quantity of bone tools[73] and fewer animal bones. The Bear Ruin, on the other hand, representing a later horizon in the Forestdale Valley,[74] yielded a considerable number of elements in both categories.

SHELL

Another notable absence was marine shell. The destruction of this material by soil chemicals must be considered as a possibility, because Dr. Buehrer's analysis of the trash shows it to be acidic in nature. The calcium carbonate of shell would thus have been destroyed. But

---

[72]E. W. Haury, 1936, pp. 36, 70.
[73]P. S. Martin, J. Rinaldo, M. Kelly, 1940, pp. 70-73; P. S. Martin, 1943, pp. 224-29.
[74]E. W. Haury, 1940, pp. 113-16.

while the conditions were not conducive to the preservation of shell, one must also consider the possibility that this substance was never present. In the Bear Ruin several centuries later shellwork was rare,[75] and there is an evident increase in shell in the later sites of the valley. It is to be regretted that the evidence of the Bluff Site in this connection is not definitive; otherwise it might be possible to judge the time of appearance of this foreign material in this locality.

DATING THE BLUFF SITE

There are two approaches to the problem of the age of the Bluff Ruin. The first is by archaeology, which allows, at best, only a relative assignment of time; the second is by dendrochronology, much more precise and satisfying to the demands of historical reconstruction. The results of these two methods, different though they be, should complement each other when all the data have been assembled.

Looking at the problem from the archaeological point of view, the establishment of a local chronology from about 700 to 1400 by previous investigations offers limiting dates, or a range within which the occupation of the Bluff Site could not fall. Of the two possibilities, then, later than 1400 or earlier than 700, only the latter alternative needs to be considered for reasons stated below.

First of all, the typology of the pottery, stone tools, and architectural features foreshadows the cultural pattern of the Forestdale Phase of about A.D. 700. But lacking were the quantity of pottery, some pottery types, and the general attainment level of the later inhabitants of the area, suggesting that the Hilltop Phase was a logical antecedent to the Forestdale Phase. In addition to this purely local consideration is the fact that trade pottery foreign to the site, as Adamana Brown and Gila Plain, occupy early positions in the chronologies where these types were at home. Furthermore, the absence of Basketmaker pottery in Hilltop Phase contexts leads to the suspicion that this stage of culture had waxed and waned before the Basketmaker produced fired pottery. The slab-lined Basketmaker type houses of the Cottonwood Phase, later than the rock-cut houses of the Hilltop Phase by stratigraphy, may be roughly equated with similar structures to the north, which again hold an early position in Anasazi prehistory. Hence, these few details lead to the assumption that the Bluff Site was occupied, not only before 700, but probably before 400, the time generally conceded to mark the appearance of an indigenous fired pottery among the Basketmaker. The Cottonwood Phase, with its few sherds of Lino Gray, may be logically correlated, then, with Basketmaker III. This line of reasoning is shown to be approximately correct when we examine the results of tree-ring dating.

The collection of charcoal consists of about 190 numbered fragments, coming from ten different architectural units. The first study of the 1941 samples by Mr. Ralph Patton and subsequent careful

[75]E. W. Haury, 1940, p. 117.

analysis of all material by Dr. A. E. Douglass[76] showed that many of
the specimens were from the same tree, as for example the twenty-four
pieces from House 5, which gave Sequence A. In addition to this
situation, which markedly reduced the size of the sample, a good many
pieces were undatable because of ring compression, the records were
too short, or the wood was juniper. In the final analysis, the dating
results rest on nine, possibly ten, individual trees, these having come
from six different houses.

Dr. Douglass' summary[77] may be further condensed as follows:

House	No. of Trees	Dates
1	1	310 ± 15
2	1	306 + x
3	1	288 + x
5	3 or more	318 (Bark date)
		320 ± 5
6	2 (?)	287 + x
		303 + x
21	1	312 ± 10

While this may not appear to be a very imposing array of dates on
which to rely for so important a step as the age assignment of the
Bluff Site, particularly as the dates fall well towards the early end of the
present tree-ring calendar, any doubts that may arise should be dispelled
by the fact that all of the dates cluster in a limited time range and
that satisfactory cross-dating exists. Only two specimens, from Houses
2 and 5, with dates of 302 and 318, respectively, gave what appear
to be the bark dates, or the actual cutting time of the trees. On all
other specimens the true outside, or final ring was not preserved, and
these dates are followed by the symbols + x. The range for all dates,
taking the latest in each case where a number of specimens of a
single tree are represented, may be stated as 285 + x to 318. Allow-
ances for rings lost on outsides might well shorten this range of years
to amount to less than a score. Thus, the dates we have offer no discordant notes within themselves, and the houses in question may be
considered as having been constructed in the final years of the third
and in early decades of the fourth centuries A.D. This does not, of
course, date the duration of the occupation but gives us only an anchor
point within it.

Another important observation to be derived is that all houses in
the above list, on architectural type and associated pottery, were placed
in the Hilltop Phase before the dates were known.

It is to be regretted that no dates were forthcoming from those
houses (11, 14, and 19) assigned to the Cottonwood Phase. This
would have provided a desirable check in the archaeological interpre-

---

[76] A. E. Douglass, 1942, 1944.
[77] A. E. Douglass, 1944, p. 13.

tation, but since the preceding and succeeding phases have been dated, the time for the Cottonwood Phase is thereby roughly blocked out.

SUMMARY AND CONCLUSIONS

The present work in the Bluff Site has resulted in the recognition of two sequent phases of occupation in the Forestdale Valley not determined in prior studies. These phases have been called the Hilltop and Cottonwood, the former having been the older. Both were lineally ancestral to the Forestdale Phase, which had an estimated temporal range of from about A.D. 600-800, with reliable tree-ring dates in the neighborhood of 700. The two new phases are synoptically defined below:

HILLTOP PHASE

Area.—Known only in the Forestdale Valley at present.
Age.—Range of tree-ring dates, A.D. 287 + x to 320 ± 20 (nine trees). Estimated inclusive dates, 200 to 400.
Excavated site.—Bluff Site (Ariz. P:16:20).
Unexcavated sites.—Ariz. P:16:28 and Ariz. P:16:58.
Environment.—Forested, elevation 6,500 feet.
Determinants
  Architecture
    A. Round to oval pit houses (average diameter, 4.8 m.) excavated into bedrock, occasionally with rubble wall if bedrock sloped; usually, but not always, parallel-sided lateral, slightly inclined, entrance; hearth unspecialized, near center when definable; floor pits; bench, deflector, ventilator absent.
    B. Proto-kiva: Large (10.3 m. diameter), round, four-post roof support plan; hearth off-center; no bench, deflector, or ventilator detected.
  Economy
    A. Hunting of slight importance; greater dependence upon food gathering and agriculture. No positive evidence of corn, but milling stones were well developed.
    B. Large hearths or earth ovens, stones used in cooking process.
  Pottery
    A. Indigenous
      Painted types.—None.
      Utility types.—Alma Plain, Bluff and Forestdale varieties; Woodruff Smudged.[78] Little pottery of all types produced.
    B. Intrusive
      Painted types.—Red-on-buff (late Pioneer (?) Period, Hohokam).
      Utility types.—Adamana Brown, Gila Plain.

[78]May be intrusive.

Stone
  A. Ground
     Basin metates, but predominantly bulky, troughed, open one end and strongly concave in both axes, near end shelflike; manos unshaped pebbles and shaped oval to subrectangular types; mortar (converted metate) and small pebble type; unshaped pestles; small oval mortarlike grinding stones; flat grinding slabs; rubbing stones, unshaped; angular and pebble hammerstones (one pitted); rough stone discs; polishing stones; rasps; tubular pipes.
  B. Chipped
     Core choppers; primary flake scrapers; flake knives; side, hollow, and ground edge scrapers; gravers; characteristic projectile point leaf-shaped with straight base and rudimentary stem, also shallow lateral notched and diagonal notched forms; drills.
  C. Ornaments
     Absent.
Bone
  No finished tools found.
Shell
  None found.
Miscellaneous objects of clay
  Large sherd containers, perforated and unperforated potsherd discs; human figurines.
Disposal of dead
  Semiflexed burials; without offerings.
Physical type
  Evidence not decisive, but apparently meso- or brachycranial.

COTTONWOOD PHASE

Area.—Known only in the Forestdale Valley.
Age.—Probably about A.D. 400-600; no tree-ring dates.
Excavated sites.—Bluff Site (Ariz. P:16:20).
Unexcavated sites.—None known.
Environment.—Forested, elevation 6,500 feet.
Determinants
  Architecture
    Subrectangular pit houses, slab lined, built in trash; hearth near center, four-post roof support plan, side entrance.
  Economy
    Same as Hilltop Phase.
  Pottery
    A. Indigenous
      Painted types.—None.
      Utility types.—Alma Plain, Forestdale variety (produced in

considerable abundance); Forestdale Smudged; Woodruff Red.

B. Intrusive

Painted types.—None.

Utility types.—Adamana Brown; Lino Gray (?); Gila Plain.

Stone

A. Ground

Metates troughed, open one end, thin; some earlier types probably also used; manos as in Hilltop Phase, but also longer, parallel-sided examples; pebble and tabular rubbing stones, latter characteristic; mortars as in Hilltop Phase; angular pebble hammerstones; polishing stones; polished discs; "medicine" stone.

B. Chipped

Generally as in Hilltop Phase, but broad and deeply notched projectile point largely replaced earlier unnotched type.

C. Ornaments

No data.

Bone and shell

No data.

Disposal of dead and physical type

No data.

With the phase summaries out of the way, brief consideration needs to be given to the chronologic position which the Hilltop and Cottonwood Phases hold in the local sequence, as well as to suggest possible correlative phases in adjoining areas. This can best be done in the form of a chart (Fig. 34). For the complete local, or Forestdale, sequence we have drawn on the excavations of four seasons. The details of those phases following the Forestdale await publication.

Approximately 1100 years of unbroken human history can be recorded for the Forestdale Valley, beginning in the third century of the Christian Era and ending about 1400. Cultural progress has been measured by the familiar device of phases, each one having a number of traits continuing from the immediate predecessor, but individualized by the addition of new ones. A case in point would be the Cottonwood Phase, which had pottery and the majority of the stone tools of the Hilltop Phase, but was distinguished by a greater output of pottery and by the intrusion of Basketmaker elements, the slab house, and a new metate form from the north. The Hilltop Phase inaugurates the sequence and represents the earliest evidence we have of the area's human occupants. In keeping with the current taxonomic procedure in southwestern archaeology, this pattern of development is called the Forestdale Branch.

A succession of this sort offers an opportunity to determine changes in the over-all pattern as possible indication of the blending of different cultural units. The work in the Forestdale Valley was begun in 1939 with the expectation of adding to our knowledge of the Mogollon

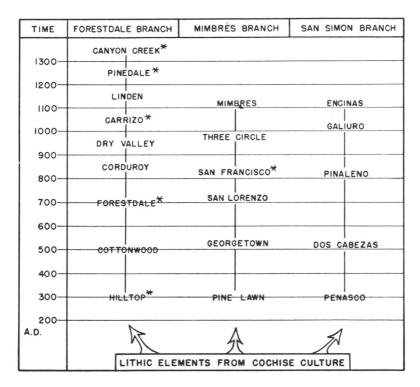

TIME	FORESTDALE BRANCH	MIMBRES BRANCH	SAN SIMON BRANCH

Figure 34.—Chart provisionally correlating the phases in the three branches recognized at present as beginning the Mogollon Complex. Asterisk indicates horizons dated by tree rings.

Culture, and the Forestdale Phase was eventually recognized as being a composite of both Anasazi and Mogollon elements. Phases subsequent to the Forestdale horizon show a progressive increase in Anasazi features and a diminution of those believed to be Mogollon.[79] The addition of two early stages poses the question as to whether or not the oldest material is fundamentally Mogollon, or whether even then mixture was already apparent. Obviously this has a direct bearing on the general problem of the separateness of the two groups. It is our firm conviction, based on the data enumerated herein, that the Hilltop Phase was as nearly "pure" Mogollon as has yet been described, excepting possibly the Penasco Phase of southeastern Arizona.[80] An important argument in support of this is the pottery, which was both

---

[79] A fuller discussion of this will appear in the final report of the Forestdale studies.
[80] E. B. Sayles, 1945 pp. 65-66.

older than and unlike the earliest Anasazi earthenware. But by about 500, or during the Cottonwood Phase, undoubted Anasazi elements appear, e.g., slab houses and pottery, beginning the hybridization of the two groups which eventually led to the almost complete suppression and replacement of the original culture. As we see it, therefore, Forestdale prehistory is more than the story of a single ethnic unit. It involves the synthesis of two.

Referring to Figure 34 again, two other phases, Pine Lawn in the Mimbres Branch[81] and Penasco in the San Simon Branch,[82] are shown as the approximate contemporaries of the Hilltop Phase. Geographically these lie in west-central New Mexico and southeastern Arizona, respectively. Culturally, in so far as general level of attainment was concerned, in the ceramics and in a number of lithic elements, these phases have much in common. Similarities between the Hilltop Phase of the Bluff Site and the Pine Lawn Phase of the SU Site are most pronounced. It may be inferred that these are early regional variations of an essentially similar cultural unit, and probably of approximately the same age.

In each of these areas, too, the subsequent phases have a distinctive quality about them, and regional histories are becoming apparent which, although they started on much the same cultural plane and complex, were deflected this way or that by the effects of contacts established with other culture units later on.

The San Simon Branch, for example, retained perhaps the parent Mogollon tradition for the longest time, from the Penasco to the Encinos Phase, when Hohokam culture factors became prominent.[83]

The Mimbres Branch[84] manifests hybridization with the Anasazi somewhat earlier and the Forestdale Branch, geographically nearest the Anasazi and, in predictable fashion, shows blending with this northern group in a minor way in the Cottonwood Phase and markedly in the Forestdale Phase, earlier than either of the two preceding branches. Subsequently the Anasazi factors easily predominate.

At this point it is well to introduce a question voiced by Gladwin[85] "As to whether we should continue to regard the Georgetown and San Francisco Phases as representative of Mogollon."

With the idea that the Mimbres sequence (Georgetown, San Francisco, Three Circle) should not be called *The* Mogollon Culture, we are in full accord. These are but phases locally evolved from a broad base and will be matched by other regional developments from the same base as more work is done, just as Chaco, Mesa Verde, and Kay-

[81]The Mogollon Branch in P. S. Martin, 1943, p. 122; E. W. Haury, 1936, p. 123.
[82]E. B. Sayles, 1945, pp. 65-66.
[83]E. B. Sayles, 1945.
[84]Martin's Mogollon Branch, 1943, p. 122.
[85]H. S. Gladwin, 1943, p. 15.

enta became differentiated from a common cultural denominator, Basketmaker III for the Anasazi. In addition to Gila Pueblo's original Mogollon studies, Sayles' work at Cave Creek and the San Simon Village, Martin's at SU, and ours in the Forestdale Valley may be listed as pointing to the eventual establishment of local chronologies, all of which were rooted to the same cultural complex.

LENGTH OF PHASES

The number of years to be assigned to a given phase is information which tree rings do not specifically provide, although they do yield dates within such a range. How much time is to be allotted per phase, therefore, is an estimate, and stated figures should be regarded as such.

For the Hilltop Phase we have calculated a 200-year period from A.D. 200-400, allowing approximately a century before and after 300, where the tree-ring dates clustered. This seems reasonable, because the pottery presumably present at this time does not represent the first ceramic efforts. Some prior acquaintance with this art may be predicated, and the same attitude will apply with respect to architecture. The year 200 is thus stated as an arbitrary figure to acknowledge that something preceded the first dated remains, but we are fully aware that this date may be either too liberal or too conservative. The phase ending date of 400 is based on the fact that at about that time the Basketmakers appear to have learned the art of pottery making. The total lack of Basketmaker pottery in Hilltop Phase contexts, therefore, is some basis for the claim that there was no appreciable overlap between the Hilltop Phase and the Lino Phase of the Basketmaker, the initial period of pottery production among that group.

As for the Cottonwood Phase, the evidence from the Bluff Site suggests a relatively short period, but there is always the possibility that the full range was not represented. Nevertheless, an arbitrary 200-year period, from 400 to 600, is allotted in order to close the gap between the end of the Hilltop Phase and the estimated beginning of the Forestdale Phase.

After the Forestdale Phase there was an evident shortening of the phase durations, due to accelerated culture progress. These are fairly well tied down by tree-ring dates.

MOGOLLON DERIVATIONS

It is appropriate to raise the question as to what preceded the Hilltop Phase; from what sort of complex did this early pottery culture spring? In the first place, it does not seem likely that we can anticipate finding locally an earlier phase with pottery as a diagnostic. The simple reason for this is the fact that it would be difficult to find indigenous pottery in less quantity than here and convince oneself that it really belonged to the culture. Pottery in smaller amounts would be about the same as having no pottery at all. Hence, it may be speculated that the roots of the Hilltop Phase dip back into a preceramic horizon. No sites of this description have been found in the Forestdale Valley, although a search was made, both in the hills adjoining the valley and in the eroded channel of the creek, where it was felt that buried sites might occur.

Any connection with a preceramic culture must be based chiefly on lithic continuities, and the only presently known relatively dated complex to turn to is the San Pedro Stage of the Cochise Culture.

Those traits which occur in the San Pedro Stage and in the Hilltop Phase may be briefly listed: basin metates, small mortarlike stones; pestles; pebble mortars; choppers; ground edge scrapers; gravers; and on the negative side, an absence of grooved mauls and axes. The projectile point type does not conform, and the Hilltop Phase has a few polished stone objects not seen earlier. The similarities outweigh the dissimilarities, and a cultural continuum looms as a distinct possibility. This belief is greatly strengthened by the findings in the Cave Creek Site,[86] where the link between the preceramic San Pedro Stage and the earliest ceramic horizon, the Penasco Phase, has been more critically assessed. The relationship is equally clear here. At the SU Site, Martin,[87] too, has sensed this continuity.

In practically all studies of southwestern archaeology, the student has been dealing either with cultures in which agriculture and pottery were firmly rooted or with those that were wholly without them. One of the critical points in the study is to find out when and where these more advanced traits came in. It now begins to appear that early sites of the Mogollon Culture will give us the answer, and that the time may be near the beginning of the Christian Era.[88]

RECAPITULATION

Finally, the more significant aspects of the excavations in the Bluff Ruin may be recapitulated as follows:

1. The aggregate of traits comprising the Hilltop Phase does not conform to the contemporary pattern of Anasazi or Hohokam Cultures, but it does agree, on the whole, with other early horizons of west-central New Mexico and southeastern Arizona which have been regarded as manifestations of a third culture unit, the Mogollon. The founders of the Bluff Site are therefore believed to have been representatives of this group.

2. The Hilltop Phase, in so far as present investigations show, was the oldest in a long series of developmental stages evident in the Forestdale region, dated by tree rings to the late third and fourth centuries A.D.

3. The Bluff Site is a manifestation of the Mogollon Culture in the northern limits of the Mogollon area and in immediate geographic

[86]E. B. Sayles, 1945.
[87]P. S. Martin, 1943, p. 124.
[88]See also E. W. Haury, 1943, for further discussion of this problem.

relationship with the Basketmakers of the Anasazi. The argument that Basketmaker-Mogollon differences were environmentally caused is thereby weakened.

4. The ruin excavated has yielded the earliest dated pottery in the Southwest, and the scarcity of this trait suggests that pottery was new to the culture. While the pottery was simple, it was well made technically, and the inventive stage must yet be sought.

5. The absence of Basketmaker pottery in Hilltop Phase contexts and of tree-ring dates earlier than 400 for Basketmaker pottery points to the possibility that Anasazi ceramics developed after the acquisition of pottery by the Mogollon Culture, probably from a Mexican source.

6. The presence of Hohokam intrusive sherds in the Hilltop Phase at about 300 supports the estimates for the early (the time of Christ or before) beginnings of that culture.

7. The presence of what appears to be a prototype of the great kiva in the Hilltop Phase suggests the desirability of reviewing the history of that architectural form in the Southwest.

8. There are good indications that lithic traits of the Hilltop Phase were derived from the San Pedro Stage of the Cochise Culture.

9. The influence of Anasazi (Basketmaker) on Mogollon, or vice versa, produced the Cottonwood Phase, and with each succeeding phase in the local prehistory, Anasazi cultural elements were in the ascendency.

10. The wide geographic spread of the brown ware complex (Mogollon), in which the Bluff Site is but one focal point, and the early date based on tree rings support the contention that this culture, along with the Hohokam and the Anasazi, entered into the basic composition of the higher Indian populations of the Southwest since the time of Christ.

APPENDIX

ANALYSIS OF SOIL SAMPLES

By T. F. Buehrer

The material submitted was a siliceous sand, the particles of which had a coating of humic organic matter. To determine whether particles of bone, as such, were present in this fine sand and which is presumably the product of weathering of sedimentary parent material over a long period of time, it is necessary to adduce evidence from various sources: (1) microscopic examination; (2) qualitative analysis; and (3) quantitative analysis.

Microscopic examination.—Examination of the material under the microscope revealed the presence of siliceous particles in dominant amounts, organic matter particles, but no particles exhibiting the characteristics of bone. When acid was added to the slide, there was no visible evolution of carbon dioxide, as would be expected from the chemical composition of bone, which is $Ca_3 (PO_4)_{23}$. $CaCO_3$ and $MgCO_3$ commonly associated with desert conditions. There were observed to be present, however, some particles of fluor-apatite, a mineral related to bone in chemical composition, which is usually associated with the minerals in granite and which resists rapid weathering. Hence one might expect to find calcium and phosphate in an acid extract of such a sand, even though bone were altogether absent.

Qualitative analysis.—As observed under the microscope, when acid is added to a sample of the sand in a test tube trial, no effervescence whatever is observed. It seemed of interest, however, to ascertain whether or not calcium and phosphate, as well as other constituents, might be found in the HCl extract of the material. In such an extract we should obtain only the *inorganic* phosphate, for the organic (humic) fraction would not become soluble under these conditions. The results were as follows:

Ca	Considerable		
Fe	High		
CO_3	None	pH	6.32
PO_4	Appreciable		

We must note first of all that since the pH of this sand when moistened with water (CO_2-free) was found to be 6.32, hence on the acid side of neutrality, the sand as it exists at present must have resulted from acidic leaching conditions. Most of the carbonic acid soluble materials have therefore been removed. For that reason it is evident that neither carbonates nor bone would be present. The presence of calcium and of phosphate, both in considerable amounts, must therefore be attributed to the solubility of the native mineral phosphates, notably fluor-apatite, which has been found present in the microscopic examination. The presence of ferric iron in this connection has no

368

significance, it being present universally in various forms in rocks and soils.

Quantitative analysis.—It seemed of interest, further, to determine the essential constituents quantitatively, in order to account for the presence of phosphates in various forms in the material. We may assume for the present that phosphates are (or may be) present in any one of three forms: (a) fluor-apatite; (b) organic matter; and (c) water-soluble form.

The following quantitative results were obtained:

Total organic matter .... 1.83 per cent
Total soluble salts .... 0.205 per cent

Ratio
$Ca:PO_4$

Insoluble inorganic fraction — Ca, 0.648 per cent
PO₄, 0.379 per cent 4:1
Water-soluble inorganic fraction — Ca, None
PO₄, None
Organic matter fraction — Ca, 0.061 per cent
PO₄, 0.291 per cent 1:2

The foregoing findings are very significant. It will be noted from the formula for bone shown above that the ratio of $Ca:PO_4$ in bone should theoretically be $3Ca:2PO_4$. If it is assumed that the calcium and phosphate in the above fractions came from bone originally, we should theoretically obtain the ratio 3:2, provided there had occurred neither a loss nor a gain in either of these constituents.

The water-soluble fraction was found to contain no calcium or phosphate. In the insoluble inorganic fraction the $Ca:PO_4$ ratio was found to be 4:1, whereas in the organic (humic) fraction it was 1:2. Neither of these ratios conforms to that of bone, from which we may conclude that if bone was originally present as such, it has entirely disappeared through ordinary weathering processes, and that the calcium and phosphate now present in the material as obtained by analysis must have come from the calcium and phosphorous-bearing minerals associated with the sand. As shown in the foregoing there were no carbonates in the material; hence we must conclude that the phosphate found in the inorganic fraction must have come largely from fluor-apatite still remaining in the material as the primary mineral. The organic phosphorus is evidently a residuum from the bacterial decomposition of phosphorproteins associatetd with the lignic portion of the humus and fairly resistant to weathering. It has no genetic bearing, however, on the original presence of bone except as a concomitant organic material associated with the original bone.

The above deductions lead to the conclusion that there is no bone in the material examined. Since bone contains on the average 39 per cent Ca and 55.3 per cent PO₄, and since the inorganic fraction showed only 0.379 per cent PO₄, it is evident that at most the material could not contain more than 0.7 per cent of bone even if present.

BIBLIOGRAPHY

Colton, H. S. and L. L. Hargrave.
> 1937   *Handbook of Northern Arizona Pottery Wares.* Museum of Northern Arizona, Bulletin No. 11. Flagstaff, Arizona.

Douglass, A. E.
> 1942   *Checking the Date of Bluff Ruin, Forestdale: A Study in Technique.* Tree-Ring Bulletin, Vol. 9, No. 2, pp. 2-7. Tucson, Arizona.

Gladwin, H. S.
> 1942   *Excavations at Snaketown, III — Revisions.* Medallion Papers, No. XXX, Gila Pueblo. Globe, Arizona.

Gladwin, H. S., E. W. Haury, E. B. Sayles, and N. Gladwin.
> 1937   *Excavations at Snaketown, Material Culture.* Medallion Papers, No. XXV, Gila Pueblo. Globe, Arizona.

Guernsey, S. J.
> 1931   *Explorations in Northeastern Arizona — Report on the Archaeological Field Work of 1920-1923.* Papers of the Peabody Museum of American Archaeology and Ethnology, Harvard University, Vol. XII, No. 1. Cambridge, Massachusetts.

Haury, E. W.
> 1936a   *Some Southwestern Pottery Types, Series IV.* Medallion Papers, No. XIX, Gila Pueblo. Globe, Arizona.
> 1936b   *The Mogollon Culture of Southwestern New Mexico.* Medallion Papers, No. XX, Gila Pueblo. Globe, Arizona.
> 1940   *Excavations in the Forestdale Valley, East-Central Arizona, with an Appendix, The Skeletal Remains of the Bear Ruin,* by Norman E. Gabel. University of Arizona, Social Science Bulletin No. 12, Vol. XI, No. 4. Tucson, Arizona.
> 1942   *Some Implications of the Bluff Ruin Dates.* Tree-Ring Bulletin, Vol. 9, No. 2, pp. 7-8. Tucson, Arizona.
> 1943   *A Possible Cochise-Mogollon-Hohokam Sequence.* Proceedings of the American Philosophical Society, Vol 86, No. 2, pp. 260-63. Philadelphia, Pennsylvania.

Hough, W.
> 1903   *Archaeological Field Work in Northeastern Arizona; the Museum-Gates Expedition of 1901.* Annual Report of the U.S. National Museum for 1901, pp. 279-358. Washington, D.C.

Martin, Paul S.
> 1943   *The SU Site — Excavations at a Mogollon Village, Western New Mexico — Second Season 1941.* Anthropological Series, Field Museum of Natural History, Vol. 32, No. 2, Chicago, Illinois.

Martin, P. S., J. Rinaldo, and M. Kelly.
> 1940   *The SU Site — Excavations at a Mogollon Village, Western New Mexico, 1939, with Reports on Pottery and Artifacts and an Appendix on Skeletal Material.* Anthropological Series, Field Museum of Natural History, Vol. 32, No. 1. Chicago, Illinois.

Mera, H. P.
> 1934   *Observations on the Archaeology of the Petrified Forest National Monument.* Technical Series, Bulletin 7, Archaeological Survey, Laboratory of Anthropology. Santa Fe, New Mexico.

Morris, E. H.
> 1939   *Archaeological Studies in the La Plata District, Southwestern Colorado and Northwestern New Mexico.* Carnegie Institution of Washington Publication No. 519. Washington, D.C.

Roberts, F. H. H., Jr.
    1929   *Shabik'eschee Village — A Late Basketmaker Site in the Chaco Canyon, New Mexico.* Bureau of American Ethnology, Bulletin 92. Washington, D.C.

Sayles, E. B.
    1945   *The San Simon Branch — Excavations at Cave Creek and in the San Simon Valley: I, Material Culture.* Medallion Papers, No. XXXIV, Gila Pueblo. Globe, Arizona.

Sayles, E. B. and E. Antevs.
    1941   *The Cochise Culture.* Medallion Papers, No. XXIX, Gila Pueblo. Globe, Arizona.

PART IV

The
Forestdale Valley
Cultural Sequence

—

THE FORESTDALE VALLEY
CULTURAL SEQUENCE

Before continuing with the synopsis of Forestdale Valley prehistory and history, a few procedural points need to be made. To segment nearly two millennia of time into manageable units so we can discuss them, the concept of the phase is used. In simple terms, this device identifies steps in the spectrum of time that are distinguished from others by one or more cultural attributes unique to them. The distinctiveness of attributes may be due to fresh introductions from the outside, to inventions, or to the normal process of cultural evolution. Groups of attributes present, the absence of traits, and nonmaterial qualities round out the way the behavior and life style of a people may be measured. Once that has been accomplished, then comparisons between phases are possible and the course people are following becomes clearer.

Because of the differences in the intensity of archaeological investigations or the richness or the poverty of cultural manifestations along the time scale, the fullness of the story, phase by phase, will vary. Thus, some phases are weakly defined while others are supported by a rich body of detail. Time controls are equally variable because of a spotty tree-ring record and thin stratigraphic or typological data. The dates and the duration of some phases must be established by extrapolation and by inferences based on other available data. In rounding out the Forestdale story, some reliance has been placed on data drawn from sites lying outside the bounds of the valley. Comparability of cultural remains in ruins within and without the valley allows that to be done logically.

The dates assigned to the phases are predicated foremost on guidelines provided by tree rings. It is clear, however, that tree rings establish only a few points along the calendar that serve as anchorages from which further assessments may be made. The dates from the Bluff and Bear ruins and Tla Kii are cases in point. Such dates themselves do not reflect durational times for phases. Time estimates are also supplemented by tree-ring data from ruins outside the Forestdale Valley.

The following review of Forestdale prehistory does not pretend to enumerate all of the minutiae of variations in cultural attributes but, rather, to present the story in its larger perspective. Detailed data either have been published or are on file in the Arizona State Museum archives.

DATING THE FORESTDALE PHASES

In establishing a cultural chronology on the basis of conventional lines of evidence such as typological change, stratigraphy with its relative temporal values, and tree-ring dating that at best only roughly places most measurable events in our calendrical system, there are problems when one tries to calculate the elapsed time between recognizable changes in architecture and material products in a way that gives beginning and ending dates. Our concept of time seems to be satisfied best when lines are drawn on a chart separating what are conceived as episodic events. Neat and tidy as that is, such a process does not portray what happened, if we perceive cultural progress to be a continuing, subtle, and relatively smooth on-going process. Because we have tree-ring data from the Forestdale Valley over a longer stretch of time than we do for most other places in the Southwest of comparable size, the temptation is greater than usual to devise an orderly, tastefully simple, time plan. But I feel uncomfortable in doing so, even though it has been a customary way for me to present ideas of time.

Instead, in the accompanying cultural time chart (Table 1), lines between phases have been omitted, and the name of the phase is placed where it seems best to express the climaxing of the cultural components that characterize the stage. What seems reasonably certain is that we are dealing with time limits in prehistory that start as early as about A.D. 200 and end as late as about A.D. 1450. The cultural nuances recognized in the succession must then be accommodated within those limits. The phase placement is based on the clustering of tree-ring dates, if available locally or regionally, when comparability of cultural remains is demonstrable. Dates from Dry Valley phase trash-filled pits provide the principal discordant note in the sequence.

The stratigraphic position of Carrizo phase remains, above those of Dry Valley origin and solidly dated at A.D. 1100, leads to an inferred age for Dry Valley phase in the tenth century, even though the tree-ring dates are contradictory. That disparity aside, Table 1 is based on over 650 tree-ring dates, about 75 from the Forestdale Valley proper and the rest from related sites in the region (Bannister, Gell, and Hannah 1966; Bannister

Table 1
PHASE CHRONOLOGY IN THE FORESTDALE VALLEY

Date	Phase	Tree-Ring Dates (Bannister, Gell, and Hannah 1966)	Site
1900	Alchesay	1881 (bark date)	Mormon "temple"
1800			
1700	Skidi	No data	
1600			
1500	Hiatus		
		Over 500 dates, 60% between	Show Low Ruin (AZ P:12:3)
1400	Canyon Creek	A.D. 1335–1384, about 30 provenience units	(see also Red Rock House, Grasshopper Pueblo, Canyon Creek Ruin)
		A.D. 1068–1378,* 78 dates;	
1300	Pinedale	39 dates between 1275–1325; 4 proveniences	Pinedale Ruin (AZ P:12:2)
1200	Linden		
		A.D. 1008–1115,* 52 dates;	
1100	Carrizo	12 structures; 6 other proveniences; 28 dates between 1100–1115	Tla Kii Ruin (AZ P: 16:2)
1000	Dry Valley	Data ambiguous	Tla Kii Ruin (AZ P:16:2)
900	Corduroy	No data	Tla Kii Ruin (AZ P:16:2)
800			
700	Forestdale	A.D. 563–702,* 10 dates; 4 structures	Bear Ruin (AZ P:16:1)
600			
500	Cottonwood	No data	Bluff Site (AZ P:16:20)
400			
300	Hilltop	A.D. 238–322,* 7 dates; 2 structures	Bluff Site (AZ P:16:20)
200			
100			
A.D. 1			

*All vv.

and Robinson 1971). All in all, they present an exceptionally convincing culture history, the tenor of which is consistent with what is known of other parts of the Southwest.

HILLTOP PHASE

No evidence has been found in the Forestdale Valley to suggest that nonsedentary and nonagricultural people ever occupied it. No doubt the big game hunters of ten millennia ago and their successors up to the time of Christ passed through—and even foraged and hunted in the valley—but if so, their traces have not been found. The surveys in the area produced no lithic assemblages without pottery.

Hence, the story of man's use of the valley begins with the earliest verifiable vestiges preserved for us in the Bluff Site

(AZ P:16:20; Part III), a fascinating, though unimpressive, community of pit houses. Architectural wood from these houses produced a set of tree-ring dates clustering near A.D. 300.

The evidences of occupation during this time are confined to the rocky tops of ridges and hills, a residence pattern that has given the name to the phase—Hilltop. It is important to note that the Bluff Site was not the only one in the valley. The Red Hill Site (AZ P:16:58) at the northwestern edge of the valley, and AZ P:16:28 located on a ridge east of the Bluff Site, are further examples, although no work has been done in them and the identification is based on surface indications. Because the extensive surveys in the Grasshopper area have produced no comparable sites, it may well be that Forestdale was near the western edge of the distribution of this early aspect of the Mogollon culture. Southeasterly manifestations, those that were studied by Martin and colleagues in the Reserve area for so many years (Martin and others 1940 *ff.*), and Crooked Ridge Village in the Point of Pines country (Wheat 1954), are believed to be representative of the Mogollon core tradition and, therefore, closely related to the Bluff Site.

The Bluff Site dates have been given much attention by tree-ring analysts, and rightfully so, because of the importance attached to them. They were not only among the earliest dates in the Southwest, but also brought the antiquity of the Mogollon complex into focus. On their correctness, to a large extent, depended the archaeologists' confidence in the concept of the Mogollon culture and the nature of its correlation with other Southwestern groups. The initial publication dealing with Bluff Site dates was by Douglass (Appendix C), followed by some observations inspired by their earliness (Haury, Appendix E). Later Douglass (1944, Appendix D) presented a full tabulation of the dates and critically reviewed the sequences, not an unusual procedure for him but the attention he gave to the Bluff Site dates revealed his recognition of their importance. Further discussion ensued in 1947 (Part III: *Dating the Bluff Site*) and the dates were tabulated again in 1951 by Smiley. As a part of the comprehensive review of all Southwestern dated ruins, the results of the last inspection given the dates were published by Bannister, Gell, and Hannah (1966: 34). Although the findings of that investigation did not wholly confirm the correctness of all previously dated specimens, the "... placement of the site in time has not been substantially altered." The dates from few sites have been so thoroughly scrutinized as these, and unless one totally rejects tree rings as an effective means of dating ruins, the Bluff Site dates may be accepted as correct. This, then, raises a number of fundamental questions that must be addressed.

Although Douglass (Appendix C) noted three other sites, all Basketmaker II (Anasazi), that yielded tree-ring material as early as that from the Bluff Site, the difference was that the Anasazi units represented a cultural horizon without pottery. When the Bluff Site dates were established, they proved to be the oldest ones with pottery in the Mogollon area. Martin and his colleagues (1952: 496) extended the age of Mogollon pottery back to about 150 B.C., not only making the earliness of pottery in the Bluff Site more plausible, but also providing consistency with the position taken by the Hohokam specialists that Hohokam and Mogollon pottery-making had early and not totally dissimilar beginnings.

A noteworthy factor in the Bluff Site was that so little pottery was recovered, a meager 2900 potsherds in two seasons of work (Part III: *Pottery*). Coupled with that was a low number of types, a total absence of painted pottery, and a simple inventory of vessel forms. In short, Bluff Site pottery represents a tradition in its incipient stages, an expected state of affairs if we are indeed dealing with a cultural manifestation in the fringes of its range of distribution and at a time soon after its carriers had acquired pottery.

Of further note, Basketmaker III pottery was totally absent in Hilltop phase contexts, though it was present later in the Cottonwood phase. Intrusive fragments of Hohokam-derived pottery, mostly Gila Plain, were present, further reinforcing the fact that Hohokam ceramics were already well established by that time.

We see then, on the basis of the data at hand, that in the early centuries of the Christian era, between A.D. 200 and 400, a people with sedentary inclinations moved into the Forestdale Valley, searching out high places for residences. The valley floor seems to have been avoided. The motivation for this choice may have been the greater ease of self-defense offered by promontories, but possibly also the newcomers saw this as a way of finding the warmer spots in the valley and thereby escaping the down-valley drainage of cold air. These people, by architecture, ceramics, and general life style were allied with those whose areal range extended far to the east and south and who left behind them the remains that we know as the Mogollon culture.

Domestic structures were pit houses, in the generic sense, and were generally circular and side entered. Of special interest in the Bluff Site was the fact that bedrock was on the surface, and that if the houses were to be built in the customary fashion, excavation into bedrock was necessary. That this was done not only reflects a tenacious obedience to tradition, but it also speaks of the energy of the people. Houses were generally devoid of internal features such as formal hearths, bins, floor partitions, deflectors, benches, and antechambers. The architectural mode is consistent with, but somewhat simpler than, that of the early pit houses in the Reserve and Point of Pines regions.

Of special note was the presence within the village confines of a large circular structure, 10.3 m in diameter and also excavated into bedrock, believed to be the prototype of later Great Kivas (Part III: *Houses, House 5*). Five tree-ring dates, derived from architectural wood associated with the structure, ranged from A.D. 238 to 322 (Bannister, Gell, and Hannah 1966: 34), though none of them were bark dates. This feature may well be the oldest structure of its kind yet discovered in the Southwest. The presence of this building, unique because of its size, in what otherwise appears to be a relatively simple and rustic community, tells us that the society may have been more complex than we supposed it to have been. A coercive religious system, strong enough to demand the erection of a major structure overcoming natural obstacles, suggests possible equivalent advances in other respects of the society that are not reflected by the material remains.

The food base was corn agriculture, with hunting and gathering as important supplements. The presence of corn is inferred from the metate form, since direct evidence of the grain was not found. Because corn was known elsewhere in the Southwest by this time, the credibility of the inference is increased.

Luxury items such as ornaments appear to have been absent. Smoking, as evidenced by a stone pipe, was practiced (Kaemlein 1958). Semiflexed earth burials without grave offerings were the norm.

The founders of the Bluff village, with roots deeply embedded in the Mogollon culture, provided the basal complex from which the later stages directly developed.

COTTONWOOD PHASE

The Cottonwood phase was minimally described in 1947 by Haury and Sayles (Part III: *Summary and Conclusions, Cotton-*

wood Phase), and in the intervening years no new information has been brought to bear on the further understanding of it.

In addition to the rock-hewn pit houses of the Hilltop phase, the Bluff village also included three slab-lined houses (Houses 11, 14, and 19 in Part III), an architectural form attributed to the Basketmaker tradition. In association with these houses were Basketmaker metates, Lino Gray sherds (a Basketmaker pottery type), and an increase in ceramic yield from the house fills, indicating these structures were not only different but also later. Because these traits did not fit the pattern of elements outlined for the Hilltop phase, a new phase, the Cottonwood, was established. Admittedly, this phase does not have the substance most of the others do, but the step is supportable on two counts: it recognizes for the first time the presence of Anasazi characteristics, marking the beginning of an amalgamation that is to increase in intensity with time; and it adds a stage in the development system that helps to bridge a time gap between the Hilltop and the Forestdale phases.

The information available does not allow a full resolution of either the exact time or the span of time ascribable to the Cottonwood phase, for there are no tree-ring dates. The phenomena noted most likely fit somewhere in the period from A.D. 400 to 600. Slab architecture among the Basketmakers had a long history, which means that its presence in the Bluff Site was not time-specific. The appearance of Lino Gray pottery does have significance, however, if A.D. 450 is accepted as about the time when pottery first appeared among the Anasazi. The construction of House 11 in Hilltop phase trash is a further indication of lateness.

It is not likely that the Bluff Site was occupied for 400 years, or even 600 years, if one takes at face value the chronology that has been developed. Yet, the tree-ring dates for the Hilltop and Forestdale phases, clustering about A.D. 300 in the former and spreading through the seventh century in the latter, require a closing of the gap if the continuity of occupancy in the valley is a valid concept. Although this idea may be debated, I prefer it to one that might contend that occupancy of the valley was discontinuous and that what we see are the remains of periodic living by unrelated or even by the same peoples. The spotty record of occupation is most likely due to the incomplete nature of our excavations.

The significance of the Cottonwood phase, thin as the evidence is, centers on several points that merit emphasis. As already noted, it represents the time when the Anasazi-Mogollon merger was beginning, at least in the Forestdale Valley. That phenomenon was to strengthen with the passage of time and result in a cultural blend that is considered in the Epilogue. Further, and of equal importance, is the fact that the information peculiar to the Cottonwood phase permitted the correlation of the Anasazi and Mogollon sequences for the first time, a fundamental step if interregional problems are to be examined and understood.

FORESTDALE PHASE

The Bear Ruin (AZ P:16:1) was first seen during Gila Pueblo's survey of the Mogollon Rim country in 1931. Its uniqueness and possible earliness were recognized at that time, but excavations were delayed until 1939. That work (Part II) led to the delineation of the Forestdale phase, the earliest one to be outlined in the sequence for the valley at the time. The main characteristics of the horizon are reprinted here in Part II: *General Discussion and Conclusions.*

It must be noted that the nearness of the Bear Ruin to the region dominated by sites attributable to the Basketmakers, yet with contrasts in the artifactual materials, heightened the interest in it as a possible further contributor to the then-developing concept of the Mogollon people. The results were not disappointing in that respect. Furthermore, having developed a grasp of one moment in the local sequence, established by tree rings, we were in a good position to move up or down the time scale in expanding the culture history of the area.

On the basis of tree-ring dates, reviewed successively by a number of people (Part II; Appendix B; Douglass 1941; Smiley 1951; Bannister, Gell, and Hannah 1966: 29–30), we conclude that construction of several buildings in the Bear Ruin took place in the seventh century A.D. Consistent loss of outside rings denies the assignment of exact dates to any of the structures. There are indications that the earliest construction took place close to A.D. 600 and that the occupation extended into the eighth century.

As an aside, it is worth reflecting on the importance of the time factor as an essential key in demonstrating the uniqueness and individuality of a cultural manifestation. With firm dates, distant and different complexes can be brought into synchrony. Not until that has been achieved is it possible to measure the extent of shared characteristics or the degree of variability as indicators of the closeness of relationship. Specifically, the tree-ring dates from the Bear Ruin permitted equating the Forestdale phase with the White Mound phase of the Anasazi, 160 km (about 100 miles) to the northeast on the Puerco River, a site of the Anasazi tradition (Gladwin 1945: 11 *ff.*). At the same time, those dates demonstrated that the Forestdale phase was slightly antecedent to the San Francisco and Kiatuthlanna phases. The net effect of these observations was to make possible the beginning of an Anasazi-Mogollon phase correlation.

The dominant pottery of the Forestdale phase is typologically linked with the Mogollon pottery tradition extending far to the east and south. The painting of pottery locally was unknown at this time, although some foreign painted pottery was acquired. The Bear Ruin people produced a limited amount of Forestdale Plain (Part II: *Pottery, Forestdale Plain*), a hybrid of Lino Gray and Alma Plain, suggesting the fusion of two ceramic traditions, a phenomenon that was to extend to other aspects of culture as well. Forestdale's proximity to the Basketmaker domain may have been partly responsible for that, but it has been tempting also to see the Mogollon people as receptors and therefore more responsive to a growing Anasazi vitality.

The sixth and seventh centuries also saw continuation of contacts between the Mogollon and the Hohokam that started as early as the Hilltop phase. These relationships are demonstrated largely through the exchange of ceramics. Bear Ruin, for the first time, provided some inkling of how the Mogollon and Hohokam sequences related (Part II, Fig. 32). It is gratifying to note that the suggested correlations have been supported by more recent findings (Wheat 1954: 91–92; Neeley 1974). Information drawn from the Forestdale phase context helped materially in bringing Anasazi-Mogollon into chronological adjustment, and now by adding the Hohokam, a three-way correlation has become possible (see also Haury 1976: 329–330).

In sum, the definition of the Forestdale phase may be recognized as a meaningful step ahead in the history of the then unfolding concept of the Mogollon as contemporary with, but different from, the Anasazi and Hohokam complexes.

CORDUROY PHASE

One of the unexpected dividends of our work in a small pueblo, Tla Kii Ruin (AZ P:16:2), a few hundred meters down valley from the Bear Ruin, was the discovery of several pit houses, reviewed in detail in Part I. The contents of those houses and the related cultural vestiges provided a much-needed chronological and typological link between the well-established pit house architectural tradition of earlier phases and the move toward the construction of contiguous stone houses on the surface of the ground. That link was equally well demonstrated by the ceramic tradition.

The phase takes its name form Corduroy Creek, which has carved the valley immediately south of Forestdale, a somewhat more rugged terrain including volcanic formations that render it less inviting than the valley of Foresdale Creek. Forestdale Creek empties into Corduroy Creek, whence it continues its way to join Carrizo Creek.

The lack of tree-ring dates from the pit houses of this phase forces the use of other criteria in determining its age. The dates of the Forestdale phase in the A.D. 700s, and those of the Carrizo phase at about 1100, leave a block of time of some 400 years without clear evidence of the cultural thread. Typological considerations strongly suggest that the pit houses associated with Tla Kii Ruin, and particularly the houses of the succeeding Dry Valley phase, are architectural forms intermediate to the Forestdale-Carrizo sequence. Ceramic typology also required placement of the Corduroy complex in the same temporal position. The similarity of Corduroy pottery to types elsewhere that have been dated was also an aid in reaching that decision. The best judgment at the moment is that the Corduroy phase remains in Tla Kii Ruin may be assigned to some interval in the ninth century. The shortened duration of the phase over earlier ones may be viewed as an indication of the speeding up of the process of cultural evolution, as was suggested in 1947 (Part III: *Summary and Conclusions, Length of Phases*).

Although living in pit houses in the Corduroy phase was still the vogue, we found too few of them (only three) to determine whether or not significant architectural changes had taken place between them and the pit houses of the earlier Forestdale phase. The use of stone partially encircling one house was a feature not seen previously. A Great Kiva attributable to this phase was not found. The presence of that feature somewhere in the valley may be postulated, for prototypes in the two earlier phases are known, as are examples in later times.

A dramatic change in the pottery tradition distinguishes the Corduroy phase from others. To this time the potters were content to make plain brown, gray, and red pottery, all fired in an oxidizing atmosphere. Pottery with intentionally smudged interiors, a technique used locally at least as early as the Forestdale phase, required a reducing atmosphere, a not-too-difficult feat because smudging was confined to bowl interiors and simple inversion of the vessel was all that was needed. The key innovation was the production of painted pottery in the black-on-white idiom of northern neighbors. Black-on-white pottery not only required the adoption of a different clay, the sedimentary clays of the Plateau in contrast to the residual and alluvial clays of traditional use for brown and red pottery, but also the application of a white slip, the use of black paint, and a more careful control of the fire to achieve a predominantly reducing atmosphere. In other words, acceptance of new ceramic habits also required getting used to a set of new materials in achieving the end product. The results, in fact, reflect the ineptness of the potters. Apart from often poorly bonded slips, a certain clumsiness in applying designs and excessive heat in the firing process produced an inordinately high percentage of defective pieces, including the blistering of surfaces and extreme warping of the vessels (Part I, Fig. 52*h*). The adoption by Mogollon people of Anasazi ceramic technology started the trend that was to expand geographically to the south and east, eventually to become superbly crystallized in the pottery of the Mimbrenos.

The black-on-white pottery produced by Corduroy phase people reflects stylistic elements drawn from such established Anasazi types as Red Mesa, Kiatuthlanna, and Kana-a Black-on-white. In broad terms, Corduroy Black-on-white equates with Pueblo I, but it also incorporates elements and treatments leading into Pueblo II. From this base, the tradition of black-painted white pottery continued for at least 300 years and, in general, compared favorably in kind and style of decoration with the ceramics produced north of the White Mountains.

DRY VALLEY PHASE

Dry Valley is a short, inconspicuous tributary joining Corduroy Creek from the north about 5 km east of Forestdale. The name was applied to a single architectural feature, several burials, and cultural residue in Tla Kii Ruin that, on stratigraphic and typologic grounds, were recognized as being intermediate in age between the Corduroy and Carrizo phases. Although the bulk of the material unique to this phase is small, it nevertheless forges another link in the succession of horizons in the local sequence.

The ambiguity in tree-ring data, as noted before, forces the use of speculative dates. While in all probability the materials recovered are close to A.D. 1000 in age, a tenth century time assignment has been given the Dry Valley phase.

The pottery, as discussed in Part I, typologically connects Corduroy and later black-on-white types. What may be termed the Anasazi "mode" has now become fixed, but the earlier mistakes in pottery production have not been entirely overcome. Some elaboration in the ceramic complex has taken place, as, for example, the addition of new decorative styles drawn from neighbors to the north and east, and the first examples of all-over corrugated pottery, along with the retention of neck corrugation.

Unit Structure 2 (Part I, Figs. 12, 13) was the only architectural feature related to the Dry Valley phase. While a single room cannot be accepted as indicative of the house-building mode of the phase, it does provide an interesting and possibly illuminating example of the transition from subsurface pit house living to surface stone construction. A shallow pit of square rather than round form, the edges circled with building blocks to increase the wall height, embodies about all the steps one could prescribe as essential in making the change from subsurface to surface living. It may not be as simple as that, however, for it would be a great stroke of luck to find the only structure exemplifying the transition. The fact remains that before the Dry Valley phase, pit house living was the norm, and after it, stone surface pueblos were the accepted residential style. In all probability, several small two- to four-room pueblos noted in the survey (for example AZ P:16:57) may be placed in this phase also. I see this architectural transition as a further step in the "Anasazization" of the Mogollon people, with the change in ceramics beginning somewhat earlier.

The amount of Dry Valley refuse, often mixed with that of the Corduroy phase, hints of a somewhat larger occupation of the period than we were able to identify. The removal of building stones from Unit Structure 2 suggests that the same fate befell other contemporary units during the building of the Carrizo phase pueblo and that our excavations failed to produce the foundations of them. Hints of older materials under the pueblo along with Unit Structure 1 may be all that remained of the Dry Valley community.

CARRIZO PHASE

The name is taken from Carrizo Creek, one of the main north-south drainages below the Mogollon Rim and one to which Corduroy and Forestdale Creeks are tributary. The time represented is that moment in the cultural chain of events when the multiroomed, sometimes multistoried, pueblo buildings were expanding in number, size, and range through the Mountain zone.

The type ruin that has provided the principal information for the phase components is the Tla Kii Ruin (AZ P:16:2). It has erroneously been called the Forestdale Ruin (Bannister, Gell, and Hannah 1966: 31), a name that since Hough's time has been used as a synonym for Tundastusa or as a general term, "Forestdale Ruins," in reference to the several large ruins of the valley. Compared with them, Tla Kii was a small community.

This pueblo of 21 rooms, with a detached small kiva and a more distant Great Kiva, has yielded a much richer array of tree-ring dates than we have had for other phases. Suffice it to say that 46 of the 52 dated charcoal specimens from 20 proveniences establish a period of time from A.D. 1080 to 1115, with a clustering of terminal dates in the early twelfth century reflecting the years when the pueblo was built (Bannister, Gell, and Hannah 1966: 31–33). The six earlier dates, none representing the time of tree-cutting, range from A.D. 1008 to 1070 and may possibly derive from Dry Valley phase activities. In round numbers, the eleventh century is assigned the phase but, admittedly, Tla Kii spanned the end of that century and extended at least into the second decade of the twelfth century.

The sequence of room block additions (Part I, Fig. 15) suggests episodic construction, though in relatively quick succession, and the marked differences in masonry (Part I, Figs. 16*b* and 17) may mean the addition to the community of Anasazi social units. The architectural style by now has become what may be called "pure" Anasazi, completely replacing the Mogollon pit house tradition. The small unfinished (or razed) kiva relates to the Anasazi tradition, too, although for the Great Kiva there are prototypes in the Hilltop and Forestdale phases indicating the feature may have had early Mogollon roots. If one makes the assumption that the Great Kiva was initially a Mogollon feature, but one adopted early by the Anasazi who quickly elaborated it (namely, Chaco and Aztec examples), then the rooms on the southern margin of the Tla Kii Great Kiva may reflect an Anasazi treatment not inconsistent with what happened in the domain of domestic architecture. Especially noteworthy is the detached location of the Great Kiva, as though the sacred space circumscribed by it was not to be profaned by the secular building, a relationship that was soon to change.

Except for the utility vessels, the pottery of the Carrizo phase is dominantly Anasazi. The black-on-whites are decorated in styles that have a wide distribution on the Plateau. Puerco and Wingate black-on-reds have made their appearance as imports, but the polychromes of the White Mountain series are yet to evolve. The early form of McDonald Corrugated, painted but lacking indented patterns, had been developed, and represented the first step in a series of later variations on the theme of modifying corrugated pottery.

The Carrizo phase appears to be the time when the local population began to increase and when village units grew in size, as seen in later phases. Intensifications of Anasazi elements in Tla Kii may signal the fact that in-migration was taking place as at least one, and possibly the major, cause for population growth.

LINDEN PHASE

To continue the Forestdale phase sequence, we must depend on the work of others in sites of the region or on our own observations of the later ruins in the valley. Although we did limited testing in AZ P:16:9, a Linden phase site, the investigation of the late phases was not a part of the original study plan, although in retrospect it would have been desirable to do so.

The Linden phase, roughly assigned to the twelfth and probably early thirteenth centuries, without benefit of tree-ring dates, takes its name from an early-day hamlet a little over 6 km (3.7 miles) east of Pinedale. Near Linden stands a large ruin known as Pottery Hill. It was studied by Hough (1903: 297–301); from it he recovered pottery types matching those of AZ P:16:9 in the Forestdale Valley. We therefore selected AZ P:16:9 as the local type site for the Linden phase. It is located about 1.6 km (1 mile) west of Tla Kii on gently rolling terrain along the north edge of the valley floor. It was here that the Mormon settlement of Forest Dale of the late 1870s centered, and near the southern margin of AZ P:16:9 the log church-school building was erected and stood until about the mid-1900s.

Arizona P:16:9 is a compact cluster of rooms, possibly as many as 75 in number. Though surface indications cannot always be correctly read, the existence of two stories is suspected. Tight spacing, an increase in community size, and probably multiple stories represent the new features that distinguish Linden phase architecture from earlier times. Another significant change is the incorporation of a Great Kiva within the room block on the south and west sides (Appendix A). Previously the Great Kivas were detached and independent from the secular rooms. We know nothing of the small kivas or even if they existed. Refuse is scattered widely and has a depth of over 1 m at a distance of 25 m east of the room cluster. In 1944 we made several tests in the trash to verify the ceramic complex seen on the surface. The range of pottery types recovered— Alma Plain (Forestdale variety), Corduroy Black-on-white, and others—indicated that the village had considerable time depth, going back at least to the Corduroy phase. Our present concern, however, is only with the latest pottery, the most readily recognized diagnostic of the Linden phase.

Black-on-white pottery dominates in the painted category but, as with most of the valley's black-on-whites, type assignment is difficult. Stylistically, a combination of Puerco and Tularosa is the best characterization of it (Fig. 1*a*, *b*, *d–j*). The Black Mesa style evidently had little or no effect on potters. Poorly executed brushwork and occasionally a hint of glaze paint are notable. The Snowflake style (Fig. 1*c*), so prominent in the Carrizo phase, has almost vanished. In sherd form it is difficult to distinguish some Linden phase black-on-white pottery from that of the Carrizo phase, but there is a greater prevalence of Tularosa-style related material that forecasts Pinedale style Black-on-white. The significant ceramic attributes not seen before are St. Johns Polychrome (Fig. 1*k*, *l*); Wingate Polychrome (Carlson 1970: 17–19), syn. Houck Polychrome (Colton and Hargrave 1937: 122–123); and Springerville Polychrome (Fig. 1*m*; Danson 1957: 93), the last being the latest in the series and suggesting that AZ P:16:9 may have extended well into the 1200s.

McDonald Corrugated of the Carrizo phase is present with painting over corrugation but without indented patterns. Also present is the derived form, exhibiting paint-filled indented patterns, which makes its appearance for the first time.

A small corrugated vessel found with a burial exhibits four mechanically produced rim notches arranged as though indicating the cardinal points of the compass, a form of ceremonial "killing" relatively common at Point of Pines in ruins of comparable age.

In sum, architecture and pottery are the principal criteria that allow us to see the Linden phase as a connecting link between the Carrizo phase and the next step up in time, the Pinedale phase.

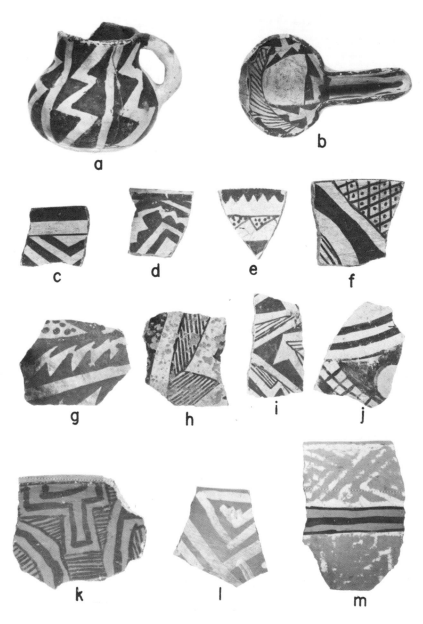

Figure 1. Linden phase black-on-white pottery from Arizona P:16:9: *a, b, d–j,*
Puerco-Tularosa styles; *c,* Snowflake style; *k, l,* St. Johns Polychrome; *m,*
Springerville Polychrome. Height of *a* is 7.7 cm.

PINEDALE PHASE

Although Hough's (1903, Pl. 10) work in Tundastusa produced ceramics that I regard as indicators of the Pinedale phase, the best information about it comes from other sites. The phase takes its name from the Pinedale Ruin located about 1 km east of the settlement of Pinedale. Pinedale Ruin, first visited in 1897 by Fewkes (1904: 164–167), encompassed possibly as many as 200 rooms. During 1977 and 1978 it was totally destroyed by bulldozers during the recovery of pottery and other goods that fed the thriving primitive art market. The destruction of Pinedale Ruin represents a tragic and irretrievable loss to southwestern prehistory, because it had great potential in shedding light on the thirteenth century Indian occupation close to the Mogollon Rim. The ruin was examined briefly in 1929 by members of the Third National Geographic Society Beam expedition while searching for timbers that would unite the two segments of the tree-ring chronology as then known (Haury and Hargrave 1931: 44 *ff.*). Although the four architectural units sampled, three rooms and a kiva, yielded construction dates from about A.D. 1275 to 1325 (Bannister, Gell, and Hannah 1966: 36–37), certain pottery types present suggest somewhat earlier beginnings. For our purposes, a time range of about A.D. 1200 to 1300 has been assigned to the Pinedale phase. The recently excavated Chodistaas Site at Grasshopper, a regional correlate of the Pinedale Ruin, dates from about 1270 to 1300 (Crown 1981).

We do not know the nature of Tundastusa, its exact size, or room arrangement during the Pinedale phase. For that reason, the Pinedale Ruin best exemplifies the architectural form of the time. It was larger than AZ P:16:9 twofold, a possible 150 rooms, multistoried, the room blocks clearly arranged around a well-defined plaza, which, until demonstrated otherwise, was a new feature in the stream of architectural development in the region. It must be noted, however, that all sites of the Pinedale phase were not large, for the Chodistaas Site was only a 20-room structure that still incorporated a plaza. Great Kivas related to this time have not been recognized, but judging from their presence and location in later phases, they could be found only by completely excavating plazas of which they were a part. It appears that with increasing secularization of the Great Kiva, it eventually degenerated into a plaza. Small rectangular kivas for the phase have been reported (Haury and Hargrave 1931: 47–52).

The pottery of the Pinedale phase includes several distinctive types. The first, Pinedale Black-on-white, usually exhibits a decorative treatment derived from the Tularosa style of painting. Precise brushwork and a mineral paint, often with glaze qualities, are distinctive characteristics. While bowls tend to be small (seldom more than 20 cm in diameter), the jars may be large and, from the aesthetic point of view, are some of the handsomest ever produced in the Southwest. Pinedale Black-on-white was the last type regionally in the long tradition of reduction-fired, black-painted pottery made of kaolinitic clay. Pinedale Black-on-red and Pinedale Polychrome were derived from St. Johns and Springerville polychromes. They are also useful diagnostics for the phase. Associated, though less common types, are Pinto Polychrome and Pinto Black-on-red, representing the beginning of the Salado pottery series that became dominant in central Arizona. Stylistic similarity to the indigenous wares bespeaks a close relationship.

The utility pottery is notably crude; the refined and well-executed corrugated forms of earlier phases have degenerated materially. McDonald Corrugated was no longer being made, and smudging of bowl interiors was losing favor as a technique in pottery production.

The size of Pinedale Ruin, as well as others that were contemporary but continued on into the Canyon Creek phase (such as Tundastusa, Kinishba, and Grasshopper), reflects a growing population. While we cannot express quantitatively the rate of growth or be certain as to the cause, normal increase stimulated by favorable environmental and genetic factors seems more probable than extensive in-migration. The phenomenon of growth, in fact, was not limited to the Forestdale Valley, for the ruins of the Hopi area, Zuni, Point of Pines, and the southern desert manifest the same condition.

CANYON CREEK PHASE

The pueblo (Anasazi) occupation of the Forestdale Valley was brought to a close about A.D. 1400 to 1450. The final and culminating century or more in valley prehistory is known as the Canyon Creek phase, named for the Canyon Creek Ruin (Haury 1934), located about 55 km (35 miles) to the west. Canyon Creek Ruin is a convincingly dated cliff house of about 60 rooms. Thirty-one tree-ring dates from 18 rooms determine the time of construction to have been from A.D. 1327 to 1348 (Bannister and Robinson 1971: 12–13). Other ruins of the same

phase are Red Rock House, a nearby cliff ruin with dates from
A.D. 1345 to 1362 (Bannister, Gell, and Hannah 1966: 44–50),
and the solidly dated Showlow Ruin with over 500 dates, 60 percent of which "cluster between A.D. 1335 and 1384" (Bannister,
Gell, and Hannah 1966: 47). These data, plus information from
other sites that need not be recounted here, establish the Canyon
Creek phase as the best dated in the sequence. A time of A.D.
1300 to 1400 is assigned with the recognition that the ending
date may need to be stretched into the mid-fifteenth century. In
the Forestdale Valley, Tundastusa is the type site for the phase
and the only ruin that manifests this late occupation.

The architecture of Canyon Creek phase ruins brings us to
what may be called the apogee of the pueblo mode, the climax
in both size and complexity in the many-century-long evolution
of Forestdale Valley house building. The only map we have of
Tundastusa is Hough's (1903, Pl. 3), a curious layout displaying
a large circular area that he called an acropolis with circum-
ambient rooms, beyond which lay concentric and radial stone
alignments extending down the hill from its highest point.
Several large room blocks with a plaza extend to the west.
Efforts to verify the detail of this plan in later years were not
wholly successful, but enough remains to indicate Tundastusa
did indeed have an unusual plan and represented a community
of more than 200 rooms. The strangeness of the layout may
have been dictated by the topography on which it was built, an
uneven area sloping gently to the south and abruptly to the
east. The Showlow Ruin (Hough 1903, Pl. 21; Haury and Hargrave 1931, Fig. 2) is more representative. While in gross
outline Hough's and my plans are similar, his accommodates
far fewer rooms. On the basis of limited excavations that
clearly demonstrated room size and orientation, I calculate a
community of over 200 rooms, approximating Tundastusa's
size. Of importance is the presence of two plazas, creating a
building roughly E-shaped in plan. Hough's map shows the
north plaza was divided by a construction that strongly suggests
the north part of it may have been a rectangular Great Kiva, a
feature present at Grasshopper, Kinishba, and in the Point of
Pines Ruin. These instances demonstrate that the Great Kiva
had not only been transformed from its early round shape to a
rectangular one, but that it also had been incorporated within
room blocks and was becoming more plazalike and, possibly in
the process, more secular in its function.

Returning to the community size factor, the main ruins at
both Grasshopper and Point of Pines, relatable by cultural

components to the Canyon Creek phase, are indeed large, and best underscore the idea that the maximum population was reached at this time. The Grasshopper Ruin encompassed at least 500 ground-floor rooms and much of the pueblo was multiple-storied, while the Point of Pines Ruin had 800 ground-floor rooms and much of it, too, was at least two-storied. Other sites like Kinishba, a large ruin at Cedar Creek, and still others west of the White Mountains bear testimony that largeness and room blocks arranged around plazas were the architectural modes for the phase.

Whether or not Great Kivas were always present in Canyon Creek phase sites is not known. Topography precluded incorporating them in cliff houses and some of the smaller sites appear to be without them. Only diligent excavation proves their presence in the larger ones, because they can easily be mistaken for plazas. Those that are known at Grasshopper, Point of Pines, and Kinishba all have southeast entries and a variety of internal features. They stand out as unique elements in Southwestern pueblo architecture. Small kivas are uncommon. The Canyon Creek Ruin (Haury 1934: 52–54) and Red Rock House (Bannister, Gell, and Hannah 1966: 50) both have second-story rooms that may have served as kivas. The most convincing evidence for small kivas comes from Point of Pines (Smiley 1952), where they are rectangular, equipped with formalized features, and detached from room blocks.

The pottery of this time period is its most distinguishing hallmark. Fourmile Polychrome is not only one of the most exuberant and vibrant kinds of pottery ever produced in the Southwest, but it is also one of the most easily identified, the one which provokes the fewest differences of opinion when examined by several specialists. Distinctive pottery types associated with Fourmile Polychrome are Kinishba, Showlow, and Cibecue polychromes. The uniformity of Fourmile Polychrome makes one wonder whether or not it was produced in a few places and distributed to many (Whittlesey 1974). As at Grasshopper and the Point of Pines villages, Fourmile Polychrome was undoubtedly an import in Tundastusa, though the potters there were closer to the kind of clay needed to produce it. A lively trading system that distributed Fourmile Polychrome so widely may have provided the potters who made it with the stimulus to create the bizarre and striking pieces that so readily identify it. The notable departure from the formal and staid art canons of earlier potters is seen in the high incidence of a black copper-lead glaze paint in sweeping noninterlocking and unbalanced spirals, in the avoidance of bilateral symmetry in patterns, and in a trend toward the depiction of life forms, including kachina figures. It was a heady time for the potters, brought to an end, however, as the Canyon Creek phase, for unexplained reasons, drew to a close. Only a collateral pottery tradition, that of the Zuni area, survived into historic times.

In reflecting on the continuity of life in the valley of Forestdale Creek, Hough (1903: 290) long ago found the failure of the pueblo dwellers to persist to our day a course of wonderment. Their withdrawal was the single most disruptive event affecting the long human tenure of the region.

What force or combination of forces brought the large communities of the Canyon Creek phase to their knees and ultimately to extinction remains one of the fascinating problems in southwestern archaeology. The phenomenon would be an inviting one to attempt to solve if it applied only to the Forestdale Valley. But it goes far beyond, because almost as though synchronized by some widely pervasive power, the same fate befell the "urban" communities in the vast areas north, west, and south of the White Mountains, in central Arizona, and in the valleys of the Gila River and its principal tributaries in the desert zone. Addressing that larger problem lies beyond the bounds of a consideration of the Forestdale Valley. It is enough to report that the end of Forestdale's prehistoric pueblo occupation was linked firmly with events that took place elsewhere.

Where Tundastusa's people went, perhaps as many as 500, an equal number or more from the Showlow Ruin, and those of many other pueblos in the White Mountain area of the same age, is problematical. The general complexion of the Canyon Creek phase cultural complex is similar to that of the protohistoric Zuni. By a process of elimination one can say that the country east, south, west, and immediately north of the Forestdale Valley was empty of pueblo-building people after A.D. 1450. Excepting the Rio Grande Valley, only the Zuni region to the northeast of Forestdale and the Hopi area some distance to the north demonstrate a continuity of the historic present to the prehistoric past. The number of large late prehistoric and early historic ruins near Zuni (for example, Hawikuh), hints of an abnormal growth at about the time the White Mountain region was depopulated. It is tempting, therefore, to see the Forestdale people settling in with their probable kinsmen at Zuni when conditions for survival became intolerable in their old home territory.

In reviewing the destiny of a people, one is inclined to believe that the abandonment of all large ruins, sharing similar cultural remains reflective of ethnic identity, came at the same time, at least within a matter of months or a few years of each other. However, in all likelihood, the phenomenon of vacating large villages and giving up territory was not that rapid. While our dating controls do not really permit us to develop a convincing time table of withdrawal, pueblo by pueblo, there are hints that some villages lasted longer than others. The Pinedale community died before the Showlow village; Tundastusa may have died between those two. The point is that rather than to consider the end of the Canyon Creek phase as a catastrophic event, the evacuation of the domain controlled by these people may have extended over some time, an action calling for viewing the termination of the Canyon Creek phase in alternative ways. Notwithstanding this possibility of slow abandonment, we can accept categorically the fact that large-scale, settled pueblo community living came to an end in the Forestdale Valley and in neighboring valleys some time in the late fourteeth century or early fifteenth century.

SKIDI PHASE

Following the withdrawal of the pueblo-building Indians from the Forestdale Valley, the record of human use of the area grows dim. In all probability, the next people to see this miniature paradise were the Apache, but we have, as yet, no definitive evidence to indicate when they appeared. Apache reoccupation of some of the pueblos can be demonstrated by the wickiup circles and rearrangements of stone on the collapsed buildings. The nature of these constructions clearly tells us that the pueblos were in a ruined state when the Apaches settled on top of them. Hough (1903: 291) observed wickiup circles on Tundastusa and evidence of Apache presence was found on the Bluff Site (Part III: *Apache Use of the Bluff*). In other areas, several roughly laid stone structures occur on AZ P:16:5 and a rock cairn stands on AZ P:16:9, both sites in the Carrizo Valley. An impressive array of 14 house circles was noted on the Willow Creek Site (AZ W:10:105) in the Point of Pines area. The stone house rings are nestled in the hollows formed by the collapse of pueblo rooms (Asch 1960). Apache material remains have also been recovered in caves of the Nantack Ridge (Gifford 1980). The stratigraphic positions of all of these manifestations place the arrival time of the Apache after the pueblo collapse, and the fact that the pueblos were in advanced states of ruin hints of a substantial hiatus between the two occupations. If one believes that the Puebloans vacated the area by A.D. 1450, and allowing 100 to 200 years for the collapse of their houses, a 1600 or 1700 date for Apache arrival might be reasonable. While I lean toward the idea that the Apache were not a factor in Puebloan withdrawal, information passed on to me by Grenville Goodwin lingers in the mind and raises another possibility.

He once asked me, "Where in the White Mountain area does one find the most recently inhabited pueblos?" My reply included mention of Tundastusa, Grasshopper, Kinishba, and other large communities on Cedar, Carrizo, and Cibecue creeks. He then commented that the existing Apaches in the western part of the Fort Apache Reservation, where most of the mentioned ruins are to be found, demonstrate the strongest parallels with Puebloans in social attributes. He specifically referred to such items as clan names and ritual practices that he speculated had been borrowed by the Apaches from the Puebloans. In his landmark book on the Western Apache he does not pursue the problem, though it remains in my mind as a tantalizing possibility.

While we must leave the beginning date for the Skidi phase open, the first extensive contacts of the Apache with Europeans can be more easily established, at least in round numbers. By 1850, contact with military and other forces had been established and the native way of life was about to change. The mid-nineteenth century, therefore, ushers in the Alchesay phase, which will be discussed shortly.

The word *Skidi*, as here applied to the initial and pre-White Apache occupation of the Forestdale Valley, is taken from an Indian by that name, ". . . a prominent Apache, who has his cornfields near the mouth of the washes where there are springs" (Hough 1903: 290). These fields were near the impressive site of Tundastusa, standing on land claimed by Skidi. Unfortunately, the name Skidi has been corrupted to Skiddy, probably by map-makers, for the USGS maps show a Skiddy Ridge and Skiddy Canyon from which the term has crept into the archaeological literature (for example, Skiddy Canyon Ruin; Hammack 1969).

ALCHESAY PHASE

The mid-nineteenth century has been selected as the beginning time of the last episode in Forestdale Valley history. Although

Apache-White contacts then were far from serene, 1857 was "the first remembered unwarlike relation with the Americans . . ." by the Cibecue group (Goodwin 1942: 22), that part of the widely dispersed Apache tribe geographically the closest to the Forestdale Valley. The troubles, however, were not over.

The White Mountain Reservation was established by Executive Order on November 9, 1871, and by Act of Congress in 1897 that part of the Apache domain north of the Salt or Black River was designated the Fort Apache Reservation (Kelly 1953: 23). Uncertainties as to whether or not the Forestdale Valley was included in the Reservation was the basis for turbulent times with Mormon colonizers, as we shall see in a moment.

When the Apaches first began to plant cornfields in the Forestdale Valley is not easily established. Goodwin (1942: 18–19) reports that from 1845 to 1855 a conflict arose between several clans of the Carrizo group, forcing one of them to move out of Carrizo Creek where they had resided for a long time. They went to the Forestdale Valley to continue customary farming practices, suggesting that the valley was then empty and open for settlement. Whether they stayed the year around or used the valley only seasonally, we do not know.

In 1877, the valley was discovered by a White man, Oscar Cluff, who settled there and was shortly followed by others, marking the beginning of a short-lived Mormon community. Oscar's brother, Alfred, arrived in 1878 and named the settlement Forest Dale, a name applied to the valley and the creek.

The history of the Forest Dale community, its ups and downs and the uncertainty as to whether or not the valley was in the Reservation, has been recounted by McClintock (1921: 171–173). While much of the information is not germane here, it does serve notice that when we enter the realm of history, the amount of data available for writing a synopsis of events becomes enormous in contrast to the thin skeleton of the story we have at our disposal from archaeological exploration. Furthermore, the criteria we depend on change. Material culture attributes are replaced by social, economic, political, and religious factors recorded for us in written accounts. While archaeology deals with people, the individuals are anonymous and faceless; in history, personalities, named people, become the focus and agents of actions. The moment of Apache-White contact in the Forestdale Valley is of some interest to our theme.

Gen. E. A. Carr, of Fort Apache, is said to have assured the colonizers that the valley was not in the Reservation and therefore was open to settlement. This must have been more than upsetting to the Indians. As a palliative, two missionaries

Figure 2. Remains of the "temple" built in 1881 in the Mormon community of Forest Dale. Photo by E. W. Haury, 1941.

". . . secured permission from the Commanding Officer of Fort Apache to allow about a dozen families on the creek" (McClintock 1921: 172). Word came through that the valley was on the Reservation and the Indians "demanded everything in sight." By 1880, all White families had gone.

In 1881, in response to rumors again placing the valley outside the Reservation, twenty Mormon families returned, establishing a ward. Confident in the community's future, a sturdy log structure intended to serve as a church and school was erected (Fig. 2). The logs harvested for the building were cut after the end of the growing season in 1881, as determined by tree-ring dating (Scantling 1940; Bannister, Gell, and Hannah 1966: 38), from which construction after August of that year may be inferred.

Troubles arose once again when the Indians arrived in 1882 to plant crops. By treaty from Fort Apache, they were allotted 30 acres as theirs to cultivate. But the conflict was not over. There are hints in the records that at the behest of nearby White ranchers, the Reservation boundary was indeed changed to include the Forestdale Valley once and for all. This spelled doom for the Forest Dale community. The ill-advised treaty allowing the Indians the use of the arable land was overthrown by Lt. Charles B. Gatewood who, at the same time, ordered the settlers to vacate the valley by the spring of 1883. Abandonment was complete by summer. Hough (1903: 289) observed that the Apaches burned the Mormon buildings except the church; but there appears to be no verification of that fact either in the historical records or in the physical evidence of burning. In the 1940s, when we worked in Forestdale, the shell of the Mormon log "temple" stood as a desolate reminder of Apache-Anglo troubles. It has since been destroyed.

Regrettably, during our several years of archaeological studies, we did not systematically record all Apache wickiups, standing or in ruins, and the few frame houses attributable to the Apache as the basis for estimating the intensity and persistence of their use of the region. Nor was any effort made to establish the group identity of the Indians using the valley. Goodwin's earlier reference suggests they were allied with the Carrizo-Cibecue people.

Our observation indicated that year-round residency did not occur, that a limited number of families arrived in spring to prepare the ground for planting corn. Perhaps no more than 25 acres were under cultivation in 1940. Even after planting, there were extended times when no Apaches were seen. Later in the season, when the corn was maturing, they returned and stayed through the harvest.

Some use of the valley was also made by the Apache for grazing cattle. While we saw considerable evidence of them, the animals themselves were rarely observed, usually disappearing in the undergrowth when humans approached. They doubtless carried the brands of the people who cultivated the valley.

One might ask that if the Forestdale Valley was subject only to seasonal use, how could it have been profitable for the Forestdale Trading Post, built about 1935 on the drainage in Skiddy Canyon north of the main valley, to have stayed in business? Although the valley was readily accessible from the north via Show Low for a long time, the rugged terrain to the south discouraged easy links with the Carrizo and Cibecue settlements. Construction of U.S. Highway 60 in the early 1930s opened the country to through travel. The trading post, catering to the traveling public as well as to the Indians, was lucrative enough to make the venture worthwhile.

The pattern of Apache use, as Hough observed it at the turn of the century, as we saw it 40 years later, and as one sees it today, has changed little. Apache dependence on the resources of the valley has been and remains desultory. Agricultural and grazing lands, and a base for hunting and plant collecting, were the prime attractions.

Except for the Mormons; the fishermen in the early days when the waters of Forestdale Creek were ample enough to support trout; the hunters who dropped over the Mogollon Rim into the vast wilderness below; the occasional explorers, including Hough, the archaeologist, in 1901; still later the archaeologists from the University of Arizona; and finally the construction of U.S. Highway 60; non-Indian impact on the Forestdale Valley has been minimal.

The rapid population increase along the southern edge of the Colorado Plateau in the communities of Show Low, Pinetop, Lakeside, Pinedale, and Heber, preferred retirement spots for the residents of the hot and dry valley of the desert, has not affected the Forestdale Valley. Providentially, this choice microcosm has been spared development and overuse because of its Reservation status.

Beyond the confrontation of two alien peoples in the Alchesay phase, the period is also distinguished by the fact that for the first time in nearly two millennia of human tenancy of the valley, investigators set out to piece together that story. The scars of that effort are lasting but perhaps the loss is offset by the information gained.

REGIONAL NOTE

The succession of phases we have reviewed for the Forestdale Valley represents a uniquely long glimpse of what happened in a small southwestern mountain valley. The legacy the residents of the Forestdale Valley left us through the centuries is that as long as comfortable arrangements between the land user and the land, between the land user and his neighbors, have been worked out, stability and prolonged survival are almost certain to follow. The worth of studying a microcosm like Forestdale in depth becomes apparent when, taken with others such as Grasshopper, the Vernon and Reserve areas, and Point of Pines, the means have been established to reach sensible and coherent understandings of human experiences applicable to a large subsection of the Southwest. In general, the archaeologist must look at the nuts and bolts of culture, the details of masonry, pottery, the tools of varied materials that kept life and limb together, and the environment in which people existed, to comprehend how and what makes the complicated cultural contraption work.

Although the progress of Anasazi evolution over a wide area was similar in its broader aspects, regional variability at any one moment in time can be recognized. The difference from region to region, even from valley to valley, led to substantial resistance by several conferees to the adoption of the Pecos Classification in 1927. The notion was entertained by some that variability in space at a given moment argued against the effectiveness of an all-encompassing taxonomy. The benefits of doing so, however, overruled; the classification was accepted as workable, and the experiences of the last fifty years suggest the decision was sound, as long as one kept in mind that the cultural stages and, to a certain extent, the attributes, did not evolve uniformly in space and time. Now that we have learned much from wide-ranging studies in the Mogollon territory, we see that the same phenomenon exists there. The generalization can be accepted that responses to locale and time leave their imprint on the products and on the levels of progress of a people in place-specific ways.

This observation then raises the question of the applicability of the chronology developed in one place, such as the Forestdale Valley, to a larger region. While I think we can see certain similarities in broad stages of cultural advances between Forestdale and neighboring areas, it is not valid to superimpose the chronological template of Forestdale elsewhere and expect total agreement. This tenet is clearly brought out by the fact that the intensive studies by the University of Arizona's Field School at Grasshopper, only 35 km to the west, reveal a somewhat different succession of cultural manifestations. Even so, enough data of a compatible nature are left when a composite of all regional histories is made to give us a working base line for the Mogollon, an essential step if integration with the Anasazi and Hohokam is to be achieved.

Most of the Forestdale cultural record is impersonal, a deficiency that can never be corrected. We tend, therefore, to look at archaeology as detached from the world of the individual. Thin as the connective tissue to the historic present is in the Forestdale sequence, the Skidi and emphatically the Alchesay phases reinforce the fact of continuity, the aboriginal American in contact with people of European descent, a new and alien culture. At last we are brought to the moment when, with the aid of written and remembered records and sure dates, we can speak of Chief Alchesay and his influence in determining the destiny of his people. He brought us to the threshold of history.

EPILOGUE: THE MOGOLLON AND ANASAZI

Our work in the Forestdale Valley contributed measurably to the evolution of the Mogollon concept. Following the proposal that cultural remains in the mountain zone of the Southwest were dissimilar to those of the Basketmaker-Pueblo on the Colorado Plateau and to the Hohokam in the desert, numerous debates ensued pivoting heavily on the question of the relative ages of the complexes. The early dates published in the Bluff Site report (Part III; Haury and Sayles 1947), ranging in the A.D. 200-to-300-year period and an important element in our arguments, strangely seem not to have registered, for they were ignored or little mentioned in the literature. One could only infer that because the Bluff Site dates were as early (or perhaps earlier) as the oldest dates published for Basketmaker II, eschewing them was the easy way out of a dilemma. Yet, the solid evidence of early age provided by the Bluff Site was eventually one of the keys leading to the acceptance of the Mogollon as a cultural, as well as a taxonomic, unit. That step further identified the Forestdale Valley as one of the principal building blocks in the development of the Mogollon story.

The proximity of the valley to the Anasazi domain made the contrast between the two sets of cultural materials available for study all the more impressive. Martin's work, with that of his colleagues, added territorial breadth and helped confirm the time-depth of the remains attributed to the Mogollon, and also further refined the concept. Wheat's (1955) synthesis and more recently Martin's (1979: 61–74) summation have imbued the Mogollon concept with an aura of respectability, and, as mentioned in the Prologue, its pedigree has been strengthened further by conferences solely devoted to it. With this amount of attention, the concept is certain to be altered and embellished far beyond the original formulation of the 1930s.

Apart from the sharply contrasting environments between the Colorado Plateau and the Mountain zone, the material remains of the former inhabitants also show substantial differences that, taken with the demonstrably great antiquity for the Mogollon complex, add validity to the separation of the groups, at least taxonomically, and probably in reality.

As time passed, the Anasazi bloomed with exceptional cultural vitality, resulting in architectural, ceramic, and other material advances as well as enriched ritual symbolism, far outstripping their southern neighbors in sophistication. Considering what appears to have been the receptor nature of the more colorless Mogollon people, one may infer that they viewed the Anasazi achievements with favor and adopted some of them. This process led to the transformation of traditional pit house living to pueblo living, with its concomitant change in attitudes of residence, that is, a shift from an uncongested life style based on the open deployment of buildings to a cheek-by-jowl existence in multistoried buildings. Along with that came the adoption of new ceramic techniques, especially for the production of "fancy" pottery, while the essential fabric of the utility wares was retained. A person knowledgeable in Anasazi remains, taken blindfolded to such sites as Grasshopper, or the late and large (800-room) Point of Pines Ruin, surely would say, on the basis of the architecture, blindfold removed, that those were sites of the Anasazi.

One hears references to the "swamping" and "takeover" of the Mogollon by the Anasazi and the inclusion of ruins and complexes within the Mogollon rubric that do not seem to belong there. I cringe, for example, when the large, late pueblos like Tundastusa, Grasshopper, Kinishba, and Point of Pines Ruin are labeled as Mogollon, or when St. Johns Polychrome is called a Mogollon pottery type.

There appears to be little difficulty with calling the Basketmaker pit house-to-pueblo transition Anasazi; there are problems, however, with saying the Mogollon pit house-to-pueblo transition is solely Mogollon. Both continua involve more than just architecture, because other Mogollon attributes survive late in time and the resulting cultural amalgam shares something of both. A useful, descriptive compromise label for the communities in the eleventh century and later that contain features of both cultures is Mogollon-Pueblo, first suggested by Joe Ben Wheat in 1955. It is less acceptable to call them Mogollon, glossing over the highly indicative and readily identifiable attributes that spell an Anasazi heritage.

These problems, and more, should lead eventually to a reevaluation of the Mogollon idea. Not to do that means that Mogollon encompasses so much that it becomes meaningless and, at the same time, what we think of as Anasazi has been seriously impaired by nibbling away at it.

Having expressed that view, it seems appropriate for me to restate what I perceive the outstanding Mogollon characteristics to have been. But capturing the essence of a people in words from their meager remnants, the mode of living, the relation to the earth, the outlook, and much more, is not an easy task. How does one distinguish the Visigoths from the Catalans, the Aztec from the Chibcha? And how different were the Mogollon from the Hohokam and the Anasazi? The archaeologist is denied the criteria such as language, social customs, political and religious systems, and view of self that are used to differentiate living societies. Hence, the determinations are less precise, but I believe them to be real nonetheless.

The most striking of Mogollon attributes was a preference for a mountain habitat. Their range encompassed most of the mountainous terrain in the Greater Southwest, as much or more than the homelands of the Anasazi and Hohokam combined. This territorial homogeneity is coupled with a long tenancy, beginning at least at the time of Christ and stretching down through the centuries little changed until, as a receptor people, they absorbed many dominant elements of the Anasazi and thereby lost much of their identity. Their social values dictated pit house living, the houses dispersed openly in what appear to have been autonomous villages, usually associated with an impressively large structure presumed to have had ritual uses. Stable village life was based on an agricultural economy supplemented richly with other natural plant resources and the products of the hunt. They buried their dead, varying locally as to manner. The details of their domestic structures and their crafts, notably pottery, differ markedly from the equivalent products of the Anasazi and Hohokam, providing the archaeologist with the most readily identifiable criteria. The pottery was a brown ware oxidized fabric, in early times much of it receiving intentional smudging, texturing, and occasionally a red slip; and only some centuries into pottery-making was it painted in simple red patterns on polished brown surfaces. Although the Mogollon people may have inspired pottery production among the Anasazi by about A.D. 400, a topic that needs further exploration, they had little else to give their neighbors, and as a consequence were willing absorbers of the advantages offered by others. Compared with the Hohokam and Anasazi, their material culture was lusterless. During the eleventh century A.D. they ceased to exist as a discrete Mogollon people. By then, pueblos were being built, and black-on-white and polychrome pottery was being made in what was once Mogollon territory. Although the roots of the original culture were still there, they were plated with the elements of another people to the extent that they had given up their birthright.

I do not pretend to know what linguistic, racial, and genetic
factors may have separated Mogollon from Anasazi people, or
even if those distinctions existed; but it is clear that life styles,
most of the material possessions, and doubtless the psychological outlook of the people who lived in a place like Grasshopper
Pueblo, were Anasazi and not Mogollon. The problem boils
down to the academic question of whether or not, and when, the
life of the people changed to more resemble one or the other. To
say that thousands of people who inhabited the many late and
large pueblos in the White Mountain region, as well as the
Salado people who lived in myriad pueblo communities during
the thirteenth and fourteenth centuries in central and southern
Arizona, were Mogollon, is to water down the concept of Mogollon so far that it loses its meaning. If one believes—and there is
some support for the idea—that remnants of the thousands of
pueblo-dwelling White Mountain and Salado people of the fifteenth century survived in the late prehistoric and early historic villages of the Zuni, then the proponents of the more
inclusive Mogollon concept would have to say that Zuni is
Mogollon and I doubt if there is any enthusiasm for that.

The observation is in order that if the modern pueblos carry
the legacy of the people who built the many notable ruins on the
Plateau (cause for little argument), and if the Pima-Papago are
the likely candidates as modern representatives of the Hohokam, the Mogollon of Arizona and New Mexico then are left
without equally obvious or eligible descendants. The easy
answer is that, indeed, there may have been a "swamping of
these Mogollon by the Anasazi and their absorption was so complete that we see no regional survivors. However, to the south, in
Mexico, a different picture emerges. The 50,000 or more people
who inhabit the backbone of the Sierra Madre Occidental, the
Tarahumara, are a conservative, change-resistant, mountain-
dwelling people. They are agricultural, and while they keep
domestic animals, they eat little meat. Much that they have and
do, and notably their ceramics, fits the template devised for the
Mogollon. Even their little dependence on meat seems to match
the scarcity of bones in most Mogollon sites. I hypothesize that
the Tarahumara are in contention as descendants of a broad-
based Mogollon cultural group, whose territory at one time far
exceeded in extent the relic Sierra Madre area inhabited today.
Perhaps the Mogollon-Anasazi controversy will be illuminated
when some imaginative and industrious investigators dig in
the still-inhabited caves of the Tarahumara, linking their

culture stratigraphically and typologically with the archaeological remains in Chihuahua, identified as Mogollon years
ago (Sayles 1936: 88; Gladwin 1936: 94; Lister 1958: 110 *ff.*), and
from there establishing connections with the Mogollon who
once lived in New Mexico and Arizona. It may even be that
such investigations could cause us to reassess our notion of
Mogollon territoriality, and that what we see as Mogollon north
of the International line was in truth no more than a robust
arm from a heartland centered in the Sierra Madre Occidental
of Mexico.

A large homeland, community living based on the family as
suggested by the architecture, an apparent easy adaptability to
variations in the environment, and a long unbroken heritage
tell us that the Mogollon were in prehistory the kind of
"enduring" people Ned Spicer saw the Yaqui to be in history.

REFERENCES
(Prologue, Parts I and IV, Epilogue)

Asch, Constance M.
1960   Post-Pueblo occupation at the Willow Creek Ruin, Point of Pines. *The Kiva* 26 (2): 31–42

Bannister, Bryant, and William J. Robinson
1971   *Tree-Ring Dates from Arizona U–W, Gila-Salt Rivers Area.* Tucson: Laboratory of Tree-Ring Research.

Bannister, Bryant, Elizabeth A. M. Gell, and John W. Hannah
1966   *Tree-Ring Dates from Arizona N–Q, Verde-Show Low-St. Johns Area.* Tucson: Laboratory of Tree-Ring Research.

Bluhm, Elaine A.
1957   The Sawmill Site, a Reserve phase village, Pine Lawn Valley, New Mexico. *Fieldiana: Anthropology* 47(1). Chicago: Field Museum of Natural History.

Breternitz, David A.
1959   Excavation at Nantack Village, Point of Pines, Arizona. *Anthropological Papers of the University of Arizona* 1. Tucson: University of Arizona Press.

1966   An appraisal of tree-ring dated pottery in the Southwest. *Anthropological Papers of the University of Arizona* 10. Tucson: University of Arizona Press.

Bueher, T. F.
1947   Analysis of soil samples. In "An Early Pit House of the Mogollon Culture," by Emil W. Haury. *University of Arizona Bulletin* 18(4), *Social Science Bulletin* 16: 90–91. Tucson: University of Arizona.

Carlson, Roy L.
1970   White Mountain Redware: a pottery tradition of east-central Arizona and western New Mexico. *Anthropological Papers of the University of Arizona* 19. Tucson: University of Arizona Press.

Colton, Harold S.
1955   Pottery types of the Southwest. *Museum of Northern Arizona Ceramic Series* 3B. Flagstaff: Museum of Northern Arizona.

Colton, Harold S., and Lyndon L. Hargrave
1937   Handbook of northern Arizona pottery wares. *Museum of Northern Arizona Bulletin* 11. Flagstaff: Museum of Northern Arizona.

Cosgrove, Harriet S., and C. Burt Cosgrove
1932   The Swarts Ruin, a typical Mimbres site in southwestern New Mexico. Report of the Mimbres Valley Expedition,

Cosgrove, Harriet S., and C. Burt Cosgrove *(continued)*
seasons of 1924-1927. *Papers of the Peabody Museum of Archaeology and Ethnology* 15(1). Cambridge: Harvard University.

Crown, Patricia L.
1981   *Variability in Ceramic Manufacture at the Chodistaas Site, East-central Arizona.* Doctoral dissertation, University of Arizona, Tucson. Ann Arbor: University Microfilms.

Danson, Edward B.
1957   An archaeological survey of west-central New Mexico and east-central Arizona. *Papers of the Peabody Museum of Archaeology and Ethnology* 44(1). Cambridge: Harvard University.

Dittert, Alfred E., Jr.
1959   Culture Change in the Cebolleta Mesa Region, Central Western New Mexico. MS, doctoral dissertation, University of Arizona, Tucson.

Douglass, Andrew Elliott
1941   Age of Forestdale excavated in 1939. *Tree-Ring Bulletin* 8(1): 7-8. Tucson: University of Arizona.
1942   Checking the date of Bluff Ruin, Forestdale: a study in technique. *Tree-Ring Bulletin* 9(2): 2-7. Tucson: University of Arizona.
1944   Tabulation of dates for Bluff Ruin, Forestdale. *Tree-Ring Bulletin* 11(2): 10-16. Tucson: University of Arizona.

Euler, Robert C., George J. Gumerman, Thor N. V. Karlstrom, Jeffrey S. Dean, and Richard H. Hevly
1979   The Colorado Plateau: cultural dynamics and paleoenvironment. *Science* 205: 1089-1101.

Ferg, Alan
1980   Forestdale Black-on-red: a type description and discussion. *The Kiva* 45(1-2): 95-118.

Fewkes, Jesse Walter
1904   Two summers' work in Pueblo ruins (summers of 1896-97). In *Twenty-second Annual Report of the Bureau of American Ethnology*, pp. 17-196. Washington.

Gifford, James C.
1980   Archaeological explorations in caves of the Point of Pines region, Arizona. *Anthropological Papers of the University of Arizona* 36. Tucson: University of Arizona Press.

Gladwin, Harold S.
1936   Discussion. *In* "An Archaeological Survey in Chihuahua, Mexico," by E. B. Sayles, pp. 89-105. *Medallion Papers* 22. Globe, Arizona: Gila Pueblo.
1945   The Chaco Branch: excavations at White Mound and in the Red Mesa Valley. *Medallion Papers* 33. Globe, Arizona: Gila Pueblo.

Gladwin, Winifred, and Harold S. Gladwin
1934   A method for designation of cultures and their variations.

Medallion Papers 15. Globe, Arizona: Gila Pueblo.

Gladwin, Harold S., Emil W. Haury, E. B. Sayles, and Nora Gladwin
1937   Excavations at Snaketown, material culture. *Medallion Papers* 25. Globe, Arizona: Gila Pueblo.

Goodwin, Grenville
1942   *The Social Organization of the Western Apache.* Chicago: University of Chicago Press.

Hack, John T.
1942   The changing physical environment of the Hopi Indians of Arizona. Reports of the Awatovi expedition. *Papers of the Peabody Museum of Archaeology and Ethnology* 35(1). Cambridge: Harvard University.

Hammack, Laurens C.
1969   Highway salvage archaeology in the Forestdale Valley, Arizona. (Contribution to Highway Salvage Archaeology in Arizona 9.) *The Kiva* 34(2-3): 58-59.

Haury, Emil W.
1934   The Canyon Creek Ruin and the cliff dwellings of the Sierra Ancha. *Medallion Papers* 14. Globe, Arizona: Gila Pueblo.

1936a   The Mogollon culture of southwestern New Mexico. *Medallion Papers* 20. Globe, Arizona: Gila Pueblo.

1936b   Some Southwestern pottery types, Series IV. *Medallion Papers* 19. Globe, Arizona: Gila Pueblo.

1940a   Excavations in the Forestdale Valley, east-central Arizona. *University of Arizona Bulletin* 11(4), *Social Science Bulletin* 12. Tucson: University of Arizona.

1940b   Progress report on excavations at Forestdale. In *Yearbook of the American Philosophical Society*, pp. 186-188. Philadelphia: American Philosophical Society.

1940c   New tree-ring dates from the Forestdale Valley, east-central Arizona. *Tree-Ring Bulletin* 7(2): 14-16. Tucson: University of Arizona.

1941   Progress report on excavations at Forestdale. In *Yearbook of the American Philosophical Society*, pp. 222-225. Philadelphia: American Philosophical Society.

1942   Some implications of the Bluff Ruin dates. *Tree-Ring Bulletin* 9(2): 7-8. Tucson: University of Arizona.

1950   A sequence of Great Kivas in the Forestdale Valley, Arizona. In *For the Dean*, edited by Erik K. Reed and Dale S. King, pp. 29-39. Tucson: Hohokam Museums Association, and Santa Fe: Southwestern Monuments Association.

1976   *The Hohokam: Desert Farmers and Craftsmen, Excavations at Snaketown, 1964-65.* Tucson: University of Arizona Press. Second Edition, 1978.

Haury, Emil, and Lyndon L. Hargrave
1931   Recently dated Pueblo ruins in Arizona. *Smithsonian Miscellaneous Collections* 82(11). Washington.

Haury, Emil, and E. B. Sayles
1947   An early pit house of the Mogollon culture. *University of*

Haury, Emil, and E. B. Sayles *(continued)*
  Arizona Bulletin 18(4), *Social Science Bulletin* 16. Tucson:
  University of Arizona.
Hough, Walter
  1903 Archaeological field work in northeastern Arizona, the
        Museum-Gates Expedition of 1901. In *Annual Report of the
        U. S. National Museum for 1901*, pp. 279-358. Washington.
Judd, Neil M.
  1964 The architecture of Pueblo Bonito. *Smithsonian Miscel-
        laneous Collections* 147(1). Washington.
Kaemlein, Wilma
  1958 Museum Notes (Tubular stone pipe from Bluff Site). *The
        Kiva* 24(1): 25.
Kelly, William H.
  1953 Indians of the Southwest, a survey of Indian tribes and
        Indian Administration in Arizona. *First Annual Report of
        the Bureau of Ethnic Research*. Tucson: University of
        Arizona.
Lassetter, Roy
  1939 Fifth annual Tree-Ring Society conference held at summer
        field camp of Arizona State Museum at Forestdale, Arizona,
        July 22-23, 1939. *Tree-Ring Bulletin* 6(1): 2-3. Tucson:
        University of Arizona.
Lister, Robert H.
  1958 Archaeological excavation in the northern Sierra Madre
        Occidental, Chihuahua and Sonora, Mexico. *University of
        Colorado Studies, Series in Anthropology* 7. Boulder: Uni-
        versity of Colorado.
Litzinger, William Joseph
  1979 Ceramic evidence for the prehistoric use of *Datura* in
        Mexico and the southwestern United States. *The Kiva*
        44(2-3): 145-158.
Mangelsdorf, Paul C., and E. Earle Smith, Jr.
  1949 New archaeological evidence on evolution in maize. *Botani-
        cal Museum Leaflets* 13(8): 213-247. Cambridge: Harvard
        University.
Martin, Paul S.
  1943 The SU Site, excavations at a Mogollon village, western
        New Mexico, second season, 1941. *Field Museum of Natural
        History, Anthropological Series* 32(2). Chicago: Field Muse-
        um of Natural History.
  1979 Prehistory: Mogollon. In *Handbook of the North American
        Indians*, edited by William C. Sturtevant, vol. 9: 61-74.
        Washington: Smithsonian Institution.
Martin, Paul S., and John B. Rinaldo
  1947 The SU Site, excavations at a Mogollon village, western
        New Mexico, third season, 1946. *Field Museum of Natural
        History, Anthropological Series* 32(3). Chicago: Field Mu-
        seum of Natural History.

1950a Turkey Foot Ridge Site: a Mogollon village, Pine Lawn Valley, western New Mexico. *Fieldiana Anthropology* 38(2). Chicago: Field Museum of Natural History.

1950b Sites of the Reserve phase, Pine Lawn Valley, western New Mexico. *Fieldiana: Anthropology* 38(3). Chicago: Field Museum of Natural History.

Martin, Paul S., and Elizabeth S. Willis

1940 Anasazi painted pottery. *Field Museum of Natural History, Anthropology Memoirs* 5. Chicago: Field Museum of Natural History.

Martin, Paul S., John B. Rinaldo, and Ernst Antevs

1949 Cochise and Mogollon sites, Pine Lawn Valley, western New Mexico. *Fieldiana: Anthropology* 38(1). Chicago: Field Museum of Natural History.

Martin, Paul S., John B. Rinaldo, and Eloise R. Barter

1957 Late Mogollon communities. Four sites of the Tularosa phase, western New Mexico. *Fieldiana: Anthropology* 49(1). Chicago: Field Museum of Natural History.

Martin, Paul S., John B. Rinaldo, and Elaine A. Bluhm

1954 Caves of the Reserve area. *Fieldiana: Anthropology* 42. Chicago: Field Museum of Natural History.

Martin, Paul S., John B. Rinaldo, and M. Kelly

1940 The SU Site, excavations at a Mogollon village, western New Mexico, 1939. *Field Museum of Natural History, Anthropological Series* 32(1). Chicago: Field Museum of Natural History.

Martin, Paul S., John B. Rinaldo, Elaine A. Bluhm, and Hugh C. Cutler

1956 Higgins Flat Pueblo, western New Mexico. *Fieldiana: Anthropology* 45. Chicago: Field Museum of Natural History.

Martin, Paul S., John B. Rinaldo, Elaine A. Bluhm, Hugh C. Cutler, and Roger Grange, Jr.

1952 Mogollon cultural continuity and change. The stratigraphic analysis of Tularosa and Cordova caves. *Fieldiana: Anthropology* 40. Chicago: Field Museum of Natural History.

McClintock, James H.

1921 Mormon settlement in Arizona. In *Arizona Historical Society Archives*, pp. 170–173. Phoenix.

Neely, James A.

1974 The Prehistoric Lunt and Stove Canyon Sites, Point of Pines, Arizona. MS, doctoral dissertation, University of Arizona, Tucson.

Plog, Fred

1974 *The Study of Prehistoric Change*. New York: Academic Press.

Reed, Erik K.

1951 Turkeys in Southwestern archaeology. *El Palacio* 58(7): 195–205.

Rinaldo, John B.
    1959   Foote Canyon Pueblo, eastern Arizona. *Fieldiana: Anthropology* 49(2). Chicago: Field Museum of Natural History.
Rinaldo, John B., and Elaine Bluhm
    1956   Late Mogollon pottery types of the Reserve area. *Fieldiana: Anthropology* 36(7): 149–187. Chicago: Field Museum of Natural History.
Roberts, Frank H. H., Jr.
    1931   The ruins at Kiatuthlanna, eastern Arizona. *Bureau of American Ethnology Bulletin* 100. Washington.
Sayles, E. B.
    1936   An archaeological survey of Chihuahua, Mexico. *Medallion Papers* 22. Globe, Arizona: Gila Pueblo.
Sayles, E. B., and Ernst Antevs
    1941   The Cochise culture. *Medallion Papers* 29. Globe, Arizona: Gila Pueblo.
Scantling, Frederick H.
    1940   Tree-Ring dates from a Mormon church. *Tree-Ring Bulletin* 7(2): 14. Tucson, University of Arizona.
Smiley, Terah L.
    1951   A summary of tree-ring dates from some Southwestern archaeological sites. *Tree-Ring Research Bulletin* 5, *University of Arizona Bulletin* 23(4). Tucson: University of Arizona.
    1952   Four late prehistoric kivas at Point of Pines. *University of Arizona Bulletin* 23(3), *Social Science Bulletin* 21. Tucson: University of Arizona.
Stafford, C. Russell, and Glen E. Rice
    1979   Studies in the Prehistory of the Forestdale Region. MS, OCRM Report 47(1–3). Tempe, Arizona.
Wendorf, Fred
    1953   Archaeological studies in the Petrified National Monument. *Museum of Northern Arizona Bulletin* 27. Flagstaff: Museum of Northern Arizona.
Wheat, Joe B.
    1954   Crooked Ridge Village (Ariz. W:10:15). *University of Arizona Bulletin* 25(3), *Social Science Bulletin* 24. Tucson: University of Arizona.
    1955   Mogollon culture prior to A.D. 1000. *American Anthropologist* 57(2), Part 3.
Whittlesey, Stephanie M.
    1974   Identification of imported ceramics through fundamental analysis of attributes. *The Kiva* 40(1–2): 101–112.
Wilcox, David R.
    1977   Assessment of Cultural Resources Subject to Direct or Indirect Impact by the Proposed Route 48, Fort Apache Indian Reservation. MS, on file at the Western Archeological and Conservation Center, National Park Service, Tucson.

Appendix A
A SEQUENCE OF GREAT KIVAS IN THE FORESTDALE VALLEY, ARIZONA*

EMIL W. HAURY

Pueblo architecture in the Southwest is distinguished apart from its compact, adjoined, many-storied living rooms, by subterranean ceremonial rooms, called kivas. Still in common use today among the Pueblo Indians, the kiva is known to have had a long history, the origins extending well back into antiquity. Any consideration of the kiva as an architectural unit must first of all recognize the likelihood of two separate origins for the small clan kiva on the one hand and for the so-called Great Kiva, or super-ceremonial room, on the other hand. As to the former, the theory has prevailed that the small kiva of a thousand years ago was an architectural survival of the pit house or living room in vogue during the early and formative stages of the Puebloan peoples. New excavations in the San Juan drainage, such as J. O. Brew's recent report[1] on Alkali Ridge, tend to confirm this theory, placing the development not only with respect to place but also as to time.

For the Great Kiva, the picture is by no means so clear. In the first place only a handful, relatively speaking, have been excavated and the geographic range of those which have been studied is, on the whole, somewhat greater than for the small kiva. Whereas formerly the Great Kiva was considered to be an intimate associate of the Chacoan Culture, F. H. H. Roberts[2] demonstrated that this feature extended well beyond the limits of the pure Chaco Culture, the presumed center of its development. The Forestdale examples extend the range still farther to the southwest into Arizona and there are surface indications of Great Kivas south of the Black River on the San Carlos Indian Reservation. A number of large structures, quite certainly not domiciliary, have been found in villages of the Mogollon Culture as well as in the towns of Puebloan folk, both laying claims to considerable age. This raises tantalizing problems as to origin, in time and in space, and as to what relationship, if any, existed between the large and small forms of the kiva. Space does not permit a full inspection of these problems but I do feel it worthwhile to present data which has a bearing on the problem.

---

*Reprinted, courtesy of Southwest Parks and Monuments Association, from *For the Dean*, edited by Erik K. Reed and Dale S. King, pp. 29–39, 1950.
[1]Brew, 1946, pp. 203 ff.
[2]Roberts, 1932, pp. 86–98.

This information is drawn from the studies in the Forestdale Valley, near the northern boundary of the Ft. Apache Indian Reservation, conducted in 1939-44 by the University of Arizona. Here we had the unusual opportunity to examine the characteristics of three large kivas through excavation and of a fourth through surface examination, all assignable to different culture levels and representing a span of time approaching 1000 years. To my knowledge we have not had an occasion to view a similar sequence in any other locality so far examined.

The Forestdale Valley lies at an elevation of 6500 feet above sea level just below the Mogollon Rim, the southern escarpment of the Colorado Plateau. It is a short valley, drained by Forestdale Creek which flows successively into Corduroy and Carrizo Creeks, Salt River and finally into the Gila. The habitable portion of the valley is reduced to some three miles in length by a lava flow which long ago blocked the lower reaches. Obviously, the arable land and several unfailing sources of water were chief attractions to Indians since the early centuries of the Christian era. Our survey noted some 50 sites, large and small, within the confines of the valley, representing an occupational range from the early centuries of the Christian era to about 1400, excluding the use of the valley by the Apache more recently. Of special interest is the fact that the earliest settlements are attributable to the Mogollon Culture which by 700 was being replaced by Puebloan people who eventually dominated the region.

In order of time, the villages excavated by us and which have supplied the data used here are:

1) Ariz. P:16:20, or the Bluff Ruin, dated by tree-rings to about A.D. 300. This is the oldest Mogollon Village so dated and is distinguished by round to sub-rectangular pit houses excavated into the sandstone bedrock and by a small amount of brown pottery. The single large room, more or less centrally located in the village, and here called a kiva, was completely excavated.[3]

2) Ariz. P:16:1, the Bear Ruin[4], a pit house village of about 700 (roughly comparable to late Basketmaker III), showing a fusion of Mogollon and Anasazi characteristics; kiva completely excavated.

3) Ariz. P:16:2, a small 21-room pueblo with adjacent Great Kiva, dating about 1100, or early Pueblo III in the local chronology. About half of this kiva had been washed away by an early erosion channel of Forestdale Creek; what remained was entirely cleared of fill.

4) Ariz. P:16:9. A large pueblo occupied about 1200-1300 (estimated) in which our digging was limited to a few exploratory tests, representing the full local Pueblo III stage.

In all of the foregoing villages there were cleared, or tested, circular structures distinguishable from domiciles by size and in most cases by shape and interior plan. Although this architectural type appears first in a ruin of the Mogollon Culture and later occurs in villages of the

---

[3]Haury and Sayles, 1947.
[4]Haury, E. W., 1940, 1940a.

Pueblos, I am assuming, in drawing inferences presented later, that essentially the same social force impelled the construction of all and that they represent various developmental steps of a single architectural form. Whether the idea of a large room presumably devoted to ritual use had already permeated both groups by the early centuries of the Christian era from some more ancient source, or whether it was inspired by one of the two groups and adopted by the other, is unanswerable now.

The fifth and most recent example used in this series is drawn from Kinishba some 40 miles southeast of the Forestdale Valley. Kinishba was inhabited by the same culture group represented in the Forestdale Valley during the 14th century at Tundastusa, the largest ruin in the area. Although W. Hough[5] tested Tundastusa in 1901, his work was not extensive enough to prove or disprove the presence of a Great Kiva.

The inclusion of the large plaza of Group I of Kinishba Pueblo in a Great Kiva sequence demands a word of explanation, since Dr. Cummings did not specifically identify it as a kiva[6]. The area in question is designated as a large patio and lies within a massed block of rooms except on the north side where a wall separates it from a smaller patio in which there is located a small kiva-like structure. The area concerned is generally rectangular, the maximum dimensions being about 17.6 x 18.8 m. The whole patio is surrounded by a stone-faced bench from 1.0 to 1.25 m. wide and 0.50 m. high, suggesting the counterpart of a kiva bench. Heavy posts in the facing walls of the east and west sides indicate that a portico type roof protected the bench proper. Entrance to the area was gained from the southeast through a long covered corridor between living rooms. This passage turned to the west outside the patio wall and led to a doorway into the plaza itself at the midpoint of the southern wall. Another door in the north wall connected with the small patio, thence to the outside through a corridor on the west. Doors of living rooms clustered about the larger patio opened directly into it. Another important feature is a masonry "altar" placed near the southern entrance, consisting of a rock platform flanked on the east, south, and west sides by low walls. Quoting Dr. Cummings, "Here undoubtedly were placed their sacred images, their painted stone tablets, and other proper offerings on the occasion of a sacred ceremony."[7] No mention is made of a hearth or fire area.

Although this patio obviously was primarily secular in function, the aforementioned features are certainly indicative of other functions, too, and I believe it may be regarded as a late, though altered, form of the Great Kiva; hence its inclusion here.

A further word is due concerning the dating of these structures. With the exception of Ariz. P:16:9, all dates are based on tree-rings.

---

[5]Hough, 1903, pp. 290–291.
[6]Cummings, 1940; see map opposite p. 2., also pp. 16–18.
[7]Cummings, 1940, p. 18.

Summarized, the information is as follows:
> *Bluff Ruin*
> From the kiva: 320 ± 5 (2 trees); 318, Bark date (1 tree).
> Range for the ruin as a whole: 285 + x to 320 ± 2 (9 or 10 trees).
> *Bear Ruin*
> From the kiva: 667 + x (1 tree).
> Range for the ruin as a whole: 636 + x to 667 + x (3 trees).
> *Ariz.* P:16:2
> From the kiva: 1008 + x to 1121 + x (9 specimens, ? trees). Roofing
logs were badly shattered when superstructure collapsed and specimens probably come from all parts of radii of large logs, accounting
for the great range, actual construction was probably near 1125.
> Range for the ruin as a whole: 1008 + x to 1121 + x (13 specimens, ?
trees).
> *Ariz.* P:16:9. No tree-ring dates; 13th century placement based on
presence of ceramic types dated elsewhere.
> *Kinishba:*[8] No tree-ring dates from patio. Range for the ruin as a
whole: 1238 ± 5 to 1306 ± 5 (6 specimens).

It is likely that the final abandonment of Kinishba was near 1400.
While the few tree-ring dates do not so indicate, the patio was
doubtless in use to the last; at any rate, well within the 14th century.

In the accompanying text figure [Fig. 1] will be found the essential
facts covering the various buildings discussed. Omitting the descriptive feature, we may proceed directly to the more general problems.
This sequence offers glimpses into the situation over a span of
approximately 1000 years, spotted in the 4th, 7th or 8th, the 12th,
13th, and 14th centuries. Large gaps are left in the earlier part of the
sequence, but it is likely that few basic changes could be detected until
about 1000 or after.

Perhaps of chief importance in recognizing trends is the relationship
of the large units to the domestic structures. In the Bluff and Bear
Ruins, both pit house villages, the buildings were independent of all
others but convenient to them. The nature of pit house architecture does
not readily permit any other scheme. This same placement was present
even in Ariz. P:16:2 at a much later date where, while the kiva was associated with a 21-room pueblo, it was located some 25 meters southwest
of the living units. For Ariz. P:16:9 the evidence is clear that the kiva
and living quarters have been moved together and probably joined,
judging from the surface evidence, but the kiva remains open on the
west and south, being only partially incorporated within the pueblo.

This situation is paralleled in The Village of the Great Kivas[9] in
Great Kiva No. 1. Kiva No. 2 in the same village was independent of the
pueblo, but no time difference could be detected between the two to
support, in this case, the idea of gradual consolidation of the Great Kiva
and the pueblo.

---

[8]Baldwin, 1935, p. 30.
[9]Roberts, 1932, Plate 1.

RUIN	PLAN	TIME	DIAM.	DEPTH	WALLS	ENTRY	BENCH	ROOF	HEARTH	REMARKS
KINISHBA ARIZ. V:4:1	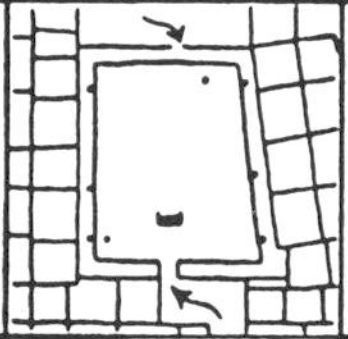	1300-1400 PUEBLO IV	17.6 x 18.8 m.	SURFACE	STONE, FORMED BY ROOMS	SOUTH & NORTH	LOW, COMPLETE	PORTICO OVER BENCH	?	GREAT KIVA SECULARIZED BY INCORPORATION WITHIN PUEBLO, CHANGING IT INTO A PLAZA.
ARIZ. P:16:9	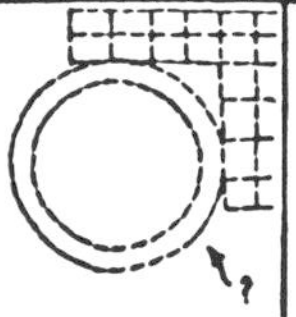	1200-1300 PUEBLO III	Ca. 17.0 m.	1.5± m.	STONE ?	?	?	?	?	PARTIAL INCORPORATION WITHIN PUEBLO.
ARIZ. P:16:2.		1100-1200 PUEBLO III	19.0 m.	1.25 m.	STONE	STAIRS, SOUTH-EAST	COMPLETE EXCEPT FOR STAIRS	4 – POST SUPPORT	?	SEVERAL ANNEXED ROOMS BUT KIVA DETACHED FROM 21-ROOM PUEBLO.
BEAR RUIN ARIZ. P:16:1	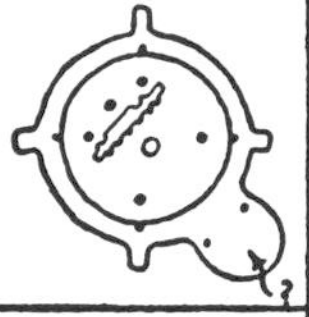	600-700 LATE BM III	15.3 m.	1.75 m.	PLASTERED CLAY	SOUTH-EAST	COMPLETE	4 – POST SUPPORT	NEAR CENTER	INDEPENDENT OF LIVING ROOMS, SPECIALIZED FEATURES APPEAR.
BLUFF RUIN ARIZ. P:16:20		A.D. 300-400	10.3 m.	1.45 m.	BEDROCK	?	NONE	5 – POST SUPPORT	SOUTH OF CENTER	INDEPENDENT OF LIVING ROOMS.

Figure 1. Chart summarizing essential data on Forestdale Valley Great Kivas and Kinishba Plaza. Up is north on all plans.

If the main Kinishba plaza is in fact a late survival of the Great Kiva as is inferred, then complete incorporation in the pueblo has had three notable effects: a) incorporation within the pueblo dictated alteration in form from round to rectangular, so as to take full advantage of the space created by joined rectangular rooms; b) because the plaza was surrounded by living rooms which opened into it, the area became secularized; c) secularization rendered the underground nature of earlier kivas impractical as well as eliminating the necessity of a roof.

It is strange indeed that the Great Kiva, the most spectacular and dramatic feature of pueblo architecture, should have died out by about 1300, as would seem to be indicated by its absence in ruins dated after 1300, but its translation into a plaza, reserved in part for ritual, as suggested at Kinishba, may be the answer. Logically this might be carried one step farther to explain the plazas in modern pueblos where public rituals are still staged.

I am well aware that examples can be cited for Great Kivas *within* plazas. The trend cited here may have applied only to the ruins of the White Mountain area. It is not intended as an argument to explain the origin of the plaza *per se*.

If the examples we have are typical for the area, then an increase in size, early to late, is apparent, climaxing in Pueblo III, but still retaining large proportions in the unroofed Kinishba plaza of Pueblo IV. Here the mechanical restrictions of roof spans were lifted and the size could have been expanded at will. The Chacoan Great Kivas vary in diameters from 14.7 to 23.7 m,[10] a range within which this series also fits, excepting the smaller Bluff Ruin structure.

As for depth, and again by Chacoan standards, Forestdale kivas were shallow. At that, the Bluff Ruin kiva was originally excavated to a maximum depth of 1.45 m in solid sandstone bedrock, not a simple undertaking. The others, however, were not so limited by nature, yet they did not have any great depth. Evidently the necessity for great depth was not felt so keenly in this area, marginal in kiva distribution, a fact which may have had a bearing in the ready translation of the underground room to the surface patio of Kinishba.

Only in the late forms were stones used to line either the outer wall or as facing for the bench. This probably has no great significance other than reflecting the degree to which stone was used in the architecture as a whole. Upended slabs were not employed at all. With the emergence of the kiva from below ground to ground level, a new problem of walling was posed and this was met by simply letting the walls of living rooms combine to make the enclosure.

While there is no evidence of how entrance was gained to the oldest structure in the Forestdale series I am inclined to regard this as having been through the side. A suggestion of such a feature occurred off the south arc of the Bluff Ruin kiva, a position in keeping with the

---

[10]Roberts, 1932, p. 96.

arrangement of the hearth and roof support, but it could not be outlined. The evidence is also unclear for the Bear Ruin kiva, but access may have been through the large annex on the southeast. In Ariz. P:16:2 side entrance from the southeast was definite, a wide stairway of dirt steps and pole and stone treads having led from the surface to floor level. For Ariz. P:16:9 there are no data, but the Kinishba patio was entered from the southeast corner of the pueblo, leading to a door through the south wall of the enclosure. A fairly consistent pattern of side entry from the southeast is thus indicated for the Great Kivas of the Forestdale area.

The information is not sufficiently representative to say much about interior fixtures, other than that the bench is present, except in the Bluff Ruin kiva. There was no pilastering in those excavated, there appear to be no vents, and there are no sub-floor vaults. A *sipapu* was recognized in only one instance, the Bear Ruin kiva. In short the specialization of Chacoan kivas is absent. This may mean either that Chaco influence was so dilute as to be ineffective because of distance, or more probably, it may be explained on the basis of a local tradition of long standing calling for fewer features.

In presenting the foregoing information of Great Kivas in the Forestdale area and including Kinishba near Fort Apache, I am not endeavoring to make out a case for the independent development of the superceremonial room locally. It is doubtful if the actual growth, step by step, can ever be pinned down to one locale. Rather it would appear that this took place over a wide area and that local developmental patterns will eventually be recognized. I do believe that this series represents one such local manifestation, and that the units listed, whether fitting or not the orthodox definition of a Great Kiva, are nevertheless related historically by actual functions in the religious systems of the times represented.

BIBLIOGRAPHY

Baldwin, G. C.
   1935   "Dates from Kinishba Pueblo." *Tree Ring Bulletin*, Volume 1, No. 4, p. 30. Flagstaff.
Brew, J. O.
   1946   Archaeology of Alkali Ridge, Southeastern Utah, with a Review of the Prehistory of the Mesa Verde Division of the San Juan and Some Observations on Archaeological Systematics. *Papers of the Peabody Museum of American Archaeology and Ethnology*, Harvard University, Vol. XXI. Cambridge.
Cummings, B.
   1940   Kinishba, A Prehistoric Pueblo of the Great Pueblo Period. Published under the Auspices of the Hohokam Museums Association and the University of Arizona. Tucson.

Haury, E. W.
  1940   Excavations in the Forestdale Valley, East-central Arizona. *University of Arizona Social Science Bulletin* No. 12, Vol. XI, No. 4. Tucson.
  1940a   "New Tree-Ring Dates from the Forestdale Valley, East-central Arizona." *Tree-Ring Bulletin*, Vol. 7, No. 2, pp. 14-16. Tucson.
Haury, E. W., and E. B. Sayles
  1947   An Early Pit House Village of the Mogollon Culture, Forestdale Valley, Arizona. *University of Arizona Bulletin*, Vol. 18, No. 4. Tucson.
Hough, W.
  1903   Archaeological Field Work in Northeastern Arizona. The Museum-Gates Expedition of 1901. Smithsonian Institution. Washington.
Roberts, F. H. H., Jr.
  1932   The Village of the Great Kivas on the Zuni Reservation, New Mexico. *Bureau of American Ethnology, Bulletin* 111. Washington.

Appendix B
NEW TREE-RING DATES FROM THE FORESTDALE VALLEY, EAST-CENTRAL ARIZONA*

EMIL W. HAURY

During the summers of 1939 and 1940, the Department of Anthropology and the Arizona State Museum of the University of Arizona conducted archaeological studies[1] in the Forestdale Valley, situated in the northern part of the Fort Apache Indian Reservation. This valley was formed by Forestdale Creek which heads below the Mogollon Rim, flowing in a southwesterly direction where it soon empties into Carrizo Creek and eventually into Salt River. It is in the heart of the western yellow pine belt of Arizona and that portion of the valley where the present archaeological work was done has an elevation of 6,580 feet above sea level.

Two ruins were involved in the excavations. The first, a pit house village of the seventh century (the Bear Ruin, Arizona P:16:1) shows a mixture of Anasazi and Mogollon culture characteristics. The second was a thirty-room stone pueblo (Arizona P:16:2) of early eleventh century times.

In the Bear Ruin fourteen domestic buildings and one large kiva were excavated. These ranged in depth from 0.5 to 2.0 meters and showed a variety of treatments insofar as structural details were concerned. The four-post roof plan, bench, deflector-ventilator complex, central hearth and bins would identify these rooms with those of the Anasazi area. On the other hand the long side entrance, the hearth type consisting of a floor excavation without lining or coping, and the lack of stone construction and floor ridges, suggest an architectural affinity with the Mogollon culture. Shapes of houses were both rectangular and round, and there appears to be relatively little cultural significance in these variations. The kiva, a large structure with a maximum diameter of 15.3 meters, was equipped with a bench, a large recess to the southeast, and four small directional recesses.

Although a number of these structures had been burned, datable charcoal in very limited amounts was found in only two: House 1 and the kiva. All specimens were badly shattered, and in no instance was the outer ring preserved to yield the true cutting date.

*Reprinted, courtesy of the Tree-Ring Society, from *Tree-Ring Bulletin*, Vol. 7, No. 2, pp. 14-16, 1940.
[1]With the aid of two grants from the American Philosophical Society of Philadelphia.

Table 1
TREE-RING DATES FROM THE BEAR RUIN

Number	Ruin	Room	Outside dated ring	Inside dated ring	Radius, mm.	Species	Form of specimen	Estimated rings lost at outside	Number absent in series	Estimated bark date
15b	Ariz. P:16:1	1	636	580	45	W.Y.P.	chcl.	40±10	0	676±10
18	Ariz. P:16:1	1	667	586	65	W.Y.P.	chcl.	10± 2	1	677± 2
67	Ariz. P:16:1	kiva	667	611	28	W.Y.P.	chcl.	8± 2	0	675± 2
52	Ariz. P:16:2	1	1098	1050	35	W.Y.P.	chcl.	5± 3	0	1103± 3
54	Ariz. P:16:2	7	1095	1046	23	W.Y.P.	chcl.	5± 3	0	1100± 3
61	Ariz. P:16:2	7a	1107	1067	20	W.Y.P.	chcl.	10± 5	0	1117± 5
55	Ariz. P:16:2	kiva 1	1117	1052	20	W.Y.P.	chcl.	3± 1	0	1120± 1
56	Ariz. P:16:2	kiva 1	1087	1056	12	W.Y.P.	chcl.	30± 5	0	1117± 5
57	Ariz. P:16:2	kiva 1	1113	1062	8	W.Y.P.	chcl.	5± 3	0	1118± 3
58	Ariz. P:16:2	kiva 1	1111	1062	20	W.Y.P.	chcl.	5± 4	0	1116± 4
59	Ariz. P:16:2	kiva 1	1117	1062	9	W.Y.P.	chcl.	3± 1	0	1120± 1
60	Ariz. P:16:2	kiva 1	1008	968	10	W.Y.P.	chcl.	?	0	1008+x
62	Ariz. P:16:2	kiva 1	1070	1016	15	W.Y.P.	chcl.	40±30	0	1110±30
68	Ariz. P:16:2	kiva 1	1121	1085	25	W.Y.P.	chcl.	2± 1	0	1123± 1
69	Ariz. P:16:2	kiva 1	1083	1048	35	W.Y.P.	chcl.	25±20	0	1118±20
66	Ariz. P:16:2	kiva 2	1108	1063	20	W.Y.P.	chcl.	5± 2	0	1113± 2

As will be seen in the following tabulation [Table 1], none of the final rings on the specimens from the Bear Ruin were later than 667. These are judged to be somewhere near the true outside, (excepting specimen 15b) and consequently the number of rings which must be added to compensate for the loss is probably small. It is believed that 675 will represent the approximate date of cutting of these timbers.

The Bear Ruin may be equated with the end of the Basketmaker III period of the Anasazi. This contemporaneity is further borne out by Basketmaker III pottery types which reached the village as trade pieces. Specifically, these were Lino Grey and White Mound Black-on-white. Ceramically, this village was closely aligned with Mogollon culture, there being present as indigenous types: Alma Plain, Forestdale Red (a derivative of San Francisco Red) and Forestdale Smudged, a thin, highly polished and smudged ware which appears to be a contribution of the local potters to the ceramic technology of the Southwest.

As far as is known, this village is the first one excavated to date in which smudged pottery occurred in any appreciable amount (15%)

during the seventh century. This type which has been found in small amounts in ruins of the same time level[2] is almost certainly attributable to the Forestdale Area source. Another type of pottery which shows the blending of the two fundamental cultures concerned was Forestdale Plain, a hybridization of Alma Plain and Lino Grey, paralleling in a way the mixed character of the architecture.

An interesting detail, insofar as pottery is concerned, was the absence of local painted ware. Apparently the emphasis was on the development of the smudging technique, and the painted pottery of the Mogollon, Hohokam, and Anasazi which reached the village did not stimulate local production.

In the pueblo, situated a few hundred meters southwest of the pit house village, approximately a third of the rooms were cleared, together with an associated Great Kiva measuring over 19 meters in diameter and a poorly preserved small kiva. Culturally, this pueblo may be placed as early Pueblo III and ancestral to several large pueblos in the valley which represent the full Pueblo III and Pueblo IV periods.

Once again the charcoal material from the pueblo and Great Kiva was badly shattered, and in no cases could the cutting dates be determined. The tabulation reveals that there were no dates later than 1121 and that the dates cluster in the early 1100s. Judging from the amount of remodeling in the building itself, the founding of the structure must be placed somewhere in the eleventh century and the end of its existence may be assigned to the early part of the twelfth century.

The most noteworthy architectural feature is the Great Kiva, entered by means of a long and wide stairway. The tree-ring dates, although somewhat unsatisfactory, would show construction early in the twelfth century. This makes the building contemporary with the Great Kivas of Chaco Canyon and probably those near Zuni excavated by Roberts.[3] A local development rather than direct diffusion from the Chaco Canyon area is implied by differences in detail, especially since the large kiva in the Bear Ruin which is more than three centuries older would appear to serve as a prototype.

---

[2]Morris, E. H., The beginning of pottery making in the San Juan Area: unfired prototypes and the wares of the earliest ceramic period, Anthrop. Papers, Amer. Mus. Nat. Hist., *28, II*, 186, 1927.
Roberts, F. H. H., Jr., Shabik'eschee Village: a late Basket Maker site in the Chaco Canyon, New Mexico, Smiths. Inst. Bur. Amer. Ethn. Bul. *92*, 108, 117–118, 1929.
Gladwin, H. S., Haury, E. W., Sayles, E. B., and Gladwin, N., Excavations at Snaketown, *I*, Medallion Papers 25, Gila Pueblo, Globe, Arizona, 1937, p. 215.
[3]Roberts, F. H. H., Jr., The village of the great kivas on the Zuni reservation, New Mexico, Smiths. Inst. Bur. Amer. Ethn. Bul. *111* 1932.

These results from the Forestdale Valley are, it is hoped, only the beginning of a long chronology based on tree-rings which will eventually accrue from work there. The area is ideally situated with respect to the necessary tree-ring materials; and culturally, the region provides what appears to be an unbroken sequence of occupation from the seventh to the end of the fourteenth centuries, not counting the more recent Apache remains which are also available. The research program includes a complete survey of all cultural resouces of the valley.

Appendix C

CHECKING THE DATE OF BLUFF RUIN, FORESTDALE
A STUDY IN TECHNIQUE*

A. E. DOUGLASS

In April, 1942, Mr. Ralph Patton, graduate student in the Department of Anthropology, University of Arizona, and member of the class in Dendrochronology, secured a date at about A.D. 310 on some twenty specimens from the Bluff Ruin at Forestdale, near Showlow, Arizona. He had assisted in the excavation of the specimens and was assigned to the study of that collection as research work in the Laboratory of Tree-Ring Research. Soon after getting this result, he was obliged to leave for Alaska to be gone six months. At the end of that time his work in Alaska was extended. Dr. Emil W. Haury, as Head of the Department and Director of the excavations at Forestdale (sponsored jointly by the Arizona State Museum and the American Philosophical Society) was anxious to have a more complete report on the age of Bluff Ruin because it showed signs of being very early. It might supply important information in the prehistory of the Southwest, since there were only four known sites whose ring records were giving any real information about the 200s or earlier. Accordingly, on his request and after some delay, the writer began what was expected to be a brief review of Bluff Ruin specimens. But due to novel conditions encountered, it has extended into a number of weeks.

LOCATION

Bluff Ruin is located on the top of a bluff-faced hill at the south edge of a shallow valley and about 1.5 miles southwest of the previous Forestdale excavations.[1] Its elevation above sea level is about 6600 feet. The ruin is surrounded by ponderosa pines and common pinyons and is about 150 feet above the flat valley floor, which is perhaps a half-mile wide. The intermittent stream along the valley has cut a bed about ten feet deep. Boring tests in living trees made by Mr. Edmund Schulman show that the pines produce large complacent rings on the valley floor, and rise into good sensitivity, though with many doubles, upon the steep slopes.

*Reprinted, courtesy of the Tree-Ring Society, from *Tree-Ring Bulletin*, Vol. 9, No. 2, pp. 2-7, 1942.
[1]Haury, Emil W., New Tree-Ring Dates from the Forestdale Valley, East-central Arizona, *Tree-Ring Bulletin*, Vol. 7, No. 2, pp. 14-16, 1940. Note: the details here given are essential to an interpretation of the trees' reaction to their climate.

The previous excavations in this vicinity, chiefly in 1939–40 on the valley floor at Little Bear Camp, had revealed some 50 charcoal specimens which were dated without difficulty in the early 700s with rings largely running through the 600s,[2] and these rings were of the sort found in the living trees, rather large, with frequent easily recognized doubles and microscopic or locally absent small rings in the years that commonly showed those characters in the well-known Pueblo chronology. There were some slight modifications of a few details.

We recognized long ago that much older ring records would be fewer in number from any one ruin, and dating would be more difficult, and each area might have special problems. Of this, the 1941 collection from Bluff Ruin has turned out to be an illustration. Since other sites will be found that present even more difficult problems, it seems worthwhile to place on record those encountered here and the procedures used in meeting them.

THE COLLECTION

About 175 numbered specimens were collected in 1941 from Bluff Ruin. Every individual piece had a separate number. In some cases, quite a number must have come from one tree; and that suggested the first point in technique in these early sites. In establishing a date, it is almost essential to have ring records from two or more trees. Hence, it is important to know how many different trees are represented in the dating specimens. So, it would help the dendrochronologist greatly if, as far as possible, the fragments of one log are grouped under one number at the time of collection.

In the work Mr. Patton had time to do, he listed the full set of specimens received at our laboratory, grouped them as to source, and picked out a couple of dozen that looked datable, made readings and skeleton plots, and derived the outside date of about A.D. 310 as stated above.

DATE CHECKING

Sequence A. The specimens which Mr. Patton had dated, about twenty in number, were carefully reviewed; all pinyon charcoal, with ring records usually 40 or 50 rings in length and ring widths of one or two millimeters. When combined, they gave a typical pueblo chronology from about A.D. 235 to near A.D. 310, the exact identity at the end being slightly uncertain because no very small 302 ring had been found. But soon one or two of Patton's group were found to show 302 as a microscopic ring only present locally. Then other specimens not on Patton's dated list, such as FST– 279 and 282, were found to give 302 as a perfectly evident but small ring. He would have found these easily if he had had more time in his study. Thus in this pinyon charcoal there

---

[2]*Op. cit.;* and Douglass, A. E., Age of Forestdale Ruin Excavated in 1939, Tree-Ring Bull., Vol. 8, No. 1, pp. 7–8, 1941.

were important verification features that came out on the second careful review, and Patton's dating was sustained. The ring record so worked out was called "Sequence A." It will be noticed that we designate a ring by its date.

But the situation was unsatisfactory because all of these dates came apparently from one single pinyon tree. If these were the only datable specimens from the site, the result, though strong, might have to be held for verification. But there were 150 other numbered pieces.

Sequence B. Among the specimens, all charcoal, set aside by Patton, were two numbered B-21, and one numbered B-14, with 100 or more crowded rings that showed no apparent resemblance to Sequence A, but which cross dated together strongly, especially in the early half. This sequence was called Sequence B. Later, other numbered specimens were found belonging to this series until about ten were unmistakable. All members of this sequence group were obviously so much alike that they could be regarded as from one tree, a pine about 120 years of age, about four inches in diameter and with outer parts full of crowded rings. Very careful sketches and reading were made and skeleton-plotted and compared with the standard skeleton plot of the Pueblo area in all possible dates from A.D. 130 to beyond 750 without result.

So increased care was taken in reviewing the remaining specimens. Two-thirds of them were either (a) erratic pinyon, unreadable, (b) compressed pinyon, also unreadable, (c) juniper, possibly scopulorum, with satisfactory ring series for confirming a chronology, but poor aids in building one; this inadequacy is due to complacent series and occasional confusing doubles that so far have not been distinguishable as such; (d) besides these were some fragments of readable ring records too short to be of service.

Sequence C. Two other sequences appeared; one, "C," was a supersensitive pine of which there were three serviceable fragments. Of these, the best was FST-199 with some 50 rings; its largest ring was some 4 mm. thick and yet here and there were one, two, or three rings of about 0.1 mm. thickness. This sequence was sketched and skeleton-plotted and compared with the known Pueblo chronology over the same centuries from A.D. 130 to the late 700s. The difficulty rested, of course, in the possible uncertainty in the microscopic rings. After long study, it was located at A.D. 242 to 290, with 279 slightly uncertain. Two other specimens, FST-245 and 257, had the same ring type and other similarities, and fitted fairly well into the last 30 rings of the satisfactory number 199. These three could have come from one tree. Later on, another specimen in this group was found, FST-202, which gave a sensitive sequence from 231 to 285.

Sequence D; FST-163. Four specimens, FST-163, 200, 289, and 144, not crossdated, were grouped in Sequence D. The last two, numbers 289 and 144, were short and not readily solved; so they are not discussed here because they are not vital to this dating. Numbers FST-163 and 200 had been preserved through the centuries in part because they were tough pine knots.

In the vicinity of knots, rings grow in different directions and also at different rates. The identification of the sequences might depend on one or both of its extreme parts and the location of these is not known. So it seemed urgent as a policy to lay bare the outside very gently, beginning in places not likely to contain the end rings but near enough to get their time-direction and begin the construction of an individual chronology of the specimen. FST-163, 10 inches long and at first named the "Stick," was the most promising. Practically every square centimeter was shaved and the sequence was read and sketched. Special difficulty came when very thin ring layers advanced toward an unrelated outside angle of the wood. Important cases like that remained until a very sharp razor blade was available. The plot of this record was compared with the known Pueblo area plot without success.

After failing to date specimens from the master plot, the next step was to see if they resembled each other in such a way as to correct each other's omissions. This was done by skeleton plots.

FST-200-201. The one remaining workable piece was a small pine section, FST-200. It had different ring curvature and type, and different wood density and color from the other pieces in hand and therefore probably came from a different tree, which made it valuable. As the reading of these various ring sequences progressed, and many specimens were examined for the third or fourth time, number 201 was found to resemble number 200; then it apparently was identical; later still, it was found actually to fit the other, showing that they were parts of an original single piece.

VERIFIED PREDICTION

"Then number 200, with excellent sensitivity, was found to resemble closely number 199 in the C group, which had been dated. Thus the common interval was about A.D. 240 to 275. Number 199 extends to about A.D. 285; number 257, on microscopic examination proved to show rings out through 306 . . . . Since number 199, a fine series, showed 257-8 as exceedingly small, the assumption of their absence in number 200 would bring an almost perfect sequence in that specimen."

The preceding words under quotation were written for an early draft of this paper, during the first examination of numbers 200 and 201. Two weeks later, a new surface was cut on an untouched part of FST-200, and there were the rings 257-8, as anticipated. That is what we mean by a "verified prediction." A photograph of these rings is show in the illustration [Fig. 1]. This "verified prediction" experience completely settled the matter of date of Bluff Ruin in the mind of the writer. It is the acid test of crossdating and has happened hundreds of times in the experience of most of us.

Provisional Dates. A ring pattern in the 240s showing in FST-199 and 200 led to the provisional dating of the inner part of Sequence B placing it near A.D. 212, where there is a short pattern that resembles

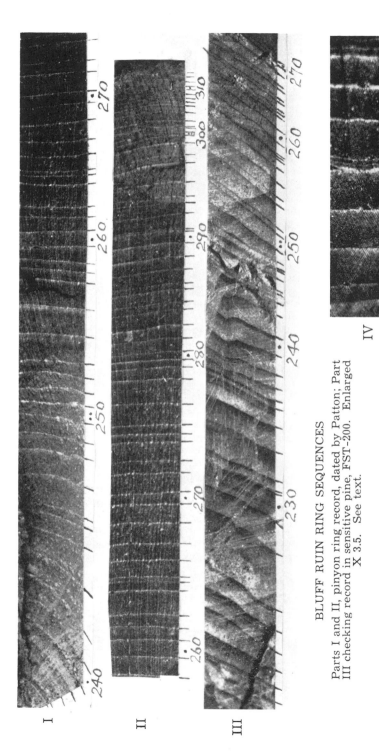

BLUFF RUIN RING SEQUENCES

Parts I and II, pinyon ring record, dated by Patton; Part
III checking record in sensitive pine, FST-200. Enlarged
X 3.5.   See text.

Part IV. "Predicted" rings A.D. 257 and 258
(at the arrow) in specimen FST-200. Enlarged
X 12.

Figure 1. Tree-ring specimens dating the Bluff Ruin.

distinctive features in MLK-153 and 110. This will be discussed at a future time. This would bring the outside of Sequence B near 320 and probably FST-163 near the same time.

PHOTOGRAPHIC RING RECORDS

The accompanying illustration [Fig. 1] shows early sequences in trees from the Bluff Ruin at Forestdale. Excellence of photograph has been sacrificed a little to the preservation of specimens. In this way, the small pieces of charcoal and wood do not have to be altered in a fashion that might sometime prevent further investigation of the ring structures if thought desirable in climatic studies. The first and second strips carry the typical pinyon sequence dated by Mr. Patton. Three specimens are used; the earlier one 234 to 253 was designated by him as B-3; the central specimen from 253 to 295 was B-8; and the outer part from 295 to 316 came from specimen FST-279. B-3 and FST-279 are enlarged X 3; B-8 is enlarged X 6. The rings are quite readable from 234 to 310 or later. The outer edge of each ring is marked by a line below; a very small ring present in the specimen is marked by two close parallel lines, as at 302. A missing ring is marked by an inverted V as in the third strip, at 229. This third photograph was taken from specimen FST-200. The two predicted rings at 257 and 258, which give great strength to the dating, are shown in the fourth strip. Enlarged X 12.

There is a weak spot at 243 in the "double" which, in the short space it is visible, seems to have a sharp outer edge. Considering the action of modern trees in that locality, this is the best interpretation until confirmation or correction is secured. It does not affect the dating of the ruin.

THE DATING CHECKED

The dating of Bluff Ruin secured by Mr. Patton is considered checked and sustained. The sequences supporting this dating are therefore (1) sequence A, 234 to 320 ±, pinyon, 20 or more specimens, one verified prediction, at 302; (2) sequence C, 231-306, highly sensitive pine, specimen numbers FST-199, 202, 245, and 257, verified predictions at 291, 297, and 302; and (3) sequence D, 224 to 275, very sensitive pine section, specimens FST-200 and 201 with very strong verified prediction at 257 and 258.

There are four sites from which dated ring records in the 200s have been obtained, namely, Mummy Cave and Red Rock Valley in northeastern Arizona, Durango in southwestern Colorado, and Kanab in southern Utah. Forestdale is added as fifth in that list with a construction date not far from A.D. 330 ± 10.

Appendix D
TABULATION OF DATES FOR BLUFF RUIN, FORESTDALE, ARIZONA*

A. E. DOUGLASS

Introduction. A general discussion of the age of Bluff Ruin was given in a previous article: "Checking the Date of Bluff Ruin, Forestdale; A Study of Technique," *Tree-Ring Bulletin,* vol. 9, no. 2, October, 1942 [Appendix C]. Herewith are (1) a list of the dated specimens from this site, (2) data which bear upon the accuracy of the dating, and (3) items that will assist in future attempts to make this dating more complete. The table [Table 1] follows the plan used in this Bulletin except for the estimated bark dates which are discussed in the text.

Wherever possible, specimens are identified by the FST numbers in Emil W. Haury's record, with the addition of Ralph T. Patton's numbers in a separate column under the group letter B (the latter were assigned, on opening the packaged collections in the laboratory, before full identity was obtained). The next columns give the first or inside dated ring, the last or outside dated ring, and the overall distance in millimeters from one to the other. Listed also are the number of locally absent rings within the series, the species, the ring type, and by footnotes the evidence of nearness of the outside ring on the specimen to the true outside or bark date.

We use here the same sequences described in 1942 with the addition of Sequence F and a slight modification in C and D.

The significance of center and bark dates. The dates of center are obtained directly, and enable one to estimate the number of trees. If specimen centers show very different dates then there are two or more trees depending upon the number of such separated dates. The importance of the number of trees is related, of course, to the general interpretation of ring sequences that crossdate, for such crossdating between different trees is the intrinsic evidence of climatic effect. In this instance, it implies a record of seasonal rainfall.

The bark date, on the other hand, has to be estimated as a rule, and is primarily of archaeological importance, since it is commonly the date at which the Indians cut a living tree for use in house building or for firewood.

Evidence of bark date may be found in several ways. The best of all is the presence of bark, but this is very rare. The next is the presence

---

*Reprinted, courtesy of the Tree-Ring Society, from *Tree-Ring Bulletin,* Vol. 11, No. 2, pp. 10–16, 1944.

434 APPENDIX D

Table 1
TREE-RING DATES FROM THE BLUFF SITE

FST Spec. Number	(B) Number	Species	Inside Dated Ring	Outside Dated Ring	Length, mm.	Number of Absent Rings	Ring Type
			SEQUENCE A				
....	1	PNN	231	274	36	0	B
....	2	"	224	280	39	0	AB
....	2a	"	242	267	22	0	AB
....	3	"	231	274	42	0	AB[4]
....	4	"	248	285	27	0	AB
....	5	"	235	274	38	0	AB
....	6	"	243	294	37	0	A
....	7	"	261	304	9	1	A
....	8	"	252	295	30	0	A[1,4]
....	9	"	249	279	39	0	AB
....	11	"	259	293	21	0	B
260	17	"	267	305	32	1	B[2]
264	....	"	275	305	28	0	B
266	20	"	260	301	40	0	B[2]
268	12	"	262	302	30	0	B[2]
271	16	"	260	304	40	0	AB[2]
278	15	"	262	312	40	0	AB[2]
279	....	"	280	316	21	0	B[2,4]
280	....	"	268	299	40	0	AB
282	19	"	274	309	20	0	B[2]
283	....	"	272	305	25	0	B
284	18	"	258	300	41	0	B[2]
287	....	"	277	317	26	0	AB[1]
288	13	"	255	305	41	0	B[2]

[1]Converging rings in outer part; also called starvation rings.
[2]Shows outside curvature, probably somewhat worn.
[3]Shows predicted rings.
[4]Photograph published October, 1942.

on the specimen of an outside surface that obviously follows the contour of some one ring. Sometimes the outside does not follow a ring perfectly and then its probable date has to be approximated from rings that are themselves dated with precision. Hence, though we give the dates of rings with utmost care, we cannot give cutting dates always with the same exactness.

Another evidence of bark date is the sharply decreasing average size of the rings which normally occurs near the outside when the food supply of the tree becomes too small. These rings may be called "converging" or "starvation" rings, and usually occur at some distance from the tree center. Very shallow or very limited soil such as gathers

Table 1
(continued)

FST Spec. Number	(B) Number	Species	Inside Dated Ring	Outside Dated Ring	Length, mm.	Number of Absent Rings	Ring Type
			SEQUENCE B				
232	....	"	218	281	14	5-6	
233	21	"	191	314	37	4±	AB[2]
234	....	"	191	318	29	4-6	[2]
235	....	"	284	318	9	0?	
236	....	"	232	320	23	6±	[2]
237	....	"	224	280	11	6	BC
238	....	"	205	312	26	4±	[1]
272	14	"	192	307	40	6±	
			SEQUENCE C				
199		PP	244	288	29	0	AA
200		"	220	262	40	1	A[1,3,4]
201		"	219	270	45	0	A
202		"	231	286	28	5	A
245		"	262	293	36	2	A
247		"	285	302	27	0	A[3]
257		"	272	306	36	1	A
			SEQUENCE D				
160		PNN	190	265	23	0	B[1]
163		"	200	285	30	0	B[1]
164		"	257	296	37	0	B
			SEQUENCE F				
F 14-15		PP	173	302	65	0	AB[1,2]

in small cracks in rocks cannot maintain a large tree. Hence, the tree grows rapidly while very small and then its rings begin to diminish sharply in average size and may finally become much too faint for the investigator to distinguish even under the microscope. Such rings are excellent internal evidence of nearness to the cutting date of the tree.

We have used another indicator of nearness to the cutting date, the "sap-heart contact." It is the date at which the tree's heartwood changes to sapwood. There is a tendency to a characteristic number of rings in the sapwood of Douglas fir and ponderosa pine. This number may be added to the sap-heart date to get an approximate cutting date.

Finally, evidence may be obtained from a large group of charcoal pieces by plotting them individually, after dating, in progressive order of their outside dates, which may thus be found to approach a definite date without going beyond it. This method has been used to secure approximate dates in large collections of charcoal pieces, to which it is specially applicable, since charcoal beams are frequently found broken into numerous pieces.

Sequence A. All charcoal. This is the original sequence dated by Patton in the early months of 1942. A recent study by microscope showed the cells in all specimens to be mostly under 0.03 mm in width and the rings to have many resin ducts and narrow latewood, hence the species is taken to be pinyon (*Pinus edulis*), common in the vicinity of Forestdale. There are over 20 specimens belonging in this sequence. However, they probably came from only two or three trees which were burned into charcoal and badly broken. All of them are from the Great Kiva.

These specimens give a beginning date for the ring series about A.D. 234 and indicate probable bark or cutting dates near A.D. 315 ± 10.

Sequence B. Charcoal and wood. Sequence B, also based on Great Kiva specimens, was recognized by Patton as different from Sequence A. It is pinyon as identified under the microscope. The series has about 120 rings in it and represents two or more trees as indicated by different average ring-size and general appearance. This group is specially valuable because a number of specimens show the outside curvature of the tree. In the previous mention of this sequence (October, 1942) a provisional dating was assigned which has been verified in the present review. Some of these specimens carry a ring series of more than 100 years with not more than three or four absences. As presumed, the three small rings A.D. 210, 212, and 214 agree with similar rings in MLK–153 which came from Red Rock Valley in the northeastern corner of Arizona. By this dating we secure the real use of the excellent outside curvature of some of these pieces. In FST–234 the curvature is continuous around some 80° of the circumference and rings can be seen following this curvature through most of that distance. Since the outside ring is now dated at A.D. 318 the cutting date, estimated at 320 ± 2, becomes a very good date for the ruin and supports the age previously obtained.

Sequence C. Wood, with some charcoal surfaces. This is the highly sensitive ponderosa pine sequence. In some cases, a ring may be twenty times as large as the next following ring. A diminution much less than this ratio may appear in other trees that crossdate perfectly well so that most doubtful cases encountered have been solved satisfactorily by the use of other specimens. Careful comparisons between these specimens indicates that FST–199 from House 3 is a different tree from FST nos. 200, 201, and 202 from House 1. No. 202 shows very high sensitivity with one or two depressed rings a small fraction of a millimeter in thickness. This possibly is not from the same tree as the other two. Nos. 245, 247, and 257 all look alike and are doubtless out of one tree coming from House 2. No. 247 comes very close to the original outside as judged by its curvature. A.D. 302 may be the true outside ring. From the straightness of the rings in some cases the diameter of the tree could be 12 inches or so. However, where the tree is part wood and part charcoal, as in all these specimens, there may be substantial distortion of the curvature of the rings.

The dated sequence extends from A.D. 220 to 305 with center at 191 or 192 and one absence at A.D. 229. Rings A.D. 285–286 are sometimes microscopic and one possibly absent; 291 is sometimes doubtful as the ring representing it could be taken as a double of the preceding year; 294 is sometimes absent. Specimen FST–247 gives the series from 285 to 302, and shows all these absent rings. They are, therefore, classed as predicted rings and have established the correctness of the dating. FST–199 performs an important service because it overlaps FST nos. 245, 247, and 257 from House 2 in its outer parts and FST nos. 200, 201, and 202 from House 1 in its inner parts, thus producing one continuous sequence from A.D. 224 to 306 with only A.D. 229 persistently absent [Fig. 1].

FST–200, FST–201 and FST–202 are highly sensitive ponderosa pines from House 1. These show strong compression in the rings at the outside and therefore give a close approach to the cutting date of the trees. The rings may be traced toward the center to about A.D. 224 with accurate dating; then come more difficult rings to the center near or before A.D. 200 with doubles which make date identification uncertain. The later rings can be identified into the 270s but probably extend ten years beyond that. The diminishing size of these starvation rings indicates a small loss on the outside. Part of this series has been published (1942) in a photo group. The bark date of this sequence is A.D. 306 + X.

Sequence D. Wood. Sequence D from House 6 was known in the first discussion of this dating as the "long stick" from its principal specimen FST–163. It has some 85 rings in it. This sequence also includes FST–160 and FST–164. This series is characterized by long intervals of complacent rings separated by brief sets of very small rings. FST–164, pinyon, shows a strong dating at A.D. 296 with probably a small loss on the outside.

FST–163 finally yielded a satisfactory date of A.D. 285 for its last ring. This was accomplished by the aid of the previous successful dating of the B sequence and a good skeleton plot of it. This dating was of course verified by the comparison of the ring sequence in the wood and charcoal with the minutely memorized picture of practically all other known specimens covering the same period of time. The actual appearance of the rings themselves in comparison with all other presentations is of course the final arbiter of the genuine quality of dating. Certain other features will be referred to below. The bark date of this sequence may be taken as A.D. 285 + X.

Sequence E. No completely satisfactory dates were found in Sequence E from a stratigraphic location called E–5. Three ponderosa pine specimens, FST–124, FST–125, and FST–127, probably came from the same tree. Dating was prevented by too many double rings. FST–140, a ponderosa, also has double rings. FST–144 and FST–146 are pinyon;

Figure 1. Early ring record at Bluff Ruin. FST–233, pinyon magnification x6. Ring A.D. 229 absent. Compare the chronology with that in MLK–153, January 1939 *Bulletin*, p. 21.

Table 2
DISTRIBUTION OF TREE-RING SPECIMENS
FROM THE BLUFF SITE

Location	Specimen	Location	Specimen
House 6	F-1	House 15	F-2
	F-9*		F-8
House 14	F-4*		F-10
	F-5*		F-12*
	F-13*	House 19	F-6*
House 11	F-3		F-7
	F-11	House 21	F-14
			F-15

*Juniper

FST-144 has a provisional dating of its last ring at A.D. 257, the inner ring being at 209. Further study may give more weight to this date. FST-146 shows strong outside curvature on a radius of about 50 mm and a fairly definite outer ring, but the dating is not satisfactory.

Sequence F. The following notes represent a preliminary study only. The 1944 collections at Bluff Ruin were contained in 15 packages. These were numbered 1 to 15 as opened, under the group letter F. The specimens were distributed as follows [in Table 2].

Six specimens, starred, are juniper and their study was postponed. Five of the others were found to have difficult ring series probably impossible to date. Thus there were left F-1 in House 6, F-3 near House 11, and F-14 and F-15, parts of one tree, in House 21. Each of these shows a significant relation to the tree's outside. F-1, probably pinyon, is a half section with a smooth unmarred outside. It gives a suggestion of dating in the 260s but has one or two disagreements that have kept it out of the dating tables for the present. F-3, ponderosa pine, seems to have a trace of bark, so its date could become valuable. Dr. Haury thought it might be many years later than the Kiva specimens dating near A.D. 320. Many of the narrow rings are hard to distinguish on account of spots of gum, both in charcoal and wood. It will need careful preparation before a reliable reading can be made.

F-14 and F-15, two parts of the same tree with nearly the same central date, are large fragments of ponderosa pine, each about 14 inches long, together giving a ring record from A.D. 173 to 302. The records from about A.D. 256 to 302 are exceedingly good but the intermediate interval from 236 to 256 is badly distorted from injury and the repair work of the tree. The ring type is excellent and the details resemble Durango specimens particularly. Thus this is a valuable contribution to the dendrochronology of the second and third centuries. The bark date of these two specimens is 304 + X.

Ring A.D. 229. Practically up to the time of this writing (October, 1944) the complete absence was assumed of any ring for A.D. 229. Sequence A did not extend that far back. Sequence B simply omitted one ring in that vicinity. Sequence C showed A.D. 231 as a microscopic ring while 229 was absent. Sequence D has only just been dated. The easier sequence on the large end of FST–163 had A.D. 229 absent but the supposedly more difficult sequence at the small end showed 229-31 as two microscopic rings separated by a larger one, which is exactly the form these rings take in the Durango and Red Rock Valley sequences.

The group near A.D. 212. Sequence B has this group very prominent— A.D. 210 very small, 212 and 214 micro, and 217 micro and locally absent. The small rings A.D. 210, 212, and 214 resemble a similar series in MLK–153 from the Red Rock Valley. The same sequence in FST–163 has A.D. 212 normal instead of small and in this resembles the Durango record. This resemblance to Durango specimens is carried only partially to the center. The rings A.D. 199 and 201 are only slightly smaller in the C sequence but the small rings at 194-195 are small as in Durango and Red Rock Valley.

Possible extra ring in the 240s. FST–200, FST–201, and FST–202 show the series of small rings beginning at A.D. 243—three rings almost exactly alike followed by larger rings 246-7-8. There is an annual-like extra ring between A.D. 244 and 248, which, however, in one instance at least looks like a part of the preceding ring. This extra ring does not appear in any other ring record we have which presents that decade. This fact together with the strong tendency to false rings in the Forestdale area leads us to the present opinion that it does not indicate an extra year. However, more specimens are needed to completely disprove its annual character in view of the relatively limited number on which the early centuries of the Central Pueblo Master Chronology is based.

Appendix E
SOME IMPLICATIONS OF THE BLUFF RUIN DATES*

EMIL W. HAURY

Dr. Douglass' preceding article on the analysis of tree-ring material from the Bluff Ruin (Arizona P:16:20, Arizona State Museum Survey) in the Forestdale Valley, east-central Arizona, is an extremely important addition to our growing southwestern archaeological picture. So that the full significance of this work will not be lost, the following archaeological notes are appended.

The cultural remains of this village so far unearthed include eight pit houses of round or roundish form (average diameter about 3.5 meters) but otherwise quite featureless, scooped out of the solid sandstone bedrock; there was one large (over 10 meters in diameter) round structure which must probably be classed as religious rather than domestic. All cultural material was exceedingly scarce. Stone implements include both basin and crudely troughed metates. Manos are large, generally of oval form. Present also are small stone vessels or mortars, tubular stone pipes, and a small amount of chipped scrapers, knives, and straight-based, leaf-shaped projectile points. Bone implements were almost entirely lacking and pottery was present but in small quantities. One extremely fragmentary burial suggested that inhumation was practised.

The chief pottery type was a smoothed plain brown ware, and there were small amounts of polished smudged and red types. There was no painted pottery. The pottery is manifestly in the Mogollon tradition and the relative unimportance of it in the culture suggests that the horizon was near the threshold of the introduction of ceramics.

Basketmaker or Anasazi sherds of any description were not found, although such are present in later phases.[1] Intrusive pottery assignable to the Hohokam Culture includes Gila Plain and several painted sherds too extensively eroded for phase identification.[2]

---

*Reprinted, courtesy of the Tree-Ring Society, from *Tree-Ring Bulletin*, Vol. 9, No. 2, pp. 7–8, 1942.

[1]Haury, E. W., *Excavations in the Forestdale Valley, East-Central Arizona.* Social Science Bulletin, No. 12, University of Arizona, pp. 84–85, 1940.

[2]In view of the early date of this village and the presence of Hohokam pottery, interesting light is cast on Gladwin's revision of the Snaketown chronology. Gladwin, H. S., Excavations at Snaketown, III: Revisions. Medallion Papers No. 30, Gila Pueblo. 1942.

The Bluff Site bears certain unmistakable marks of relationship with the S U Site in New Mexico excavated by Martin[3] which, although not dated as yet by tree-rings, is estimated to be early. It seems, furthermore, to be the basic culture of the Forestdale Valley. Some centuries later it amalgamated with the Anasazi to constitute the Forestdale Phase as determined in the Bear Ruin.

Of the four localities mentioned by Dr. Douglass producing ring records through the A.D. 200s, Mummy Cave, Red Rock Valley, Durango, and Kanab, the terminal dates of the records from the latter two areas point to a Basketmaker II or non-pottery level of culture. The Mummy Cave record, with outside date in the 300s is probably associated with Basketmaker II and the status of the Red Rock Valley specimens has not been accurately determined. In this light the 4th-century date for the Bluff Site would appear to give us the earliest ruin with a pottery complement yet dated by tree-rings. Ever since considerable age has been claimed for the Mogollon Culture and particularly the proposal that Mogollon pottery may have been in existence before Anasazi ceramics, the lack of tree-ring dates has been cited as the central argument against it. While the evidence from the Bluff Site is still not conclusive it is nevertheless in support of this line of reasoning. Additional work in the Bluff Ruin is indicated and unfortunately this must wait until after the war, when a detailed report will be issued.

---

[3]Martin, P. S., Rinaldo, J., and Kelly, M., *The S U Site: Excavations at a Mogollon Village, Western New Mexico.* Anthropological Series. Field Museum of Natural History, Vol. 32, No. 1. 1940.

INDEX

Note: Artifacts are listed under material of manufacture: bone, pottery, shell, stone. Specific ceramic types are listed under Pottery types; they are not indexed alphabetically by name.

Abandonment
   of Forestdale Valley, 395–396
   of rooms, 45, 46
Acorns, 64
Agriculture, 11, 15, 20, 63, 65, 147,
      148, 255, 290, 340, 360, 366,
      380, 397, 398–401, 405, 406.
      See also Corn; Forestdale Val-
      ley, terrace systems in
Alchesay, Chief, v, 402
Alchesay phase, 397–401, 402
Alkali Ridge excavations, 415
"Altar" masonry, 417
American Philosophical Society, 3,
      137, 283, 427
Amerind Foundation, xv, 193
Anasazi culture (Plateau people), xv,
      xvii, xviii, 7, 16, 104, 105, 154,
      157, 174, 180–184, 186, 188,
      190, 194, 196, 198, 200, 201,
      204, 211, 214, 223–228, 242–245,
      252, 320–322, 336, 340–341, 355,
      381, 383, 387, 403–406, 415,
      423–425, 442.
Anasazi-Mogollon amalgamation.
      See Mogollon-Pueblo amalga-
      mation
Animals. *See* Bones, animal;
      Figurines, animal; and by
      specific name
Antelope, 68, 291, 357
Antevs, Ernst, 10, 19, 20, 138, 143,
      144, 262
Antler flakers, 131, 247
Apache Indians, 3, 11, 12, 15, 16,
      137, 146, 148, 194, 287, 289,
      291, 336, 396–401, 416. *See also*
      Alchesay, Chief
Apache Tribal Council, 3, 137, 283
Archaic culture, 263
Architecture
   domestic. *See* Pit houses; Pits;
      Pueblo architecture;
      Storage structures;

Unit structures
   religious. *See* Great Kivas; Kivas
Arizona sites
   P:16:1. *See* Bear Ruin
   P:16:2. *See* Tla Kii Ruin
   P:16:5, 396
   P:16:9, 9, 388–389, 391, 396, 416,
      418, 421
   P:16:20. *See* Bluff Site
   P:16:28, 289, 378
   P:16:58. *See* Red Knoll Site
   Q:3:1, 79
   Q:13:1 (ASU), 51
   W:10:105, 396
   See also by specific site name
Arizona State Museum, 3, 72, 137,
      423
Arnold, Brigham, 138
Awls. *See* Bone artifacts, awls;
      Stone artifacts, awls
Azurite, 129, 241

Baldwin, Gordon, C., 10, 138
Balls
   clay, 250
   stone, 107, 129, 236, 243
Bandelier, A., 140
Basalt
   artifacts of, 114–117, 346, 348, 352
   sources of, 37
Basketmaker culture, xv, 8, 110,
      140, 167, 181, 184, 186 n 50,
      194, 214, 217, 223–224,
      242–244, 248, 258, 266, 269,
      270, 308–310, 315, 322, 333,
      334, 337, 340, 354–355, 356,
      358, 362, 365, 367, 381, 404,
      424, 442
Basketry, charred, 174, 252, 255
Basso, Keith, 17
Bat Cave, New Mexico, 67
Bead manufacture, 119
Beads
   bird bone, 247

443

Beads *(continued)*
shell, 131, 164, 166, 249, 255
steatite and stone, 107, 118, 119,
    348, 355
turquoise, 107, 117–118, 236, 243,
    255
Bear, 147
Bear Ruin (AZ P:16:1), xix, 3, 8, 11,
    12, 17, 18, 20, 27, 51, 73, 81,
    82, 109, 131, 133, 136–279,
    283, 285, 299, 302, 320, 322,
    323, 326, 329, 331, 334, 337,
    339, 356–358, 375, 382–383,
    416, 418, 421, 423–425, 428,
    442
Benches
in domestic structures, 23, 24, 26,
    31, 32, 152, 154, 160, 162,
    167, 171, 180, 182, 183, 255,
    423
in kivas, 19, 47, 53, 176, 179, 255,
    417, 420, 421, 423
Bins, 45, 167, 181, 184, 306, 319, 423
Bird bones, 131, 147, 245, 247
Bird effigy, 120–122
Birds, 63, 68–69, 147, 148
Bison, 68, 147
Black-billed Magpie, 63
Black Mesa, Arizona, 20, 107
Bluff Site (AZ P:16:20), xix, 3, 8, 11,
    12, 16, 51, 67, 133, 282–371,
    375, 377–383, 396, 403, 416,
    418, 420–421, 427–442
Bone artifacts
awls, 129, 245–247, 248, 255
cylinder, 247
dice, 131, 164, 247, 249, 255
discs, 247
incised, 247, 249
lacking at Bluff Site, 357
needles (bodkins), 247, 249, 255
scrapers, 131, 247, 248, 255
spatulates, 247
tubes, 131, 164, 198, 247, 249, 255
whistles, 247, 255
See also Antler flakers
Bones
animal, 55, 62, 63, 66–69, 129,
    147–148, 192, 193, 245–249,
    289–291, 357. *See also*
    Hunting
human, 60–62, 196–199, 264–270.
    See also Burials

Bracelets, 118, 131, 249, 255
Brachycephals. *See* Physical types,
    of Mogollon
Brew, J. O., 10, 415
Burials, 19, 23, 25, 34, 46, 58, 60–62,
    64–65, 71–73, 79, 80, 82, 90, 92,
    107–109, 111, 117, 118, 129,
    131, 196–199, 236, 241, 249,
    255, 264–270, 289, 324, 361,
    380, 385, 389, 405, 441.
    See also Bones, human;
    Grave goods
Burt, W. H., 138
Butler, B. D., 283

Canyon Creek phase, 16, 63, 69,
    131, 392–396
Canyon Creek Ruin, 141, 392–393,
    394
Cardium elatum shell, 249
Carey, Linda, 4
Carr, Gen. E. A., 398
Carrizo Creek, Arizona, 142, 384,
    386–387, 397, 416, 423
Carrizo phase, 16, 21, 28, 31, 32, 45,
    52, 53, 58, 60, 62, 63, 70, 72,
    89, 92–103, 111–118, 123–127,
    129, 131, 376, 384, 386–388,
    389
Carrizo Valley, 336
Cattle grazing, by Apaches, 400, 401
Cave Creek site, 214, 259, 261, 320,
    333, 337, 365, 366
Cedar Creek, 397
Chaco Canyon area, xvi, 221, 415,
    420, 421
Chaco Canyon Conference, 140
Chaco-type architecture, 39, 41, 52,
    420, 421, 425
Chalcedony, artifacts of, 126, 127,
    229, 348, 352
Charcoal, 42, 55, 59, 423, 425, 428,
    432, 435–439
Chert, artifacts of, 116, 124–129,
    229, 234, 236, 238–241, 342,
    348–352
Chihuahua, Mexico, 221, 407
Chinking stones, 31, 39
Chodistaas site, Arizona, 391
Chrysocolla, 241
Cibecue, Arizona, 144
Cibecue Creek, 397
Cinnabar, 241, 242

Civilian Conservation Corps, 3, 283
Classification, of Southwestern
    cultures, xv-xix, 8, 89,
    258-263, 402, 403-407
Climate, in Forestdale Valley,
    144-146, 148, 290
Cluff, Oscar, 398
Cochise culture, 20, 67, 188, 193,
    194, 245, 261, 262, 340, 355 n
    54, 356, 357, 366, 367
Coconino sandstone, 142, 229, 285
Colorado Plateau, xv, 8, 12, 13, 62,
    94, 104, 107, 139, 140, 142,
    220, 401, 403, 416
Colorado River, 13
Concretions (stone balls), 107, 129,
    236, 243
Connolly, Florence.
    See Shipek, Florence
Conus shell, 131
Cooking stones, 236, 245, 255, 256,
    261, 323, 360. *See also* Food
    preparation; Hearths; Heat-
    fractured stones; Pits, storage
    and warming
Corduroy Creek, Arizona, 13, 142,
    384, 385, 387, 416
Corduroy phase, 20, 23-25, 27, 28,
    30, 31, 62, 63, 71-83, 85, 89,
    91, 104, 107, 111-119, 124-129,
    131, 317-318, 339, 341, 349,
    350, 355, 356, 383-386, 389
Corduroy Valley, Arizona, 51
Corn, 55, 63, 65, 67, 146, 148, 194,
    244, 255, 380, 397-401.
    See also Agriculture
Cosgrove, Harriet, 10
Cotton, 179
Cottonwood phase, 16, 67, 285, 289,
    307-311, 314-315, 317,
    320-322, 333, 339, 341,
    344-346, 348-350, 352,
    354-367, 379-382
Covers. *See* Pottery vessels,
    covers for
Cox, Stephen, xix
Coyote, 291
Cranial deformation. *See*
    Deformation, cranial
Crooked Ridge Village, Arizona, 378
Cross dating, 79, 227-228, 253, 431
Crystal, quartz, 129, 236
Cummings, Byron, 137, 141, 417

Cylinder, bone, 247

Dating
    of Forestdale Valley cultural
        sequence, 3, 11, 12, 15, 19,
        67, 79, 91, 214-215, 242,
        252-254, 321-322, 328, 329,
        334, 336, 337, 358-367,
        375-402, 403, 416, 423-442
    tree-ring, xviii, 8, 12, 19, 37,
        47-51, 54, 59, 91, 92, 102,
        144, 154, 179, 214, 216, 218,
        227-228, 242, 252-254, 294,
        296, 300, 302, 319, 335, 337,
        340, 358-367, 375-402,
        417-418, 423-442
Datura fruit, 79
Deer, 63, 68, 129, 147, 245-247, 291,
    357
Deflectors, 26, 43, 154, 157, 160,
    163, 170-172 177, 181, 182,
    255, 423
Deformation, cranial, 255, 264, 267,
    269, 324
Depopulation. *See* Abandonment
Dice, bone, 131, 164, 247, 249, 255
Dioritic material, artifacts of, 236,
    241
Dipper. *See* Pottery, ladles
Discs
    bone, 247
    pottery, 112, 250-251, 255,
        341-342, 361
    shell, 249
    stone, 47, 52, 348, 361, 362
Dogs, 69, 148
Domestic structures. *See* Pit houses;
    Pits; Pueblo architecture;
    Storage structures;
    Unit structures
Donner, William, 3, 137, 283
Doorways. *See* Entryways
Douglass, A. E., xviii, 10, 359, 378,
    379, 427-440, 442
Dry Valley phase, 16, 20, 25, 31, 32,
    34, 37, 54, 58, 60, 62, 63, 70,
    82-94, 97, 111-118, 120,
    124-127, 129, 131, 376, 384-387

Edwards, Ida, 4
Effigy vessels, 99
Elk, 68
Ellis, Florence Hawley, 10

Encinos phase, 364
Entryways, 23, 24, 26, 27, 31, 43, 47, 52, 157, 160, 163, 164, 167, 168, 171, 173, 174, 180–183, 255, 296, 299, 302, 306, 307, 314, 316, 317, 319, 360, 361, 380, 394, 417, 420, 421, 423, 425. *See also* Hatchways
Erosion cycles, 19, 34, 51, 144, 146, 416
Ezell, Paul, 10

Fauna. *See* Bones, animal; and by specific name
Feathers, 63, 68. *See also* Birds
Ferg, Alan, 72
Fewkes, J. W., 140, 391
Field school, in Forestdale Valley, 3–5, 8
Figurines, clay, 111, 112, 174, 249–250, 255, 341–342, 361
Finger grooves, in manos, 115, 116, 233, 344, 345
Fire clouds. *See* Pottery, fire clouds on
Firepits. *See* Hearths
Fish, 69
Floor sill, clay, 303–304
Floor trench, 179
Floors, 23, 24, 26, 28, 42–43, 47, 153, 154, 157, 160, 163, 167, 168, 170–172, 174–176, 184, 293–322
Flora, I. F., 10
Food
  preparation of, 188, 190, 192–194, 236, 244, 245, 255, 256, 261, 322–324. *See also* Cooking stones; Hearths
  sources of, 63–69, 147, 244, 291. *See also* Agriculture; Bones, animal; Corn; Gathering; Hunting; Plants
Forest Dale, Arizona, 388, 398–400
Forestdale Canyon, 13
Forestdale Creek, 13, 17, 19, 20, 34, 37, 46, 51, 69, 142, 143, 148, 190, 342, 384, 387, 416, 423
Forestdale phase, 16, 20, 24–25, 27, 71–73, 81–82, 109, 131, 151–270, 285, 299, 322, 331, 333, 339, 354–356, 358, 360, 363, 382–384, 387, 442
Forestdale Ruin. *See* Tla Kii Ruin

Forestdale Valley
  description of, 13–16, 142–148, 286–287, 416
  terrace systems in, 10, 13, 17–20, 143–144, 149, 150, 287
Fort Apache, Arizona, 144, 146
Fort Apache Indian Reservation, 3, 137, 142, 283, 397, 398, 416, 423
Four-mile Ruin, 141
Fox, gray, 147

Galbraith, F. W., 138
Galena, 241
Gaming piece, 131. *See also* Dice, bone
Garnets, 198, 236
Gatewood, Lt. Charles B., 400
Gathering, 15, 67, 360, 380, 401. *See also* Food; Plants
Gems, 198, 236
Georgetown phase, 67, 183, 212–214, 220, 261, 262, 321, 364
Getty, H. T., 10
Gila Basin, Arizona, xvi
Gila Butte phase, 79, 206, 210, 217–218, 220, 253
Gila Pueblo Archaeological Foundation, xv, 7–10, 13, 139, 141, 188, 217, 220, 320, 337, 382
Gila River, 13, 94, 140, 395, 416
Gladwin, Harold S., 7, 139, 364
Gladwin, Nora, 261
Glycymeris shell, 131, 249, 255
Goodwin, Grenville, 397, 400
Gopher, 147, 291
Grasshopper area, Arizona, 378, 391, 401
Grasshopper Pueblo, Arizona, 392–394, 397, 402, 404, 406
Grave goods, 23, 62, 64–65, 71–73, 79, 80, 82, 90, 92, 107–109, 112, 117, 118, 129, 131, 196–199, 200, 236, 241, 249, 389
Great Kivas, 11, 19, 47–52, 92, 144, 175–179, 184–186, 380, 384, 387–389, 391, 393, 394, 415–421, 423, 425, 436, 441
Grid system, at Bear Ruin, 149
Growing season, length of, 146
Gulf of California, 13

Gypsum, 129, 241

Hack, John T., 20
Hafting, of stone tools, 127
Hale, Thomas, 10
Haliotis shell, 131, 249
Hall, Edward T., 10
Hargrave, Lyndon L., 4, 10
Harris Site, New Mexico, 8-10, 139,
    140, 151, 212, 219, 225, 260,
    304, 321, 333, 337, 355, 357
Hastings, Russell, 7, 139
Hatchways, 43, 154, 155, 177,
    180-182. *See also* Entryways
Hawikuh village, 395
Hawk, 147
Hawley, Florence. *See*
    Ellis, Florence
Hearths (firepits), 23, 24, 26, 31, 32,
    37, 42, 43, 46, 60, 149, 150,
    153-155, 157, 160, 163,
    166-168, 170-172, 174, 176,
    180-184, 188-195, 255, 287,
    299, 302, 306, 307, 319,
    322-324, 347, 360, 361, 421,
    423. *See also* Cooking stones;
    Food preparation;
    Heat-fractured stones;
    Pits, storage and warming
Heat-fractured stones, 23, 188, 229,
    245, 287, 323. *See also*
    Cooking stones; Hearths;
    Pits, storage and warming
Heber, Arizona, 119, 144
Heineman, R. E. S., 138
Hematite, 121, 129, 241, 242, 353
Hilltop phase, 15, 16, 63, 67, 285,
    289, 294-307, 312-317,
    319-323, 333, 339, 341, 344,
    346-367, 377-380, 387
Hohokam culture, xv, xvi, 7, 110,
    128, 131, 183, 188, 193, 194,
    238, 243-245, 249, 253,
    339-340, 342, 360, 364, 367,
    405, 406, 425, 441
Hopi area, 20, 392, 395
Horn. *See* Antler flakers
Hough, W., 140-142, 285, 388, 391,
    393, 395, 396, 400, 401, 417
Hunting, 15, 63, 65-69, 147-148, 255,
    290, 357, 360, 377, 380, 401,
    405. *See also* Bones,
    animal

Incising
    on bones, 247, 249. *See also* Dice, bone
    on pottery, 82, 83, 202, 211, 212,
        255
In-migration, Forestdale Valley,
    37, 392
Interments. *See* Burials
Iron
    concretions, 129
    in pottery clay, 201

Jar stoppers, clay, 250. *See also*
    Pottery vessels, covers for
Jarosite, 241
Jasper, artifacts of, 352
Jeddito Valley, Arizona,
    217, 225, 253
Jennings, Mr. and Mrs. Thomas,
    138, 283

Kachina figures, on pottery, 395
Kaibab limestone, 229, 342
Kaolinitic clay, xvii, 392
Kiatuthlanna phase, 108-109, 383
Kiatuthlanna village, 141
Kidder, A. V., xv, xvi, 259, 262
"Killing" of artifacts, 231, 244, 389
Kinishba pueblo, Arizona, 138, 141,
    392-394, 397, 404, 417-421
Kivas, 47-54, 92, 175-179, 182, 252,
    255, 263, 300-302, 320, 360,
    367, 380, 387, 391, 394,
    415-421, 423, 425. *See also*
    Great Kivas

La Playa, Sonora, 193
Laboratory of Anthropology,
    Santa Fe, xv, 141
Ladders, 43, 160, 164, 177, 181, 184
Ladles. *See* Pottery, ladles
Lakeside, Arizona, 144, 146
Lange, Richard, 119
Lassetter, Roy, 10
Lava, artifacts of, 114, 229-233,
    235, 244, 255, 342, 344-346,
    348
Lava flow, in Forestdale Valley,
    142, 342, 416
Lee, Mrs. Gordon, 138
Lids. *See* Pottery vessels, covers for
Limestone, 229, 236, 344
Limonite, 129, 241
Linden phase, 16, 388-390

Little Colorado River area, 13, 141, 260
Looms, evidence of, 179
Lowry Ruin, 9
Lugs, *See* Pottery vessels, lugs on
Lukachukai area, 225

Malachite, 129, 241
Manzanita berries, 64
Martin, Paul S., xviii, 9, 10, 259, 320, 365, 366, 378, 379, 403, 442
Masonry. *See* Pueblo architecture
McGregor, John, 10
"Medicine" stone, 348, 362
Menstrual hut(?), 31
Mera, H. P., 141, 206, 212, 220, 333
Mescal, 194
Mica, in pottery paste, 333-335
Mimbres potters, 111
Mimbres Valley, New Mexico, 7, 8, 132, 139, 183, 225, 262, 331, 364
Miniature vessels, 111, 198, 200
Minerals, 129, 241-242, 353. *See also* Paint pigments
Mogollon physical type, 255-257, 260, 264-270, 361
Mogollon-Pueblo amalgamation, xix, 3, 12-13, 133, 140, 186, 188, 204, 208-209, 217, 244, 256-263, 285, 321-322, 363-365, 367, 381-407, 416, 442
Mogollon Rim, 12, 13, 119, 139, 141, 225, 382, 416
Mogollon Village, New Mexico, 7-10, 139, 151, 183, 188, 202, 214, 219, 225, 260, 337, 355, 357
Mormon culture, 148, 388, 398-401
Morris, Earl, 8, 10, 139, 214
Mortar, 31, 37, 42, 45
Mule deer. *See* Deer
Mummy Cave, Arizona, 432, 442
Museum of Northern Arizona, xv
Museum-Gates expedition, 140

Nantack Ridge, Arizona, 396
Nantack Village, Arizona, 25
Nassaris shell, 131
National Geographic Society, 141
Navajo culture, 194
Necklaces. *See* Beads; Pendants

Needles, bone (bodkins), 247, 249, 255
Nesbitt, Paul, 10, 183, 220, 259, 262
New Mexico Q:1:14. *See* Harris Site

Obsidian, artifacts of, 127, 229, 238, 342, 352
Olivella shell, 131, 164, 249, 255
Olivine, 198, 236
Ornaments. *See* Beads; Bracelets; Gems; Pendants
Ovens, earth. *See* Hearths; Pits, storage and warming
Owl, horned, 147

Paint
  carbon, 72, 223
  glaze, 78, 86, 97, 389, 392, 394
  on sherd disc, 251
  on stone artifacts, 117, 122, 233, 417
Paint pigments, 121, 129, 223, 241, 242, 353
Painted slabs, 122, 417
Palette, sherd, 251
Patayan culture, 194, 211, 218
Patton, Ralph, 283, 358, 427-432, 433, 436
Peabody Museum Expedition, 253
Pecos, New Mexico, xv
Pecos Classification, xv, 89, 402
Pecten shell, 131
Penasco phase, 363, 364, 366
Pendants
  bird effigy, 117
  turquoise, 117, 236, 243, 245, 255
Petrified Forest area, 72, 141, 210, 212, 216, 220, 333, 355 n 54
Petrified wood, artifacts of, 124-127, 229, 234, 236, 238, 239, 342, 350-352
Phase concept, 375-377
Physical types
  of Anasazi (Basketmaker), 256, 257, 260
  of Mogollon, 255-257, 260, 264-270, 361
Pigment. *See* Paint pigments
Pigummi oven, 194
Pima-Papago Indians, 406
Pine Lawn area, New Mexico, xviii, 7, 9, 10, 67
Pine Lawn phase, 364

Pinedale, Arizona, 144, 146
Pinedale phase, 16, 106, 131, 389, 391–392
Pinedale Ruin, 391, 396
Pipes
   clay, 249, 255
   stone, 245, 348, 355, 361, 380, 441
Pit houses, 7, 11, 16, 20, 23–28, 31, 62, 70, 71, 73, 80, 107, 112, 132–133, 151–174, 252, 255, 256, 260–261, 263, 289, 291–322, 354, 358, 360, 361, 378, 380, 381, 383–384, 386, 387, 404, 405, 415, 418, 423, 425, 441
Pits, storage and warming, 23, 24, 26, 31, 32, 34, 45, 46, 54–60, 62, 63, 70, 82, 115–117, 120, 124–127, 129, 154, 155, 160–162, 164, 166–168, 171, 173, 174, 179, 181, 184, 188–195, 255, 293, 294, 306, 307, 314, 317, 319, 323, 324, 360. *See also* Bins; Hearths; Storage structures
Plants, 64, 67, 147, 163, 287, 291. *See also* Food; Gathering
Plaster, 42, 47, 152, 154, 160, 176, 190, 299, 302, 303, 306, 307, 314, 316, 317, 319
Plateau people. *See* Anasazi culture
Plazas, 34, 391, 393, 417–420
Pluvial Period, 144
Point of Pines ruins, Arizona, 52, 69, 85, 94, 378, 380, 389, 392–394, 396, 401, 404
Population estimates, 16, 17, 36, 37, 51, 60, 388, 392, 394
Postholes, 23, 24, 26, 28, 45, 47, 52, 154, 155, 157, 158, 160, 162, 163, 167, 168, 170, 172–175, 179, 180, 183, 299, 306, 308, 314, 319. *See also* Roofing
Potsherds
   containers, 341–342, 361
   in mortar, 42
   in pits, 55, 58
   worked, 112–113, 250–251, 255, 341–342, 361. *See also* Pottery, scrapers
Pottery
   analysis of, 70–71
   Apache, 336

   applique decoration on, 329
   ball, 250
   Black Mesa style, 89, 97, 107, 389
   black-on-red, 16, 72, 83, 91, 102, 103, 113, 388, 392
   black-on-white, 16, 23, 27, 28, 31, 32, 56, 58, 60, 70, 75–82, 85–91, 99, 102, 103, 106, 107, 109, 111–113, 133, 146, 211, 214, 216, 217, 220, 223–224, 227, 253–254, 317, 324, 341, 385, 386, 388, 389, 392, 405, 424
   brown ware, xvi, xviii, 7, 9, 11–12, 16, 23, 104–112, 204, 211, 212, 218, 220, 254, 258, 293, 296, 299, 300, 302, 304, 308, 312, 314, 317, 322, 330–331, 333–334, 341, 355 n 54, 358, 360, 362, 367, 384, 405, 441
   clays for, xvii, 97, 104, 201, 385, 392
   construction of, 73, 75, 78, 85–87, 101, 106, 201–211, 217, 223, 326–330, 334, 385
   corrugated, 16, 31, 32, 56, 60, 82, 85, 91, 93–97, 106, 112, 151, 207, 386, 388, 389, 392
   corrugated black-on-white, 99
   crazing of, 78, 202
   Deadmans style, 89
   dippers. *See* Pottery, ladles
   discs, 112, 250–251, 255, 341–342, 361
   figurines, 111, 112, 174, 249–250, 255, 341–342, 361
   fire clouds on, 78, 83, 86, 205, 207, 209, 326
   glaze paint on, 78, 86, 97, 389, 392, 394
   gray ware, 27, 72, 73, 75, 79–81, 104–111, 200, 204, 208, 211, 212, 216, 217, 220, 223, 224, 253, 254, 314, 317, 331, 334, 338, 341, 358, 362, 381, 383, 384, 424, 425
   Hohokam, 17, 27, 81, 82, 103, 108, 110–111, 200, 211, 217–220, 223, 225, 228, 253, 254, 334–335, 360, 367, 379
   incised, 82, 83, 202, 211, 212, 255
   intrusive, 79–82, 90–92, 103, 211–228, 253, 333–342, 360,

Pottery *(continued)*
    362, 367, 441
  kachina figures on, 395
  Kiatuthlanna style, 107–110
  "killing" of, 389
  knobbed, 79, 107
  ladles, 86, 93, 111
  miniature. *See* Pottery vessels,
    miniature
  mottling on, 201, 221, 327
  neck-banded, 16, 23, 27, 28,
    73–75, 83, 106, 200, 211–215,
    223, 225, 227, 255, 317
  neck-corrugated, 60, 82, 83–85,
    92, 106, 386
  oxidizing firing of, xvii, 75, 104,
    201, 209, 218, 223, 326,
    384, 405
  painting on, 72, 78, 79, 85–91,
    93–103, 106, 107, 385, 405.
    See also Paint pigments;
    Pottery types
  pipes, 249, 255
  polishers. *See* Stone artifacts,
    polishing stones
  polychrome, 16, 17, 106, 151,
    389, 392, 394, 404, 405
  Pueblo I, 317, 335, 341, 342
  Pueblo III, 335–336
  Puerco style, 87, 89, 97, 100
  Red Mesa style, 107, 108
  red ware, 23, 27, 28, 32, 72, 83,
    93, 106, 113, 200, 206,
    209–212, 215–216, 218, 220,
    221, 225, 226, 252, 254, 255,
    258, 259, 261, 262, 300, 302,
    314, 317, 322, 332–333, 338,
    362, 384, 385, 424, 441
  red-on-buff, 81, 82, 211, 217, 219,
    253, 254, 335, 360
  reducing firing of, xvii, 75, 85,
    104, 201, 206, 223, 384, 392
  Reserve style, 32, 87, 89, 97,
    107, 113
  scoring on, 211, 212, 217, 255,
    296, 302, 308, 331
  scrapers, 82, 113, 164, 251–252,
    255, 324, 341–342
  smudged ware, 16, 23, 27, 28, 32,
    56, 72, 80, 82–83, 92–93,
    107, 112, 113, 200, 201,
    205–207, 211, 212, 216, 217,
    219–227, 250, 252, 254, 258,

    293, 300, 302, 306, 314, 317,
    330–332, 338, 360, 362,
    384–385, 392, 405, 424, 425,
    441
  Snowflake style, 32, 56, 87, 97, 389
  temper, 75, 82, 85, 92, 101, 201,
    205, 207, 209, 223, 327,
    329, 330, 334, 338
  Tularosa style, 89, 389, 392
  unfired, 97, 209 n 77
  See also Grave goods; Paint
    pigments; Pottery types;
    Pottery vessels
Pottery Hill site, 388
Pottery types
  Acquarius Brown, 211, 218, 254
  Adamana Brown, 204, 211, 212,
    220, 254, 293, 308, 314,
    317, 333–334, 341, 355 n 54,
    358, 360, 362
  Alma Incised, 82, 202, 211, 212,
    255
  Alma Neck-banded, 23, 27, 28,
    73–75, 83, 200, 211–215,
    225, 255
  Alma Plain, 23, 27, 28, 60, 71–73,
    82, 85, 92, 106, 112, 113,
    200–204, 208, 209, 212, 216,
    219, 225, 226, 254, 293, 296,
    299, 300, 302, 304, 306, 308,
    312, 314, 317, 326–330, 332,
    338, 341, 360, 361, 383,
    389, 424, 425
  Alma Scored, 211, 212, 255, 296,
    302, 308, 331
  Black Mesa Black-on-white,
    87, 89, 90–91, 103
  Cebolleta Black-on-white, 89, 91
  Chaco Black-on-white, 102, 103
  Cibecue Polychrome, 394
  Corduroy Black-on-white, 16, 23,
    27, 28, 75–79, 80, 82, 102,
    113, 389
  Deadmans Black-on-red, 91, 103
  Deadmans Black-on-white, 90
  Fine Paste Brown, 293, 296, 299,
    300, 302, 304, 308, 312,
    314, 317, 330–331
  Forestdale Black-on-red, 72, 83
  Forestdale Plain, 27, 28, 72, 107,
    200, 204, 207–209, 216, 254,
    256, 314, 331, 383, 425
  Forestdale Red, 23, 27, 72, 83,

200, 206, 209–212, 225, 252, 254, 331, 333, 424
Forestdale Smudged, 23, 27, 72, 80, 82–83, 92, 107, 112, 113, 200, 205–207, 211, 212, 217, 219, 220, 221, 224–226, 250, 252, 254, 314, 317, 330–332, 338, 362, 424
Fourmile Polychrome, 17, 394
Gila Butte Red-on-buff, 81, 82, 211, 217, 219, 253, 254
Gila Plain, 81, 103, 110, 211, 217, 254, 296, 299, 300, 306, 308, 333–335, 341, 358, 360, 362, 379, 441
Gila Polychrome, 17
Gila Red, 221
Holbrook Black-on-white, 89, 91, 103, 113
Kana-a Black-on-white, 385
Kana-a Gray, 73, 75, 79–81, 212, 216
Kapo Black, 221
Kiatuthlanna Black-on-white, 78, 79, 81, 82, 385
Kinishba Polychrome, 394
Linden Corrugated, 93
Lino Black-on-gray, 211, 212, 216, 218, 227, 254
Lino Gray, 27, 72, 80–81, 200, 204, 208, 211, 216, 217, 220, 223, 224, 253, 254, 314, 317, 331, 334, 338, 341, 358, 362, 381, 383, 424, 425
Lino Smudged, 211, 216–217
Los Lunas Smudged, 221
McDonald Corrugated, 16, 60, 85, 93–97, 112, 207, 388, 389, 392
Mimbres Black-on-white, 111
Mimbres Boldface Black-on-white, 111
Mogollon Red-on-brown, 211, 214, 216, 218–219, 227, 254
Pinedale Black-on-red, 392
Pinedale Black-on-white, 99, 389, 392
Pinedale Polychrome, 17, 392
Pinto Black-on-red, 392
Pinto Polychrome, 392
Puerco Black-on-red, 91, 103, 388
Puerco Black-on-white, 87
Ramos Black, 221

Red Mesa Black-on-white, 79, 385
Reserve Black-on-white, 112
Reserve Plain, 220
Reserve Smudged, 92
Rio de Flag Smudged, 220, 221
Roosevelt Black-on-white, 111
Salado Red, 221
San Francisco Red, 210, 211, 215–216, 225, 226, 255, 259, 261, 262, 424
San Lorenzo Red-on-brown, 218–219, 227
Showlow Black-on-red, 102, 103, 113
Showlow Polychrome, 394
Snowflake Black-on-white, 89
Sosi Black-on-white, 89
Springerville Polychrome, 389, 392
St. Johns Polychrome, 16, 151, 389, 392, 404
Three Circle Neck Corrugated, 83
Three Circle Red-on-white, 111
Tonto Red, 221
Tularosa Black-on-white, 111
Tularosa Fillet Rim, 102, 103
Tularosa White-on-red, 102, 103
Tusayan Corrugated, 91
White Mound Black-on-white, 27, 81, 102, 109, 112, 113, 211, 214, 216, 220, 223–224, 227, 253, 254, 424
Wingate Black-on-red, 91, 103, 388
Wingate Polychrome, 389
Woodruff Brown, 204, 220, 258, 333
Woodruff Red, 200, 210–212, 216, 220, 255, 258, 300, 302, 314, 317, 332, 362
Woodruff Smudged, 27, 200, 206, 211, 212, 216, 220, 254, 258, 293, 300, 302, 306, 317, 331–332, 338, 360
Pottery vessels
covers for, 174, 250, 348
knobbed, 79, 107
effigy, 99
handles on, 86, 93, 99, 202, 204, 208, 209, 223. *See also* Pottery vessels, lugs on
lugs on, 202, 204, 208, 210, 223
miniature, 111, 198, 200

Pottery vessels *(continued)*
  seed jars, 93, 327–330
  warped, 75, 77, 85, 97, 106, 107,
    385
Prairie dog, 147
Pueblo architecture, 16, 17, 20, 27,
    28, 31, 37–42, 46, 302, 307,
    308, 314, 316–320, 322, 358,
    360–362, 364, 381, 386–389,
    391, 393, 417, 420
Pueblo living, beginning of,
    132–133. *See also* Mogollon-
    Pueblo amalgamation
Puerco River area, 141, 196, 210,
    216, 220, 221, 223, 225, 383
Pyrolusite, 241

Quartz
  in jar with Burial 2, 198
  in pottery temper, 75, 82, 85, 92,
    101, 201, 205, 207, 209, 223,
    327, 329, 330, 334, 338
Quartz crystal, 129, 236
Quartzite, 114–116, 123, 124, 192,
    229, 235, 342, 344, 346,
    348–350

Rabbits, 63, 68, 129, 147
Racial types. *See* Physical types
Racoon, 147
Rainfall. *See* Climate
Rasps, sandstone, 348, 361
Rat, 147
Realgar, 241, 242
Red Hill Site. *See* Red Knoll Site
Red Knoll Site (AZ P:16:58),
    16, 289–290, 378
Red Mesa area, 78, 107
Red Rock House, 393, 394
Red Rock Valley, Arizona,
    432, 436, 440, 442
Reed, Eric, 10
Reeds, in roofing, 44
Reserve area, New Mexico,
    7, 83, 92, 107, 220, 259, 378,
    380, 401
Reserve phase, 92, 220
Residence locations, 15–16, 20,
    290–293, 378, 379, 404, 405.
    See also Pit houses;
    Pueblo architecture
Rinaldo, John, 10

Rio Grande area, 221
Roberts, F. H. H., Jr.,
    141, 214, 415, 425
Roofing, 43–47, 52, 154, 155, 163,
    167, 174, 175, 179, 183, 184,
    255, 299, 306–308, 314, 319,
    417, 418, 421, 423.
    See also Postholes
Roosevelt Lake area, Arizona, 58

Salado culture, 58, 221, 392, 406
Salt, 69
Salt River, 13, 69, 416, 423
Salvaging, prehistoric, 31
San Francisco phase, 157, 180, 183,
    212–214, 242, 260, 262, 364,
    383
San Francisco River area, 85, 331
San Lorenzo phase, 213, 214, 242
San Pedro stage, 261, 262, 340,
    355 n 54, 366, 367
San Simon site, 259, 320, 365
Sand, added to plaster, 42
Sandstone
  architectural use of, 28, 37, 47,
    163, 166, 168, 171, 172,
    182, 314
  artifacts of, 114–116, 122, 229,
    230, 232, 233, 244, 342–348
  sources of, 37, 342
Santa Cruz phase, 128, 253
Sayles, E. B., 10, 12, 20, 214, 259,
    261, 262, 283, 337, 365, 407
Scantling, Frederick H., 138
Schroeder, Albert, 10, 138
Schulman, Edmund, 10, 427
Scrapers. *See* Bone artifacts,
    scrapers; Pottery, scrapers;
    Stone artifacts, scrapers
Scraping spoons. *See* Pottery,
    scrapers
Sedentary period, 131
Senter, Donovan, 10
Settlement patterns.
    See Residence locations.
Shabik'eschee village, 184
Sharp-shinned Hawk, 63
Shell artifacts, 107, 131–132, 164,
    198, 249, 255
Shipek, Florence Connolly, 138, 283
Showlow Ruin, 393, 395, 396
Sierra Ancha region, 141
Sierra Madre Occidental, 406, 407

Sipapu(?), 32, 167, 421
Skeletal remains. *See* Bones, human;
    Physical types
Skidi phase, 396-397, 402
Slab houses. *See* Pueblo architecture
Sloan Creek, 119
Slutes, Frances T., 283
Smithsonian Institution, 141
Smoking, prehistoric. *See* Pipes
Snaketown site, 206, 217, 220, 253,
    259, 261, 262, 336. *See also*
    Pottery, Hohokam
Soil analysis, 368-369
Spicer, E. B., 407
Spier, L., 141
Spiked vessels. *See* Pottery vessels,
    knobbed
Stallings, W. S., Jr., 10
Starkweather Ruin, 183
Steatite, 107, 118, 119, 348, 355
Stone artifacts
    abraders, 233, 243
    abrading slabs, 233, 243
    axes, 116, 236, 243, 244
    axe-sharpening stone, 116
    blades, 237-238, 243, 245, 255
    choppers, 123-124, 236, 243, 342,
        349, 355, 357, 361, 366
    discs, 47, 52, 348, 361, 362
    drills, 119, 129, 238, 243, 255,
        352, 361
    gravers, 126, 241, 243, 255, 351,
        356, 361, 366
    grinding slabs, 346, 361
    hafting of, 127, 357
    hammerstones, 116, 166, 192,
        234-235, 243, 342, 346-348,
        361, 362
    knives, 127, 238-239, 243, 255,
        350, 352, 361, 441
    manos, 46, 55, 114-116, 148, 149,
        173, 174, 192, 230-233, 243,
        244, 255, 294, 296, 324,
        342-345, 355, 361, 441
    mauls, 116-117, 166, 192, 235-236,
        243, 244, 255, 357
    "medicine" stone, 348, 362
    metates, 46, 63, 114, 116, 148,
        149, 157, 160, 163, 192,
        229-233, 243, 244, 255, 291,
        296, 310, 315, 322, 324,
        342-344, 354, 355, 357, 361,
        362, 366, 381, 441
    mortars, 114, 233, 243, 255, 344,
        346, 355, 361, 362, 366, 441
    ornaments. *See* Beads; Bracelets;
        Pendants
    painted slabs, 122, 417
    pestles, 233, 243, 346-347, 355,
        361, 366
    pipes, 245, 348, 355, 361, 380, 441.
        See also Pipes, clay
    polishing stones (polishers), 116,
        234, 243, 244, 326, 348,
        361, 362
    projectile points, 127-128, 238,
        243-245, 255, 342, 352, 356,
        361, 362, 366, 441
    rasps, 348, 361
    rubbing stones, 116, 192, 346, 348,
        354, 361, 362
    scrapers, 124-126, 239-241, 243,
        245, 255, 349, 350, 356,
        357, 361, 366, 441
    toothed tools, 126-127
    vessels, 236, 243, 255, 441
Storage pits. *See* Pits, storage and
    warming
Storage structures, 28, 174-175,
    180, 184, 255. *See also* Pits,
    storage and warming
Students, at field schools,
    4-5, 138, 283
SU site, 214, 259, 320, 321, 324,
    333, 337, 355, 356, 357,
    364-366, 442
Subsistence. *See* Agriculture;
    Gathering; Hunting

Tarahumara Indians, 406, 407
Teiwes, Helga, 4
Temperature. *See* Climate
Terrace systems. *See* Forestdale
    Valley, terrace systems in
Third National Geographic Society
    Beam Expedition, 141, 391
Three Circle phase, 67, 182, 183,
    260, 364
Tla Kii Ruin (AZ P:16:2), xix,
    3-133, 151, 217, 283, 375, 383,
    385, 387-388, 416, 418, 421,
    423
Tonto Basin, Arizona, 111, 221
Toys, 198. *See also* Pottery vessels,
    miniature
Transitional Life Zone, 147

Tree-Ring Conference, Fifth
    Annual, 10
Tree-rings. *See* Dating, tree-ring
Trischka, C., 193
Trout, 69
Tubes. *See* Bone artifacts, tubes
Tundastusa pueblo, 9, 15–17, 63,
    133, 140, 142, 285, 387,
    391–397, 404, 417
Turkey Creek Ruin, Arizona, 52
Turkeys, 63, 68–69, 147, 148
Turquoise, 107, 117–118, 121, 198,
    236, 243, 245, 255, 355
Turritella shell, 131
Turtle, mud, 147
Twin Butte site, 72
Unit structures, 25, 27–34, 37, 46,
    56, 70, 386
University of Arizona, 3, 8, 137,
    141, 283, 401, 402, 416, 423,
    427
University of New Mexico, 140
"Utah" metates, 230, 243, 244,
    344 n 50

Vahki phase, 261
Ventana Cave, 337, 356
Ventilators, 26, 27 153, 154, 157,
    158, 160, 163, 174, 180–183,
    255, 423
Viking Fund, Inc., 12, 283
Vickrey, P. E., 3
Village of the Great Kivas, 141, 418
Volcanic activity, 142

Walls
    kiva, 47, 51, 417, 420
    pit house, 23, 24, 26, 152, 154,
        157, 160, 163, 167, 168,
            170–172, 174–176, 182,
            293–322
    pueblo (stone), 16, 17, 20, 27, 28,
        31, 37–42, 46, 302, 307, 308,
        314, 316–320, 322, 358,
        360–362, 364, 381, 386–389,
        391, 393, 417, 420
Walnuts, 64, 291
Warfare, 148, 400
Warped vessels. *See* Pottery vessels,
    warped
Water sources, 16, 20, 146
Weaving, evidence of, 179
Weckler, Joe, 10
Wendorf, Fred, 72
Wheat, Joe Ben, 403, 404
Whistles, bone, 247, 255
White Mound phase, 81–82, 210,
    214, 383
White Mound Village, 141, 181,
    205 n 71, 206, 214, 216, 220,
    223–224, 253
White Mountain Indian
    Reservation, 7, 398
White Mountains, Arizona, 7, 12,
    16, 106–107, 141, 142, 395, 406
Wickiups, Apache, 15, 16, 289,
    396, 400
Willow Creek Site, 396
Willow trees, 144
Wilson Creek, 119
Withers, Arnold, 138
Wood, roofing of, 44. *See also*
    Petrified wood; Roofing
Wristlet. *See* Bracelets

Yaqui Indians, 407

Zuni area, 141, 392, 395, 406, 425